Dr. Perlman, who lived in and closely studied several *favelas* over a period of six years, contends the prevailing wisdom is false. She provides persuasive ▓▓▓▓▓▓▓▓▓▓▓ idents of *favelas* are well organized and c▓▓▓▓▓▓▓▓▓▓▓▓ re middle-class norms and values; econ▓▓▓▓▓▓▓▓▓▓▓e; politically, they are neither apathetic▓▓▓▓

Many new insights ▓▓ ▓▓▓▓-world urban poverty are presented in this book; it will have a lasting impact on the course of future research, and perhaps of policy as well.

Continued on inside back cover

1 WEEK
Date Due

THE MYTH OF MARGINALITY

THE MYTH OF
MARGINALITY
Urban Poverty and Politics
in Rio de Janeiro

JANICE E. PERLMAN

University of California Press
Berkeley • Los Angeles • London

University of California Press
Berkeley and Los Angeles, California

University of California Press, Ltd.
London, England

Copyright © 1976, by
The Regents of the University of California

ISBN 0-520-02596-2
Library of Congress Catalog Card Number: 73-87246
Printed in the United States of America

To my grandparents

migrants themselves, who have provided an inspiring
example through their courageous spirit in seeking a
new world, loving sacrifice in raising their families,
and gentle dignity in the conduct of their lives

Contents

List of Tables and Figures

Figures

Foreword
by Fernando Henrique Cardoso

T he concept of marginality, like all myths, exerts a magnetic
attraction. It offers a compelling yet simple explanation of a
complex social reality and an ideology that appeals to deep-
rooted social prejudices. Were it merely an illusion, marginality would
not have attracted so much attention and energy; nor would it have
brought the author to take up the challenge of research in the favelas.
This only happened because the myth of marginality hides behind it
something very real. Until the inner structure of the myth is discovered,
one remains trapped within the bonds of its ideology which the myth
affirms as if it were an absolute. And so, when an author finally succeeds
in demystifying the ideology which surrounds the heart of the myth, the
result is immensely rewarding.

Janice Perlman undertook painstaking research in her quest for a
synthesis which would not only reject the ideal of marginality but also
find something to replace it. When I first met her she had just finished
her field work in the favelas of Rio, where she had put to use her background as an anthropologist as well as her training in sociology and
political science. She was immersed in the analysis of her questionnaires and life-history matrices, determined to find a way to recreate and
interpret the world of the favelados.

Returning to Cambridge, Massachusetts, she continued her creative search at M.I.T., trying to make the computers answer the challenge of the sphinx: myth or reality? Is there really a "culture of
poverty"? What is the political potential of the favelados for the rectifi-
cation of an injust social order? Would they really be only poor wander-
ers in search of paternalistic support? Could it be that their recent
migration explains the apathy of the favelados? Or do all these questions
only distort the main purpose of the analysis?

I met Janice again in the spring of 1970, at a Conference on
Authoritarian Brazil at Yale. She had reached that crucial moment
which defines the stature of a researcher; the theoretical clues which
had led her into her field work in the first place had been cast into
doubt, and new theories, especially those of Latin American scholars,
seemed increasingly attractive. Janice did not hesitate: she rejected

much of her former conceptual framework and reexamined her data in the light of her new insights.

I find this book especially important because it is based on the genuine first-hand experience of one researcher, who stands apart from the large group of social scientists who have tried to understand "marginality" without doing the empirical research. The critical achievement of this book is that it does not stop at the level of a critique. Rather, it proposes a route toward a deeper understanding of the concepts of marginality, its roots and functions. In proposing this new route, it shows that the favelados are not politically and economically marginal, but are instead repressed and exploited.

One of the major difficulties of exposing this viewpoint is that favelados have been seen as an ecologically defined group rather than as part of a social system. To fully test the reappraisal proposed in the conclusion of this book would require concepts, sampling techniques, and units of analysis different from those which first oriented the research. But it is precisely that creative tension in the book which illuminates the contradiction between a "positivist" approach and methodology on the one hand and "dialectical" thinking on the other. This tension characterizes the crisis of the social sciences in the United States at the present moment. For me, one cardinal virtue of this work is that the author refuses to use pseudo-scientific arguments to obscure the problems posed by this confrontation between two divergent conceptions of science, conceptions which have very different consequences in experience and in action.

Indeed, in order to bring about a veritable Copernican revolution in the theory of marginality, it is not enough to simply show that empirically there is less apathy, social disorganization, underemployment, or unemployment than is commonly supposed by those who defend the status quo of increasing marginalization, which is typical of dependent capitalist states. This book shows us the existing patterns of migration, the problems of urban adaptation, and the limits of credibility of the hypothesis of cultural, economic, social, and political marginality of the favelados in Rio de Janeiro. The results are convincing. However, despite the fact that from these many angles the favelados are not "marginal," and indeed are similar in their patterns of behavior to "non-favelados," the fact remains that their lack of economical, cultural, and political resources is real. This explains why Janice Perlman chose to concern herself not so much with the needs of the "marginals" in comparison with the supposedly "integrated" populations, but with the poverty, the exploitation, and the systematic repression which, although affecting the entire social pyramid, are most visible in the favelas. The next step would be to reconstruct the history of this exploitation and to establish the mechanisms through which, in a varying but persistent manner, the means of exploitation and repression are recreated. They are continually recreated by the structural condition which characterizes the formation and initial stages of capitalist accumulation and by its distinctive form of social classes and the division of labor, including the division between country and city.

Although this book includes no history of this sort, there are sufficient indications to show the reader how and why relations of exploitation seem at first glance to be the result of social processes (such as immigration, illiteracy, and cultural deprivation) which have little to do with industrial development, economic growth, and capitalistic development. That is why observers and analysts often initially stigmatize favelados as "marginals," going so far as to hold them responsible for not entering the world of abundance represented by the city.

Upon discovering that this situation is mythical and that the favela is the synthesis—perhaps accentuated—of a broader world of social exploitation in which it is integrated, one takes the first step in breaking the former static and judgmental view of marginality. Consequently, the analysis illuminates the dialectical relationship between the world of the disinherited and the poles of dynamism and economic growth of the system. The favela itself emerged historically as a problem only after economic growth and urban development brought masses of immigrants to the cities. Rural poverty, although filtered and gradually adapted to "urban industrial civilization" through the step-by-step pattern of migration, invaded the metropolis and forced government and church authorities, politicians and social scientists, to an awareness of the scandal of a form of economic development which, despite its dynamism, maintains and intensifies the pattern of social disparity that characterizes underdeveloped societies.

Janice Perlman, in exposing the myth of marginality, highlights that part of it which exists in reality and which provides the effective social support for the whole myth. She offers us solid empirical data, and shares with us her direct, empathetic understanding of the human beings studied. Her book is a major contribution to our theoretical understanding of marginality and urban poverty in developing nations, not only in Latin America but throughout the Third World.

Preface

This study was originally intended to explore the impact of urban experience on the migrants and squatters of Rio de Janeiro. Much had been written about the explosive waves of cityward migration throughout Latin America and other areas of the Third World, and I felt it would be important to look at the process of adaptation and understand how people change—or do not change—as a result of exposure to urban life. After living in the squatter settlements of Rio, however, and becoming familiar with the realities of the Brazilian situation, I decided that the critical question is not how these people adopt urban lifestyles or become "modernized" by urban exposure, but rather how they interact with and are acted upon by the rest of society, and how they fit into national social, economic, and political structures. It became apparent that the set of stereotypes which I call the "myths of marginality" are so widespread and deeply entrenched that they form an ideology—indeed, a political weapon—for justifying the policies of the ruling classes, upon which the very lives of the migrants and squatters depend. I decided then to explore the validity of prevailing wisdom on this topic, and to study the terms of migrant integration in the favelas or shantytowns of Rio de Janeiro.[a]

The roots of this book are embedded in a history of personal involvement in Brazil spanning over a decade. My first contact with the country was in 1962, when I traveled throughout Latin America as a member of a Cornell University theatrical group. We spent six weeks in Brazil, visiting every major city and many smaller ones.

It was a time of great expectancy in the country. Whether they hoped for it or feared it, most Brazilians believed that a social revolution was imminent. The President, João Goulart, was talking of *reformas de base* (structural reforms), and was being pushed ever more to the left on land and tax reform issues by his communist brother-in-law, Leonel Brizola, the Governor of Rio Grande do Sul. Miguel Arraes, another powerful force on the left, was Governor of Pernambuco, and Francisco Julião was organizing Peasant Leagues throughout the Northeast.

[a]*Favela* is the generic Brazilian term for a squatter settlement (an illegal land occupation) and *favelados* are those who live in them. These, and several other frequently used Portuguese words, will be treated as English words (not italicized) after their first occurrence in the book.

Students were engaged in a nationwide strike demanding one-third representation in all university decision-making and highly politicized labor leaders were trying to mobilize the work force. It was in no small part the energy of this particular historic moment, and this sense that every person's skills and efforts would count in creating the "new Brazil," which captured my lasting interest in and commitment to the country.

The following summer I returned to do anthropological research in a series of small fishing and agricultural villages on the northeast coast of Bahia. What I found was not a people ready to follow the revolution-ary banner, but a people newly aware of expanded horizons and ready to forsake the lifestyles of their ancestors for a fresh start in the cities. Few of them were literate, or had job skills transferable to the competitive urban labor market, or had lived anywhere outside their own village. I wondered what would become of these people, and thousands like them, as they arrived in the cities to inevitably make their homes in the favelas on the hillsides, swamps, and vacant lands, or in the remote *subúrbios*.

The long-awaited "revolution" arrived on April 1, 1964—not from the left as anticipated, but from the right in the form of a military coup.

The squatters, who by then represented 15 to 45 percent of the popu-lation of every major city, had been counted on by leftist theorists to play a supportive role in the expected overthrow of the government. But partly because they had been hardest hit by the chaotic conditions and rampant inflation of the Goulart period, and partly for other reasons, a good number of them descended from their hillsides and marched alongside businessmen and housewives in support of law and order, tradition, family, and private property. A number of my Brazilian friends had their personal lives so heavily committed to a different outcome that the double shock of the coup and its popular celebration pushed them into psychic breakdowns. Many others were imprisoned, tortured, driven under-ground, or forced into exile.

A desire to understand the egregious political miscalculation of the students, professionals, and leftists in general became one of my reasons for undertaking this study. It became clear to me that the only valid way of even beginning to comprehend the reality of the *favelados* would be to actually live among them and participate in their daily lives.

Despite the coup—and in part because of it—in 1965 I co-directed a work-study project in two fishing villages outside of Recife. Some 30 Brazilian and 15 American students participated. Our experience with the community leaders, the local power structure, and the charismatic and radical Archbishop, Dom Helder Câmera, heightened my political awareness and showed me yet another facet of the problems of the powerless in Brazil. We found that the factories which had been located in the area to develop the Northeast had destroyed the traditional village economy by polluting local rivers, while failing to provide new jobs because production was so highly automated. Adults were growing sick from eating the contaminated fish and crabs, and children were dying. When finally forced into negotiations, the factory owners claimed that it would take 15 years to generate the profits needed to dispose of their waste products in a less harmful manner, and that in the meantime nothing could be done. It was clear that the people could not wait and that many of the families would be forced to leave the region and become migrants in search of survival.

In 1966, I was invited to teach in the Graduate School of Political Science at the Federal University of Minas Gerais. The students had been involved in a study of the political culture of social classes in their city and were trying to acquire the theoretical and methodological skills with which to analyze their results. Before we could work together, however, we had to engage in the inevitable credibility struggle which I faced anew each time I worked with a different group in Brazil. Survey research itself was suspect as a methodology (for bearing the stigma of intellectual imperialism), and the motivation of an American so closely involved in Brazil warranted questioning. During the months I was there, however, I developed a strong friendship and working relationship with the students. This experience was invaluable in helping me to distinguish the really important issues for research and debate from the popular topics of discussion among Brazil's *esquerda festiva* (coffee-house radicals).

In early 1968 I went to Brasília to teach at the university and study the impact of city life on the migrants who had settled there. I intended to compare the urban experience of three groups: laborers who had come to construct the capital, middle-class bureaucrats working in the various government agencies, and members of the political elite who were running the country.

After six months of investigation, however, I became convinced that Brasília was so atypical that no useful generalizations could be derived from studying it. Given my interest in the marginality or integration of migrants in an urban context, it seemed more useful to look at an older city that had grown organically rather than by architect's design. After considering São Paulo, Recife, Salvador, and Rio de Janeiro, I chose Rio because it was such a striking example of the situation I wished to explore. There were more squatters and squatter settlements in Rio— over one million residents in 300 favelas—than in any other Brazilian city. Also, I was offered an ideal institutional base for the study at IBAM, the Brazilian Institute for Municipal Administration. The institute had recently opened a new Urban Research Center and needed a consultant on research priorities and a staff trainer in research methodology.

I began serious work on the Rio favela study in September 1968, and worked through November 1969, when it became politically unfeasible for me to remain in Brazil. In the late fall of 1969, the military government passed a decree prohibiting foreign scholars from taking research materials out of the country without examination and possible confiscation by the military. Shortly thereafter, I received word that the Ministry of War suspected me of being an "international agent of subversion" for living in the favelas and for having certain friends, and that a warrant for my arrest was pending. Fortunately, I had finished collecting and coding all the information I needed for the study. I had the data keypunched and transferred to a small magnetic tape, and I left the country as quickly as possible.

Despite this threatened interference by the Brazilian military regime, being a foreigner proved a significant advantage for research in the squatter settlements. If a Brazilian university student had spent as much time as I did asking questions, attending local festivals, parties, religious gatherings, and political meetings, it would have seemed suspicious. Any native Brazilian would have instantly betrayed—by dress, speech, and manner—his or her class background, and people would have grown uneasy at seeing expected class roles altered. But as a foreigner, I was an unknown quantity. My friendliness and interest came as a pleasant surprise, and curiosity was considered natural in someone from a faraway place. The favelados expressed neither deference nor condescension toward me. Certain political questions, which would have seemed either ludicrous or suspicious coming from another Brazilian, seemed merely ignorant or innocent when asked by a foreigner. I explained my presence by saying I was trying to learn about life in the city and about how it differed from the other places the people had lived in before. This was a topic of general interest among the favelados, so no one thought it strange. As time went on, there was even a certain amount of jealousy on the part of people who had *not* been interviewed.

I also found that being a woman was an advantage in conducting research in the favelas. Since women in Brazil do not fit into any of the intrusive "expert" roles—such as politician, civil servant, or journalist— it was relatively easy for me to ask what might have been sensitive questions, and to be considered non-threatening or even inconsequential. Being a woman was also a help in the official world of government institutions. My non-threatening role, coupled with the mechanical machismo of the Brazilian bureaucrat, allowed me access to official documents, maps, and aerial photographs which had been denied previous researchers.

Of course, not being Brazilian invited perils of its own. I worked closely with Brazilian students from the outset in an attempt to avoid the ethnocentricism of the foreign scholar who descends on a country and imagines that because he has studied it, learned the language, or even lived there, he has the same understanding and sensitivity to the nuances of the culture as the natives. I involved the students in the crucial decision-making and implementation of the study, from the formulation of the pre-test questionnaire to the final data analysis.

The study was carried out in 1968 and 1969 as the research for my doctoral dissertation. It was done in three types of squatter settlements in Greater Metropolitan Rio de Janeiro: (1) a favela on a hillside in the midst of an upper-class residential and commercial area; (2) a favela in the industrial periphery of the city; and (3) a subúrbio—a group of neighborhoods in an outlying satellite, or dormitory city. I lived in each of the favelas or neighborhoods for a period ranging from a few weeks to several months, using a mixture of informal and formal research techniques.

In each of these communities, 250 people were interviewed; 200 of them were chosen at random from men and women 16 to 65 years of age, and 50 were community leaders chosen on the basis of positional and reputational sampling techniques. The interview schedule grew out of participant observation in each of these communities, in-depth non-structured interviews, and an open-ended pre-test questionnaire. The final survey instrument included four main sections: social background, urban experience, attitudes and values, and political styles. In addition, year-by-year life histories were compiled for each person, covering all changes in residential, occupational, educational, and family histories. (See Appendix for research methods.) The data thus collected form the backbone of this book.

In the summer of 1973, I returned to Rio to update my study for this book, and to follow the lives of those favelados who had been removed from their homes and relocated in public housing projects. I also visited squatter settlements and alternative low-cost housing projects in other areas of Brazil in order to place my Rio experience in broader perspective.

In the course of over a decade's work on this project, I have become indebted to many people whose help—extended or brief, substantive, methodological, or spiritual—was crucial to its successful completion. It is impossible here to thank all the countless individuals who have contributed, but I would like to name just a few whose assistance deserves special mention.

First and foremost are the migrants and favelados who shared with me the stories of their lives and opened their homes and hearts to me as friends. I am also grateful to all the members of the Brazilian research team, including the co-directors Cristina Silva and Tarcisio Dalsenter, and the architects Gilda Pôrto and Eloisa Mello.

Many other Brazilians gave me the benefit of their insights and experiences. For practical guidance, the originators of CODESCO— Silvio Ferraz, Carlos Nelson, Sylvia Wanderley, and L. A. Machado— were invaluable; and for theoretical guidance, the CEBRAP group was extremely helpful, expecially Fernando Henrique Cardoso. I am also grateful for the suggestions and guidance of José Artur Rios, Hélio Jaguribe, Manoel Berlinck, and Diego Lordello de Mello, the Director of IBAM.

In various stages of the study, I have been aided and inspired by Professors Frank Bonilla, Philippe Schmitter, Lisa Redfield Peattie, John Turner, Anthony Leeds, Joan Nelson, Frederick Frey, Gino Germani, Alex Inkeles, Jorge and Elizabeth Balan, and Manuel Castells.

In the preparation of the manuscript I benefited immensely from the help of Curt Lamb, Paulo Vieira da Cunha, José Fernando Pineda, Alexandra Marmot, Richard Conley, Timothy Smith, Thomas Brom, William Greenbaum, Norma Montgomery, and Grant Barnes.

The financial support for my initial study came from the National Institute of Mental Health, the National Science Foundation, and Latin American Teaching Fellowships.

Computer costs and technical assistance for the data analysis were arranged through grants from M.I.T. The follow-up study was made possible through the Latin American Studies Center at Stanford University, and the cross-city comparison was facilitated through the support of Rubens Vaz da Costa, then President of the Brazilian National Housing Bank. In the past year, further data analysis and rewriting the manuscript for the final draft has been supported by the Institute for Urban and Regional Development, the Center for Latin American Studies, and the Institute for International Studies, at the University of California, Berkeley. Refinements on the consideration of the concept of marginality were done while preparing a report for a World Bank Task Force on Urban Poverty, over the summer and fall of 1974.

PART I
THE SETTING
AND THE
PEOPLE

Chapter One
Cities and Squatters

Favelas, like the one in Plate 1, were by the late 1960s the home of a third of the population of Rio de Janeiro. The two favelados shown in Plate 2, relaxing in front of the local Youth Athletic Club, are not unlike millions of other squatters all over Latin America. They work hard during the week—one as a shoe salesman, the other as a waiter—to support their wives and children. For recreation they belong to the Juventude A.C. (Youth Athletic Club); it is the night of a big dance and they are waiting for the decorations to arrive so they can help put them up.

Outsiders might say that the first picture sums up the chaotic, jerry-built, overcrowded nature of squatter settlements and that the second shows two ne'er-do-wells lounging on the street when they should be working. But careful examination reveals a more complex reality. Beneath the apparent squalor is a community characterized by careful planning in the use of limited housing space and innovative construction techniques on hillsides considered too steep for building by urban developers. Dotting the area are permanent brick structures that represent the accumulated savings of families who have been building them little by little, brick by brick. The sign of the local athletic club is newly painted, and the two men in front of it are neatly dressed in middle-class styles acceptable anywhere in the world. They are both wearing leather shoes and wrist watches, symbols of their achievement in the urban environment.

These different perceptions of the favela and the favelados are a unifying thread throughout this book. Although common understandings are rare among scholars, policy-makers, leftists, rightists, and middle-class liberals, they all hold strikingly similar stereotypes regarding city-ward migrants. The common belief is that in postwar years of rapid urbanization, the city has been invaded by hordes of rural peasants. These migrants are seen as arriving lonely and rootless from the countryside, unprepared and unable to adapt fully to urban life, and perpetually anxious to return to their villages. In defense, they isolate themselves in parochial ruralistic enclaves rather than take advantage of the wider city context. Their "filthy and disease-ridden shantytowns" supposedly mani-

1

PLATE 1.

fest all the symptoms of social disorganization—from family breakdown, anomie, and mutual distrust to rampant crime, violence, and promiscuity. The rural-born migrants are seen as clinging to maladaptive rural values, or taking on the equally self-defeating traits of the "culture of poverty." Either choice produces high degrees of fatalism and pessimism, and a total inability to defer gratification or plan for the future. Such people are accused of being parasites or leeches on the urban infrastructure and on its limited resources. Most important to many analysts, squatters and migrants pose the threat of a "seething, frustrated mass" apt to fall easy prey to the appeals of radical rhetoric.

I call these beliefs the "myths of marginality." The characteristics of the urban poor are drawn from a wide range of popular studies, academic theories, and local prejudice. How the myths of marginality evolved, how much truth they reflect, and what their consequences are comprise the

PLATE 2.

focus of this study. I shall begin by setting the entire issue of marginality and squatter settlements in the broader context of urbanization and migration.

THE PHENOMENON OF URBANIZATION

Although cities can be traced back 5,500 years, only very recently has urban existence begun to define the life situations of great masses of people.[1] No society before 1850 could be described as more urban than rural.[2]

Only 1.7 percent of the 900 million people on the globe in 1800 lived in cities of 20,000 or over.[3] In the last 150 years this has changed radically. Between 1800 and 1950, while the world's total population increased two and a half times, urban populations increased twenty-fold. By 1950 just over a fifth of the world's population lived in cities over 20,000 and about an eighth in cities larger than 100,000. And the rates have continued to climb.[4] Within the next 30 years the number of people living in cities will equal twice the population growth of the entire world over the last 6,000 years. The largest urban complexes (100,000 and over) will contain over one-quarter of the world's population by 2000 and over one-half by 2050.[5]

Urbanization in the Third World. This process is even more striking in the so-called pre-industrial three-quarters of the world. Until the turn of this century, rates of urbanization were about the same everywhere. Initially "advanced" countries urbanized more rapidly, but in recent decades there seems to have been a steady decline in rates of urbanization in many of these countries and an enormous increase in the rates for developing nations.[6]

All over Asia, Africa, and Latin America, people are flocking to the cities at unprecedented rates. In the last ten years, an estimated 200 million people moved from the countryside to the cities of these three continents.[7] In the Third World many cities are growing at rates so high (5 to 8 percent per year) that they double their populations every 10 to 15 years.[8] This constitutes one of the most important migrations in human history. Yet there is little understanding of the social, cultural, economic, and political consequences for the migrants, the cities, and the larger society.

Urbanization in Latin America. With nearly half of its population in cities, Latin America is well above Asia and Africa in absolute degree of urbanization and just below Europe, Anglo-America, and Oceania. In terms of rates of growth, the region's urban population is now growing at *twice* the rate of total population and *four times* that of its rural areas.[9] It has been implicitly assumed that the process of urbanization experienced by Latin American cities is similar to the one of developed nations during the period of industrialization, and that since the rates of urbanization in the Latin countries are higher, then internal migration must be proceeding at a greater level. While rural and urban rates of natural population growth are not significantly different in most Latin American countries, the overall growth rate for rural areas is 1.5 percent a year as against 5 to 7 percent for urban areas.[10] This point is important because people perceive the phenomena of urban overpopulation as essentially a problem of overmigration. However, recent statistical evidence modifies this assumption. Kingsley Davis has argued that for underdeveloped countries, the rapid growth of cities is due at least partly to the rapid decline of mortality and the relatively constant birth rate.[11] In an analysis of the effects of migration on city growth, Arriaga found that "of the total growth of cities 20,000 and over, 58 percent in Mexico, 66 percent in Venezuela, and 70 percent in Chile, is due to natural growth of the cities."[12] The same evidence is given by George Vernez for Colombia, where less than 50 percent of the city growth is accounted for by migration.[13]

Urbanization in Brazil. Brazil provides a useful and interesting context in which to study urbanization. It has one of the highest rates of urban growth in Latin America, and probably in the entire Third World. Brazil has been a "predominantly urban nation"—that is, with more of its population living in the cities than on the land—for only the past decade. The watershed year was 1963, but throughout the 1960s there was an enormous exodus from rural to urban areas.[14] One out of every five Brazilians became a cityward migrant in that decade. There is no sign yet in the 1970s of a decrease in either absolute numbers or rates of migration. Tables 1 and 2 show the comparative growth rates of rural and urban areas in Brazil from 1940 to 1980. According to these projections, the rural-urban ratios will have been completely reversed by the end of this period—from one-third of the population in the cities in 1940, to two-thirds in cities by 1980.[15]

Of all Brazilian cities, Rio de Janeiro is among the fastest growing and demonstrates in striking form the widening gap between urbanization rates and absorption of the labor force into the industrial sector. At the time this study was conducted, the favelas of Greater Rio numbered close to 300 and held a population of about one million, or one-seventh of the total population of the metropolitan area. While the city of Rio itself was growing at 2.7 percent per year, these favelas—and the surrounding *subúrbios*—were expanding by 7.5 percent per year.[16]

CONTROVERSIES OVER URBANIZATION

This rapid expansion of squatter settlements takes on added meaning in the light of the insufficient expansion in the absorptive capacities of these same areas. Few if any major cities in developing nations are growing fast enough in terms of job opportunities, urban services, infrastructure, facilities, and governmental capabilities to absorb current population growth. This disparity in which urbanization outpaces industrialization and the creation of adequate urban institutions is known as "overurbanization" or "hyperurbanization."[17] To provide a comparative example, Brazil, Venezuela, and Argentina fall in the same category as Sweden, France, and Canada in terms of percent of population in cities of over 20,000; but in terms of industrial employment these Latin American countries, at 7 to 12 percent, are far behind the 20 to 30 percent figure for developed nations.[18]

Brazil clearly illustrates this tendency, which is tied in with the entire process of industrialization and economic development experi-

TABLE 1

Evolution of the Rural and Urban Population of Brazil

(1000 inhabitants)

Year	Urban	Percent	Rural	Percent	Total
1940	12,880	31.2	28,356	68.8	41,236
1950	18,783	36.1	33,162	63.9	51,945
1960	32,005	45.1	38,988	54.9	70,993
1970	52,905	55.8	41,604	44.2	94,509
1980	80,000	66.7	40,000	33.3	120,000

SOURCE: Instituto Brasileiro de Geografia e Estatistica, *Sinopse Estatistica do Brasil* (Rio de Janeiro, 1972), p. 43.

TABLE 2

Comparative Increase of Urban and Rural Population in Brazil

Decade	Urban Population	Rural Population
1940-1950	5,903,000	4,806,000
1950-1960	13,222,000	5,826,000
1960-1970	20,900,000	2,616,000
1970-1980	27,170,000	-1,604,000

SOURCE: Instituto Brasileiro de Geografia e Estatistica, *Anuarios Estatisticos* (Rio de Janeiro 1940, 1950, 1960, 1970).

enced in the recent history of the country.[19] The urban labor force, for example, increased by 9.2 million in the decade 1950-1960, but 62 percent of this added group were unemployed. Some .6 million went into industry, and 2.9 million into services; the rest, 5.7 million, were termed "inactive."[20] Added to the problem of unemployment or "inactivity" is the relative increase in the "tertiary" sector, which often means "disguised unemployment" or extremely low productivity at best.[21]

By contrast, the Brazilian economist Celso Furtado sees the primary dilemma as one of *overmechanization* more than overurbanization, although these perspectives are certainly not mutually exclusive. He believes the process is caused by a borrowed highly capital-intensive technology which permits Third World countries to increase industrial output without expanding industrial employment. In the 1950s Brazil's urban population increased 6 percent per year and its industrial productivity by 9 percent while its employed labor force grew by a mere 2.8 percent. In agriculture, where technological advances are less common, productivity rose by 4.5 percent in the same period and the employed work force by 3.5 percent annually, nearly keeping pace.[22]

Regardless of whether the main sources of hyperurbanization are migration, natural growth, or overmechanization, the phenomenon presents planners with one of the greatest challenges of our times.[23] While macro-solutions are clearly necessary in the long run, the poor themselves improvise critical solutions in the short run. In terms of income, many remunerative occupations not formally recognized as employment support entire families.[24] Also, unemployment, although high, is often short-term among city residents and is usually alleviated in part by *biscates* (odd jobs). There are often several wage earners in one family, and several jobs are frequently held by a single family member.[a] In the realm of housing, shantytowns, squatter settlements, and peripheral satellite towns are actually self-created solutions to the severe housing shortage and the failures of the market mechanism.

These "problems" or "solutions" (depending on one's viewpoint) fit within a long-standing set of controversies. The scholarly debate over the characteristics of cities and whether their growth should be encouraged or discouraged has a history almost as long as that of the city itself. One early viewpoint—associated with Maine, Morgan, Toennies, Durk-

---

[a]Broadly speaking, there are three problems associated with the measurement of unemployment. First is idleness enforced by circumstances on a large part of the available working population for some part of the year, month, or day. This is what is usually called open underemployment. Second, there is a problem of very low productivity— productivity so low that those who are nominally engaged in work, if judged by their net contribution to social output, would seem to be unemployed. This is usually called disguised underemployment. And third, there is full continuous and open unemployment of the labor force. Official statistics only include open unemployment and thus result in very low figures of unemployment for the local labor force. The criteria used for the definition of the labor force raise still other measurement problems. These include the definition of work or economic activities, the reference time period, and limit of amount of time worked above which a person may be classified as economically active, age limits in enumerating the economically active population, and the treatment of certain population groups such as unpaid family workers. Yuki Muira, "A Comparative Analysis of Operational Definitions of the Economically Active Population in African and Asian Statistics," *U.N. Population Conference*, vol. 4 (Belgrade, 1965), pp. 373-379; and Nurual Islam, "Concepts and Measurements of Unemployment and Underemployment in Developing Economies," *International Labor Review* 80, no. 3 (March 1964): 204-256.

heim, Simmel, and others—contrasts status-oriented, face-to-face relationships in villages with the depersonalized and formalized ones characteristic of city life. This position, crystallized in the work of Louis
Wirth, held that by the very nature of the segmented roles, secondary
relationships, and complicated class structure of cities, contacts between people become impersonal, transitory, and lead to "immunization
of self against others."[25] Thus kinship ties weaken, neighborhood solidarity wanes, and mental breakdown, delinquency, and crime of all
sorts result. In this tradition Robert Redfield defined his folk-urban
continuum moving from the small, isolated, homogenous, collectively
based rural village to the large, central, heterogeneous, socially disorganized city.[26] In the United States there has been a long tradition of
anti-urbanism; and in Europe it occasionally has even reached the point
of agrarianism, as in Spengler's *Decline of the West.*

The anti-urban position and all that it implies about personal,
family, and community disorganization has been severely challenged by
Oscar Lewis, who studied the small village of Tepoztlan in Mexico and
then traced the histories of one hundred families who migrated to the
city. In his report entitled "Urbanization Without Breakdown," Lewis
suggests that the city is not the impersonal world of social and psychological disorientation postulated by existing theory.[27] He found stable
family life, few abandoned mothers and children, relatively good health,
little mental disorder, no striking generational cleavages, and continued
traditional respect for parents and authority. In many ways the necessities and ambiguities of city life had strengthened both the extended
family structure (through the godparent system) and religiosity, with
Catholicism often supplementing Indian beliefs.[28] The data from the
present study tests in the context of Rio de Janeiro which of these
models is more accurate for describing the urban poor.

Parallel scholarly traditions have glorified the city in history as the
pinnacle of high culture, the noble best that human civilization is
capable of producing. Many Latin American scholars, intellectuals, and
politicians have tended to regard their cities as the best of the Spanish
and Portuguese cultural heritage.[29] Although pro-urban in this sense,
they are effectively aligned with many anti-urban elements because they
see rural migration into the cities as an invasion of undesirables into the
sanctuaries of civilization.

Rapid Urbanization: Blessing or Curse? There are three schools of
thought concerning the fate of migrants in the city—a negative, a posi-

tive, and a cynically accepting.[30] The first sees overurbanization as a disaster, merely transferring rural poverty to the cities and creating a parasitic, hard-to-modernize sector in the urban social system.[31] In the words of Barbara Ward, "when the unskilled poor come to the cities in advance of industrialization, it leads to squalor, despair, disorder, and violence."[32] Many of these pessimists point to what they consider the dire political implications of overurbanization. The core of their argument, considered more fully in Chapter Six, is that the frustration of migrant hopes leads to demoralization and radicalization.[33]

Positive thinkers, on the other hand, see rapid urbanization as a blessing, albeit sometimes in disguise. They dispute the notion that the high growth rate of cities has been economically undesirable. John Friedmann, for example, sees urbanization (including "hyperurbanization") as "an essential condition for the rapid expansion of national economies."[34] He argues that even with limited industrial opportunities, a massive rural-urban influx is a more favorable sign of economic advance than is limited urbanization: "The latter implies a static condition, while the former is a sign of flux and disruption of old patterns which leads to economic betterment."[35] Furthermore, poverty is not unique to the city and conditions are as bad, if not worse, in the countryside. E. J. Hobsbawm stresses the "obvious superiority" of city life, even in the poorest favela or barriada, to life in the countryside,[36] and Sjoberg adds that city dwellers in most modernizing countries actually enjoy many economic, educational, and social benefits over villagers and that social scientists are often misled by "the greater concentration and higher visibility of poverty in the city."[37]

The idea that rapid urbanization leads to "modernization" of attitudes is another theme.[38] An ECLA (Economic Commission for Latin America) report typical of the mid-1960s concluded that the rapidity of Latin American urbanization is "a seemingly hopeful circumstance," adding the query, "is it not precisely the big city that is . . . the vehicle of modernity?"[39]

Historically, cities have always been associated with modernization—in the fertile crescent, in Southwest Asia, in Medieval Europe, during the Industrial Revolution, and now in the development of the Third World. In Daniel Lerner's famous paradigm, urbanization and industrialization are seen to lead to higher levels of literacy, media exposure, and "empathy" (or psychic mobility) which, to him, is the keynote of the modern style, and a prerequisite to responsible political participation.[40] Empirical studies using individual rather than macro-level data, however, have suggested that length of urban experience per se has little effect on either individual modernity or political participation. In Alex Inkeles' data, education and factory experience accounted for most of the differences between individuals in these regards.[41] Perhaps urbanization facilitates modernization not through individual psychological change but through change in class structure, such as "by replacing old elites with middle and working-class groups."[42]

The third school of thought on rapid urbanization tends to be more accepting than the negative school and more resigned than the positive. Like the early Chicago School of Sociology, it sees the poor and minorities as a possibly undesirable but nevertheless natural and inevitable part of the urban landscape, and likens the developmental process to the growth of a garden, weeds and all.

A variation from all of these views is common to many radical Latin American social scientists today. They challenge the basic assumptions that the poor are the problem, that urbanization leads to perhaps lagging but certainly improved conditions for all sectors, and that poverty is a by-product of the modernization process. Anibal Quijano and André Gunder Frank, for example, contend that urbanization intensifies internal colonialism and stimulates underdevelopment, and that rational guidance of the urbanization process has no potential unless external dependency can be eliminated.[43] This view is discussed further in Chapter Four.

Migrants: Who, Why, and How? To understand these problems of over-urbanization, some knowledge of the causes of migration and the characteristics of migrants is necessary. The way these are understood not only affects judgments about urbanization per se but also contributes substantially to policy regarding the migrants themselves. There are three major issues concerning cityward migration. First, who migrates—are they all from the lowest social level, all from the countryside, all from the poorest class? Second, do persons migrate because of the push of bad conditions in the countryside or because of the pull of excitement and opportunity in the city? Finally, do migrants come in a once-and-for-all move, or in stages from smaller to larger places, or in seasonal back-and-forth patterns? And related to this, do they come alone or with others, having urban contacts or not? Data addressing these issues for the case of Rio is presented in Chapter Three, so at this point we will only highlight the parameters of the debate.

It has been commonly assumed that those who leave the countryside simply couldn't survive there, that they are the most poverty-stricken, diseased, hopeless elements of rural society.[b] Jorge Balan's review of the literature found three dominant assumptions: that migrants of rural origin predominate among migratory streams to the big cities; that the majority of migrants come from the bottom of the stratification system; and that there are large native-migrant differences in socioeconomic status. Interestingly, none of these held up when he tested them empirically.[44] In addition, other recent research indicates that "migrants to large cities are universally above national averages for education, skill, and acquaintance with urban ways, and in some cities they suffer no handicap in the labor market vis-à-vis native urbanites."[45] Moreover, because "migration is selective, the more dynamic members of the rural population are the ones that go to the cities."[46]

As for push vs. pull factors, it has generally been assumed that people migrate because they are driven off the land by depletion of the soil, poor climatic conditions (especially flood or drought), continually smaller subdivisions of plots for subsistence agriculture, or consolidation of land and mechanization of agriculture.[47] However, many Asian countries experienced severe land pressures before they experienced any urban growth, and many Latin American and African countries have experienced rapid urban growth in the absence of any land pressures.[48] Recent research on the topic has raised questions about the assumed importance of push factors in migration. For example, when rural areas of Brazil are divided into zones of varying degrees of poverty and economic-climatic depression, the rates of out-migration are fairly constant from each. No greater migration is evident from areas where push factors should be strongest.[49]

The arguments for pull factors have been based on the metaphor of the "attraction of the city lights" as well as the increased opportunities for jobs and social services. In newly developing countries much of this pull was created by the demand of growing industries for cheap and abundant sources of labor; but while migrants may still come for job opportunities in the Latin American case, the unskilled nature of the migrant is a liability rather than an asset, partially because of the more

[b]The problem of selectivity in migration is not empirically established in the literature. Most of the approaches have compared the characteristics of the migrants in their place of destination with the local population, which obviously does not prove or disprove the point. Comparison of out-migrants with a reference group in their place of origin might be more fruitful but entails its own methodological and substantive problems.

ed technology now being used in factories. Thus the real pull
ge of an open door and unlimited options for the future, in
contrast to the dead-end of life in the countryside.

Finally, there is the question of how migration takes place. Is it
direct or stepwise? Is it done by individuals, by family groups, or by
whole clans? Do migrants have someone to turn to in the city or not? The
literature is full of contradictions and conflicting evidence on these
issues; certainly the variation in patterns from country to country is
enormous.[50] Lucian Pye's contention that migrants are "lonely people"
may well be true in some contexts and not in others.[51] According to
Wayne Cornelius (for Mexico City) and Anthony Leeds (for Rio and
Lima), it is largely untrue. Both found that migration takes place very
much within a social context. Not only do many migrants come with
others, but often close ties are retained with the places of origin; moreover, most migrants have friends and relatives in the city who can help
in the initial adaptation period.[52]

THE PHENOMENON OF SQUATTER SETTLEMENTS

Squatter settlements of the Third World, by whatever name—
bandas de miseria in Argentina, *gececondu* in Turkey, *bidonvilles* in
Algeria, *favelas* in Brazil—all reflect the same interplay of social forces.
Because "standard" housing is so scarce relative to need, and even the
least expensive dwelling units cost so much more than the low-income
family's ability to pay, vacant lands in and around the central city
become natural squatting grounds for thousands of migrant families. In
the late 1960s such settlements represented about one-third of the population of Rio, 45 percent of Mexico City and Ankara, 35 percent of
Caracas, 25 percent of Lima and Santiago, 15 percent of Singapore,
12 percent of Istanbul, and as much as 65 percent of Algiers.[53] These
proportions constantly rise, for as Richard Morse points out, "if urban
growth rates are 2-3 times rural rates, we must remember that 'marginal'
growth rates in the city may be 2-3 times the general urban rates."[54]

In Latin America, there are in total about 20,000 to 30,000
favelas. Approximately 300 of these are in Rio, the site of the greatest
concentration of favelas in Brazil, and very likely in all of Latin
America. The *Official Bulletin* of the Brazilian Secretariat of Social
Services describes a favela as "a group of dwellings with high density of
occupation, the construction of which is carried out in a disorderly
fashion with inadequate material, without zoning, without public ser-

vices, and on land which is illegally being used without the consent of the owner."[55]

Actually, there are all types of favelas; some are spread out rather than overcrowded; some have orderly street patterns and open spaces (such as those in Lima which were planned with the aid of university architecture students); and many of them have been vastly improved over time in terms of construction materials and urban services. What ultimately distinguishes a favela, then, from many otherwise similar lower-class communities is its illegal status in terms of land use.

From outside, the typical favela seems a filthy, congested human antheap. Women walk back and forth with huge metal cans of water on their heads or cluster at the communal water supply washing clothes. Men hang around the local bars chatting or playing cards, seemingly with nothing better to do. Naked children play in the dirt and mud. The houses look precarious at best, thrown together out of discarded scraps. Open sewers create a terrible stench, especially on hot, still days. Dust and dirt fly everywhere on windy days, and mud cascades down past the huts on rainy ones.

Things look very different from inside, however. Houses are built with a keen eye to comfort and efficiency, given the climate and available materials. Much care is evident in the arrangement of furniture and the neat cleanliness of each room. Houses often boast colorfully painted doors and shutters, and flowers or plants on the window sill. Cherished objects are displayed with love and pride. Most men and women rise early and work hard all day. Often these women seen doing laundry are earning their living that way, and many of the men in bars are waiting for the work-shift to begin. Children, although often not in school, appear on the whole to be bright, alert, and generally healthy. Their parents, as will be shown in Chapter Five, place high value on giving them as much education as possible. Also unapparent to the casual observer, there is a remarkable degree of social cohesion and mutual trust and a complex internal social organization, involving numerous clubs and voluntary associations.

The earliest documented account of a favela in Rio was in the 1920 census, which reported an agglomeration of 839 houses on the Morro da Providencia organized by veterans of the Canudos campaign, an uprising in Bahia.[56] The first major wave of rural-urban migration in Brazil in the early 1930s led to a rapid growth in favela population. An abrupt fall in world prices for Brazilian agricultural products depressed the already low standard of living of many rural areas. Simultaneously, the new government was stressing the development of industries to supply internal markets. A resulting increase in new factories created a concomitant demand for a labor force in a manner reminiscent of the classic "industrialization-first" model. These events were paralleled by, and probably contributed to, a rapid rise in construction costs and land values. Housing became scarce and expensive. Urban services, including transport from surrounding suburban areas, were primitive. New migrants searching for homes were joined by many city dwellers no longer able to afford the rents, even on *cortiços, avenidas* and *cabeças de porco* (various forms of tenement apartments rented by the room). Squatting on hillsides around the central city, with the dual advantage of being rent free and centrally located, became the best solution for many.[57] Thereafter, favelas increased steadily: by 1950 favelados represented about 8.5 percent of Rio's population; by 1960 they were 16 percent and by 1970 about 32 percent. About one million favelados lived in Rio in 1968-1969.[58]

There are few signs that favelas are a temporary phenomenon, even though most governments speak of eradicating them and substituting public housing. In all of Latin America, states Friedmann, "substandard housing—the slum, the rancho, the barriada, the favela, the villa de miseria—may well be regarded as a semi-permanent feature of the urban landscape. . . . It will exist for as long as there is massive urban poverty and continued rapid migration to cities."[59]

CONTROVERSIES OVER SQUATTER SETTLEMENTS

The way favelas are perceived, especially by those in power, largely determines what policies are imposed on them. In order to clarify existing perceptions, I organized an informal conference of urbanists, architects, and planners with experience in the favelas. We met in January 1969 in Rio and developed a simple simulation game dealing with the future of the favelas over the next ten years. In the process, three major viewpoints, synthesizing both scholarly opinion and popular ideas, began to emerge. They saw the favela, respectively, as pathological agglomeration, as community striving for elevation, and as inevitable blight. These views are the natural concomitants of the three major attitudes toward rapid urbanization discussed above.

Favelas as Pathological Agglomerations. In this viewpoint the favela is seen as a disorderly agglomeration of unemployed loafers, abandoned women and children, thieves, drunks, and prostitutes. These "marginal elements" live in a "subhuman" condition without piped water, sewage systems, garbage collection, and other basic urban services in an unclean and unhealthy atmosphere. In appearance an eyesore, the favela detracts from the picturesque panorama of the city. Economically and socially it is a drain, a parasite, demanding high expenditures for public services and offering little in return. Favelados stick largely to their separate enclaves, they do not contribute skills or even purchasing power to the general welfare, and they are a public menace. Furthermore, the lands they occupy are often of high financial value, thus preempting more profitable use and lowering district property values.

Flowing from this image is the clear policy implication that both the city and the squatters would be better off if the favela no longer existed. Considerations of health, economic efficiency, esthetics, and political stability all point in the same direction: eradicate the favela. In the first place, migrants should be discouraged from moving to the city. Those who do persist in coming should be forced to bear their share of the costs of urbanization. Housing and sanitation codes and zoning laws should be rigidly enforced. Whenever possible, inhabitants should be removed to more remote areas where land values are low and where they could occupy low-cost public housing which would meet "minimum standards."

This negative picture is the prevailing myth on the subject.[60] It is held not only by some scholars and academicians but also by large segments of the general public in Latin America, and, most important, by government officials and policy-makers.

Favelas as Communities Striving for Elevation. The counter-vision sees the favela as a community inhabited by dynamic, honest, capable people who could develop their neighborhoods on their own initiative if given the chance. Favelados contribute to the economy as workers and consumers and through improvements they make on their land and houses. Over time the favela will evolve naturally into a productive neighborhood, fully integrated into the city. The entrepreneurial capacity and organizational skills of residents show clearly in self-help collective efforts in house building (*mutirão*) and public works in the community and in their elaborate network of social and political organizations. These supposed "backwaters" are, in fact, central to the cultural identity of Brazil. Much of the spirit for which Rio is famous— the samba, the colorful slang, the spiritist cults—springs directly from the favelas. This fits into a general body of literature on the nature of the slum. For example, John Seeley, Marc Fried, and Peggy Gleicher have pointed out many sources of satisfaction in the slum, such as "variety, adventure, convenience, loyalty, a sense of community, and mutual self-help."[61]

A group of Brazilian sociologists who had worked intensively in the favela found the following: "The favela is used as a scapegoat for many embarrassing social problems that are unresolved: low growth rate of the gross national product, high rates of inflation, etc. . . . These definitions of the favela are so deeply ingrained . . . that many favelados themselves, principally the poorest strata, are convinced of their own inadequacies. The crucial fact is that the urban structure has impeded the development of the favelado and obstructed his channels of access to formal education, thereby eliminating the possibility that he can resolve the urban problems relating to the favela on his own."[62]

Because of this attitude, these sociologists contend, "all the plans relating to the favelas so far are based on middle-class social norms of morale and propriety which have no value whatsoever for the specific circumstances of the favela." They cite, for example, the assumption that living in a government housing project is "better for the favelado," and the fact that the building code (*Código de Obras*) expressly forbids making any improvements in houses, public spaces, or services in the favela.

The kinds of policy recommendations flowing from this viewpoint and the first one are diametrically opposed. Rather than removal of the favelas, this second outlook would lead to an official policy of legalization and "urbanization" at the locale.[c] This policy would give favelados title to their land, provide easy access to credit, long-term loans, and technical assistance, thereby allowing them to be the agents of their own self-improvement.

Favelas as Inevitable Blight. The third and intermediate view of the favela is that it is a natural, though unfortunate, consequence of rapid urban growth. It is recognized that the city cannot grow fast enough to provide adequate employment or to offer adequate urban services. The existence of widespread unemployment or underemployment and of inadequate infrastructure in the favela is seen as the normal outgrowth of rapid rural-urban migration. Favelados are recognized as useful in providing cheap labor and easily bought votes, though they are still

[c]Unless otherwise specified, we will use the term "urbanize" in the Latin American sense, which means to provide with urban services and infrastructure—primarily water, electricity, drainage, sewage, and paving where necessary.

regarded as underproductive economically, naive politically, and rather undesirable socially.

The proponents of this attitude take the paternalistic view that favelados are like children—they need to be guided, taught, and educated by the good will of those more fortunate. The policy implications of this line of reasoning are that the favelados should be helped within the limits of what is feasible, so that they can be recuperated, *os pobres coitados* ("the poor things"), without necessarily modifying the basic structure of the situation. The most appropriate programs are palliative types of assistance such as distribution of food and clothing, organization of health services, mother's clubs, and so on. Through these policies it is believed that the worthy favelados will overcome the many obstacles and become integrated into society.

Each of these viewpoints and its policy outcomes is based on a set of assumptions about the nature of the inhabitants of the favelas. The analysis of these assumptions—their roots, their validity, and their implications—forms the backbone of this study.

Chapter Two
Two Favelas and a Subúrbio

B ecause of its high levels and rates of urbanization, Brazil is an ideal site for studying the consequences of cityward migration. Contrasted with most other Latin American countries which have only one major city, Brazil has nine urban centers: São Paulo, Rio de Janeiro, Belo Horizonte, Recife, Porto Alegre, Salvador, Curitiba, Fortaleza, and Belém. The two cities with the highest growth rates and most severe problems of rapid urbanization are Rio and São Paulo. The problems that squatter settlements pose are probably most severe in Rio, which has experienced less industrial growth, and has much less space than does São Paulo. Rio is squeezed into a small strip of land between the ocean and the mountains and, unlike São Paulo, has no convenient area in which to expand outward. São Paulo also has an abundance of inner-city tenements which serve as alternatives to favelas. These factors, combined with the sensual attractiveness and fame of Rio, have produced some 300 favelas—by far the most for any city in the nation.

Herded into flatbed trucks, crowded into railroad cars and buses, wearily finding their way on burro and foot, thousands of Brazil's poor stream daily into the cities. One of the first steps of the study was to select sites representative of those in which recent, long-term, and second-generation migrants lived. I approached the problem in a variety of ways. I waited at the truck stops, depots, and crossroads around Rio and traced the routes of the newcomers in their search for shelter, jobs, companionship, and social amenities. At some disembarkment points I waited with the few people who had received word that family or friends were arriving, and then went "home" with them. I also followed up those with no one to meet them, many of whom spent the first night on the street. Most families *did* have friends or relatives in the city, whom they managed to locate eventually. Others had met someone on the trip who knew of a job or a place to go, or in their first wanderings had managed to find a construction site or favela where they could squat temporarily. Girls arriving to be maids went directly to their employer's homes. Sometimes single young men with a little money found and went to a cheap room in a pension or private home.

Those who are homeless, jobless, and without connections of kin or fellow-villager are picked up by Albergue, a state institution that provides a number of services to migrants while they look for a means of subsistence. One week of free room, board, health care, and child care is provided. Each morning at six o'clock all adults must be out hunting for jobs and cannot return until nightfall. A second week's stay is granted in some cases. If no home or job can be arranged within this time, the family is shipped back to its place of origin at the state's expense.

Talking to the migrants and officials at Albergue reinforced what I had observed when accompanying families directly to their destinations within the city. There were only two options for migrants arriving in Rio: either they went to favelas or to outlying dormitory communities called subúrbios.[a] Weeks of interviews with every public and private agency dealing with migrants, favelas, and low-income housing further confirmed this conclusion.

By contrast, the major writings on settlement patterns in Latin American cities claim that inner city slums, not favelas or subúrbios, are the most common reception points for migrants. Turner and Mangin, for example, had found that in Lima such centrally located and cheaply rented houses provided the first urban residence ("bridgehead" stage) for the vast majority of migrants, who later organized invasions, became squatters, and finally built up working-class neighborhoods on the outskirts of the city ("consolidation" phase). Similar patterns also had been documented for other cities, including Santiago and São Paulo.[1] Therefore, upon arriving in Rio I spent a good deal of time in the inner-city slums—the cortiços, cabeças de porco, vilas and avenídas, and lotes proletários. I found that the inhabitants of these tenement-type residences are in fact not migrants, but mostly Portuguese, Spanish, and Jewish families who have been in the city for generations and never quite "made it."[2] The slum is simply not a place where rural migrants come— probably because there is little space available, low turnover, much crowding, and often prohibitions against children. In recent years many

---

[a] I will treat the word subúrbio, like favela, as part of our common vocabulary, using the Portuguese word so as not to confuse it with American notions of middle- and upper-class suburbs.

of these tenements have been torn down—in Rio's first urban renewal effort—thereby aggravating the overcrowding in those that remain. Finally, although rates are cheap, there are still monthly payments to be made in contrast to the favelas, which are totally free.

In searching for a way to grasp the range of urban experience, I discovered three distinctly different environments to which migrants could come and in which second-generation favelados could raise their families. These were: (1) favelas on the hillside in the South Zone of Rio, that is, the commercial and upper-class residential area; (2) favelas in the North Zone of Rio, the industrial periphery and working class residential area; and (3) the subúrbios in the Baixada Fluminense (the lowlands in the state of Rio de Janeiro), a group of satellite towns or dormitory cities.

The extent of the urbanized area of Greater Rio de Janeiro is indicated in Figure 1. As shown, it includes portions of both Guanabara and the State of Rio. The Baixada Fluminense is the area encompassing the municipalities of Nova Iguacú, Duque de Caxias, Nilopolis, and São João de Meriti. Figure 2 displays the relative locations of the South Zone, North Zone and Center of Rio, and indicates the pattern of favela location.

The three areas—the South Zone, the North Zone, and the State of Rio Subúrbios—differ in many respects. Proximity to "demonstration effects," heterogeneity of city contacts, relations with external agencies, employment styles, neighborhood condition, security of tenure, land values, and density of occupation, for example, varied significantly between them. It seemed important, then, to study in depth at least one community in each of these locations.

In each area I became familiar with about 10 to 20 of the communities; from these I eventually picked three which seemed typical and in which I had established relationships with some of the residents. These three were Catacumba in the South Zone, Nova Brasília in the North Zone, and Duque de Caxias in the Baixada Fluminense (within which I chose five low-income neighborhoods and three favelas). The exact research sites are indicated on the map in Figure 2.

I used a mixed methodology involving participant observation, open-ended interviews, contextual analysis, survey data, and longitudinal life-histories (with year-by-year residence, job, family, and educational changes recorded for each person). This combination of qualitative and quantitative investigation seemed most useful for counteracting prevailing ideologies and misunderstandings. Also, it was essential to

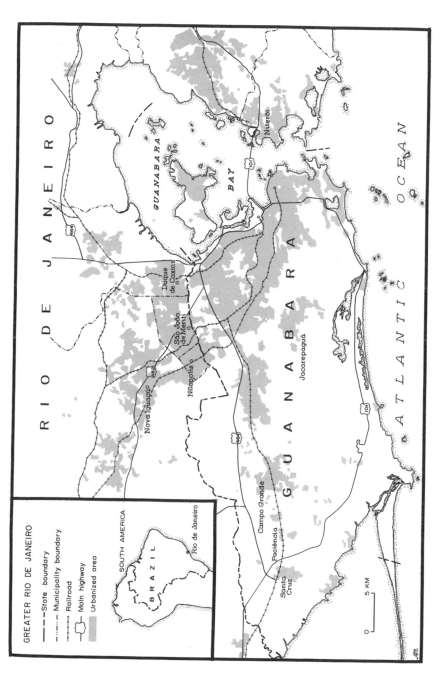

1. The Urbanized Area of Greater Rio de Janeiro.

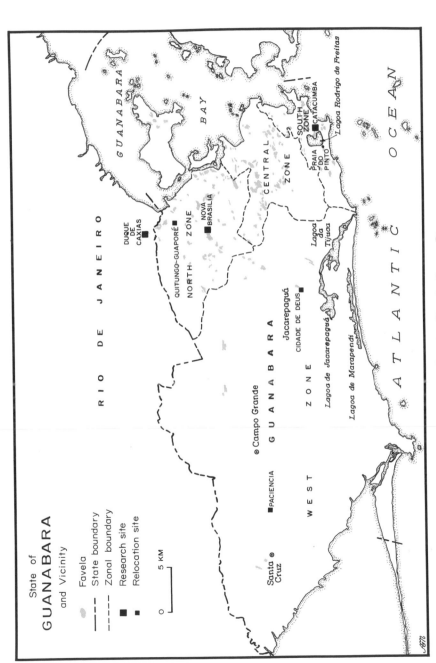

State of
GUANABARA
and Vicinity

Favela
State boundary
Zonal boundary
Research site
Relocation site

0   5 KM

RIO DE JANEIRO

GUANABARA BAY

ATLANTIC OCEAN

DUQUE DE CAXIAS

QUITUNGO-GUAPORÉ

NORTH ZONE

NOVA BRASILIA

CENTRAL ZONE

SOUTH ZONE

CATACUMBA

Lagoa Rodrigo de Freitas

PRAIA DO PINTO

Lagoa da Tijuca

Campo Grande

GUANABARA

Jacarepaguá

CIDADE DE DEUS

Lagoa de Jacarepaguá

Lagoa de Marapendi

WEST ZONE

PACIENCIA

Santa Cruz

2. Favelas and Relocation Sites in Greater Rio.

interview the favela leaders, internal organization directors, and re-
spected notables, as well as the general population. Most of the discussion throughout this book is based on the 600 men and women in the
random sample, but the 50 "elites" from each community are often used
for purposes of comparison. (For detailed description of the methodology, the questionnaire formulation, sample selection, interviewing
procedure, and use of the longitudinal life-history matrix, see the
Appendix.)[b]

Because each of the three communities has characteristics of its
own which influence the urban experience and political situation of its
residents, it will be useful to describe each of them in some detail as to
location, physical properties, history, urban services, community solidarity, and prospects for removal.

The South Zone: Catacumba

Situated in the heart of the upper-middle-class and upper-class
residential and commercial district of Rio, the South Zone is the location of the most famous tourist spots in Latin America—Copacabana,
Ipanema, and Leblon. No part of the South Zone is more than a five-
minute walk from the beach. The area is full of bright shops and chic
boutiques and has bustling street fairs almost every day of the week.
Above all, it is one of the most densely populated areas in the world.
There one finds what the Brazilians most value—*movimento* (action).

Needless to say, South Zone land values are extremely high. Squatter settlements grew there by accretion (not by invasion, as in Lima),
spreading up the steep, rocky hillsides where no regular construction
could take place, thus reversing the American pattern of rich residents
on the hills and poor ones in the flatlands. Ingenious stilt-like supports
were developed to buttress the precarious perches of shacks on the hillside. With removal a constant threat, investments were rarely made to
convert the mud or wood houses into brick or cement (except those along
the roadside). Rather, money was generally invested in movable objects
such as television sets, refrigerators, and other items of this nature
rather than in permanent improvements or house construction. Some

[b]The actual survey instrument used, along with the frequency distributions for the
random and elite samples, and a complete description of the research procedure may be
found in Janice Perlman, *Methodological Notes on Complex Survey Research Involving
Life History Data*, Institute of Urban and Regional Development, Monograph no. 18,
University of California, Berkeley, 1974.

effort was made, however, to provide adequate infrastructure (primarily water spigots, electricity, drainage, and paving).

The South Zone can also be characterized by its distinctive job market. Nowhere else in Rio are there so many opportunities for what is known in Portuguese as *biscate* (odd-jobbing), and nowhere so many little *bicas de emprêgo* ("spouts" or "founts" of employment) for women and children as well as men. By virtue of its location in the heart of Rio's affluent society, there is a constant supply of service jobs available for those who look. A family can easily multiply its sources of income by the wife taking in washing, ironing, or sewing, daughters selling sweets, and sons shining shoes, watching parked cars, or selling scraps. And construction work or repair work is often available for able-bodied men.

The hillside on which Catacumba is located overlooks a beautiful fresh-water lagoon, the Lagoa Rodrigo de Freitas. It faces on Avenida Epitácio Pessoa, a main route from the South Zone to the center of the city, and can be seen—a busy beehive rising from the bay—all along the drive around the lagoon (see Plate 3). On the other side of the lagoon are luxurious, modern apartment buildings, an exclusive yacht club, and a race track.

History and Ownership. [3] No one in the favela or any official agency knew for sure who owned the land. One source contends that Catacumba derives its name from the fact that Indians buried their dead there (the name literally means catacombs). [4]

A small, undated, and anonymous history in the archives of the Rio Social Work Library states that Catacumba, called Chácara das Cata-cumbas at the end of the past century, was leased by the Baroness of Lagoa Rodrigo Freitas. When she died she gave the land to her slaves, who considered the land their own. In 1925 the federal company which formerly owned the land divided it and began to sell it. Thirty-two people bought sections. The heirs of the Baroness complained to the courts. At this time the owner of some adjacent land decided to "re-vindicate" for himself possession of the entire site. Thus there began the long litigation that continues to this day in the federal courts. When no one could be officially proclaimed owner of the land, the first squatters' shacks appeared. There was little development during the 1930s and the first major invasion of migrants took place in 1942. In 1952 a second wave brought refugees from the drought-stricken Northeast. The court eventually decided that the buyers of 1925 should retain title to the land, but litigation and appeals are still going on.

Some believe that Catacumba belongs only in part to the variety of private contenders, and in part to the Brazilian Air Force. At the time this book was being written, Catacumba had been eradicated for five years. Although developers and profiteers could hardly wait to start putting up luxury hotels and high rise condominiums, no construction had begun because of the continuing legal battles.

Population. Facts concerning Catacumba's population are at least as confusing as those concerning its history. Since favelas are not officially recognized, they do not appear on government maps or in any consistent form in census data. Estimates of the number of inhabitants as of 1969 ranged from 1,410 units with 6,000 inhabitants to the enormous figure of 7,000 shacks and 28,000 people.[5] In our study we identified 1,457 shacks, many of them multiple-family dwellings. There was an average of 5.9 persons per dwelling, giving an overall population of about 8,600.[c] Most of the recent increase in population at that time could be attributed to natural increase alone; there was simply no more room for shacks to be built and no more room within existing shacks to accommodate new arrivals. Those newcomers who chose to live there were forced to pay exorbitantly high prices for the privilege of occupying a shack and its land.

Physical Properties. Catacumba covers a relatively small area—about 26 acres or one twenty-fifth of a square mile.[6] It is quite densely settled as shown in the frontispiece, creating a colorful patchwork quilt effect fully displayed to view because the hillside is so steep. It is divided into three distinct areas corresponding to the three adjacent slopes on which it is located. What looks like an undistinguished mass to outsiders is divided by residents into sub-units. The one closest to Copacabana-Ipanema is called Passarinheiro and is considered a calm and desirable place to live within the favela. The big new Assembly of God meeting house is located along the road in this section, as is the Youth Athletic Club. On the middle hillside is Maranhão, named for its first settlers who came from that state. The third slope is Café Globo, distinguished by the Police Station along the road at that point and the garbage-burning chimney there.

---

[c]The true figure is probably slightly higher than this because a number of shacks were so well hidden from the view of a random walker or our photographers in the bay that they were never included in our sample. Probably most accurate was the figure of 9,000 in the government study, the result of a door-to-door census in the favela in preparation for removal and relocation.

PLATE 3. The Favela of Catacumba,
a busy beehive along Avenida Epitácio.
Reeds in foreground are at lagoon's edge.

In addition to this horizontal sectioning there is a fascinating vertical stratification as well, corresponding roughly to social class and length of time in the favela. Generally, along the road are the concrete and brick houses belonging to the earliest and most affluent residents. (About 10 percent of houses in Catacumba are made of bricks and concrete.)[7] The better commercial enterprises, shops, and stores within the favela are also located at the bottom on the hill along the Avenida Epitácio Pessoa. Further up, the typical house construction is wood (79 percent of all the houses), and near the top, wattle and daub or scraps. Life in the upper levels of the favela has a reputation for being tougher and more dangerous. Certainly there are more hardships there—even getting there is hard, as the access paths dwindle from cement and stone to dirt and finally to steep rocks.

Urban Services. Access to urban amenities in Catacumba follows the same horizontal stratification. The closer to the road, the easier the availability of water, sewage, electricity, and garbage collection. Water is provided at 15 collectively used spigots located near the road. Most favela residents (89 percent) are serviced from these, while a few have arranged for piped-in water. Because pressure is so low, there are often long lines at the pumps. The inconvenience falls hardest on those living highest in the favela, who must descend all the way to street level and climb back up the steep, rocky trails with the large tin cans on their heads. Young boys can be hired for the enervating wait and long climb, but the few cents per trip mounts up for poor families.

Only 50 percent have any sort of toilet facilities inside or connected to their homes. Even if they do, sewage is not removed in closed pipes but runs down the favela in open channels and collects in troughs beside the sidewalk at the bottom.

One dwelling in five has no electricity at all. Half of the residents are supplied by extensions from 300-odd houses where "meters" (*relógios*) have been installed by the light company. This is a major source of complaint among residents. People are charged by the number of outlets, about U.S. $1.25 per outlet per month, no matter how much electricity is used. Because so many lines extend from one trunk, often there is not enough power to use a sewing machine, watch television, listen to the radio, or do ironing in the evening hours when lights are also on. Electric service is thus totally inadequate, and costs considerably more than the rate charged by the light company in other parts of the city. Even electricity supplied by the central *cabine* which the State Commision of Electric Energy (C.E.E.) installed a few years ago is overpriced, with the directors of the local "Light Commission" making a personal profit from it.

Garbage disposal is facilitated by four large incinerators within the favela—which are great fire hazards—and four large depositories along the road where residents may bring garbage to be collected once a week by the city's trucks. Again, any service the city provides is sporadic and won at a high cost in terms of bargaining for other benefits.

Commerce. Catacumba has a lively and diversified commercial life within its boundaries. There are ten large grocery stores, five bars (*boutequíns*), over 100 small shops (*tendinhas e biroscas*), two shoe stores, two clothing stores, six barber shops, a beauty parlor, a newspaper stand, a pharmacy, a chicken and egg shop, a furniture store outlet, and several repair shops. Unfortunately, prices within the favela are often higher than elsewhere, but merchants do offer certain advantages to their customers: they extend credit when needed, allowing families to get along when the breadwinner is unemployed; they divide merchandise into small packets to allow purchase of small amounts at one time (a single cigarette, a few slices of bread);[d] and some establishments, especially bars, serve as social gathering places and local news centers.

Associations. The most important membership organization in the community is the Residents' Association, SOMAC (Sociedade dos Moradores e Amigos de Catacumba). It was founded in 1961 and has held elections for officers every two years since then. Its membership in 1968-1969 was registered as 1,600.[8] According to its president, Waldevino, about 500 persons participate, but our observations indicate about 50 people who are consistently active in the affairs of the organization. Only one general assembly was held during the year of my research, and it was poorly attended. The statutes of the organization give some indication of its priorities. The following rules were framed on the walls of the headquarters: (1) Respect the association and its premises. (2) No drinking on the premises. (3) Playing of checkers, dominos, and the like is permitted but not for money. (4) No one may appear at headquarters after 6 o'clock in shorts, bathing trunks, barefooted, or shirtless whether you are a member or not. (5) Anyone getting into a fight will be immediately suspended from the association. (6) Anyone who doesn't pay his dues for one month will have three months'

---

[d]More expensive for the favelado in the end, but in the short run it allows him to buy what he needs with available income.

punishment of not enjoying the association's benefits. (7) Anyone not paying for two months will be punished likewise for a six-month period, and after three months will be dismissed from the association. (8) This applies also to the officers, except that in their cases they are removed from office after the second month of non-payment.

Among benefits provided by the association are a medical clinic (half-price for members) open three afternoons a week and, supposedly, the services of a social worker and dentist, although these never seemed to materialize. The major stated purpose of the organization was to represent the favela in disputes with the outside world, demands for urban services, and in the struggle against relocation.

The second most powerful organization in Catacumba is the Electricity Commission, which had been in existence a little over a year at the time of this study. It was started by a counter-elite and supported by the C.E.E. (State Commission of Electric Energy) because some people were dissatisfied with "exploitation" in the provision of electricity and convinced that the Residents' Association was not doing an adequate job.

There are a number of social and recreational associations in the favela as well: six soccer clubs, a samba school, and a Youth Athletic Club which gives dances and parties. Finally, there are several religious centers, including the Assembly of God, a number of *terrenos macumbistas* (Afro-Brazilian spiritualism), a ten-year-old Catholic church visited weekly by a priest, and various small sects and meeting houses.

Schools. Catacumba has no official schools. At least two women take care of youngsters during the day privately, and give some instruction, but there is no regular instruction on any level and no adult literacy course. Women who work as maids often use their patron's address so their children can qualify for the regular school system (see Plate 4).

Economy. Catacumba has a considerably lower incidence of unemployment than the typical favela. As mentioned earlier, its location is such that it services the affluent residents of Copacabana, Ipanema, and Leblon. The study indicated that there are over twice as many people working in construction and domestic services in Catacumba than in either of the other two sites and only half as many men who have never worked. It should be pointed out, however, that many of the jobs are quite unstable, with high turnover rates, and that a person will say he is working at biscate (odd-jobs) rather than unemployed even if he is only fixing a few appliances here and there or washing or watching cars from

PLATE 4. Woman supervises her children at play from her window high in the favela. She wishes there were a school in Catacumba which they could attend.

time to time. Here is a description of work activity in the area by one newspaper reporter:

> At five o'clock in the morning Catacumba begins to disgorge its inhabitants. Butlers, cooks, and nursemaids descend the steps leaving for the homes of the "ladies." Workers, in large part construction laborers, form lines at the two bus stops or set off by foot in the direction of Copacabana, Ipanema, and Leblon. . . . A little later those who come down from their houses have a different appearance: it is the time of the public functionaries, of the children who are going to school, and of the enormous number of washerwomen who leave their houses early to take advantage of the weak morning sun for their scrubbing and later the stronger sun to dry the clothes they've washed. . . . The favela almost in its entirety already shows—by eight o'clock in the morning—ample proof of its energy and work force.[9]

Removal. As far back as residents can remember, they have lived in constant fear of being evicted from their homes and forced to relocate elsewhere. Eighty-five percent of the random sample we interviewed in Catacumba could recall a specific threat of removal and recount the measures taken to forestall or avoid eviction. Commissions had been organized to go to the governor's palace with petitions, the mass media alerted to create a public opinion favorable to the squatters, protests and appeals staged, and "pull" with influential friends or politicians used. All of these activities took place after 1960, when Guanabara became an autonomous state (with the transfer of the Federal District to Brasília) and before the military takeover in 1964. In that era public opinion counted, populist norms prevailed, and the votes of a million favelados in Rio could not be ignored. Most of the urban services that now exist in Rio's favelas were gained as a result of their bargaining power during that period.

The story of Catacumba has an abrupt ending. It was decided by CHISAM, the federal agency created for the purpose in 1968, to remove all Rio favelas within the next three years. In August 1969, the Secretary of Social Services had started a house-to-house census of Catacumba to ascertain salary rates and decide where each family should go. The Association of Residents was co-opted into a uniformed vigilante committee of 31 men to guard against improvements being made on any of the homes, to see that no one entered or left the favela without authorization, to keep any new families from moving in, and to preserve the general tranquility.[10] Although families bemoaned their fate, no opposition was voiced publicly.

An article in the *Jornal do Brasil* on May 10, 1971, announced that by that date 41 of 300 favelas had already been removed, including Catacumba. The causes and consequences of this massive removal policy are discussed in Chapter Seven.

THE NORTH ZONE: NOVA BRASÍLIA

The North Zone is located on the periphery of the city, in an industrial district, and has a predominantly working and lower-middle-class population. It is neither as densely populated as the South Zone nor as urbane in the range and intensity of its recreational and social activity. Land values are lower, and space somewhat more abundant, so that the shacks (*barracos*) can be slightly more spread out. Often there is room for a little gardening, a pig, or a couple of chickens. Because the North Zone is more remote, the threat of removal is also less pressing and people are somewhat more secure in their tenure. Thus construction, especially in the older and more established parts of the favelas, is often of brick or concrete. Fair amounts of resources have been devoted to basic facilities. Residents have fewer contacts with the full variety of urban life present in the South Zone, and being more distant from the city's affluent areas they have less direct exposure to "demonstration effects." However, the bus trip to central Rio is only 30 minutes to an hour from most places, so the city still is quite widely used.

Generally, less service jobs but more factory jobs are available, although the favelados do not always qualify for these. It is harder to supplement family incomes with odd jobs, children's chores, or even women's domestic services, since there is no local elite for whom to perform these services, and often they must be done in spare moments, near the location of the home. One important concomitant of this is that there are fewer opportunities for establishing patron-client relationships with influential people; thus, many of the needs that would be taken care of through personal contacts in the South Zone here have to be dealt with collectively by the favela as a whole. For example, where no patron exists to help get one's children into school, or see to it that medical care is provided in case of emergencies, the alternative is likely to be a petition for a local school, or a pressure group to have a clinic installed in the local Residents' Association. In line with this, the residents' associations in the North Zone are often stronger and more active than those in the South Zone, and there seems to be more pride and self-identification in being a favelado, and less tendency to mimic middle-class patterns.[11]

Location, Population, and Physical Description. Nova Brasília is located in the heart of the North Zone, surrounded in large part by factories. The community faces on the Avenida Itaoca and is bordered on the side and back by Caminho Itaré and Rua Campos de Paz. Like all Rio's favelas, it appears on official maps as a vacant green hillside. In 1967 the main entrance road, Rua Nova Brasília, was legalized after a long battle by the Residents' Association. Shown in Plate 5, this road is the major pedestrian access into the favela, although another route on the back of the hillside, which is passable by jeeps and sturdy automobiles, allows shops and stores on the upper levels to be supplied. Figures 3 and 4, drawn from an aerial photo, indicate the main streets, the pattern and density of dwellings, the sample chosen, and the stratification scheme.

As in Catacumba, the part of the favela nearest the main front road is the oldest, richest, and best developed. Higher up, the houses change to predominantly brick and wood, and finally to wattle and daub, giving the upper portions of the favela a distinctly rural aspect. Plate 7, taken in an older section along Rua Nova Brasília, documents the transition from a one- to two-story house. The gentle slope from Rua Nova Brasília ends in the Praça do Terço, a large open space arranged neatly around a

PLATE 5.   Rua Nova Brasília, which the residents fought to legalize, is filled with
people and activity at any hour of the day. Most of the families who live along the
street build second stories to live in while converting their main floors to shops.

garbage dump, a water tank, and a loud speaker, and populated
liberally by pigs and chickens. From Praça do Terço the hillside rises
steeply in three directions.

While Nova Brasília is about four times as large as Catacumba in
area, covering some 400,000 square meters, its population is only 50
percent greater, leaving the area much less crowded. The Serviço Social

NOVA
BRASÍLIA

■ Houses selected
    for random sample

▨ Houses selected
    as alternates

0   50   100

Meters

3. Sampling Map for Nova Brasília.

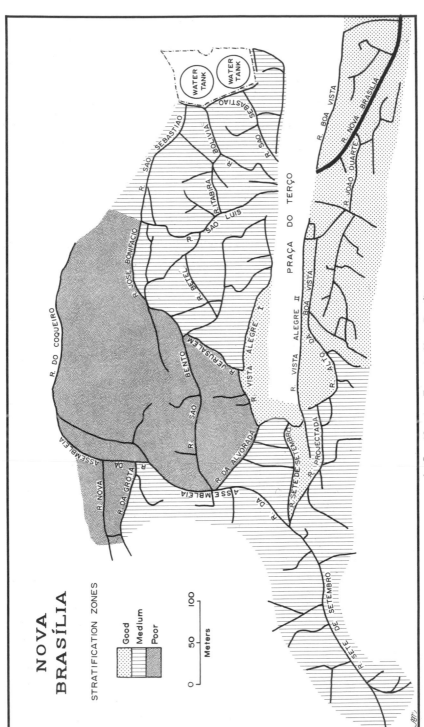

4. Stratification Zones in Nova Brasília.

and the Fundação Leão XIII estimate the population at about 15,000 distributed in 3,000 housing units. In my study, I identified 2,112 dwelling units (671 in the wealthier, 952 in the moderate, and 489 in the poorer areas), and about 12,600 residents in all.

History, Ownership, and Removal. Nova Brasília is newer than Catacumba, dating from 1942, when a few squatters began to settle on an unoccupied hillside in the area of the Praça do Terço. The neighborhood grew slowly and had no name that anyone can remember until around 1957 when the front part along the road was built up. Sr. José, one of the early settlers, recalls that at the time there were only about 2,000 people living there. In 1958 they decided to name it Nova Brasília, after the new national capital which was then under construction. Its growth has been rapid and continuous ever since. A Residents' Association study counted 8,899 inhabitants in August 1967, a date which according to Sr. Francisco marked the halfway point in a tremendous growth spurt that doubled the community's population. Most of the new growth took place in the hills in the back part of the favela which had remained almost vacant as late as 1966.

The property belongs mainly to the Instituto Nacional de Previdência Social (National Institute for Social Welfare). Aware that thousands of families were making their homes on this land, the institute tried to expel settlers and reestablish its rights of possession in 1959. Sr. José organized a delegation of six men and went downtown to look for a certain city councilman (*vereador*) who might intervene on their behalf. When the man could not be found, the group went directly to the institute's headquarters and convinced its president not to take further action. Their agreement held until 1961, when the institute mounted its second removal operation. Sr. José tells the story as follows:

> This time I organized a group of about a dozen to go down to the institute on the bus and protest. We had been given eight days' notice to move out. When twelve days had passed the police arrived to tear down houses. I said *nada disso*—none of this!—and began to organize the group to go downtown. But this was not enough because they told us that the head of the institute was away and went right on trying to oust the squatters from the property. But I was not about ready to let them get away with that. I rented eight enormous buses, filled them with all the men, women, children, chickens, pigs, and dogs I could find in the favela, and went to the Governor's Palace in Laranjeiras. We knew that the President of the Institute would be there, and we just got out, with a signed petition in our hands, and sat down in front of the palace—all of us—to see what they would do. Of course the President of the

PLATE 6.   Construction of a wattle-and-daub house by a newcomer to Nova Brasília. Houses like this are typical of the Brasilian countryside and are the easiest and least expensive for newly arrived favelados to build. As resources increase they gradually change over to wooden planks and eventually to brick if land tenure is secure enough to warrant the invest-ment. The house is made by creating a latticework of wooden boards or poles and then filling it in with a mixture of moist clay, sand, and dirt which dries into a durable stucco and can be plas-tered over and painted.

Institute had to come out and talk with us. We even called the newspapers and radio stations to come there and sent a telegram to the President of the Republic. We negotiated with him for a long time.

Finally the favelados were granted five years of grace on the insti-tute's land, after which time they had to either fix up all of their homes according to standard and resolve the title problem or be relocated. The agreement, however, was not enforced. The only people who have been evicted were about a dozen families who built their houses on the factory's land and were sent away in 1965-1966.

The part of the favela owned by this factory is an irregular space of empty green amidst dense construction and activity, clearly visible on the maps and photographs. People say there is an informal "taboo" against building in this area because of the importance of maintaining good relations with its owner, Sr. Tuffy, whose factory provides jobs for

PLATE 7.   House in transition along Rua Nova Brasília. The life cycle of this house is typical: originally a simple wattle-and-daub hut, it went through a phase of wood while bricks were being purchased one-by-one and stored in the backyard. When enough bricks had been amassed the house was carefully remade in brick. (Note the two types of brick on either side of the front door and the decorative work above the window.) Now, a second story is being added—it will remain wooden boards until it too can be transformed into brick.

many residents. Obviously, the incident of the evicted families is remembered as well. The state has initiated litigation to acquire this land from Sr. Tuffy. If it wins, which is highly likely, the land will revert to public domain and immediately be invaded by squatters. This is another reason the families are not risking their good relations with Tuffy, since they believe his days are numbered.

Although Nova Brasília meets all the criteria established by the State Planning Agency for "urbanization," and is located in a partially flat area where infrastructure would be easily installed, and is on a site of only moderate land values with low public visibility, nevertheless it falls on the list to be razed by 1976.

Associations. The Residents' Association, AMBNB (Associação dos Moradores do Bairro de Nova Brasília) originated in Sr. José's home on June 8, 1961, during the second fight against removal. It is much more

active and well organized than SOMAC in Catacumba. Besides the
delaying of removal and gaining official recognition of Rua Nova
Brasília, the association has arranged for location of a police station on
the upper hillside area called Alvorada, a fully equipped consulting
room in association headquarters, a vaccination center, a laboratory for
medical analysis, a large meeting room (including a bar and dance
floor), and—most recent of all—a new linkage of water and power
sources to supply the more remote portions of the population. The
association has obtained the service of a doctor, a dentist, a lawyer, a
part-time social worker, and a full-time receptionist to take care of
problems as they arise.

One of the first achievements of the association was the installation
of a loudspeaker system that could be heard all over the favela. Each
evening José would tell the news of the day, review the problems
facing the residents, and ask for the voluntary manpower needed to
proceed. The system is depicted in Figure 5, and also appears in Plate
7, over the house just to the left of the one in transition.

The main issues seem now to have faded into the background. José
is no longer president and the loudspeaker is used only rarely, to
announce a birthday, inform someone of a letter or telegram, help
visitors locate friends or relatives in the favela, or simply to play music.
The next item on the association's agenda is to get the city to build
covered bus stops in front of the favela on Avenida Itaoca. The present
director has promised action, saying, "It's all a question of pulling the
right strings."

From its beginning, AMBNB has had about 1,800 members.
According to the current president, Sr. Francisco, 1,200 are registered
and living in the favela, although only about 500 contribute any time or
pay the monthly dues. According to another member of the board of
directors, the figures are 400 dues-paying members and 30 to 40 who
attend meetings. This latter estimate corresponds more accurately to the
turnout in the general assembly meetings I witnessed while there.
During the study the AMBNB held 13 informal open meetings on
specific topics, 12 meetings of the board of directors, and 20 external
meetings with city officials of one kind or another.

According to Sr. Levi, who came to Nova Brasília from Minas
Gerais many years ago and has been a leader in the AMBNB since its
formation, the organization struggles constantly against popular apathy.
For most residents, participation is limited to periods of crisis. In his
words:

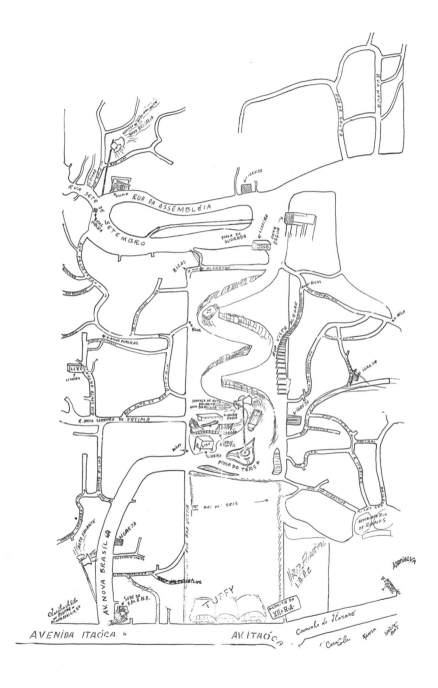

5. Sketch Map of Nova Brasília.

Those who are wealthier and better off are thinking of moving out of Nova Brasília and therefore are unwilling to devote any of their efforts to bettering the area. Those who've been here a while have become conformist, cynical, and unwilling to make the effort. The best group to try to involve are the newly arrived migrants. . . . But they, like the rest, have a very paternalistic attitude—they think that the association leaders should do everything for them. No one is willing to make any effort, or to go out of their way except for their immediate personal needs. They transfer their paternalistic attitude towards the authority and the government at large to the association.

As an example of this, he recounted the following:

The people living around the Praça do Terço—up there with the pigs, goats, and chickens hanging around the garbage dump—were complaining about the accumulation of filth and mess there and the damage to their health. Finally, after much difficulty, the association had to shovel that entire mountain of garbage all by themselves. After that, the association didn't pay much attention to that particular problem. . . . Most of the favelados have a very passive paternalistic attitude and expect the association to solve all of their problems without offering in return even the minimal cooperation or participation. . . . And when their necessities aren't looked after, they accuse the association of benefitting only its own directorate or of pocketing the public funds.

The formal organization of the Residents' Association is as impressive as any I witnessed in the favelas. The statutes are printed and bound in a handsome 30-page volume with the motto "Unida Venceremos" (United We Conquer) on the cover. Each year a full report on the accomplishments of the term is mimeographed, distributed, and filed. Careful records are kept of meetings, attendance, and business accomplished. A house-to-house census of sorts was conducted in August 1967. One of the members, the local artist, has sketched an "official" map of the area, which is on file at the headquarters and was used to identify the streets when the census was done. As seen in Figure 5, certain locations and streets of the favela were clearly more important to him than others and are emphasized on the map in various ways, such as the width of the streets Avenida Nova Brasília, Sete de Setembro, and Assembleia; and the identification of the Praça do Terço, the loudspeaker system, various garbage dumps, water tanks, and the Tuffy factory.

There are a number of less important organizations in Nova Brasília: an electricity commission (since 1967), three sports clubs, five evangelical temples, ten spiritist centers, a Catholic church, and two recreational associations.

Urban Services. When asked what the major problems of Nova Brasília were, the residents most often mentioned water, electricity, garbage disposal, and schools. While the association census of 1967 showed 35 percent of families with adequate water supply, my study, two years later, indicated 56 percent. This may be compared with the 10 percent figure for Catacumba (see Plates 8 and 9).

Electricity is an interesting issue in Nova Brasília. Many believe that ever since the Electricity Commission was established in 1967, it has made large profits and maneuvered to keep an official lighting system from being installed. Our study indicates that 45 percent of the residents still had no light whatsoever as of 1969. As with the water supply, those families in the highest and most recently settled portions of the favela have least access to urban services. The "knack" (*jeito*) of electric extensions from other houses is less frequent than in Catacumba, probably because of the greater distances between shacks. Even in the better areas many complain that there is not enough light to read the evening paper.

For sewage there is one closed pipeline along the main street and a series of open connecting channels. The system represents a slight improvement over that described for Catacumba. Garbage is supposed to be taken away three or four times a week by a truck from the Departamento de Limpeza Urbana, but residents do not collect it for easy transferral so it is generally left untouched. A central open-air incinerator was in construction in the Praça when I left. There are no gas pipelines and gas for cooking is purchased in pressurized containers (see Plate 10).

Schools. To the dismay of the residents, there are no regular educational facilities in Nova Brasília. Dna. Cecilia, who came from the backwoods of Espírito Santo some 25 years ago seeking medical help for her eight-year-old son, has been the main local schoolmistress. For a number of years she ran a tiny school in the remote Alvorado section, one of the highest areas of the favela. The Fundação Leon XIII helped out a little, but the main resource was Dna. Cecilia's compassion. "The little ones can't just be left on the street," she said. In 1967 she had about 40 students in the morning and the same number again in the afternoon. Part of her house was given over to another woman who held classes for the overflow. Adult literacy classes were held at night. In 1969, however, Dna. Cecilia became ill, and the school had to be closed. As I left the area a new one was being built with some Methodist Church funds which Dna. Cecilia had helped collect. She had gone

PLATES 8 AND 9.   People drawing water and carrying it to their homes in Nova Brasília. The collective spigots provide most families with their daily water supply and serve as a meeting place for women to exchange gossip and laughs. Plate 8 also shows the rural quality and open space of the favela and is reminiscent of paintings by Candido Portinari.

back to her home town in Espírito Santo to recuperate, and there was no telling what would happen without her energy behind the endeavor.

The nearest school is over a mile and a half away. It is a long walk, including some dangerous street crossings at places with heavy traffic and neither stoplights nor sidewalks. Parents, wary of allowing their children to make the trip alone, have formed a cooperative arrangement with a different mother accompanying the children each morning. Most of the favela's children, however, never see the inside of a classroom.

When Carlos Lacerda was governor, 1961-1963, the residents petitioned him for a school for the favela. He told them he didn't believe in putting schools inside favelas because the children there should not

PLATE 10.   Gas for cooking is purchased in metal vats and carried up to the shacks. What was a steep slippery hillside path here has been converted by the Residents' Association—in bargaining with electoral candidates— into a series of broad cement steps.

be isolated but rather should mix with those of the external community. He said he favored putting schools on the periphery of such areas. Sr. Levi told us he understood the logic of the argument but thought it shameful as a rationale for the nonexistence of educational opportunities for local children.

Commerce. Residents of Nova Brasília can buy almost anything they need in the community. As of 1969, the favela contained 47 small stores (*tendinhas*) and shops (*biroscas*)—often located in the front of dwellings—33 bars, and grocery stores (*mercearias*), 13 barber shops, six clothing stores, two butchers, three chicken and egg stalls, two pharmacies, four fruit and vegetable stands (*quitandas*), two coal and charcoal shops, a photo-development stall, a furniture store, a tailor, two beauty parlors, six drygoods shops, two construction material stores, a lawyer, and a public telephone. Entrepreneurial activity has taken a strong root in Nova Brasília, and all of it is in the hands of local residents, not outsiders. As discussed in Chapter Seven, internal development was even more impressive as of 1973. (See Plates 28, 29, 30, 31 in Chapter Seven.)

A Subúrbio: Duque de Caxias

Life in the subúrbios provides yet another kind of urban existence for the migrant. Thirty years ago, the Baixada Fluminense was a swampy wasteland, totally undeveloped and only sparsely inhabited. As the need for land around the city became increasingly desperate, four municipalities were carved out of these lowlands. These are now among the fastest growing regions in the world. The most rapidly growing of the four is Duque de Caxias, which became an independent municipality in 1943.

Caxias is divided into four districts, only the first of which is included within Greater Metropolitan Rio. Even there, only the center of town with its administrative buildings, plaza, and central market place, and a few of the adjacent, well-to-do blocks, are fully "urbanized." Land values in most of the other 32 neighborhoods are generally so low that small plots can actually be purchased for amounts within the reach of many first- and second-generation migrants looking for a place of their own.[12] This is the major alternative to the option of squatting. In order to ascertain whether the fact of ownership (or legal renter status) with its concomitant security makes a significant difference, we sampled five legal neighborhoods and three favelas within Caxias. These are shown in Figure 6. The houses, in both cases, are likely to be made of plastered concrete or brick, since even in the squatter zones the threat of removal is low enough so people are willing to invest in home improvement. Space is often available for chicken raising and gardening.

The major problem is that Caxias is about one and a half to two hours from Rio by bus and about 80 percent of its work force commutes daily to inner-city jobs. Residents often have to line up for buses or trains as early as four o'clock in the morning in order to insure arrival in the city at seven or eight when the work day begins. Transportation is extremely inadequate and the cost quite high relative to incomes (sometimes as much as a quarter of monthly earnings).

Of the 600,000 people in Caxias, almost all are first- or second-generation migrants. There is a small and growing elite, but in general the environment does not offer much in heterogeneity of personal contacts, nor much choice in style of living or recreation. There are few urban services and governmental agencies, although this is gradually beginning to change.

Location. Caxias, though closely integrated into the Greater Metropolitan Area of Rio, was located in the State of Rio (whose administrative

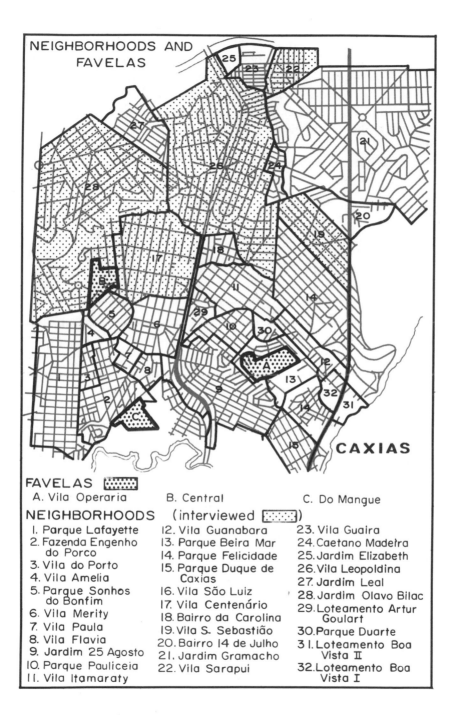

NEIGHBORHOODS AND FAVELAS

FAVELAS ▨

A. Vila Operaria   B. Central   C. Do Mangue

NEIGHBORHOODS (interviewed ▨)

1. Parque Lafayette
2. Fazenda Engenho do Porco
3. Vila do Porto
4. Vila Amelia
5. Parque Sonhos do Bonfim
6. Vila Merity
7. Vila Paula
8. Vila Flavia
9. Jardim 25 Agosto
10. Parque Pauliceia
11. Vila Itamaraty

12. Vila Guanabara
13. Parque Beira Mar
14. Parque Felicidade
15. Parque Duque de Caxias
16. Vila São Luiz
17. Vila Centenário
18. Bairro da Carolina
19. Vila S. Sebastião
20. Bairro 14 de Julho
21. Jardim Gramacho
22. Vila Sarapui

23. Vila Guaira
24. Caetano Madeira
25. Jardim Elizabeth
26. Vila Leopoldina
27. Jardim Leal
28. Jardim Olavo Bilac
29. Loteamento Artur Goulart
30. Parque Duarte
31. Loteamento Boa Vista II
32. Loteamento Boa Vista I

6. Neighborhoods and Favelas in Duque de Caxias.

capital was Niteroi), not in the State of Guanabara (whose capital was
the city of Rio).[e] The tug of allegiances between Niteroi and Guanabara
created grave problems for Caxias, especially in the building of urban
infrastructure. Logically, the services of Caxias should be planned and
coordinated with those of Guanabara and be financed through its budget, but at the time of the study the two areas were totally separate. The
mayor of Caxias, however, had contracted for the architectural firm of
Mauricio Roberto to draw up an integrated development plan and elaborate the case for a jurisdictional revision which would bring the whole
Metropolitan Area under one administrative framework. And in fact, at
this writing, the two states are in the process of becoming officially
united as one—the federal law was passed in the fourth quarter of
1974—and now it is up to the united assembly of the two states to work
out the specific details.

Caxias' situation is ideal as an industrial center for the Rio area. It
is located on the Leopoldina Railroad and bordered by two of the most
important highways in the area, Rio—São Paulo and Rio—Petrópolis. It
already has the largest oil refinery and synthetic rubber plant in Brazil; a
huge National Motor Company factory; and a variety of other industries
including pharmaceuticals, chemicals, metallurgy, and electric motors.
Over 22 percent of the industrial production of Rio comes from the 300
industrial establishments located in the city's industrial park. The vast
majority (90 percent) of local industry is owned by the national government rather than by private corporations or entrepreneurs.[13] As indicated above, only a small portion of the labor force works in commerce
or industry in Caxias, but more local jobs are gradually opening up.
Residents who hold highly skilled or professional positions can already
find good employment in the local job market.

Caxias is known all over the region for its enormous Sunday street-
market, which opens at three or four o'clock in the morning and lasts
until mid-afternoon. The stalls extend for 10 or 20 blocks along the railroad tracks and inward along the main thoroughfare. The covered portion is an immense bustling maze in which one can get lost for hours,
and people come from miles around to do their bargain shopping there.

Population. Caxias has seen phenomenal growth in the last ten years. Its
growth rate has been 8 to 10 percent per year. For example, 1960 estimates listed 17,000 dwellings in the first district; by 1968 the figure had

[e]These legal distinctions were made when the nation's capital was moved to Brasília
in 1961 and Rio ended its status as a Federal District.

risen to 82,000. Recent estimates place the population of the First District at 355,000, and that of the city as a whole at 600,000. The city covers 442 square kilometers, giving a density of 1,400 persons per square kilometer compared with 34,000 in Nova Brasília and 110,000 in Catacumba.

History. Much of Caxias is below sea level. Until fairly recently most of it was an impassable swamp. The area developed in three distinct phases. During the colonial period enormous sugar plantations were established around Guanabara Bay. Because of poor drainage, the Caxias portion was not developed until the first half of the nineteenth century, when (with proper attention to drainage techniques) the land began to flourish. In the second half of the century, the decline of sugar cane, a progressive shortage of slave labor, and improved transportation links between Rio and more remote fertile lands caused a general deterioration in the area. The Baixada rivers became totally obstructed and the region reverted to a swamp. When malaria moved in, most inhabitants moved out.

After many years, the government of President Nilo Peçanha launched a program to reclaim the area. In 1933 a sanitation program was undertaken and the water pipes of the Federal District hooked up for local service. With extension of the Leopoldina Railroad line into the area, there was a sudden surge in settlement. The Rio—Petrobrás highway opened and land speculation began in earnest. The urban phase of the municipality had begun; its rural phase had ended.

Starting in 1943 when Caxias separated from Nova Iguacú, the city began to mirror the growth of Rio itself. As urban space in Rio became saturated and new bus lines began local service, the federal government decided to locate some of its industrial enterprises in the state of Rio. The Petrobrás oil refinery opened in 1969. Private investment followed, and in a few years the industrial park in the First District developed a momentum of its own. Caxias is moving away from being a dormitory city for Rio and becoming a growth pole in its own right. [14]

Political Background. Caxias has a widespread reputation as a violent, dangerous city. It is common among the Brazilian middle class to believe all favelas unsafe—few will enter them at all—but Caxias holds special terrors. Part of this terror springs from the fact that in many areas of Caxias men still carry guns, a holdover from habits of the interior. Also, in 1962 Caxias experienced a food strike and mass uprising during which stores were robbed and looted at gunpoint, and some shopkeepers were burned to death in ovens (which they had used to hoard beans and rice in order to raise already inflated prices).[15]

The Caxias mystique also involves a dramatic figure—Tenório Cavalcanti, a charismatic and colorful leader from the state of Alagoas. Cavalcanti was an early migrant to the area and one of its first elected deputies. He gave rousing public addresses, draped in a black cloak, and "wheeled and dealed" for his constituency and himself. He lived in a "fort" he had built in the center of the city and had an armed entourage of strongmen always at his side. Cavalcanti was the prototype paternalistic, populist leader. At the time of the flood in 1958, when thousands of families from the favela of Mangue were left homeless, he arranged for the construction of Vila São José, an instant neighborhood of row houses, for displaced families. A less charitable version of the story (often there were less charitable versions) was that he appropriated public funds for the construction and then charged the residents exorbitant rents. Despite countless charges of corruption, Cavalcanti was popular enough to be considered a threat to the military regime and was therefore deprived of his political rights (cassado) in 1965. Since then he has remained in Caxias on his well-guarded fazenda with its elegant veranda, swimming pool, zoological garden, and suite of guest rooms.[f]

There is only one blatantly violent aspect of Caxias' political system, the esquadrão do Morte (Death Squad). The esquadrão is a vigilante group composed of off-duty policemen which decided to carry out justice in a quicker and more efficient fashion than possible through regular channels.

The military regime now has declared Caxias, along with many other municipalities across the country, an "area of national security." No more municipal elections are to be held. When the term of the present Prefect, Moacyr Rodriques do Carno, expires, all future officials will be appointed directly by the governor with the approval of the President of the Republic.[16]

At the local level, the mayor's assistant said the population was slowly moving toward public action. More and more, Residents' Associations, neighborhood organizations, street associations, and individuals

---

[f] I visited him there a number of times, but he was too defensive to reveal much of his political past, aside from reciting long lists of favors he had done for the people and equally long lists of lies his enemies perpetrated against him. People either give orders, he said, or follow them; as for himself, he chose giving.

(women even more than men) were coming directly to the mayor's office to demand better services. "They no longer take no for an answer," he said. They get petitions signed and keep pressuring until their demands are met. He mentioned the popularity of Umbanda and Macumba (the Afro-Brazilian spiritist cults of which there are 200 to 300 organized groups in Caxias), soccer clubs (Caxias has a new stadium), and the many recreational clubs and samba schools. He called these *pão e circenses* (bread and circuses) or *válvulas de escape* (escape valves), indicating that these kept the people from thinking about or working on their real problems.

Urban Services. In general, urban services in Caxias did not seem to be any better than those in the North and South Zone favelas. Only 17 percent of the residents we interviewed had running water indoors—more than in Catacumba (where the terrain made this such a problem) but less than in Nova Brasília. About half the Caxias households—roughly the same proportion as in the other two areas—had no bathrooms in or attached to their dwellings; and only 45 percent of the area is serviced by enclosed sewer pipes. One quarter of the houses are without electricity. Only half of the 23 neighborhoods of Caxias, technically not favelas, have official water supplies. Figure 7 shows the network of drinking water and Figure 8 that of paved roads. These and other service maps allowed us to identify those neighborhoods most similar to the favelas.

There is an acute shortage of teachers in the area, and of schoolrooms as well. The few schools that do exist are generally located in the downtown area around the central plaza. Thus, only 13 percent of school-age children are in elementary school, and only 2 percent of those eligible for secondary school have the opportunity to attend.

Favelas. Since Caxias includes both favelas and private property with the same standard of living, inhabited by migrants with the same backgrounds, individuals from both types of area were sampled. The three largest favelas in Caxias—Vila Operária, Favela Central, and Mangue—were chosen for sampling. Because of especially interesting features, favelas Operária and Mangue warrant special attention.

Vila Operária, sometimes called Beiramar or Parque Duque, was established by an invasion of some 2,000 families (10,000 people) one night in 1962.[17] The organizer and innovative leader of the invasion was José Barbosa. He decided to restrict the area to only those who were married, had children, were steadily employed, and had no police

7. Drinking Water Network in Duque de Caxias.

record. When the prefect was approached with this plan he agreed to let the invaders remain on the land. Sixteen or 17 parties immediately claimed ownership of the land and demanded payment from the government or the squatters. Ownership of the land is still in dispute.

In his own way, José has attempted to foresee the favelas' problems and deal with them in advance (see Plate 11). His first act in office was to use the dues of the first 250 persons to buy an ambulance and start a school. He has prohibited renting shacks (barracos) to avoid the speculation and exploitation often common in the favelas of Rio. To forestall formation of cliques and avoid fights and misunderstandings, José prohibited friends and relatives from locating their homes near one another.

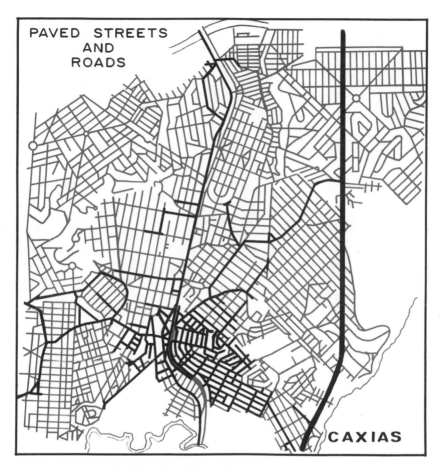

8. Paved Road Network in Duque de Caxias.

To the same end, all homes were placed under the joint legal ownership of women and men, "so that when they have a fight the women have equal rights and can't be kicked out."g After bragging at some length

---

gJosé established the precedent that in domestic squabbles the woman would come to see him. "I then call the husband to discuss the problem calmly and if he is really furious and violent, I take him to the police station to cool off." At one time when sickness abounded and 15 to 20 children were dying each month, José trained a small commission of local women to go from house to house teaching the fundamentals of hygiene, home economics, and health. Bulletins were broadcast over loudspeakers reminding mothers to boil water thoroughly before giving it to children, wash their hands before preparing food, and so on.

PLATE 11.   Favela Vila Operária in Duque de Caxias was built by an invasion of
the hillside in 1962. It supports its own schoolteachers with the revenue from the
amusement park shown in the foreground. (The two men were part of our research
team.)

that he was "born with the spirit of leadership," José remarked, disin-
genuously to say the least, that "the people around here have to take a
more responsible position in helping the government. They should not
see the government as a welfare state, and should stop having the paternalistic attitude that things are going to be done for them."

Favela Central is a "planned" favela. In order to maximize the use
of space and minimize costs of construction and infrastructure installments, the favelados decided to build adjoining row houses like those
shown in Plate 12. Beneath the drainage channel that runs down the
center of their front sidewalk, lie the water and sewage pipes. Each
family was responsible for purchasing and installing the part of the pipelines in front of their own house. The extra open space thus created is
used as a soccer field.

The favela of Mangue is located in a swamp that floods annually.
Its main street becomes a veritable river of mud in the rainy season and
the back edge of the favela is too boggy to support even the most flimsy

PLATE 12. Favela
Central in Duque
de Caxias, a
planned favela.

dwelling. When all of its dwellings were swept away in the 1958 flood, a
dozen residents decided not to go to Cavalcanti's public housing project
but to stay and reestablish a community on the spot. Mangue now has a
population of 5,000 and a Residents' Association with 250 members, of
whom 25 to 50 participate regularly.

Each year in January and February, the time of the floods, the
residents place sacks of cement in front of their doors and brick up their
windows. They take pride in photographs showing themselves waist-
deep in water in their front yards, or floating down their streets on
improvised rafts and canoes.

At the time of the interviews, the residents had been waiting three
months for the prefect's office to approve paving the main street of the

PLATE 13.   Children clowning for the camera on the sidelines of a Sunday soccer
game in Favela Central. Note the racial mixture of Portuguese, Indian, and African
descent.

favela and enclosing the open sewer (see Plate 14). A commission from
Mangue had presented a petition to the government asking for the raw
materials and agreeing to supply the labor themselves. They had
received a promise of quick action. A local leader told us it was probably only propaganda, that even the local *vereador* (city councilor) could
not help since "he had his own problems." Since the coup (*golpe*), he
explained, *vereadores* continued to be elected but no longer had any
power. "You have to be pre-selected by the elite clique in order to be
given a chance with the people. . . . People here are resigned, they ask
for something and then keep waiting passively. They are afraid of
repression."

It is especially important, given this repression and the fact that
the favelados cannot defend their own interests even when these are
abundantly clear, that the realities of their lives be brought to light.

PLATE 14. Boy playing on footbridge across the open sewer in the Favela of Mangue in Duque de Caxias is a testimony to the health hazard of this arrangement. Residents petitioned for months for approval to pave the main road and enclose the sewer but to no avail.

Stereotypes of favela parochialism and passivity are reinforced in the absence of free expression or objective outside research. Even the most basic facts—such as who the migrants are, where they come from, and why and how they come—are little known, which allows existing misperceptions and erroneous assumptions to go unchallenged.

Chapter Three
Portrait of the Migrant

Turning from the community to the individual, this chapter presents a composite portrait of the people, beginning with favelados in general and then focusing on the migrants—where they came from, what prior urban experience they had, why and how they came to Rio, and what their adaptation to the city was like. I will conclude by examining differences between natives and migrants and between residents with urban and nonurban backgrounds.

WHO ARE THE FAVELADOS?

The common stereotype of favelados as male, black, footloose, uninterested in work, and without stable family lives is misleading both in its characterization of the black male population, and in its simplification of the complex texture of the overall favela population. The basic demographic data is summarized in Table 3. Somewhat more women than men live in favelas, though sex proportions are hard to establish precisely. I took my best estimate (women as 55 percent of the population) from Catacumba, where our procedures were most rigorous. This mild imbalance probably occurs because of the wider variety of acceptable alternatives for males—such as living in military barracks, on construction sites, or in boarding houses—and because of the slightly higher migration rates for women.

Racially, 21 percent of favelados are black, 30 percent mulatto, and 49 percent white.[1] This approximate racial balance is typical of Rio's favelas, but should not be taken to reflect racial equality in the society as a whole. The third who are black represent nearly *all* of Rio's blacks; favela whites, on the other hand, are but a fraction of all whites living in the city.

The average age of the favelado is 34 years. As for marital status, 24 percent are single, 66 percent married or cohabiting (referred to as "togethered" or "married in the green church"); 5 percent separated; and 5 percent widowed. In modern urban fashion, the nuclear family rather than the extended kinship group predominates in the favela. In our sample, 90 percent of the residents belonged to nuclear family

TABLE 3
Profile of the Favelados

Characteristic	Percent of Random Sample (N=600)	Percent of Elite Sample (N=150)
Sex		
Male	41	90
Female	59	10
Race		
Black	20	12
Mulatto	30	24
White	50	69
Age		
Mean	34	41
Mode	33	40
Median	33	40
Kinship		
Family head	37	85
Spouse	38	6
Child	15	6
Other	10	4
Marital Status		
Single	24	13
Married or united	66	79
Separated	5	6
Widowed	5	3
Religion		
None	6	11
Catholic	72	66
Assembly of God	10	3
Baptist	5	3
Spiritist	4	11
Other	4	5
Education		
Illiterate	31	13
No school, but literate	9	9
First grade	9	5
Second grade	11	9

TABLE 3
Profile of the Favelados (Continued)

Characteristic	Percent of Random Sample (N=600)	Percent of Elite Sample (N=150)
Education (cont.)		
Third grade	10	14
Fourth grade	15	15
Fifth grade	7	13
Admission course for "Ginasio" or more	9	20
Occupation		
White collar	4	10
Security	1	8
Merchant	4	21
Skilled	5	5
Construction	6	13
Semi-skilled	4	14
Domestic	19	2
Unskilled	15	10
Unemployed	28	13
Underemployed	2	2
Never worked	13	1
Origin		
Rio-born	18	21
Migrants	82	79

NOTE: Percentages in all Tables are rounded off to the nearest whole number.

households, leaving just 10 percent as assorted relatives or friends. Although favelados almost unanimously described a two-child family (one boy and one girl) as their ideal, the average household actually has 4.6 children. Illiteracy in the favelas is 30 percent, only about half of that in the countryside (60 to 70 percent). Twenty-eight percent of those favelados we interviewed were unemployed; 13 percent never worked.

The differences in these indicators between the random and elite samples is shown clearly in Table 3. Both political and social leadership is made up of a male-dominated elite; women are excluded even from the local world of neighborhood influentials, in which nine out of ten leaders are men. The elite group is also predominantly white (65 percent), older than the overall average by seven years (41 years old), and twice as likely as the average favelado to be literate and employed.

Certainly all favelados are *not* migrants. Our data indicate that almost a third of Rio's favela residents are city-born; 18 percent in fact were born in Rio itself.[2] Native favelados often live in the same shanty-towns where they were born. In absolute numbers, however, migrants accounted for 494 of the 600 people in the random sample, and 119 of the 150 people in the elite sample.

About one-fifth of our sample are second-generation Cariocas (natives of Rio), and less than 2 percent are third-generation.[3] This leaves a large majority of favelados—82 percent—who have experienced migration at some point in their lives. Discounting those coming from another large city, this still leaves 69 percent who have come from municipal seats, towns, villages, or the rural interior.[a] The large proportion of migrants in our sample is an accurate reflection of the composition of the favelas. Therefore it is essential to look more closely at their individual characteristics and the larger causes of migration to the city.[4]

WHO ARE THE MIGRANTS?

The process of migration to the favelas of a metropolitan area is by no means a homogeneous or identical one for all of the migrants. Although to some extent they share the same fate and urban living conditions, their migratory experience obviously differs significantly. Some of the migrants, for example, are married males with a background in agriculture, while others are single women coming from major urban centers. Some of them come as children or teenagers, others as adults or even grandparents.

I hoped to find a pattern of basic variables that would cluster the migrant population into different sub-groups and explain the difference in their personal attributes and the degree of success in their urban adaptation.

Attempts at creating a typology of this kind were made by using a combination of variables abstracted from background data and migratory experience. No meaningful groupings could be found using criteria of age, sex, marital status, size of birthplace, motive for migration, number of intermediate moves, time in transit, or persons accompanying

[a]The Brazilian word for the rural countryside, *roça*, will be loosely translated as "farm" throughout most of the text.

migrants. All the distributions were nearly flat: equal numbers of men and women had migrated at every age; equal proportions of those coming from every region came in one or many stages. Types could be defined, but these rarely included enough members to warrant additional investigation.[b]

It was nearly as difficult to determine whether migrants came from the bottom or the top of rural social strata. Migrants had been assumed to be the most destitute of the rural poor. While it was impossible to compare Rio's migrants with those people who remained in the rural areas, my data tended to support recent empirical research showing that "migrants to large cities are universally above national averages for education, skill, and acquaintance with urban ways, and in some cities they suffer no handicap in the labor market vis-à-vis native urbanites."[5] My own experience, and the data of Morse, Beyer, Balan, Sjoberg, and Germani, suggests that migration is selective: only the more dynamic members of the rural population migrate to the cities.[6]

This selective migration tends to perpetuate a docile work force in the rural communities. In the words of the Brazilian social scientist, Octavio Ianni: "The departure of the men . . . relieves social tensions, decreasing the conflicts about work and labor. . . . Ofttimes the migrants are men of action or men with potential qualities for leadership and organization. They have a broader cultural horizon than the average, and the migration of these persons to the urban centers represents a loss of vanguard elements."[7]

Selective migration seemed evident to me on the basis of field work in Bahia, Pernambuco, and Minas Gerais. The impression was strengthened by a trip with one favela family to its "home town," Santo Antonio de Padua in the State of Rio. This village, only six hours from the city of Rio de Janeiro, had been losing its more dynamic members through migration for over 20 years. The results were striking: only the uneducated, unskilled, and unmotivated remain, eking out a meager existence that makes the favelados' life look luxurious by comparison.

Leaving relative status aside, however, we must emphasize the absolute poverty of the typical migrants in their place of origin (see Table 4). Only 5 percent could be considered even remotely middle

[b]Work in progress at the time of this writing, however, is showing that by using the two variables of distance and decade of migration an interesting typology *can* be defined, which meaningfully discriminates between sub-sectors of the migratory stream.

class, with another 14 percent working class or blue collar. The remaining 81 percent come from the lowest sector—mostly agricultural workers and some unskilled laborers. Sixty-six percent of the fathers of migrants worked in agriculture; 60 percent of them were illiterate. Even among migrants born in large cities, almost a third of their fathers worked with the *enxada* (hoe) most of their lives. Before moving, only 2 percent of migrants had white collar jobs, 7 percent blue collar. Thirty-seven percent held unskilled and agricultural jobs, and the remainder had not yet begun to work. Of those not working, about a third were under 12, a third 13-20, and a third over 20 years of age. Seventy-eight percent of the migrants were illiterate at the time of migration. Three-fourths were single when they came to the city; most of the rest were married and had children.

Where Do Migrants Come From? The predominant myth is that migrants are rural peasants coming directly from the countryside.[8] Data gathered on the topic differs: Bonilla found two-thirds of the Rio favelados he studied of rural origin,[9] while the Leeds, discussing the same city, state "our guess is that they constitute no more than 5 percent of the population."[10] My findings place the figure between these two extremes. As shown in Table 4, of the 494 people who migrated to Rio, 23 percent came from the rural countryside (*a roça*), 25 percent from a small town or village (*vila* or *povoado*), 33 percent from a provincial administrative center (*sede municipal*), and 19 percent from large cities other than Rio, usually state capitals.[11]

In Brazil, the assumption that migrants are peasants is linked with the idea of a massive exodus from the drought-stricken Northeast.[12] In fact, of the favelados we interviewed, about an equal number came from the Northeast, the State of Rio, and the Eastern states of Minas Gerais and Espírito Santo.[13] According to census figures, and our aggregate data, migration from the Northeast to Rio has been declining relative to that from the states of Minas Gerais and Espírito Santo. Recife and Bahia have recently become "poles of attraction" in their own right under the impetus of industrialization and development programs, and are deflecting some of the migration that would otherwise be directed toward São Paulo and Rio. The idea of the Northeast disaster exodus is further weakened by considering the relationship between region and size of place. Contrary to expectations, while people coming from farms were about equally divided among all regions, 40 percent of all those

TABLE 4

Profile of the Migrants

Variable	Percent of Random Sample (N=494)[a]	Percent of Elite Sample (N=119)[b]
Place of origin		
City (cidade grande)	19	19
Municipal seat (sede municipal)	33	32
Town or village (vila or povoada)	25	26
Farm (roça)	23	23
Region of origin		
Rio area	32	29
East	32	32
Northeast	32	34
Other	4	5
Class background		
Father's education		
Illiterate	60	40
Elementary incomplete	39	37
Elementary complete or more	1	22
Father's job		
Skilled or white-collar	8	10
Semi-skilled	16	16
Unskilled	6	7
Agriculture	66	59
Unemployed or never worked	4	9
Job at time of migration		
Never worked	52	37
White-collar	1	3
Blue-collar	6	12
Unskilled	11	13
Agriculture	27	33
Unemployed	3	1
Education at time of migration		
Illiterate	78	43
Literate	22	57
Migration background (class background and size of origin)		
City-born, white-collar	2	4
City-born, blue-collar	5	4

TABLE 4
Profile of the Migrants (Continued)

Variable	Percent of Random Sample (N=494)[a]	Percent of Elite Sample (N=119)[b]
Migration background (class background and size of origin) (continued)		
City-born, lumpen	11	11
Municipal seat, white-collar	3	3
Municipal seat, blue-collar	6	6
Municipal seat, lumpen	24	23
Village or farm, white-collar	3	2
Village or farm, blue-collar	4	6
Village or farm, lumpen	40	40
Age at time of migration		
1-12 years old (child)	31	30
13-20 years old (teen)	37	39
21 and over (adult)	33	31
Migrant type (age and sex)		
Female child	16	2
Male child	9	18
Female teen	24	6
Male teen	19	43
Female adult	18	2
Male adult	14	29
Marital status at time of migration		
Single without children	74	77
Married without children	4	7
Married with children	17	13
Single with children	5	3
Motive for migration		
Economic, financial	46	62
Family reasons	44	20
Health reasons	2	1
Availability of urban services	3	2
Attraction of the city	2	7
"Acts of God"	2	0
Military service	1	8

[a]In the random sample 494 out of 600, or 82.3 percent, are migrants.
[b]In the elite sample 119 out of 150, or 79.3 percent, are migrants.

coming from big cities were from the Northeast as compared with 35 percent and 23 percent from the Rio area and the East. Yet, it is supposedly the peasants, not the city dwellers, of the Northeast who have been driven to migrate by droughts, floods, scarcity of good land, and the other "push" factors so often mentioned.[14]

Prior Urban Experience. The original myth that migrants were rural peasants totally unprepared for city life was replaced by a newer, contradictory theory that they were almost totally pre-urbanized by the time they arrived in the city. Harris has argued that an "urban ethos" or urban ideology permeates towns even as small as 1,500 or 2,000 people all over Brazil.[15] The Leeds have contended further that the latifundio have strongly urban elements in organization, administration, and orientation. According to them, also, the typical "peasant" migrant has "labored on a farm, sold in the money market, become familiar with the modalities of transactions, with the urban ambience, with the urban institutions—police, bureaucrats, licensing, trade, exchange, traffic flow, transportation, etc.[16]

I went to some lengths to test this notion in my study, and found it only partially true at best. I asked people from villages, small towns, and farms how frequently they had traveled to the nearest city and for what purpose. A third (32 percent) had *never* gone or gone only a few times in their lives and thus had virtually none of the urban experience the Leeds speak of. Another 34 percent went monthly or a few times a year, the remaining 33 percent weekly or daily. Of the 244 people who came from the villages, small towns, and farms, then, only 78 had the kind of experience assumed to be the modal pattern.

In addition, the motives of those who *did* go to the cities do not add up to the kind of pre-urbanizing institutional experience the Leeds emphasize. Of those who visited cities, only 3 percent said the trip was to obtain documents, see a lawyer, or visit a bureaucratic agency or bank. Another 16 percent went to look for jobs, and the vast majority went for purchases (47 percent) or for recreation (34 percent). These latter two activities, though undoubtedly giving the migrant some experience in handling the urban environment, certainly do not prepare him for dealing with the large bureaucracies and the different roles that he encounters coming to a metropolitan area like Rio. Twice as many leaders from such rural locations, it might be noted, visited cities. Even in the countryside, leaders had been more mobile and motivated before coming to the city.

Why Do People Migrate? Migration studies frequently rely on either a "push" or a "pull" theory as the major explanation for the movement of the rural poor. The major "push" theory is that people are driven off the land by depletion of the soil, poor climatic conditions (especially flood and drought), smaller and smaller subdivision of land for subsistence agriculture, and the overall grinding poverty of remote rural areas. Sovani points out, however, that many Asian countries had land pressure before they experienced any urban growth, and that many Latin American and African countries have had rapid urban growth without any land pressure. [17]

Ianni describes the macroeconomic, structural "push" factors that also affect migration: "The rural exodus is not a unilateral fact arising from the attraction of the city and its industries. It is related also to the changes in the technical and social conditions of production in several of the agricultural regions. . . . Little by little capitalistic technology in the rural areas expanded, producing unemployment and the expulsion of a portion of the labor force." [18]

Recent empirical studies, however, have discredited the importance of push factors in migration. Germani, for example, found no correlation between the degree of rural poverty and the tendency to migrate. He believes instead that "objective factors are filtered through the attitudes and decisions of the individuals. . . . Therefore rural-urban migration is not merely a symptom, a demographic fact, and a response to a certain economic pressure, but also the expression of a mental change. . . . Thus one can say migration is a substitute for social revolution." [19] Werner Baer divided the rural areas of Brazil into zones of varying degrees of poverty and economic-climatic depression and found the rates of out-migration fairly constant from each of them. No greater migration was evident from areas where push factors should have been strongest. [20]

On the micro-level, the data are by no means definitive in resolving the main controversy as to whether push or pull factors predominate in migration. Both elements are undoubtedly present and it is a question of which are more operative under what circumstances. It is interesting to note, however, that according to migrants themselves, economic considerations are not the only factor in their decisions. Less than half (46 percent) mention an economic concern as the reason for their move. An equal number speak of family or health reasons—to join a relative or spouse, escape from a difficult family situation, find a husband or wife, or get medical treatment.[c] Only 2 percent mention clearly "push" factors such as natural disasters, climatic or soil conditions, or "acts of God," while only 5 percent say "attraction of the city itself"—which is the obvious "pull" factor. The Leeds speak of the importance of military service as a propelling force for many in migration; but only 1 percent of the rank and file and 4 percent of the leaders mention this.[21]

We found most migrants unable to describe their decision to migrate with any precision. It was clear that specific decisions involved complex factors, many of them not even conscious. Often a mixture of motives, involving pushes and pulls, works differently for persons in different life circumstances, as the following four vignettes demonstrate.

Adult men with rural backgrounds and families tend to leave their homes only when it seems impossible to stay. For example, Sebastião left a small town in Pernambuco's interior at the age of 54. He came to Rio with his wife and three of 16 children, some of whom were already in the city, because, as he put it, "I couldn't make it there anymore. . . . There weren't any more jobs to be found and the land wasn't supporting us." To make the trip he sold his only possession, one cow, and walked two days to arrive at Recife where he bought a ticket to Rio for the equivalent of about U.S. $50.00.

Contrasted with this is the case of Amaro, a younger man who came to Rio from Minas Gerais at the age of 19 to search for "better opportunities." At 17 Amaro had already left his birthplace, a *fazenda* (Brazilian-style plantation) and moved to the nearest municipal seat because "the situation was lousy and I wanted a better life." He had a brother in Rio who came to visit him and described "all the advantages in Rio, including better salaries and more *movimento*." Shortly afterward, Amaro borrowed money from his mother for the trip and convinced a cousin to go along. Amaro lived in three other favelas before settling on Catacumba as his home. The prominent factor in his decision, and that of many like him, was the desire to "be where the action is." In his mind the countryside was a dead-end where the years plodded on in dull predictability

[c]A few more men (52 percent) mentioned economic motives, a few more women (52 percent) family motives.

while the city represented the unknown, exciting, and unforeseeable future.[22]

A third example is Dona Juliana, who came to Rio from Paraiba do Norte when she was 20. She was single and worried about becoming "an old maid." Relatives arranged for her to go directly to the home of a wealthy family in Copacabana as a domestic, a common pattern among the 24 percent of migrants in this age-sex bracket. Soon after arriving she found a boyfriend and became pregnant. The family she worked for expelled her, and she moved in with her boyfriend in Catacumba. Three children later, he abandoned her. Now Dona Juliana takes in washing so she can earn some money without leaving her children for long periods of time; she lives in the worst part of the favela—an open sewer runs by her front door—and she longs for the opportunity to buy some land and have a house of her own. (Others like her, however, who also came as maids, still work, with fairly good pay, high job security, and lots of "fringe benefits" in the homes to which they were originally sent.)

Older women tend to come for family-related reasons, often to join husbands who had gone ahead to look for a job and a place to live. Dona Cecilia, the Nova Brasília schoolmistress, originally came to Rio seeking medical help for an ailing child who had swallowed some caustic soda and desperately needed help. The trip took two days of walking and three days on the train. When she arrived she looked up her husband's brother who lived in Nova Brasília, but he refused to take her in. Finally, she found a doctor who would operate on her son and who saved his life. Since then, Dona Cecilia has become one of the most active community leaders in Nova Brasília, not only setting up the school, but also organizing many of the campaigns with city officials over land titles and city services. Although barely literate herself, she has dictated a number of powerful, scathing letters to public officials and agencies, having them typed on behalf of the Residents' Association and signed like petitions.

Each of these four people, in different life circumstances, came to the city for a mixture of reasons, hardship weighing more heavily for some, the attraction of urban opportunity more compelling for others.

How Do Migrants Come? How does the migration process take place? Is it direct or stepwise? Is it done alone, in family groups, or by whole clans? Do migrants have someone to turn to in the city or not? As mentioned in Chapter One, there is much controversy in the literature on these points.

Recently many scholars have felt they had to refute the "simplistic" notion that people leave rural or small-town homes and come directly to the city, insisting instead that "step-wise" movement patterns through larger and larger cities are more common.[23] I gathered year-by-year migratory histories of each respondent in part to help resolve these controversies. To my surprise, the findings totally contradict the "step-wise" hypothesis. For each person a "string" representing the actual path he or she had taken between the four sizes of places—farm, village, municipal seat, and city—was constructed. All these strings were then compiled to see if patterns emerged. Moves between places within the same size bracket (such as farm to farm) were not counted. Of all migrants, only 8 percent came to the city in a step-wise manner (see Table 5). The rest did not necessarily come directly to Rio from their birthplace, but they had no experience in places larger than their birthplaces prior to Rio. Twenty-six percent of favelados came to Rio directly from another big city. Another 54 percent came directly from places of other size with no intermediary steps, and 12 percent took erratic paths including back-stepping to places of smaller size.[d]

Even in terms of absolute number of moves before arrival in Rio (disregarding sizes or levels of places moved to), one-step migration is the norm, not the exception. As seen in Table 6, 67 percent of the migrant population has made no residential moves whatsoever prior to coming to Rio; this conforms to the experience of Sebastião, Juliana, and Cecilia described above—all came directly from their diverse places of origin. Among those who did move before coming to Rio, two-thirds moved only once, as did Amaro. Most of the others moved twice; a small minority, 6 percent, moved four or more times.

With Whom Do Migrants Come? In an article written for the United Nations, Lucian Pye outlined three distinctive patterns of urban growth he saw as common to developing societies. The first, which he calls the "shuttle pattern," is that of a seasonal or cyclical pattern of movement between country and city—clearly inapplicable to Brazil. The last is that of migrants in "communal groupings," tribes, clans or religious groups, banding together to come to the city. Again this is inappropriate in the Brazilian context. The intermediate type, the closest possible to

[d]Step-wise patterns would be more prevalent if one considered inter-generational histories, since most parents of migrants were rural-born, even if the migrant was born in a small town or municipal seat. Migration figures for the elite are much the same as those for the rank and file.

TABLE 5
Migratory Paths to Rio de Janeiro
(N=494)

Number of Steps from Birthplace to Big City		*Percent*
No steps		
Born in a big city and never lived in any other size place (152 people)		26
One step		
Came directly to big city from birthplace		54
14% Farm to city	(82)	
15% Village to city	(89)	
25% Municipal seat to city	(147)	
Total 54%	318 people	
Two steps		
Came to city from birthplace with one stage between		6
1% Farm to village to city	(7)	
3% Farm to municipal seat to city	(17)	
2% Village to municipal seat to city	(14)	
Total 6%	38 people	
Three steps		
Came to city from birthplace with two stages between (i.e., farm to village to municipal seat to city)		0
Deviant Steps		
All other paths including downward steps (i.e., from larger to smaller places, back and forth, ending up in the city)		12
No path within these has more than 2% of population or 12 people		
2% City to municipal seat to city	(12)	
1% City to village to city, etc.	(8)	
The rest are almost all unique paths with less than 1%.		

TABLE 6
Pre-Rio Residential Moves
(N=494)

Number of Moves		Percent
None		67
One or more		33
	Total	100
One prior move		60
Two prior moves		27
Three prior moves		7
Four or more prior moves		6
	Total	100

the Latin American case, Pye describes as a "pattern of isolated individuals moving more or less permanently into psychologically and socially unprepared urban settings." He continues:

> Whether the people are pushed off the land or attracted to the promises of the city, the result is a sense of rootlessness which provides a seed-bed for all manner of anomic movements. . . . That is to say, if lonely people come to the cities in search of a better existence and cannot even find the satisfactions of employment, they are likely in time to turn to increasingly antisocial activities. [24]

The issue of anomie and anti-social activities is dealt with elsewhere. What concerns us for the moment is the notion of loneliness and isolation often associated with migration to the city.

My data do not support Pye's characterization. In the migration process I found many forces sustaining support and continuity. First, most migrants did not come to the city alone. Many observers have suggested that migrants are solitary travelers, but the fact is that only 22 percent of our sample came unaccompanied. As seen in Table 7, 64 percent came with relatives (as did Sebastião, Amaro, and Cecilia); 8 percent came with friends or acquaintances; and 7 percent with some other person (like Juliana). Furthermore, migrants do *not* arrive in the city as total strangers, with no one to turn to. As Table 7 also shows, 84 percent had friends, relatives, or both already in the city.

We can ask, then, if the 22 percent arriving alone overlap with the 16 percent who had neither friends or relatives in the city. This subgroup would indeed correspond to the traumatic adjustment situation

TABLE 7
Social Context of Migration
(N=494)

Support System	Percent
Who accompanied migrants to the city?	
No one	22
Friends or acquaintances	8
Brothers and sisters only	6
Spouse only	7
Spouse and children	15
Parents	24
Other relatives	12
Boss	4
Other	3
Who did migrants know in the city?	
Both friends and relatives	23
Relatives only	55
Friends only	5
Neither	16

which Pye and others fear may lead to disruptive behavior. However, only 3 percent (15 out of 494) fell into this intersecting category.

That is not to imply that migration is always easy and effortless. Whether or not one comes alone or with one's family, the going can be very rough if there are no friends or relatives to turn to in the city. As one family described it:

> We arrived in the city after many days and nights cramped into those boards in the back of the truck. We had no place to go. We had spent all of our money to get here. The truck owner asked each family how much money they had, and charged the entire amount as his fee. So nobody had anything left. There was no choice. Those of us who had no relatives in the city found some vacant land and built little shelters for our families to sleep in. That's how we became favelados.

When Did Migrants Come? Although migration in general has been increasing over time, it may have reached a plateau—a fact which should help quell the fears of "alarmists" (see Table 8). The breakdown by political era shows that numerically the largest cohort to enter the

TABLE 8
Historical Trends in Migration to Rio
(N=494)

Trends Over Time		Percent
Date of arrival		
By decade		
Up to 1919		0
1920-1929		2
1930-1939		6
1940-1949		17
1950-1959		37
1960-1969		38
	Total	100
By political era		
1930-1944	Vargas and the Estado Novo	14
1945-1954	Postwar era: Dutro, Vargas, Café Filho	26
1955-1963	Late populist period: Kubitschek, Quadros, Goulart	36
1964-1969	Military regime: Branco, Costa y Silva, Medici	24
	Total	100
Percent arriving without friends or relatives in Rio		
1930-1944		27
1945-1954		20
1955-1963		14
1964-1969		7

city did so during the late populist era when migration all over the country was at a peak and the bargaining power of the favelado was at an all-time high.

The trend over time shows that migrants arriving without prior contacts in Rio have become increasingly rare, which corresponds with what we know about the social network of migratory patterns (see Table 8). Among those arriving during the Estado Novo Period (1930-1944), about one in four had no contacts in the city. The percentage has decreased to 7 percent in recent years, and will probably decrease still further.

Where Do Migrants Go in the City and Why? I collected data on three aspects of initial entry into the city: route of entrance, first type of residence, and reasons for choice of location. Certain patterns of insertion into the city have begun to emerge from research on other Latin American cities.[25] I wished to test these theories in the Rio context. Again I was surprised by the findings. The typical pattern for Lima is entry into what John Turner calls the "bridgehead settlement," a zone near the center of the city and thus closest to the job market. The next phase, "consolidation settlement," usually involves moving to (or invading) a more peripheral area which has the advantage of being rent free and more spacious. Once a job has been found, transportation costs from a more distant area can be afforded.

The Leeds point out that most of Rio's favelas were settled by gradual infiltration, not by planned invasion as in Lima. However, they add:

> In both cities one of the main routes of entry for the migrant poor is by way of old decayed housing or housing apparently built for proletarian residence, e.g., the *córtiços, cabeças de porco*, the *avenidas* built on *lotes proletários* (proletarian lots) and decayed residences in Rio. . . . In Rio there seems to be considerable moving around from one to another of such residential types by a large portion of the immigrants until they settle down, move up, or move out to the favelas.[26]

This may be true for Lima, but it is not the case in Rio, as Table 9 indicates. Only 1 percent of migrants to Rio went to the central city upon arrival; only 4 percent lived in inner-city tenements (*cortiços, cabeças de porco*, or *avenidas*), and over half the migrants never moved from their initial location in the city. Sensitive to the importance of the Lima precedent, we were careful to check these findings in a number of ways. "Strings" (similar to those for migration patterns) were created for each migrant on the zones he lived in within the city. All evidence confirmed the presentation of Table 9.[e] The relative absence of post-migration residential moves received further verification. Of Catacumba resi-

---

eThere are other notable divergences from the Lima pattern. There are no provincial clubs to welcome newcomers, no planned invasions (or very few), and much lower probabilities of squatter settlements turning into recognized working class communities. The discrepancies with the work of the Leeds, again, are probably due to differences in methodology. I spoke with a few persons, notables within the community, who had entered in the Lima-like pattern, but the random sample survey turned up quite different overall patterns.

TABLE 9

Initial Residential Experience of Migrants

(N=494)

Residential Experience	Percent
Location of first residence within Rio	
Center	1
South Zone	32
North Zone	35
Baixada Fluminense	22
Subúrbios of Guanabara, Niteroi, and others	10
First type of residence within Rio	
Cortico, cabeça de porco, or avenida[a]	4
Streets	1
Pension, rented room in private home, Albergue	7
Site of work	12
Barraco in a favela	76
Number of residential moves after arriving in Rio	
None	54
One	25
Two	15
Three or more	5
Reasons for choosing initial site within Rio	
Because it was the house of a relative	41
Because it was near the house of a relative	9
Because it was the house of a friend	4
Because it was near the house of a friend	2
Because it was near or at the site of work	20
Because it was the cheapest place available	8
Because it was the only place known, or the first place anyone suggested	8
Other (more freedom there, looked like an agreeable atmosphere, found it by accident, etc.)	8

[a]In fact, when asked in a separate item, only 10 percent of the entire sample (600) had *ever* lived in one of these residential types in their entire lives.

dents who were migrants, 81 percent had started out in the South Zone; 70 percent of Nova Brasília migrants had been from the beginning in the North Zone; and of those in Caxias, 52 percent had lived initially in the Baixada Fluminense.^{f} This last figure is a bit lower than the other two because of the relatively recent development and remoteness of the Baixada satellite towns as compared with the long-standing, more accessible North and South Zone favelas. Also, there is some secondary migration out of the favelas to the satellites motivated mainly by the opportunity to legally own or rent one's house and land.

With the Lima experience in mind, I thought that migrants entering Rio would make calculated decisions about where to live based on priorities and trade-offs which vary according to stage in the life-cycle of the individual or family. Those needing to be near multiple, unskilled, service-type job opportunities would choose the South Zone; those looking for factory work, the North Zone; and those wishing to maximize security of tenure, Caxias. My expectations were not borne out. Only 20 percent of migrants said they considered such matters in deciding where to live (and all of these persons said they chose a site near their work). For most there was no "choice" at all. The most common pattern—followed by 56 percent of migrants—was to seek out the home of a friend or relative for the initial period. Another 8 percent went to "the only place they knew," or to "the first place anyone suggested," and the same number went to the cheapest place they could find.

It is interesting to note that 38 percent of migrants eventually constructed their own barracos (favela dwellings). Another 42 percent either bought a barraco or the rights to squat on a particular plot of favela land, which costs anywhere from U.S. $25 to $800 in choice South Zone locations. (The annual income of someone earning the minimum wage was about U.S. $480 at the time.) Another 11 percent rented their residence (twice as common in Caxias as elsewhere); and the remaining 9 percent "borrowed" the use of a dwelling.

The question of purposive intra-city migration can be approached from another perspective. If there are different reasons for living in different parts of the city, it should result in different profiles of residents by neighborhood. I found few such differences. In each of the three com-

---

^{f}Another 25 percent who live in Caxias started in the North Zone; 13 percent had started in the subúrbios of the State of Guanabara.

munities the distribution of persons along the following dimensions were almost identical: size and region of birthplace; frequency and purpose of pre-migration urban contact; class background; father's job and father's education; own job and education at time of migration; age at time of migration; marital status at time of migration; motive for coming to Rio; contacts within Rio. Date of arrival differed somewhat between the three areas (showing that Catacumba was the oldest and Nova Brasília the newest community), as did numbers of moves before and after arriving in Rio (a little higher for Caxias), and some variables relating to work (10 percent more persons in Catacumba came to the city alone and gave "being near work" as the reason behind their choice of residence). But overall, the profiles of the three communities were strikingly similar.

Initial Work Experience. According to the hyperurbanization theory, there are not enough jobs for the migrants who flock to the city. To some extent this is true, yet according to my data, jobs are found relatively quickly by those who look, even though they are not the most desirable or best-paying jobs. Some economists consider most of these jobs as "disguised unemployment," but the term seems inappropriate since even the least productive and lowest status urban jobs generally provide incomes enabling families to live better than they had in the country-side. A full 81 percent of migrants told us they were "better off econom-ically than people like them who had remained at home."

Of migrants arriving in the city, 45 percent did not look for a job right away for a variety of reasons. Many were too young, some had to stay home to care for children, still others lived with friends or relatives for a while before starting to earn their keep.

An investigation of those who did not seek work immediately is revealing. As shown in Table 10, the proportion varies widely with age and sex, from 77 percent of young women not looking to only 17 percent of adult men. Looking at males across all ages, those who did not look for work immediately were more likely to have friends and relatives in the city, to have come from other urban centers, and to have relatively higher class backgrounds. Thirty-four percent of men who had both friends and relatives did not seek jobs immediately as opposed to 19 percent who knew neither; 75 percent of urban-born men of skilled or white collar backgrounds didn't look for work immediately, compared with 18 percent of farm-borns with agricultural or unskilled back-grounds. It is clearly a luxury to migrate to a city and not look immedi-ately for work—a luxury that not all can afford.

TABLE 10

Job-Seeking Among Rio Migrants by Age and Sex

(N=494)

Percent Who Did Not Look for Work Immediately		
Age	Male	Female
1-12	72	77
13-20	24	47
21 and over	17	60

Of those who did look for jobs right away, over two-thirds (68 percent) found them within one month after arrival and another fifth (18 percent) within three months. Only one in seven took more than three months to find some employment.[27] Men fared somewhat better than women, except the youngest women, who had the advantage of employment as maids. The figures for Nova Brasília are about 10 percent lower than those of the other two communities, indicating that residential location does affect the ease of finding a job even though it may not be the principal factor.

Our life history strings provide an interesting insight into the job situations in various epochs of Brazil's history. I compared the early Vargas and Estado Novo Period (1930-1944), the postwar period (1945-1954), the populist period (1955-1963), and the post-coup military period (since 1964). The politico-economic situation in these various periods indeed did seem to affect migrants' chances of finding employment when they arrived in Rio. Most favorable was the postwar period, when 72 percent of all migrants who looked found jobs within a month. At this time the industrial sector was growing rapidly, an import substitution policy was creating new jobs and backward and forward linkages, and a temporary resurgence in the coffee market was creating a boom-like period for the economy. In the World War II period, Vargas identified himself strongly with the interests of the industrial bourgeoisie and the workers. He founded labor unions, instituted a minimum wage, and established the PTB (Brazilian Labor Party) as a workers' party. Under Dutra, 1945-1951, there were some setbacks, but labor's basic advantages persisted and Vargas was elected President in 1951.[28]

The worst period for migrants has been the post-coup military dictatorship. Of migrants who sought, and are seeking, work in this period, only 63 percent could find any sort of job within the first month (as compared with 72 percent in 1945-1954), and these were skewed toward precarious, underpaid types of employment.

Our data on unemployment do not show any difference in education, skill levels, or motivations of the migrants themselves during this period but rather reflect a government economic policy blatantly unconcerned with the well-being of the lower sectors. The post-coup policy of cutting back on government expenditures, freezing wages (while prices continue to soar), and courting American big business has decidedly worsened the economic situation for the favelado.

Finding Jobs. A place to live and a job are the two crucial goals of the initial adaptation period for newly arrived migrants. The role played by relatives and friends is paramount in both—a pattern which recurs in many areas of Brazilian life. Although Brazilian society is not based on extended clan or kinship groups, kinship ties are often strong. Through the godparent system (*compadrio*) friendship is often boosted to the status of quasi-kinship. Almost two-thirds of migrants found their first jobs through the help of friends or relatives (see Table 11). Another 13 percent (including somewhat more women than men) came to prearranged jobs. Only 23 percent had to fend for themselves and seek jobs alone, by knocking on doors, using newspaper ads, employment agencies, etc. As Table 11 indicates, though the jobs were not always of high quality, all but 8 percent did manage to find something.

I cross-tabulated how long it took to find a job by what kind of job was found to see if the best jobs went to those who searched immediately, or to those who could afford to take their time and be selective. The latter is confirmed by the data. Of those who spent three months or more looking for their first job, 12 percent got desirable public or private security jobs (police, guards) compared with none of those who found work within the first three months. Further confirmation that more "privileged" migrants were holding out for better opportunities comes from the fact that 85 percent of men who came from *unskilled* urban jobs or agriculture found work within a month, whereas only 65 percent of those who had previously held *skilled* employment did. Similarly, 67 percent of those who knew no one upon entry found a job within a month while only 43 percent of those with contacts did. The help of friends and relatives seems to have helped delay the timing and thereby improve the quality of employment.

TABLE 11

Initial Job Experience of Migrants

(N=494)

Job Experience	Percent
How the first urban job was found	
Prearranged	13
Through relatives	27
Through friends	36
Alone	16
Through the newspapers	3
Through an employment agency	1
Through a social worker or assistance bureau	3
Classification of first urban job	
White-collar (professional, administrative)	6
Security (public or private, police, guards)	2
Merchant or shopkeeper	1
Skilled labor	6
Construction	6
Semi-skilled labor	8
Domestic	31
Unskilled labor	18
Primary (farming or small animals)	2
Unemployed (could not find any job at all although arranged some biscate from time to time)	8
Never worked (never looked for work or held any job either before or after arriving in Rio)	13

NATIVE-MIGRANT DIFFERENCES

I sought to determine if among the whole favela population migrants differ from natives in terms of class background, education, employment, income, and other indicators of levels of living (see Table 12). In terms of both class background and educational level, birth in Rio confers certain clear benefits. Many places in the country-side simply do not have schools, so that any contact urban children have with educational facilities—even if they can't go beyond the first few

TABLE 12

Native-Migrant Socioeconomic Differences

(Percent)

Socioeconomic Indicators	Natives (N=106)	Migrants (N=494)
Socioeconomic status: Percent high (in upper third of additive measure including education, occupation, and income)	27	15
Class background: Percent low (from agricultural or urban unskilled background)	39	75
Educational level: Percent high (third grade or more)	58	25
Occupational status		
White-collar	8	4
Merchant	0	4
Blue-collar (including factory)	12	18
Domestic	24	18
Unskilled	9	8
Unemployed	29	30
Income level: Percent high (earning two minimum salaries per month or more — 320 contos or U.S. $80.00)	34	32
Household facilities: Percent high (with at least three of the four facilities: running water, electricity, closed sewage, and indoor toilet facilities)	70	59
Appliances: Percent high (owning at least four of the following five: refrigerator, iron, radio, sewing machine, television)	38	26
Property: Percent high (owning any two of the following seven items: their own shack, a residence aside from the one living in, a plot of land with building, plot without building, a store, a shop, or a car or truck)	20	23
Social Mobility: Percent high (going from low parents SES to medium present SES)	20	34

years—is a clear advantage over migrant children. Differences in household facilities emphasize a point made throughout this study—that earlier residents of the favelas (natives being earliest of all) live in the most desirable locations, with the best houses and the most access to legitimate services. These people benefit first when electricity lines, water pipes or sewage networks are constructed. Equality in property ownership as shown in Table 12, probably indicates that some migrants have maintained control of parcels of land in the country which they were reluctant to sell.

Most disturbing in terms of the future of the lower strata is the evidence from Table 12 that although educational and social mobility levels differ greatly between the two groups, income levels do not. Migrants appear to come to the city from lower class backgrounds and, over time, to acquire more education as one form of social mobility. But on the whole, education per se appears to be a relatively unimportant variable, both in magnitude and significance. Both migrants and natives are subject to a constrained choice of jobs. Their occupational careers seem little affected by the new educational opportunities open to them in the city, or even in their original communities. Such immutable variables as social background, age at job change, and age of labor force entry seem to determine occupational status.

It is nonetheless true that rural migrants generally achieve higher occupational levels than they formerly held in the countryside. Furthermore, recent migrants experience greater rates of upward mobility than either older migrants or Rio natives. Recent migrants are the least likely group to settle for unskilled positions. They also have the highest participation rate in the sample; only 23 percent of its members are inactive, compared to almost 33 percent for both older migrants and Rio natives (see Tables 13 and 14).

This degree of relative migrant mobility, however, only measures a jump from abject rural poverty to the severely limited job opportunities of the favela. In addition, migrants are positively selected with respect to age, education, ability, and ambition with regard to their community of origin. A truly successful occupational move might result in residency outside of the favela, even for workers whose career beginnings in Rio were associated with favela residency.

If the data are correct, migration simply amounts to changing membership from the lower sector of rural society to the lower sector of urban society, with no appreciable increase in income. This conclusion

TABLE 13

Job Mobility for Random-Sample Males in the Labor Force:
First Job Compared to Present Job, 1969

(N=171)

Length of Rio Residence	Upward	Horizontal	Downward	Total	Upward (Not Counting Farm to Unskilled)
1-4 years	80%	19%	2%	100%	55.93%
	(47)	(11)	(1)	(59)	(33)
5 or more years	59%	22%	19%	100%	45.34%
	(51)	(19)	(16)	(86)	(39)
Rio native	15%	50%	35%	100%	11.53%
	(4)	(13)	(9)	(26)	(3)
Total	60%	25%	15%	100%	43.85%
	(102)	(43)	(26)	(171)	(75)

Note: *Upward Mobility* includes (a) farm to unskilled, semi-skilled, or skilled;
(b) unskilled to semi-skilled or skilled; and (c) semi-skilled to skilled. *Horizontal*
indicates no change among these four categories, although jobs within them change.
Downward includes skilled to semi-skilled, or unskilled plus semi-skilled to unskilled.

Skill categories contain jobs of the following sort. *Unskilled:* messenger boys, dock
workers, doormen, garbagemen, domestic servants, assistants in construction carriers,
streetcleaners, vendors, car washers. *Semi-Skilled:* drivers, fare-collectors on buses,
graphic assistants, painters, upholsterers, soldiers, weavers, bakers, repairmen, artisans
and craftsmen, cooks, confectioners, barbers, gardeners, typists, office machine
operators, salesmen. *Skilled:* communications workers, firemen, mechanics, iron
workers, electricians, book printers and binders, cabinet makers, skilled jobs in
construction.

would have to be discounted if there were avenues of escape from the
favela to higher sectors of society, but it is our impression that this kind
of mobility is practically nonexistent. Although there were a handful of
notable exceptions, almost none of the favelados we interviewed knew of
anyone who had moved out of the favela even into a regular working-
class neighborhood. Rents are prohibitively high, and home ownership—except possibly in the subúrbios—is virtually impossible.

URBAN-NONURBAN DIFFERENCES

A possible source of contamination in the above analysis of natives
and migrants is the fact that 19 percent of migrants were born in big
cities. Although these people share with other migrants the experience
of leaving their places of origin and adapting to a new environment, they

TABLE 14

Present Job Status (1969) by Length of Rio Residence,
Percentage Distribution for Random-Sample Males
(N=244)

Length of Rio Residence	Unskilled	Semi-skilled	Skilled	Unem-ployed	Total (N)	Never Worked	Total Number
1-4 years	28.8	35.6	35.6	—	100 (59)	23.57 (18)	77
5 or more years	31.5	20.9	41.9	5.7	100 (86)	32.81 (42)	128
Rio Natives	42.2	23.0	23.3	11.5	100 (26)	33.33 (13)	39
Total	32.2	26.4	36.9	4.8	100 (171)		244

are—like the Cariocas—as least second-generation urbanites. Table 15 distinguishes between favelados of four types. First are native-born Cariocas who have never changed cities; next, those who migrated to Rio but came from other large cities. These two groups are then combined in the third column, which puts all urban-born together. The fourth group consists of those who migrated from municipal seats and the fifth combines those from either small towns, villages, or rural areas (combined for this portion of the analysis).

Differences between Rio-born and other urbanites are essentially the same as those between natives and migrants. Rio-born individuals have notably higher class backgrounds and educational levels than those born in other cities; they have better household facilities and more appliances. On occupation, income, and socio-economic status, however, the two groups are at about the same level.

Comparing all city-born favelados (Rio plus other) to those from municipal seats and the countryside gives a similar picture. Again the biggest differences show up in class background and education, which progress from lowest in the rural-born group to municipal seat, urban, and then Rio born. Differences in appliances and facilities are not great, nor are those in jobs. Income seems to improve slightly with size of birthplace. Balan's survey, too, found that "migrants coming from urban communities tend consistently to have higher socio-economic status than rural migrants."[29]

TABLE 15
Urban and Non-Urban Socioeconomic Differences,
Percentage Distribution
(N=600)

Socioeconomic Indicators	Rio Born (N=106)	Other City- Born (N=82)	Total City- Born (N=188)	Municipal- Seat Born (N=167)	Rural Born[a] (N=245)
Socioeconomic status					
High	27	24	26	19	9
Class background					
Low	39	61	49	74	81
Education level					
High	58	41	51	28	18
Occupational status					
Blue-collar	12	20	16	17	17
Domestic	24	18	21	18	18
Unskilled	12	9	10	15	15
Income level					
High	34	39	36	32	28
Facilities					
High	70	56	64	60	60
Appliances					
High	38	25	32	33	21
Property					
High	20	22	21	25	21
Social mobility (Percent going from low SES parents to medium SES)	19	30	24	35	35

[a]Village (126) and farm (119) combined.

I would add to this perspective the somber proviso that the advantages accruing to those with migration in their family histories instead of their own immediate past must not be taken to indicate a hopeful future for the lower classes generally. As Tables 12 and 15 indicate, rates of social *mobility* do not rise with urban experience. The fact that persons can improve their situation by migrating to the city does not mean that urban society will continue to reward their initiative.

Table 16 directly addresses the question of whether over time migrants diminish the gap between themselves and those born in Rio. Migrants are categorized in the columns by the amount of time they have spent in Rio, starting with those newly arrived and ending with those living in the city 20 years or longer. Some advances can be observed in socioeconomic status, income, appliances, and property ownership, although this may be due solely to increasing age. There is, however, no sign of improvement in educational level—theoretically one of the major opportunities city life has to offer. Only 4 percent of the population told us they had ever taken a specialized training course and only .5 percent attended adult literacy classes. Among the young migrants, educational attainment seemed only slightly higher with increased urban experience. In employment also, length of time in the city did not increase one's chances for a better job, nor did it increase social mobility.

Michelena found a similar pattern in Venezuela. "One would think," he says, "that horizontal and vertical mobility are associated . . . but in the case of Venezuela, internal experience and length of time or urban residence after that had no significant impact on upward social mobility."[30]

The one big increase in socioeconomic position, seen both in the Venezuelan study and in my own, comes in that first transfer from the *rural* lower sector to the *urban* lower sector. This is indeed an improvement, but neither social system seems sufficiently open to allow for movement out of the lower sector in general.

We now turn to a closer examination of the lives of people in this lower sector—those designated as "marginal" to the society, or peripheral to the mainstream of urban life. In the next chapter we expose the roots of the concepts of marginality—showing how the idea developed into a pseudo-theory—and present a set of propositions with which to test that theory.

TABLE 16
Socioeconomic Differences According to Length of Rio Residence,
Percentage Distribution Among Migrants
(N=494)

Socioeconomic Indicators	One Year (N=31)	2-4 Years (N=56)	5-10 Years (N=103)	10-20 Years (N=187)	20+ Years (N=117)
Socioeconomic status					
High	6	16	14	20	18
Class background					
Low	77	67	78	69	61
Educational level					
High	26	29	23	37	30
Occupational status					
Blue-collar	10	19	18	17	16
Domestic	6	14	25	18	20
Unskilled	26	16	12	12	14
Income level					
High	23	19	25	36	36
Facilities					
High	61	55	55	64	62
Appliances					
High	6	17	13	34	36
Property					
High	6	14	16	27	25
Social mobility (Percent going from low parents SES to medium present SES)	29	21	31	35	31

PART II
THE MYTHS OF
MARGINALITY

Chapter Four
Marginality Theory
and the Ideal Type

Although there are few areas of agreement among social scientists, policy-makers, and the general public, they all hold strikingly similar stereotypes regarding the urban poor, or "marginal" sectors of society. The phenomenon of marginality has become the key social issue in Latin America in recent years, appearing in such diverse forums as political discourses, housing programs, and scholarly research proposals. This chapter delineates the various common uses and meanings of the term, and the major academic schools of thought which have contributed to the concept in both the United States and Latin America. Rather than attempting to formulate a new theory of my own, or resolve the conflicts between the varying uses of the term, I will focus on the major themes which appear throughout the marginality literature; I will use these to construct an ideal type and set of propositions which guide the analysis of the data I gathered in the favelas of Rio. I will then be able to assess the extent to which the reality of the favela fits the notions held about it.

The concept of marginality is especially critical for study because the ideologies and stereotypes associated with it affect the lives of millions of poor urban residents and shantytown dwellers. The concept has virtually taken on a life of its own, popularized as a coherent theory even though—or perhaps because—it is based on a set of loosely related, rather ambiguous hypotheses. Also, marginality has been used in many debates as a smokescreen behind which old ideological battles—such as the nature of the social system, the process of modernization, or the implications of capitalism and imperialism—continue to be fought. I intend to briefly examine the popular uses of the term and the assumptions underlying marginality theory before turning to its academic antecedents.

COMMON-SENSE USES OF THE TERM

In Portuguese and Spanish, the very word "marginal" has exceedingly derogatory connotations. *Um marginal* or *um elemento marginal* means a shiftless, dangerous ne'er-do-well, usually associated with the underworld of crime, violence, drugs, and prostitution. This parallels a long-standing tradition in America and Europe of characterizing the poor as disreputable in one sense or another—"the dangerous classes," or "persons living in regions of squalor and woe."

In Latin America the pejorative connotations of the urban poor have deep historical roots. The city, as Lisa Peattie, Alejandro Portes, and others have pointed out, was always a fortress of high culture, the citadel of the elites, and highly homogeneous in class composition.[1] From the first "invasion" of migrants from the countryside, and the first appearance of squatter settlements on the urban landscape, the policy of the urban elite has been to treat these communities as a blight. Everything possible has been done to prevent the birth of favelas, stunt their growth, and hasten their death.

At the same time, however, the system was producing both the squatter settlements and the concentrations of unemployment in cities. The incapacity of the economy to absorb the "marginals" into the labor force accentuated the threat of social and political disruption. This contradiction between the dread of "growing barbarian masses" in the cities and the awareness of its unavoidable existence underlies the ideology of marginality and its political uses.

Paradoxically, the characteristic way to handle the dread of these masses is to profess a desire to "integrate" them into the very system which is producing the social and economic situation called "marginal."

Highly partisan social labeling is thus attributed to both squatters and squatter settlements, and it is transmitted through the socialization process. Economic interests reinforce the social biases as the cost of urban services and the price of urban land continues to rise. The migrant and squatter populations, however, continue to grow. What was considered "mainstream" and what was considered "marginal" has come to be determined less by what is done by the numerical majority or minority, and more by what is done specifically by the middle and upper classes. If the criteria for normalcy were prevalence-determined rather than class-determined, then playing the numbers (*jôgo do bicho* in Brazil) would be called mainstream, while attending the opera would be marginal.[2] Clearly this is not the case.

Unfortunately, the ideas about the marginality of the urban poor have not been confined to harmless stereotypes in the prevailing wisdom. On the contrary, these notions have been strengthened and perpetuated by the very public agencies that are responsible for shantytown policy.

A striking example can be seen in the official report of the Fundação
Leão XIII, in Rio de Janeiro:

> Families arrive from the interior, pure, and united—whether legally or
> not—in stable unions. The disintegration begins in the favela as a con-
> sequence of the promiscuity, the bad examples, and the financial difficul-
> ties there. Children witness the sexual act. Young girls are seduced and
> abandoned; they get pregnant but don't feel any shame. . . . Liquor and
> drugs serve to dull the disappointments, humiliations, and food deficien-
> cies of favela life. The nights belong to the criminals. . . . In the quiet of
> night one can hear the screams for help but no one dares to interfere for fear
> they will be next. . . . Policemen rarely penetrate the favela, and then only
> in groups.[3]

Among the general characteristics the document attributes to the
squatter community are: "irregular agglomeration of sub-proletarians
with no professional capacities, low living standards, illiteracy, mes-
sianism, promiscuity, alcoholism, the habit of going barefoot, supersti-
tion and spiritualism, lack of healthy recreation, refuge for criminals
and marginal types, and spreader of parasites and contagious dis-
eases."[4]

Lest these notions be interpreted as some sort of religious holdover
from the Fundação's Catholic origins, I hasten to point out that a very
similar set of attitudes is reflected in the publication *Seminário Inter-
universitário*, which was issued in 1967 by the six rectors of the universities around Rio. They refer to the favelas as "social cancers,"
despoilers of "one of the most beautiful landscapes of the planet," and
part of the "national patrimony" which "we have in custody for
humanity," filled with "rebels and gangsters," and so on.[5]

The Fundação Leão XIII and the Interuniversity Seminar report
identify "marginals" simply by their residence in the favelas, defining
them à priori as illegal squatters and as part of a socially disorganized
sub-group. But the term "marginality" has been used loosely to refer to a
variety of other, sometimes overlapping groups. These include the *poor*
in general, the *jobless*, *migrants*, members of other *subcultures*, racial
and ethnic *minorities*, and *deviants* of any sort. In light of the diverse
implications of these criteria, both for identifying the urban poor and for
formulating policy, it is important to establish the defining factor in each
of the five common usages.

1. Location in squatter settlements. Among those who focus on
location, or the squatter settlements per se, are architects, planners,
and housing authorities who consider favelas marginal because of the

sub-standard physical construction, high density, lack of urban services and hygiene, peripheral placement within the urban area, and illegal land occupation. While in reality these facts do not necessarily overlap, it is assumed that they do. Subsequently, analysts combined these physical traits with what they assumed to be attendant social attributes and life-styles, broadening the definition of marginality from the external habitat of the poor to their internal personal qualities. This later viewpoint has sometimes been called the ecological school of marginality. It isolates the ghetto or shantytown as a physically delineated space within which everyone is marginal, and outside of which everyone is somehow "integrated."

2. Underclass in the economic-occupational structure. The second major use of the term associates marginality with the urban underclass, the jobless, or the underemployed—those who are only precariously part of the labor market. In this use of the term, the physical boundaries of the favela and the attitudes of outsiders towards the favela would be irrelevant. The determining characteristic is an economic-occupational one dealing with lack of work or with unstable, low-paying jobs which are not part of the mainstream economy and do not contribute to it. According to this occupational definition of marginality, people who live within the favela but are employed in the dynamic industrial sector of the economy would not be marginal; conversely, people living elsewhere who are odd-jobbers would be included.

3. Migrants, newcomers, or different subcultures. A third major use of the term is in association with migrants and the migratory experience. In this case, the key identifying point is newcomer status and the transition between traditional-rural and modern-urban life. This situation of transition need not be concomitant with ghetto living or poverty, but it often is. The critical factor in this case is associated with the idea of different subcultures, part of a larger conceptual framework of cultural change and transition. From this point of view, any subculture which is different from the mainstream could be described as marginal, although other conditions usually apply. If, for example, subcultures coexist as separate enclaves or tribes, with little awareness of or contact with one another, or without feelings of superiority of one group over the others, the conditions would be most accurately described as pluralism. For marginality to apply, the diverse groups must give some degree of legitimacy to the same nation-state or larger unit, and one subculture must have higher prestige, privilege, and power than the others. Furthermore, the barrier between the groups must be at least semiperme-

able; a totally closed and deterministic caste system is really irrelevant to the concept of marginality.[6]

Beyond this, three other points are relevant. First, groups such as adolescents, career women, and the newly rich are also caught in a status dilemma and a situation of confused social identity in their transition from one subculture to another and thus may also be considered marginal.[7] Although the intensity of their asymmetrical relationship to the mainstream and the transitory or permanent condition of their respective dilemmas may differ, the critical distinction between them and the subcultures discussed in this book is that the latter are an underclass and have less power to define their situation.

Second, the marginal type may emerge among a people who have not themselves emigrated but instead have been subject to invasion from without.[8] This is especially relevant to the Latin American case, where the process of colonization implied not only conquest and invasion but daily cultural contact and use of the indigenous population. Rudolfo Stavenghagen and Pablo Gonzalves Casanova show that for the Latin American case the historical context of invasion and colonization by the Spanish and the Portuguese and their use of the native populations transformed *all* of the existing cultures into marginal status.[9]

Finally, there could be no concept of marginality without some basic notion of equality. In tribal or feudal systems the problem of marginality never arose, because in the tribal system there was no concept of superiority implied, and in the feudal system there was an accepted understanding of one's "station" in life and the hierarchical nature of society. As Gino Germani points out, only in the post-Enlightenment period, with the French Revolution and the concept of the Rights of Man, did the idea emerge that people ought to have equal privilege and opportunity in some fundamental sense.[10]

4. Racial or ethnic minorities. The definition of marginality based on racial or ethnic minority status also requires the superior-inferior status differential. The major difference in this case is the ascribed genetic trait that is the determinant of in-group or out-group participation, rather than an acquired or cultural trait. Assimilation becomes a much more serious problem as the boundaries take on immutable properties. Milton Gordon's discussion of assimilation is quite illuminating in this regard. He describes the possibility of a gradual formation of a sub-society composed precisely of racial or ethnic marginal men. For those who wish to merge into the mainstream, however, he specifies some seven stages of assimilation (including cultural, structural,

mental, identificational, and civic), the price of which is giving up one's own racial identity and ethnic culture.[11]

5. Deviants. The final situation for which the term marginality is used involves individual deviants, whether pathological or especially gifted and nonconformist. In the case of an artist, criminal, prophet, or revolutionary, marginality implies a lack of participation in the occupational, religious, or political mainstream. The individual deviant might emerge either as a passive dropout or active critic of the society, or might arise from a subculture in itself marginal. The earlier sociological meaning of "marginal man" specifically referred to an individual from a subordinate subculture who had rejected his own group but was not accepted by the dominant culture. He might become a leader of his own group, be partially accepted or rejected by both groups, or become a cosmopolitan figure, truly at the margin of all groups.

Of course, marginal individuals rarely pose a serious threat to the mainstream. Whereas an individual deviant is often treated as a psychological problem, when a marginal group reaches a critical mass it becomes identified as a social problem. Such a group can be identified by location as in the squatter settlements, by dress and dialect as are the Indians in Lima, La Paz, or Mexico City, or by the physical characteristics of race. In any of these situations, the group's visibility and clustering make it easier for the dominant class not only to stigmatize the group, but also to define its situation and manipulate it to preserve the status quo.

The favelados and suburbanos of Rio de Janeiro conform in varying degrees to the five categories of marginality just described. Specifically, they are mostly visible and identifiable as living in peripheral, substandard housing settlements, they are predominantly of migrant origin, and they are generally employed in the most unstable and least remunerative jobs. With regard to the distinctive subculture indicator of marginality, it might be argued that most favelados are eligible (even if they are not Indian or African in origin) either on the basis of their personal or parental experience in a more traditional world, or because of their special adaptation to the modern world—existing as they do within the constraints of low-income living. Obviously not all of the people in all low-income communities hold the same outlooks or behave in the same ways. Nor will they have uniform relationships within their own community or with respect to the larger society. Just as some of the national Latin American elites are more concerned with the United States or Europe as a reference group, some of the squatters (especially the local elites) may look toward the national middle and upper classes for their value orientations and economic-political interactions. They may in part serve as "brokers" between the ghetto or squatter settlements and the external urban world. Others will continue to hold their rural counterparts as a reference group and feel especially privileged to be living in the city, while still another group will undoubtedly develop its own sense of identity and perceive other squatters as the significant group for comparison. Many may find community within the ghetto while others may indeed be isolated and alienated, incorporating a number of the personality traits and attitudes considered typical of the "marginal man."

The critical point for our discussion here is that because of the living conditions of this sector of the population in favelas or in subúrbios, they have been automatically assumed to have a series of associated economic, social, cultural, and political characteristics. It is the combination and assumed systematic covariation of these dimensions which allow marginality to be used as an overall view of the lower classes and as an explanatory statement of why poverty exists. Each dimension refers to a specific way of being "outside" of the standard functioning of society, and they are seen as linked together by the spatial-ecological fact of slum residence.

SOCIAL THEORY AND THE STUDY OF MARGINALITY

The common focus of all of the many schools of thought leading into the marginality construct is that all deal at the sociocultural level with the urban poor. They often overlap, or draw upon one another, and are not discrete either in chronological sequence or in content. They have quite diverse theoretical backgrounds and use very different methodologies and analytical techniques. Many have started with a predetermined conclusion, using empirical research only to support a specific ideological position. The reference point or standard against which the marginal population is being compared is often left implicit. The traits of the marginal are supposedly the diametric opposites of modern, urban middle-class traits; but in fact there has been little empirical evidence either that all modern urban middle-class members possess these traits, or that other groups do not.

Furthermore, many of the investigations of marginality have produced contradictory findings, and it is difficult to discern whether these discrepancies are due to differences in the places studied, in the methods used, or in the theoretical and ideological perspectives adopted. Comparing different units of analysis, different time periods, different indicators of the same concept, or qualitative and quantitative studies becomes not only confusing but also meaningless.

Because of these factors any hard and fast classification or taxonomy of the schools of thought contributing to marginality is impossible. Any method used to divide the mainstreams of thought for the purposes of discussion will be somewhat arbitrary. I have chosen therefore to group the schools of thought loosely according to the backgrounds of the contributing writers, common themes and ideological perspectives, the units of analysis used, and a general chronological order. I will discuss seven approaches: (1) the psycho-sociological; (2) the architectural-ecological; (3) the ethnographic; (4) the traditional-modernizing; (5) the culture of poverty; (6) the DESAL participation ideology developed in Chile; and (7) the radicalism "theory."

Among all of these, the psycho-sociological approach was the first to use the term marginality, and it implicitly preconditioned all of the later variations on the theme. The architectural-ecological school of marginality is important primarily because of its persistence; despite its simplicity and the great amount of contradictory empirical evidence, this first view of marginality tends to determine much of the policy-making in Latin American countries. The ethnographic school has contributed to pervasive stereotypes with its catch-all notion of "peasants in the cities." The modernization school, popular in many North American universities, focuses on attitudinal prerequisites to modernity, and the parallelism between national development and sub-group or individual progress. The culture of poverty school added the critical aspect of "blaming the victim" to marginality theory, while the DESAL group has been the major popularizer of the marginality concept in Latin America. Finally, the literature on radicalism among the marginal sectors summarizes the basic fears of the ruling classes, which provide much of the motivation for government programs in Latin America.

Without attempting to criticize each school of thought in detail, I will try to present the basic tenets and internal logic of the major trends as they have contributed to the overall theory of marginality at the sociocultural level.

THE PSYCHO-SOCIOLOGICAL APPROACH

The term marginality was first used on the individual psychological level. In the article "Human Migration and the Marginal Man" (1928), Robert Park spoke of marginal man as a "cultural hybrid": "a man living and sharing intimately in the cultural life and traditions of two distinct peoples yet never quite willing to break, even if he were permitted to do so, with his past and his traditions, and not quite accepted because of racial prejudice, in the new society in which he now sought to find a place. He is a man on the margin of two cultures and two societies which never completely interpenetrated and fused."[12]

Park came to the concept through his wide interest in human migrations, cultural contacts, and culture conflicts. In his view, the cause of marginality is the internal war between two worlds, one familiar and one enticing, but neither complete within this "cultural hybrid." The cause is *not* totally individual, since the contact of two cultures, or the phenomena of mass migrations, is the precondition for the individual phenomenon to occur. Yet the symptoms are sought on the internal psychological level.

Contrary to present stereotypes, Park saw in this marginal man the hope for civilization and progress. It was his belief that innovations and major advances in culture occur precisely at periods of migration and population movement, which free the individuals involved and give rise to both turmoil and creativity. In the last sentence of his article, he states: "It is in the mind of the marginal man—where the changes and fusions of culture are going on—that we can best study the process of civilization and progress."[13] Park also refers to the conceptualization of "the stranger" in the earlier work of Georg Simmel. The stranger enters a society from the outside and remains on the periphery of it. As a transient he is in a special position of both "objectivity" and "openness," allowing him heightened perceptions and creativity.

The rest of the literature in what I have defined as the individual-psychological school is basically an elaboration on Park's initial definition. Some new elements and details have been added, but they are all in keeping with the basic framework. Perhaps most important has been the work of Everett Stonequist, whose article "The Problems of the Marginal Man" was published in 1935.

Stonequist described the marginal individual as "placed simultaneously between two looking-glasses, each presenting a different image of himself."[14] What is here termed "marginal," he states, "represents a process of abstraction, a core of psychological traits which are the inner correlates of the dual pattern of social conflict and identification."[15] The word-picture he paints of the core of psychological traits became the basis of a number of empirical studies conducted later.[16] According to this description, the marginal individual is likely to display a "dual personality" and have a "double consciousness."

He will be ambivalent in attitude and sentiments, have a divided loyalty, be irrational, moody, and temperamental. He is likely to be excessively self- and race-conscious, have feelings of inferiority, be hypersensitive and hyper- critical and so be liable to withdrawal tendencies. He will have skill in noting contradictions and hypocracies among people of the dominant culture and be contemptuous of the people below him. His heightened mental activ- ity may sometimes enable him to be creative . . . but often he is merely imitative and conformist in outlook.[17]

Stonequist believes that the marginal individual passes through a life cycle of three steps: introduction to two cultures; crisis; and adjust- ment. In the first stage, at least a partial assimilation takes place; other- wise, the individual does not experience the conflict of loyalties we are discussing. The crisis stage is characterized by "confusion, even shock, restlessness, disillusionment, and estrangement." In the third stage, a number of outcomes are possible that include becoming an accepted member of the dominant group, leader of the subordinate group (either as a "revolutionary," an aggressive nationalist, or as a conciliator, reformer, or teacher) or a totally alienated individual subject to with- drawal and isolation. The way in which this final stage is resolved and the number of people who are experiencing it simultaneously determines which way the dilemma itself will be resolved. A strong innovative culture may develop, or the process of disorganization may set in, finding expression in "delinquency, crime, suicide, and mental instability."[18]

Stonequist ends his article by saying that just as there is a life cycle for the individual, so there is a natural history for the setting:

The initial phase involves a small group of marginal individuals who are much ahead of the minority or subordinate group. . . . Gradually the group of marginal persons increases and the minority race itself begins to stir with new feelings and ideas. It makes progress in cultural development and self- respect. Then if the dominant race continues intransigently in its position and attitudes of superiority some of the marginal individuals swing about and identify themselves with the rising group. They further define the situation and accelerate the movement. In this manner, nativistic, nationalistic, and racial movements evolve from trickles into tides which have as their goals some kind of equality and independence.[19]

The issue here of inclusion/exclusion, or membership/non-mem- bership, and the intransigence of the dominant group is addressed by Robert Merton in his classic work, *Social Theory and Social Structure*. He defines marginal man as someone aspiring for membership in a certain group but ineligible for membership. Merton used the concepts of reference group and anticipatory socialization to help clarify the structural condition of this out-group member. The marginal man, the ineligible aspirant, goes through the process of anticipatory socialization in adopting the values and norms of the group he wishes to enter, and is then unable to find acceptance by that group while suffering rejection from his own group for repudiating its values. He is then the "victim of aspirations he cannot achieve and hopes he cannot satisfy."[20]

Anticipatory socialization . . . is functional for the individual only within a relatively open social structure providing for mobility. . . . By the same token the pattern of anticipatory socialization would be dysfunctional for the individual in a relatively closed social structure where he would not find acceptance by the group to which he aspires and would probably lose acceptance because of his out-group orientation by the group to which he belongs. This latter type of case will be recognized as that of the marginal man, poised on the edge of several groups but fully accepted by none of them.[21]

When this condition becomes widespread, community life and even a "marginality culture" can develop. But, as Goldberg points out, even groups that opt for maintaining their own culture are *not* communities in the strictest sense, since they don't have an economic life of their own and are linked with the larger community in many ways.[22]

A number of fascinating studies were done in the 1940s and 1950s applying the marginal man concept to various subcultural and ethnic groups. Although the work departed largely from Park's and Stonequist's foundations, it criticized their approach for overstressing personality traits and understressing exclusion from social status. Milton Goldberg, J. S. Slotkin, David Golovensky, and Aaron Autonovsky all studied American Jews. These studies agreed that American Jews "did *not* manifest the characteristics of marginal man," since they had found a "stable modus vivendi" within a culture which, although not mainstream, was as "real and complete as any other culture."[23]

Following I. L. Child's work with Italian-Americans, in which he tried to distinguish between the marginal situation per se and marginal personality traits,[24] Alan Kerckhoff and Thomas McCormick set up a study with racially hybrid American Indian schoolchildren.[25] Inspired by this project, J. W. Mann based his doctoral dissertation on a racially mixed housing project in Durban.[26] The latter two studies operationalized Stonequist's word picture by creating a marginal personality scale, which was measured in relation to the status of the group, the individual's reaction in terms of group identification, and the level of rejection or barrier. Kerckhoff, McCormick, and Mann found that the members of the minority groups in general showed no more marginal personality traits than the others, and concluded that marginal situations don't automatically give rise to marginal personalities. What they did find (corresponding nicely with Merton's definition of marginality mentioned above) is that high incidence of the marginal traits only exists among those individuals who both identified strongly with the dominant group and were rejected by it because of Indian-like or Negro-like appearance. Still, this did *not* account for even half of the psychological marginality found in the testing, showing that such personality traits simply cannot be wholly accounted for in terms of group relations.[27]

Perhaps the best summary of the work on individual marginality is H. F. Dickie-Clark's book, *The Marginal Situation*, which not only synthesizes the previous work in the field, but also points out a fact quite relevant for the study of the Latin American urban poor. Dickie-Clark shows that "the dominant group may encourage subordinates to adopt some of their attitudes (punctuality, thrift, etc.) *but*, if they want to stay dominant, they can't permit the subordinate strata to share in their powers or opportunities."[28] Herein lies a central theme of this study—the constant attempt of those in power to blame the poor for their position because of deviant attitudes, masking the unwillingness of the powerful to share their privilege.

THE ARCHITECTURAL-ECOLOGICAL SCHOOL

Analysts of Latin American urbanization originally used the term "marginal" to describe the newly established, substandard and makeshift housing settlements built by recent migrants on the fringes of the urban areas. It was the physical characteristics of these settlements—their "marginal" location with respect to the central city as well as their clearly deficient infrastructure, unsound construction, lack of sanitary services, and overcrowding—that drew the attention of observers. A marginal situation was circularly defined as a condition of inhabiting marginal neighborhoods—that is, favelas.

Policy prescriptions designed to deal with the problem of marginality were based on little empirical evidence. Journalistic reviews and inherited stereotypes provided justification for the immediate action felt necessary because of the rapid growth of squatter settlements. Marginal settlements were uniformly classified as slums, as dangerous manifestations of social disease. Housing soon became *the* pressing social issue in the developing countries of America. The problem was stated in blunt words:

> As a consequence of the migratory movement toward urban areas, and of demographic growth which has produced an abnormal increase in the population without a proportional increase in the number of dwellings, there has been registered a fact that can be generalized in spite of accidental differences: the emergence of slums. Slums are houses which, by their conditions, represent a threat against the moral code, the security and health of the family that occupies it, and of the collective in which they grow. [29]

Squatter settlements were seen as zones of total social breakdown:

> Promiscuity, sickness, lack of hygiene, family disintegration, delinquency, etc., reign in squatters. It is a growing chain of social problems that tend toward incalculable proportions, almost intractable. . . . This lack of a minimum of material commodities to live, converts the slum dweller into a sick illiterate, without fixed employment—in an individual without ambitions and rebellious. . . . Their life styles are generally primitive, anti-hygienic, anti-social, amoral—everything conspires to make them negative elements in the social system. [30]

Latin American policy-makers equated the problem of marginality with that of substandard housing. The perceivable housing deficit, a product of the rapidly accelerating pace of internal migration, was considered the main cause of marginal neighborhoods. Marginality was seen as something to be *physically* eradicated, a manifestation that had a simple cure: remove favela dwellings and provide for the public construction and financing of "adequate" low-cost housing.

Although conceptually simple, the solution was politically unfeasible. The existing needs of the urban middle and upper classes for better transportation and public services took precedence over the allocation of scarce public funds for programs of direct subsidy to the poor.

In spite of their assessment of the mounting pressures on the urban structure imposed by the migrant population, and in spite of their fear of the invading "rural hoards," the existing sociopolitical elites found no solution—and therefore offered no response—to these demands. The solution came from the migratory population itself, in the form of land invasions. As Ramiro Cardona has put it, it was the double failure of the existing system to respond to the housing demands of migrants and to control the migratory process that led to the phenomenon of land invasions. [31]

Invasions of property occurred in unoccupied plots being held off the market for purposes of real estate speculation. With de facto occupation of the sites, a burgeoning market for squatter housing (even if illegally occupied) developed. Equity on structures and improvements accumulated; and transactions between original invaders and subsequent owners conferred upon the property all the legal rights that could have been denied to the first illegal occupants. Moreover, the increased magnitude of the phenomenon lent it internal diversification. There were both recent invaders and established invaders seeking to invade elsewhere in search of better accommodations. In many places, invasions no longer obeyed a random, individual pattern but were the product of extensive organization and carefully thought-out alternatives. Arriving migrants, often paired with friends and relatives having the minimum capital necessary to join a land movement, waited for the organization of the next land invasion. In the *barriadas* of Lima, Peru, land invaders could set up a complete subdivision in 24 hours, with provision for streets, public facilities sites, and sewer drainage. Although such complex and complete squatting patterns developed in few cities, the persistence of the phenomena threatened the very fabric of property ownership and with it the operation of the single most important capital market for the great majority of the upper middle-class families in Latin America.

A number of Latin American cities designed massive programs of squatter removal and construction of low-income housing to counter the threat of an ever-expanding tide of migrants, the *superbloques* of Perez Jimenez in Venezuela being the most famous example.[32] However, the private housing industry was slow to react to the prospects of such low-profit housing. Government subsidies needed to be granted, if only to buy the previously occupied land from its original owners at the increased "market" prices. Most of the countries showed a clear structural incapacity to build housing units in adequate numbers, and indulged a bias toward architecturally "pleasing" solutions based on middle-class standards and building codes. The few units that were produced proved too desirable to be allocated to previously removed squatters. Very rapidly the field of subsidized public housing became the domain of government bureaucrats and other members of the lower middle classes. Thus, the solution to the problem became in itself a source of new, and more fundamental problems. Public housing emerged as a mechanism through which the middle sectors could profit at the expense of squatters. Lacking sufficient income and adequate occupational status, the "marginal" population was denied access to the proposed solution for its marginality. Poor people actually invaded the Caracas *superbloques*, refusing to leave or pay rent.

The most striking aspect of this phase of marginality is not its naiveté, but rather its perseverance. Of all the views on marginality, this first approach has most readily captured the allegiance of government officials in the Latin American nations. The errors of the past, however, have not gone unnoticed. The continuing support, or justification, for these policies has more recently arisen from another set of "marginal" attributes which could be called the ethnographic school.

Partly as a result of the increased contacts between squatters and governmental authorities, and further motivated by the renewed interest in squatting in face of a failure to control its growth, a new view on marginality emerged in the late 1950s advocating the eradication of squatter settlements as seedbeds of disruption and social anomie. The term "marginal" began to be applied to the characteristics not of the squatter settlement, but of the squatters themselves.

Although belatedly, the first systematic empirical studies of squatter communities were undertaken. Architects were displaced by social workers and later by anthropologists and sociologists, who first attempted to "explain" the problems of the squatters and their settlements.

THE ETHNOGRAPHIC SCHOOL

Government housing agencies believed that the provision of housing facilities for the favelados represented the formal integration of the squatter into urban life. "A house is something more than a roof" was a common motto in the early 1960s. The idea was that the individuals themselves would be "recooperated" by relocation into "standard housing." So it was up to the social scientist to describe in an "objective and scientific"manner the state of social disintegration or integration of the squatters and to explain or predict their social behavior. If squatters were a social problem for the official housing agencies, their integration into urban life was a sociological problem for the sociologists and anthropologists who would form the ethnographic school of marginality.

The theoretical framework and the methodology used by these social scientists varied widely. Much of the methodology employed for the study of the acculturation of the squatter settlers derives from previous ethnographic studies of peasant communities or aboriginal tribes. As in these studies, the squatter settlements were conceptualized as self-contained units. In the same way that anthropologists in the

Malinowsky tradition identified isolated and relatively autonomous cultures, the urban social investigators sought to describe squatter settlements as cultural entities. It was widely believed that squatter settlements were transplants of rural communities into the urban setting, which put a premium on researchers who knew something about rural customs and belief systems. The school of related research is often referred to as the "peasants in the cities" approach.[33]

There were two major objectives or goals of the ethnographic school. The first was to describe the preservation or destruction of rural attributes and institutions in the city; the second was to describe their functionality or dysfunctionality as mechanisms for urban adaptation. It was never the major concern of this school to examine whether *in fact* the assimilation of urban styles of life and attitudes by the migrants would enhance the probabilities of actively participating in the decisions and benefits of urban life. Ethnographic researchers showed little interest in testing whether the internalization of urban roles would affect migrants' chances of being accepted by the urban middle class or having upward social mobility. To have done so would have severely threatened the notion of self-contained squatter units and forced the school to take a broader structural perspective. The ethnographic school worked under the rough assumption that urban integration was simply a matter of divesting the migrants of their rural rags and dressing them up in urban finery.

Within this general outline, the ethnographic school of marginality emerges in two forms. The first attributes marginality to the persistence of rural customs and institutions in an otherwise urban setting. As Matos Mar says in his study of Lima, Peru: "It should be noted that the people who come from the rural areas into the cities bring with them their own way of life which is that of an underdeveloped people of peasant mentality, with the addition, in the case of these from the Andes region, of traditional Indian cultural patterns. . . . [The contrast] between the rural and urban ways of life . . . leads to serious conflicts which are reflected in mental, social, and economic maladjustments that militate against satisfactory integration."[34] He goes on to report high incidences of "marital instability, unemployment or underemployment, criminality and political alienation" in the *barriadas*, presumably as a consequence of the attempt to "reproduce Indian communities on an urban scale."[35]

The second form of the ethnographic school attributes the existence of marginality to the lack of community pressure to enforce more sanctions and to offer rewards to the migrant population. In other words, it attributes marginality to the absence of the internationalization mechanism of the rural community. According to Juarez Brandão Lopez, "social control of work behavior by rural patterns is principally the result of the internalization in the migrant's personality of the idea of one's duty or 'obligation.' In the absence of the community and the sanctions that enforce its laws and in the midst of the individualistic urban milieu, this social control becomes irreparably weakened."[36]

In a study of a squatter settlement in Buenos Aires, Gino Germani reports: "The degree of social disorganization observed in the villa (squatter settlement) is high, except for the earlier migrant group resident in the urbanized area, and of course, the proportion of squatters who were city born. . . . In the villa, social control is almost wholly lacking or in a sad state at the family level, at the level of the local community, and at the level of society as a whole."[37]

Andrew Pearse, who studied the favelas of Rio in 1958, reported remnants of "attitudes of rural dependence, strong family ties, and distrust of outgroups, manifested in religion and politics by the search for a *patrao*."[38]

Pearse believes the lack of responsiveness to pressures from outside the kin-group—not the breakdown of the family or clan—is responsible for the marginality of the squatter. He concludes: "The attitude which prevailed was certainly that of 'non-commitment,' or the avoidance of extra-familial obligations and entanglements. One of the corollaries was the . . . relative unimportance of approval and disapproval coming from outside the in-group."[39] According to Pearse, the lack of need for external approval in itself was a key sign of marginality.

In this Latin American sociological literature, the rural migrant living in the city is "damned if he does and damned if he doesn't." For example, if the migrant obeys the pressures of his kin-group he is considered overly traditional. But if the kin-group is in a state of social disintegration and the migrant is autonomous, he is considered to be in a state of breakdown. In both cases, he is considered unintegrated in city life. The contradiction is a consequence of the divergence between the stereotype of urban institutions on one hand, and the functional analysis of them on the other. It is also the result of conceiving the squatter settlement as a self-contained unit, without a description of the broader urban system to which migrants are supposed to adapt.

All of the above authors implicitly or explicitly assumed the existence of a rural-urban continuum, with a clear dichotomy between traditional rural patterns and modern urban life. The intellectual roots of that split are especially relevant to the growth of the traditionality/modernization school of marginality, and have been critical in creating many of the stereotypes of the squatter population.

TRADITIONALITY/MODERNIZATION SCHOOL

One of the principal schools of thought contributing to the set of attributes associated with marginality concerns the effect of rural-urban differences on the modernization and development process. The writing in this school has taken two distinct forms: the social-psychological form dealing with the assimilation of modern, urban-industrial values on the part of individuals in transition; and the political-economic form, dealing with the formation of a modern nation-state and the necessary attitudinal prerequisites of its citizenry for political and economic growth. The dimensions are interrelated, and in each case the connection with marginality is introduced through the notion that large portions of the urban poor and squatter populations are either first or second generation migrants, often from the countryside and unintegrated in city life because they lack the necessary "modern" attitudinal and behavioral syndrome.

For over a century scholars have discussed the differences between traditional or rural and modern or urban lifestyles, often using dichotomous schemes to characterize the polar extremes between the two. Among the first studies were Henry Sumner Maine's *Ancient Law* (1861), which distinguished "status" and "contract" as the basis for interpersonal and legal relationships, and Lewis Henry Morgan's *Ancient Society* (1877), which pointed out the differences between "societas" and "civitas" along the same lines. The seminal concepts in the field, however, were those of Emile Durkheim (*The Division of Labor in Society*, 1878) and Ferdinand Tonnies (*Gemeinschaft and Gesellschaft*, 1887). Durkheim's concept of mechanical solidarity versus organic solidarity departs from the distinction between community and society. He finds "mechanical solidarity" in traditional communities where each individual "replicates" the skills and knowledge of every other, and shares the same "basic personality." In complex societies with a high degree of division of labor, individuals become specialized in order to complement one another's skills, creating mutual interdependence and "organic solidarily." Tonnies also differentiated the traditional rural village, where "community" prevailed, from the large city where community is replaced by "society." The rural village is characterized by contact between all its members, and an overall sense of solidarity, while those in the city relate to each other in a series of roles which do not include their full selves, and exist as isolated units.

More than fifty years later, Robert Redfield formulated and developed the ideal of the "folk-urban continuum," which he tested in a series of communities in the Yucatan peninsula of Mexico. He characterized folk culture as small, isolated, homogenous, and collectively-based—and urban culture as essentially the opposite.[40] More recently, Talcott Parsons and Edward Shils have developed a set of "pattern variables" which can be used to distinguish traditional from modern value bases.[41] Some of the major dichotomous schemes that have been used to differentiate between rural-traditional and urban-modern life styles are listed below:

Author	Title	Year	Rural-Urban Dichotomy	
Henry Sumner Maine	*Ancient Law*	1861	status	contract
Lewis Henry Morgan	*Ancient Society*	1877	societas	civitas
Emile Durkheim	*The Division of Labor in Society*	1878	mechanical solidarity	organic solidarity
Ferdinand Tonnies	*Gemeinschaft and Gesellschaft*	1887	community	society
Max Weber	*Economy and Society*	1925	traditional authority	legal authority
Ralph Linton	*The Study of Man*	1936	ascribed status	achieved status
Robert Redfield	*The Folk Culture of Yucatan*	1941	folk	urban
Talcott Parsons and Edward Shils	*Toward a General Theory of Action*	1950	pattern variables: ascriptive diffuse affective particularistic collective quality	achievement specific non-affective universalistic individual performance

The concepts behind many of these schemes have been used—often in contradictory and ill-understood fashion—in the scholarly literature on marginality to identify traditional-rural beliefs or behaviors inappropriate in the urban setting. The problem with most of these schemes is that they focus on characterizing the polar extremes without much examination of the mechanisms through which a person or group moves from one of these polar extremes to the other.

A different approach—that based on underlying world views and gradual social pressures—stems from the seminal work done sixty years ago by Max Weber. Weber modified the view that the forces of production were the major determining factors in the organization of society with the understanding that technology and work styles were part of a larger gestalt. He explained than an individual's world view plays a critical part in determining the success or failure of the functioning of any given economic system in any given context. Thus, transformations in the technologies of production, or factors of production, take hold and are able to transform society only when there were supportive and parallel transformations in the minds of the people. There had to be ideologies available to give rationale and coherence to the material changes.[42]

Weber's work and the influence of the dichotomous studies produced the school of attitudinal modernization which flourished in the 1960s. There is much which could be said about this literature—its ethnocentricism, its lack of a sufficiently historical and structural orientation, its ideological anti-communist bias—but the salient point for our purposes is that it contributed substantially to the set of ideas about the so-called unintegrated sectors, specifically the traditional masses in the countryside and in the cities who comprise the "marginal" population.

One of the major underlying premises is that issues of national economic and political development cannot be dealt with apart from the basic values and world views of the people involved, and that in developing countries there are entire sub-groups whose values are different from, or at best in transition toward, those needed for modernization.

Many of the studies of the period, then, turned their attention to the attributes of individuals in traditional societies, regarding their orientations and world view as an explanation for the perpetuation of "underdevelopment."

Millikan and Blackmer were perhaps the first authors to address the topic of modernization from an interdisciplinary standpoint. Their work is especially representative of the traditionality/modernization school of thought: "The underlying requirement for change in all three areas (politics, economics, and social structures) is the modernization of attitudes. Modernity is a style of life. . . . The paramount requirement for the modernization of any society is that the people themselves must change."[43]

Thus, a focus of the process of change within the individual became paramount, and much attention was paid to the "obstacles to development" posed by the persistence of a traditional mentality among the population. The basic line of analysis holds that a syndrome of values, attitudes, and aspirations, variously defined by different authors but generally labeled as "attitudinal modernity," is a prerequisite not only of national economic development but of political maturity as well.

One of the principal and persistent themes throughout the literature is the integration of all parts of the society through participation in the process of nation-building.[44] The idea in economic terms is that through urbanization, industrialization, the spread of mass media, and the widening of educational opportunities, many segments of the population can be brought from the subsistence sector into the modern economy. Marginal populations will then become consumers, expanding the internal markets and stimulating further development.

There is also an underlying assumption that political participation of a democratic nature goes hand-in-hand with economic development, and that the population has to be prepared to assume the responsibilities of modern citizenship. Widespread political participation is considered to be both part of the process and an end in itself, and—by some—a buffer against totalitarianism and communism. Attitudinal modernity, or at least an uprooting and stage of transition, is a prerequisite for the mobilization and extended participation of the population in the development process.[45]

Among the attitudinal obstacles to modernization—which reappear in various forms throughout the literature—are: a lack of control over nature; feelings of fatalism and religiosity; a distrust of science, technology, and innovation; an inability to plan for the future; a lack of "empathy"; and an authoritarian, non-achievement-oriented personality type, all tied in with family, clan, and kin relationships.

The first of these, the theme of control, is clearly seen in Cyril Black's definition of modernization as an "unprecedented increase in man's knowledge of and control over his environment."[46] It is also discussed by the economist W. W. Rostow in terms of traditional man having "pre-Newtonian attitudes toward the physical world," that is, "not seeing it as subject to knowable laws or capable of productive manipulation."[47] In the traditional peasant world it is quite plausible that the population did not feel effective in controlling their environment because their practical capabilities to do so were in fact quite limited. Thus, a sense of impotence and fatalism was reinforced, along with the reverence for religion and magic which seemed the only way to interpret a seemingly whimsical and capricious world.[48]

Redfield, in *The Primitive World and Its Transformations*, describes "the remaking of the primitive world by the reflexive mind" as one of the great attitudinal changes in mankind. "The primitive world-view is overturned and man emerges from the unity of the universe and perceives himself as separate from nature and able to exert his will over it." The universe is thus reduced from "morally significant" to merely impersonal. The next step is individual "self-management." Redfield writes, "Man comes to believe in his competence to reconstruct himself and society by deliberate design." Secular-technical thinking comes to prevail over the moral-sacred, and experimentation has precedence over ritual.[49]

Belief in science and technology and the application of rational thought to problem-solving, then, develops along with an openness to innovation and experimentation, and can be used as a rough indicator of the modern style.[50] In this context, one can posit a three-step set of conditions: a belief that change is possible, a desire for change, and the mental flexibility to perceive new alternatives and adapt to new situations as they arise. This is where Rokeach's idea of "cognitive flexibility" and Lerner's notion of "empathy" become relevant to social change.[51] One needs an open mind in order to avoid the rigid dogmatism of traditional teaching and to have a sufficient tolerance of ambiguity to cope with the ever-changing conditions of transformation. But one also needs "empathy" or psychic mobility," which is the ability to imagine oneself in another's situation, if one is to cope successfully with upward mobility: "What differentiates [the transitional person] . . . from his peers is a different latent structure of both aptitudes and attitudes. The aptitude is empathy, the attitude one of desire for the things his mind visualizes."[52]

This transitional person is—within his own milieu—a deviant. Everett Hagen discusses the need for this type of deviant in his *Theory of Social Change*, contending that societal level transition requires many such personalities who—in addition to being empathetic and aspiring—accord prestige to manual and technical activity and have higher needs for achievement and autonomy than for dependency and affiliation.[53] This connects with another central theme, that of achievement motivation, or the need for achievement. David McClelland defines it as a "desire to do well not so much for the sake of social recognition, but to attain an inner feeling of personal accomplishment." In short, it is a striving for excellence.[54]

Perhaps the single thread which ties together much of this literature is the one dealing with kinship, family ties, deference to traditional authorities, and the clinging to religious beliefs. While modernization theorists differ on details, they agree that strong family ties, extended kinship networks, or "loyalties to family and clan" serve to hinder individual mobility, constrain individual achievement, limit an individual's economic advancement, and take precedence over the individual's loyalty to his nation. All of these ties slow the development of modern citizenship.

The theorists of modernization argue that for a modern nation-state to develop, the individual must be free of constraining parochial ties to tribe, clan, or family and become self-oriented rather than collective-oriented. He must not judge others by their relation to him personally, but rather by the functional role they can play in his life.[55] Religiosity advances a fatalistic world-view which is in opposition to the desired secular view. Because religion discourages tampering with time-honored wisdoms and encourages respect for traditional authorities, it is a reactionary force in the modernization process.

Alex Inkeles brings many strands of this literature together in his work on "the modernization of man."[56] He attempts to make his theories operational through the "overall modernity" (OM) scale, which he has verified in an intensive six-nation study. Inkeles' basic paradigm first distinguishes between the external components of modernization—the processes of urbanization, education, communication, industrialization, and politicization—and the internal components that accompany them. The broader, societal transformations parallel personal world-view transformations, which he codifies into nine basic elements: (1) readiness for new experience; (2) disposition to form or hold opinions on a large number of problems and issues; (3) psychological orientation to the present and future; (4) belief in planning and organizing as a way of handling life; (5) sense of personal efficacy; (6) confidence in the calculability of the world; (7) awareness of human dignity and disposition to show respect for others; (8) faith in science and technology; and (9) a belief in distributive, impartial justice. These—or, more precisely, their opposites—are critical components of the ideal type, or marginal man, that emerges at the end of this chapter.

There are a number of problems with the modernization literature, primarily stemming from a notion of development by stages following the Western model, and assuming that the characteristics of the entrepreneurial elite and the mobile middle class are necessary prerequisites for modernization anywhere. In addition, the modernization process is seen as necessary for economic expansion of the capitalist system, cultural expansion of the "American way of life," and political protection against communism. This, plus the fact that modernization is regarded as bringing "progress" in an undifferentiated manner to the whole society— ignoring the asymmetrical consequences for different social classes— helps us understand why modernization theory has had so wide an appeal to North American theorists and has so often been linked with the ideological rationale for U.S. domination in Latin America.

The way in which this modernization literature deals with the question of why underdeveloped countries remain underdeveloped is paralleled on the individual level by another body of literature contributing to the myths of marginality—the "culture of poverty" school, which poses the question of why the poor remain poor.

THE CULTURE OF POVERTY SCHOOL

The literature defining a "culture of poverty" has become yet another major source of marginality theory. Although the specific phrase is linked to the work of Oscar Lewis, the concepts have been picked up and used widely both in the United States and in Latin America. The culture of poverty literature postulates the rise of certain personality traits in response to a situation of deprivation. These traits are perpetuated through the socialization process to subsequent generations, persisting even in the face of objective changes in economic or social circumstances. This is thought to create a vicious cycle of poverty, which is supposedly more difficult to escape than the economic deprivation itself. This is what the marginality theorists refer to when they go beyond describing a marginal situation to point out specific dysfunctional personality traits. Since the perpetuation of poverty can then be ascribed to a lack of key attitudinal prerequisites or behavior patterns, the poor are in effect blamed for their own condition. Much of the logic is akin to that of the modernization literature discussed earlier. In both cases, social scientists describe the differences between the poor and an idealized middle-class norm, then concentrate on the symptoms rather than the causes of these differences. Modernization and culture-of-poverty concepts have become the theoretical justification for many social welfare programs in Latin America which in fact only perpetuate the status quo in the name of "helping the poor."

The primary theorist of the culture of poverty, Oscar Lewis, was ironically responsible for destroying the earlier simplistic notions of rural cohesion and urban breakdown.[57] Lewis's first reference to cultural traits associated with poverty appears in *Five Families* (1959), although his ideas were not yet crystallized.

In *The Children of Sanchez* (1961), he begins to specify his idea of the culture of poverty and presents a list of traits which appear—in modified and embellished form—throughout his writings, and are perhaps most clearly stated in his introduction to *La Vida* (1965) and in an article entitled "The Culture of Poverty," which appeared in *Scientific American* (1966).

It is interesting to note that despite the widespread popularity and influence the notion has had, the actual theoretical exposition of the culture of poverty is really limited to a relatively few pages of Lewis' writings in which he proposes lists of traits, mechanisms for their perpetuation, and conditions under which they will appear and flourish.

Lewis differentiates between poverty itself and its cultural aspects, claiming that the former is simply deprivation of certain wants or needs, while the latter is part of a "design for living."[58] "Poverty in modern nations is not only a state of economic deprivation, of disorganization, or of the absence of something; it is also something positive in the sense that it has a structure, a rationale, and defense mechanisms without which the poor could hardly carry on. . . . It is a dynamic factor which affects participation in the larger national culture and becomes a subculture of its own."[59]

However, the specific traits that Lewis associates with the poor are primarily negative, self-defeating attributes juxtaposed with supposed middle-class norms. In the introduction to *La Vida*, Lewis lists, among other traits, "lack of effective participation and the integration of the poor in the major institutions of the larger society; suspicion; apathy; cynicism; a minimum of organization beyond the level of the nuclear and extended family; high incidence of child and wife abandonment; strong feelings of marginality; helplessness, dependency, and inferiority; lack of impulse control; a strong present-time orientation with relatively little ability to defer gratification and to plan for the future; a sense of resignation and fatalism; and a high tolerance for psychological pathology of all sorts."[60] Lewis adds that the poor are "provincial and locally oriented, [and] usually do not have the knowledge, the vision, or the ideology to see the similarities between their problems and those of their counterparts elsewhere."[61]

Because the culture of poverty fits well within the long academic tradition of "blaming the victim," Lewis's work has inadvertently lent credibility to those who would blame the poor for their own poverty. The concept of the "disreputable poor" is well established, especially in North American sociological literature. Thirty years ago, E. Franklin Frazier described the black poor as so hopelessly disorganized and over-run with social pathologies that "they even lack public opinion, social control, and community institutions."[62]

Within this tradition in the United States are such reputable scholars and policy-makers as Nathan Glazer and Daniel Moynihan whose *Beyond the Melting Pot* ends on the same note of condescension. The well-known Moynihan Report (*The Negro Family: The Case for National Action*) describes fundamental problems lying within the Negro family that are not amenable to manipulation from outside, leading to the convenient public policy recommendation of "benign neglect."

Eleanor Leacock points out the irony that the concept of culture, which was originally adopted by the social sciences to get away from concentration on innate propensities, has been so widely applied in the "culture of the poor" that it is "almost as pernicious in its application as biological determinist and racist views have been in the past."[63] An extreme example of this tendency is the work of John Bartky concerning what he terms "dregs culture." Bartky contends that "the dregs culture child, if he is old enough, is probably being cared for by his second father and third mother"; crime is so rampant in dregs culture communi-ties that the law must work "fast and ruthlessly"; and the "storefront church in these communities is more an amusement than . . . a moral influence."[64]

These stereotypes of behavior in the poor communities appear regularly in the publications of the welfare establishment. *Growing Up Poor*, an HEW report written in 1966, echoes Lewis when it states, "the subcultural adaptation to poverty would seem to interact with the poverty situation to perpetuate lower-class status." Among other traits of the poor, the report includes "fatalistic and apathetic attitudes, magical rigid thinking, and poor impulse control."[65]

Undoubtedly the most controversial and critical aspect of Lewis's "culture of poverty" is the mechanism of self-perpetuation. Lewis describes the process in the introduction of *La Vida*: "Once [the culture of poverty] comes into existence, it tends to perpetuate itself from generation to generation because of its effect on children. By the time slum children are age six or seven, they have usually absorbed the basic attitudes and values of their subculture and are not psychologically geared to take full advantage of changing conditions or increased opportunities which may occur in their lifetime."[66]

This contention has been subject to serious criticism from several perspectives. First of all, Lewis implies that socialization is complete by the age of six or seven, a position unsupported by recent psychological research.[67] More important, Lewis states that an individual's mental set is predominant over concrete circumstances in determining behavior. This leads him to the amazing contention that the culture of poverty, and not poverty itself, is the focus of the problem. "The elimination of physical poverty per se," he says, "may not be enough to eliminate the culture of poverty."[68] The individuals Lewis portrays are ill-equipped to take advantage of new opportunities or respond to changing conditions, adding the condition of permanence to the characteristics of poor communities. It is precisely this aspect of the culture of poverty that has been most applied by the marginality theorists of Latin America.

The conditions under which the culture of poverty arises is another critical factor in Lewis's analysis. Lewis changed over time in his writings on the subject. In his *Scientific American* article in 1966, he explicitly stated that the culture of poverty is a subculture of Western society: "It arises in a setting of a cash economy where there is a high rate of unemployment, where the dominant classes hold values of thrift, accumulation, and upward mobility, and where low economic status is explained as the result of individual personal inadequacy and inferiority."[69] He describes the culture of poverty as "both an adaptation and a reaction by the poor to their marginal position in a class-stratified, highly individuated, capitalist society."[70]

Later, in the introduction to *La Vida*, Lewis states that any group that maintains personal and social integration, even if extremely poor by objective standards, is not subject to the culture of poverty. As examples, he cites non-literate primitive peoples, the lower castes of India, the Jews of Eastern Europe, and, speculatively, anyone in the socialist countries. He uses his re-visit to a slum in Havana, Cuba, as an example of this latter situation.

> The physical aspect of the slum had changed very little except for a beautiful new nursery school. It was clear that the people were still desperately poor, but I found much less of the despair, apathy, and hopelessness which are so diagnostic of urban slums in the culture of poverty. They expressed great confidence in their leaders and hope for a better life in the future. The slum itself was now highly organized, with block committees, educational committees, and party committees. The people had a new sense of power and importance.

They were armed and were given a doctrine which glorified the lower classes as the hope of humanity.[71]

Lewis finds, however, that such advanced industrial countries as the United States, though still harboring widespread poverty, have little of the culture of poverty "because of the advanced technology, high level of literacy, mass media, and high aspirations."[72] He says that probably only among the very low-income ethnic minority groups would one expect to find the telling traits, and that the civil rights movement has done much to eradicate these among the black population.

He finally concludes that the culture of poverty must be "endemic to colonialism and the early stages of capitalism." The only cure he sees is organization, solidarity, and hope. Social work and psychiatric solutions are useless; his analysis leads him to revolutionary solutions: "By creating basic structural changes in society, by redistributing wealth, by organizing the poor and giving them a sense of belonging, of power, and of leadership, revolutions frequently succeed in abolishing some of the basic characteristics of the culture of poverty even when they do not succeed in abolishing poverty itself."[73]

Unfortunately, and perhaps ironically, those who use Lewis's work on the culture of poverty tend to be selective in the passages they choose for policy guidelines. Revolutionary alternatives are dismissed, while the traits for self-perpetuating poverty in "marginal" communities have been popularized throughout Latin America. In particular, two key ideas from the culture of poverty—lack of participation and lack of integration—were developed by the DESAL group in Chile. This agency became the major exponent of marginality theory in Latin America.

DESAL's participation "theory"

While the modernization and culture-of-poverty literature dealt with marginality only by inference, DESAL, the Center for Latin American and Social Development (Centro para el Desarrollo Economica y Social de America Latina) focused directly on creating a theory of marginality and an ideological framework to go with it. For the past ten years DESAL has worked almost entirely on conceptualizing marginality, exploring its empirical dimensions, and most importantly, disseminating the emerging marginality thesis as the key concept within the Christian Democratic platform for social change. DESAL's various members, especially director Roger Vekemans (a Belgian Jesuit coming out of the European tradition of Christian Social Democracy), have been the main popularizers of the notion of marginality in Latin America. Theirs is one of the only direct statements about marginality, and much of the literature which followed on the topic merely responded to, criticized, or expanded upon their basic definition and position.

DESAL's basic precept is that the condition of marginality exists when lack of internal *integration* and political *participation* within a group reaches the extent that external management and money must be applied. These formulations were both a reaction to the policies of external aid agencies and served as guidelines for them. By projecting an implied model of harmonious social integration, DESAL's theory alluded to the church-inspired "heavenly city," and to the USAID ideal of North American democracy. DESAL sought not only to define marginality, but also to achieve a political solution whereby the haves and the have-nots would share in a unified system.

In DESAL's view Latin American countries constitute nations only in the most formal, juridical meaning of the word. Each of the countries is really a juxtaposition of two social systems. The Euro-Iberian culture has been superimposed over the native infrastructure for more than 500 years, creating a uniquely bipolar, or dual, society.

The historical circumstances of cultural superimposition, matured by centuries of dualism in the values, social structure, administration, and political regimes in Latin America, give rise to the repeated appearance of marginality within the varying social systems of the subcontinent. Marginals are not simply that group of the population that occupies the lower rungs of the social scale. They are actually *off* such a scale. Marginals have no position in the dominant social system, not even as its lower class: "It can be said of them that they are not socially and economically integrated in a society, in a class system, because they do not belong to the economic system. They are on the mathematical limit, without being, for they are not to be found in the countryside, which expels them, or in the city, which does not harbour them: . . . they are only there; they populate a piece of land which is no-man's land."[74]

Marginality is the antithesis of integration. DESAL substitutes the concept of marginality-integration for the older duality between underdevelopment and development. Duality theory in its many forms permeates a substantial body of literature dealing with modernization in developing countries.

In political terms, modernization is often associated with the increasing participation of different groups in the decision-making process, and in the sharing of the results of policies implemented through the political process. Social participation in this view becomes, quite naturally, an essential prerequisite to development. No "real" development can occur without popular participation. Where it is absent, developmental aims must depart from efforts to bring the outcast groups into the mainstream of the political process. Accepting this formulation, DESAL directly challenged the view that economic growth causes social progress and stimulates popular participation. The DESAL thesis changes the emphasis of past theories of dualism away from the problems of economic transformation and toward aspects of cultural transformation and social-political participation.

Marginality, in the DESAL ideology, implies quite literally a separation or schism betwen the social system as a whole and a specific underprivileged group. Lack of political participation by certain groups engenders a disintegration of the national fabric, as well as internal disintegration, and thus causes the situation of marginality. As Vekemans succinctly put it in a piece entitled, "A Strategy for Misery": "Marginality is characterized by a complete lack of participation in the global society. . . . Not participating actively in decisions, and not having access to the sources of power leads to the lack of passive and receptive participation in the common good, the benefits of society, or the sharing of its resources. . . . This double play of omissions is due in turn to the internal disintegration of the marginal groups and their total lack of any sort of organization."[75]

It is clear from past DESAL proposals that integration is set out as a goal, an ideal not fully existing in any social system. The degree of social and political disintegration along with the lack of participation thus becomes the essential meaning of marginality. The two dimensions to the lack of participation emerge clearly in the quote. The first comes from the lack of active, or contributive, participation in the decision-making process common to society; the second is the lack of passive, or receptive, participants in the distribution of the material benefits of society. Those goods in society that should be shared among the population are not received by marginals. They do not participate in their use or enjoyment, be they education, social security, or access to better jobs.

From this two-pronged phenomenon of participation emerges the third characteristic of marginality: the lack of internal cohesiveness in the marginalized groups, which makes the individuals helpless in the face of their condition: "Marginals do not share in the responsibilities and assignments that must be undertaken for the solution of social problems in general, and in their problems in particular. Marginal groups find themselves, therefore, lacking any organization that could link them to society and that would, furthermore, represent them to the institution of "established" society."[76] This corresponds to the accusations of the culture-of-poverty school—and all the notions of urban breakdown discussed above. DESAL's view, however, adds the critical point that the integrated part of the social system lacks mechanisms for receiving and socializing these groups. The fight against marginality must, therefore, proceed through the creation of new institutions capable of administering external help to the afflicted population.

The consequences of marginality have been catalogued by DESAL observers in five major areas—physical, cultural, social, economic, and political—each commanding specific instruments of external help. To begin with, marginal groups are physically segregated both in rural and urban areas. Those who inhabit the marginal settlements suffer diminished initiative and capacity to act—individually or collectively—in a rational manner. They face disintegration of their traditional cultural roots and at the same time are unable to acquire the traits of the dominant social sectors. Marginals, furthermore, lack either the occupational or income levels of other groups in the economy. Finally, they are politically apathetic, unable to influence or respond to the democratic process.

According to this logic, special community development projects and social change policies are required to overcome and compensate for the deficits of the marginal groups, so that all members of the nation can be integrated into a common set of functional institutions.

The clearest expression of DESAL's views comes from an analysis of the policies it has proposed. DESAL rejected from the start its initial role as a research group uncommitted to political action. Its views are now seen more clearly in the political platforms it has produced. In this practice, DESAL emulates development models nourished by the North American social sciences. At the core of DESAL's work is the model of popular participation, an amalgam of activist policies designed to combat marginality and fight the threat of communism. The program has two aspects, each requiring external intervention into the marginal sector. The goal of this process would be a form of "cultural mutation" achieved through a combination of community work and self-help programs in urban infrastructure, housing, and social welfare. The second aspect would involve the transformation of existing social institutions, so as to make them more receptive to the marginal groups. Although the policies are never fully specified, one is led to believe that their thrust would be toward greater public spending for social programs, and for more active state and international role in countervailing the increased concentration of private incomes.

DESAL in Perspective. As DESAL's director, Roger Vekemans, points out, the preoccupation with marginal groups in Latin America came in the wake of disastrous policies for accelerated economic development promulgated during the 1950s by ECLA, AID, the World Bank, and others. The purely economic measures advocated by the multinational agencies, based on the rapid development of internal industrial markets and the trickling down of opportunities to the less favored groups, failed to generate growth in the middle sectors. Instead, sustained increases in economic capacity were accompanied by an equally impressive worsening of the income distribution. Opposition to these policies led to the declaration of the Alliance for Progress, which emphasized the need for social development proceeding alongside measures to speed the rate of capital accumulation.

To many analysts, the generalized recession that began to engulf the region in the early 1960s was the product of a fundamental structure imbalance: the previous process of economic development had failed to enlarge the market for the goods and services of the modern sector. Industrial development failed to penetrate and transform the decaying traditional agricultural sectors. As a consequence, not only did income become more concentrated and serve to increase the dualistic structure of the society, but also industrial growth stagnated in the absence of a sufficient level of demand.

While community development programs had been common in Latin America for some time, the new approach of DESAL, building upon the pioneering work of the Organization of American States, was much more ambitious than earlier examples. It was perhaps the closest example of the policies proposed in the U.S. Foreign Assistance Act of 1966, known since as Title IX. The act proposed financial assistance for the development of indigenous institutions that would "sustain economic and social progress," and for civic education and training in the skills of democratic self-government.

Such an occurrence was not accidental. In a period of political reformism aiming at "change without revolution," many programs of social participation were formulated, the ultimate objective of which was to be "functional" to the *existing* systems of power relations in Latin America. DESAL programs were some of the more sophisticated and better articulated ones in this select group.

As for the specific importance of DESAL's work, it cannot be understood in isolation from its critical role in Chilean politics. DESAL served as an important ideological mentor in the Christian Democrat regime of President Frei from 1964 to 1970. Many of the urban policies then advocated were a direct result of DESAL's equating of the problems of marginality and participation. Jorge Guisti puts the period in perspective:

> DESAL's brief life in Chile began with the "boom" of Christian Democrat parties, particularly after the triumphs of Alcide de Gasperi in Italy, and of Konrad Adenauer in West Germany, following the Second World War. In both countries, Christian Democrats emerged as an efficient barrier against the impulses of powerful leftist groups, especially the Communists. The European Christian Democracy served as a base, and stimulus, for the creation of this type of political movement in other parts of the world. European leaders of the Christian Democrats, as well as Church dignitaries, turned their attention to Latin America, a continent assessed as a gunpowder barrel in the wake of the Cuban revolution. The end of DESAL, in Chile, coincided with the defeat of the Christian Democrat alliance in the hands of the leftist coalition that supported Allende in 1970. In effect, immediately following the Congressional confirmation of Allende, Roger Vekemans, director of DESAL, dissolved this organism, setting up offices in Bogota, Colombia.[77]

Ironically, in the Chilean reality, the programs, reforms, and improvements brought to the squatter settlements under the DESAL ideology had the ultimate effect of increasing the cohesiveness and political consciousness of the "marginals" once their structural situation changed during the Allende period.[78] This leads to our final component "stream" in the formulation of marginality theory—the question of radicalism.

RADICALISM, SOCIAL THEORY, AND MARGINALITY

There have been many different and conflicting conceptions of the political outlook of migrants, squatters, and "marginal" populations in general. Some, who accept Vekemans' statement that "after lack of participation, the first essential characteristic of marginality is its radicalism," hold them to be potential revolutionaries;[79] others imply with equal theoretical vigor that they are defenders of the status quo.

Squatters as Revolutionaries. A number of forceful lines of reasoning lead to the conclusion that migrants or shantytown dwellers will behave in violent and socially disruptive ways and hold political beliefs of a radical nature. This is the daydream of the left and the nightmare of the right.

One main line of argument is that migrants leave their homes with unrealistic expectations about the new life that the city can offer them. They arrive lonely and uprooted to find their hopes frustrated by insurmountable difficulties at every turn. They cannot find a decent place to live, a good job, or satisfactory educational, medical, or other services. As Barbara Ward eloquently states the case:

> All over the world, often long in advance of effective industrialization, the unskilled poor are streaming away from the subsistence agriculture to exchange the squalor of rural poverty for the even deeper miseries of the shantytowns, favelas, and bidonvilles that year by year grow inexorably on the fringes of the developing cities. . . . They are the core of local despair and disaffection, filling the jeunesse movements of the Congo, swelling the urban mobs of Rio, voting Communist in the ghastly alleys of Calcutta, everywhere undermining the all too fragile structure of public order and thus retarding the economic development that alone can help their plight.[80]

Disappointment and frustration are heightened by the affluence which the poor see around them in the city and hear extolled in the media but have no way of attaining themselves. This "demonstration effect" supposedly leads to thwarted expectations and alienation from the system. Such terms as the "want-get ratio" and the "revolution of rising expectations" filled the development literature of the 1960s. Psychological studies which suggest that frustration leads to aggression[81] were used to underwrite the theory that migrants are likely to erupt in angry explosions of violence and revolutionary activity because they cannot fulfill their aspirations. In the words of the Brazilian sociologist Soares: "When industrialization doesn't keep pace with urbanization and there is a mass of underemployed and unemployed with aspirations heightened by urban living and no possibility of satisfying these aspirations even to a minimal degree, then leftist radicalism finds fertile soil."[82] The migrant, "socially mobilized" in leaving the countryside, becomes the thwarted "mass man" of the city, easy prey for the demagogy of radical leaders. [83]

Germani traces this theme to one of the original concerns of marginality theory, the meeting of disparate cultures. According to this logic, persons living on the margins between two cultures are often faced with status inconsistencies and blocks to mobility which are firm foundations for radical political views.[84]

Many theorists, along with the DESAL group, believe that the social disorganization of the favela contributes to its radicalism as well. When traditional values (such as religiosity or respect for the family) break down or come into question, a normlessness results which supposedly renders the affected person vulnerable to those who would fill this gap with a coherent and radical world view. This is most likely to happen during what some have called the "anomic gap"—the period between the abandonment of a traditional value system and its replacement with other values. Lacking strong secondary group ties, the favelados are available for attachment to protest movements that preach direct action and large-scale change in society.

The poverty of squatter settlements, whether better or worse in absolute terms than that found in the countryside, is seen as more conducive to radicalism because of a shift in reference group. In the city, poor people are in constant contact with persons of much greater wealth. Poor women work in the homes of the rich, poor men as their chauffeurs. Favelados are in the midst of the most wealthy residential neighborhoods of the country and through their own observations, and through the media, observe upper-class styles of life daily. The "relative deprivation" that results from increasingly invidious comparisons of his own life with that of the rich presumably leads the favelado to a radical critique of society.

Urbanization itself is seen as a radicalizing force by some. In the city, people grow more aware of the effects of government policies and are exposed to new ideas about alternative ways of proceeding. The struggle for power is more visible in the city than in the countryside, where family clans often reign unquestioned and unchallenged. According to this line of reasoning, squatters learn that they too can influence politics if they act forcefully, and in unison, for radical change. Examples of countries whose governments preach power to the proletariat are discovered for the first time. It is feared, for example, that the Chinese and Cuban examples will become known to the favelado through his broadened circle of contacts and wider media use.

In contrast, Marx did not see the lumpen proletariat as a revolutionary group. In the *Eighteenth Brumaire* he defines them as not meeting the basic definitions of a class, not having manifest relationships with one another, lacking class antagonisms, and being most easily mobilized by populist mass appeals of a pragmatic rather than an ideological nature.[85] Many self-styled Marxists and neo-Marxists fall into the line of reasoning discussed above, however, believing that the uprooting of migration and the anomie of the urban experience in itself is radicalizing, and will open people's eyes to their "true" but formerly unrecognized interests. Over time, they argue, squatters will develop a revolutionary consciousness (become *conscientizado*). Franz Fanon in *The Wretched of the Earth* expressed dramatically this point of view: "The men whom the growing population of the country districts and colonial expropriation have brought to desert their family holdings circle tirelessly around the different towns, hoping that one day or another they will be allowed inside. . . . For the lumpen-proletariat, that hoard of starving men, uprooted from their tribe and clan, constitute one of the most spontaneous and the most radically revolutionary forces of a colonized people."[86]

The major flaws in this perspective are three: the equating of marginal groups with the lumpen proletariat, when in fact squatter settlements and other situations considered marginal encompass sectors of the working classes and other popular classes as well; the assumptions that an uprooted people are a revolutionary people, when in fact this may be the opposite; and, finally, the premise that migrants are uprooted, when in fact their geographical moves are often tied into a tight social network.

The Second-Generation Hypothesis. An important variant on the squatters-as-revolutionaries theory is the prediction that although the first generation of migrants to the city might be quiescent and apolitical, their children can be expected to be highly alienated and politically active. According to Samuel Huntington: "In Asia, Africa, and Latin America urban violence, political and criminal, is due to rise as the proportion of natives to immigrants in the cities rises. At some point, the slums of Rio and Lima, of Lagos and Calcutta, like those of Harlem and Watts, are likely to be swept by social violence as the children of the city demand the rewards of the city."[87]

The underlying logic is that first generation migrants still believe in the rural values of social deference and political passivity. In addition, their reference group is the villagers they left behind, not the more affluent city dwellers. The second generation of migrants, with no rural model against which to match their accomplishments, receives the full impact of their parents' rising expectations and absorbs fully the goals and style of city life. When these people find no place for themselves in elementary school, no jobs available in the economy, no way to (or room at) the top, they will become radicalized. Research in urban settings as disparate as Watts, Calcutta, and Rio, for example, indicates that those who participate in riots or vote for radical opposition practices tend to be urban poor, not first-generation migrants.[88]

Squatters as Conformists. Theories which link squatters and radicalism seem compelling. Many scholars contend, however, that the major problem to understand is the opposite—not activism but actually apathy and lack of political involvement. They say that revolts in urban centers have been few and participation of squatters in them virtually nil. In Hobsbawm's words, "It is remarkable how few riots—even food riots—there have been in the great Latin American cities during a period when the mass of their impoverished and economically marginal inhabitants multiplied, and inflation . . . was uncontrollable."[89] Halperin points out that in those (exceptional) situations in which shantytowns did vote for opposition parties, often they supported moderate, sometimes even right-wing candidates: Odria in Peru, Pietri in Caracas, Frei in Santiago and Valparaiso.[90]

From this point of view it would seem that squatters try to maximize favors from the political system and minimize risk of loss. They know they are somewhat better off in the city than in the country and are not in fact highly alienated, anomic, or frustrated. They are more concerned with getting ahead—making do with present resources—than with engaging in political struggles and ideological debates. A paternalistic ideology, combined with a "don't let them take it away" slogan would be more appealing (to *barriada* dwellers) than a revolutionary "let's rise and kill the oligarchy" approach. Probably not many inhabitants of squatter settlements would be sorry if someone else took the latter action, but they themselves are too busy trying to survive.[91]

Among those who find no radical potential among squatters there is still another level of disagreement. There are those who posit apathy and disengagement as the dominant political attitude and those who hold that a calculating shrewdness, backed by appropriate, if minimal political activity, is the prevailing pattern. In the first group are Bonilla and Michelena, who found that in Venezuela "squatter settlement political systems seem to be based on clientele relationships in which the individual squatter is an apathetic and manipulated partner."[92] In Rio's favelas, Bonilla discovered that less than one-fifth of the men and women had discussed politics at all during the last six months and that even fewer saw politics as a means to desired goals. In his words, "The urban and rural poor in Latin America do not seriously expect their governments to do anything to alleviate the situation."[93] Hobsbawm, reflecting on the fate of urban populism, generally says of squatters: "This is a population with no prior commitment—or even potential commitment—to any version of urban or national politics, or indeed to any belief which could form the basis of such politics. . . . They understand personal leadership and patronage alone, since it alone provides a link between the political worlds of the hinterland and the city. . . . Untouched by any other tradition . . . the new migrants look naturally for the powerful champion, the savior, the father of his people."[94]

Others, while agreeing that the favelas are not revolutionary, disagree that they are passive and paternalistically dependent in their dealing with the larger society. José Artur Rios, the most widely read author on the favelas in Brazil, states: "The favelados don't have a patriotic political consciousness, but they know the heart (basis, root) of politics, or the way to use it in their own interests. They are totally suspicious of the politicians, making propaganda for the candidates and promoting votes in return for favors (improvements, benefits) but they don't vote for the candidate—as they themselves declare—thus taking advantage of the system of secret ballots."[95] In this vein, the Leeds found the favelados they spoke with "keenly cognizant of what is happening inside the favela . . . and often extraordinarily well informed about . . . what is occurring in the matrix polity." They said that "along with the professional politician and administrator of the Brazilian polity, the favela residents are the most subtle and conniving politicians we have ever met anywhere."[96]

THE IDEAL TYPE AND THE PROPOSITIONS

Since it would be nearly impossible to test individually all of the separate and sometimes conflicting claims which have been made regarding the attributes associated with the marginal status of the migrant and squatter population, I have used the diverse literature mentioned above to construct an ideal type, to create in effect the polar extreme of the marginal subculture so it can be tested against the realities of the squatter settlements and the urban poor. Clearly, no one author will have ascribed to the marginal population all of the characteristics embodied in the paradigm, and undoubtedly no one squatter or migrant exists who represents them all. Marginality is obviously a question of degree rather than absolutes, and it is apparent that a person could be marginal in some senses, or in regards to certain spheres of life and certain institutions, while being quite well integrated in other respects.[97] However, by developing the ideal construct and testing the propositions which flow from it, I intend to break up the existing theoretical logjam that currently permits government policy to be carried out at the expense of the favelados. I also hope to open the question of other approaches to the entire marginality issue and to the critique of this ideal type itself by Latin American scholars, which I will discuss in the concluding chapter.

What then *is* the ideal type which can be derived from this entire discussion? To begin with, the migrants are seen as uprooted, anomic individuals or families from the countryside, knowing no one in the city and having no place to go. They never adapt well to urban life and are generally anxious to return to their home towns. They seek out others of their kind and isolate themselves in parochial, ruralistic enclaves where they live in filth and squalor. Instead of using the wider context of urban agencies, institutions, and services, the contact which could help them and also have a modernizing impact, they prefer to stay within their ghettos and protect their traditional values and life styles. Within these shantytowns there is a huge void created by the transition process. Social disorganization has resulted—evidenced in family breakdown, anomie, lack of trust and cooperation, secularization, rampant crime, violence, and promiscuity.

As the self-defeating traits of the culture of poverty replace the maladaptive traits of the culture of traditionality—or supplement them, as the case may be—the squatters become highly pessimistic and fatalistic. They show total inability to defer gratification or plan for the future. They are regarded as parasites or leeches on the urban economy, and as a drain on the limited resources for city services and infrastructure. Favelados are seen as lazy, not placing a high value on work, and contributing little either to production or to consumption. Finally, they are considered politically non-interested, non-participant, and non-supportive of the system. They are seen as a "seething, frustrated mass" apt to fall easy prey to the appeals of revolutionary rhetoric.

This word-picture can be distilled into a concise framework with four dimensions: social, cultural, economic, and political. Within each of these categories are two major propositions which flow directly from the literature. The eight propositions can be operationalized into specific concepts testable among squatter and migrant populations. The resulting theoretical framework is shown in Table 17.

I intend to use this framework both as a guideline for presenting my own data and as a way of testing the validity of marginality "theory." In the next two chapters I will systematically explore the relationship between each component concept of marginality and the reality of favela life in Rio de Janeiro, taking this as a significant example of the sector of society to which marginality refers.

TABLE 17

Marginality: The Ideal Type

Dimensions	Propositions	Concepts
Social	*Internal disorganization* The favela lacks internal social organization or cohesion; its residents are lonely and isolated.	Voluntary associations Friendship and kinship Trust and mutual help Crime and violence
	External isolation The favelado is not integrated into the city; he does not make wide use of the urban context and he never feels fully at home in it.	Urban adaptation Familiarity with city Heterogeneity of contacts Use of the city Use of urban agencies Mass media exposure
Cultural	*Culture of traditionality* The favela is an enclave of rural parochialism in the city.	Religious orientation Openness to innovation Family orientation Empathy Fatalism Deference to authority
	Culture of poverty The favelado as a reaction and adaptation to his deprivation develops and perpetuates a culture of poverty.	Suspicion of others Crime and violence Family breakdown Pessimism Aspirations

TABLE 17
Marginality: The Ideal Type (Continued)

Dimensions	Propositions	Concepts
Economic	*Economic parasitism* Favelados are a drain on the urban economy, taking out more than they give.	Employment and income Consumption Contribution to infrastructure
	Economic parochialism Both the culture of traditionality and the culture of poverty contribute to an economic parochialism in the favelado.	Work ethic Education and job training Entrepreneurial values
Political	*Political apathy* The favelado is not integrated into city and national political life.	Internal political structures Political interest, saliency, and information Electoral participation Direct political action Use of administrative channels
	Political radicalism Because of their frustration, social disorganization, and anomie, favelados are prone to leftist radicalism.	Alienation Demand for structural changes Class consciousness Nationalism

Chapter Five
Social, Cultural, and
Economic Marginality

U sing the survey data gathered in 1968-1969, I intend to test each of the eight propositions outlined in Chapter Four to determine how closely the favelados and suburbanos of Rio de Janeiro conform to the components of marginality theory. Each set of propositions and concepts will be tested in order, and in each case I will assess both the degree of marginality and the terms of integration. The first part of each discussion, then, will focus on the attributes of the favelados; the second will focus on the mechanisms of the society in which they live.

SOCIAL MARGINALITY

The propositions developed from marginality theory contend that the favela is socially disorganized and its residents isolated from the surrounding urban life. The prevailing wisdom on the topic remains Huntington's belief that "a high level of mutual distrust exists in urban slums and this consequently makes difficult any sort of organized cooperation."[1] Friendship and kinship networks—once strong in the rural villages—are supposedly weak in the cities. In addition, it is assumed that the personal frustrations of unemployment, inability to obtain schooling and health care for one's children, and failure to achieve many of the goals that lured migrants to the city are transformed into such antisocial behavior as violence, crime, and alcoholism.

INTERNAL ISOLATION

The first measure of internal disorganization concerns participation in voluntary associations. Contrary to the predictions of marginality theory, our findings show that the favelados have an extremely active associational life. As the description of Catacumba, Nova Brasília, and Duque de Caxias attests, community organization in the favela includes political associations (the Residents' Association and Light Commissions), social organizations (recreation clubs, samba schools, and soccer clubs), and religious and spiritualist groups.

Sixty-eight percent of favela residents belong to at least one community group. Two statistics will put this figure in perspective. A study in 100 poor neighborhoods in the United States revealed that less than 20 percent of the residents held membership in one or more voluntary associations.[2] Almond and Verba in their study of five national polities put the comparable figure for Americans generally—surely one of the most highly participant populations in the world—at 57 percent.[3] Favelados also feel positively about local groups, even the controversial political ones. Sixty-one percent of those we interviewed felt that Residents' Associations "worked for the good of all residents"; another 11 percent said they worked "for the good of the majority."

As for informal friendship and kinship networks, the data speak for themselves. When asked where their best friends and favorite relatives lived, over half the favelados said "within the same community." Two-thirds have very frequent (daily or weekly) social contact with these persons. This is consistent with the discovery, reported in Chapter Three, that 84 percent of migrants had friends, relatives, or both in Rio when they came, and that 73 percent arrived in the city accompanied by family or friends. A separate study of six Rio favelas carried out by Renato Boschi in the same period reached a similar conclusion—that the favela is a cohesive complex with strengths at all social levels: family, voluntary association, and neighborhood.[4]

In like manner, our evidence on mutual trust and cooperation totally discredits the marginality myths. As Table 18 shows, trust and unity are remarkably evident in the favela. Eight persons out of ten told us their neighborhood was more or less united.[5] The same high proportion said they could count on at least a few friends and neighbors when they were needed, and 43 percent said "most" of their friends could be counted on. Most striking of all, 70 percent felt that mutual help is as great or greater than it is in the countryside. The evidence refutes a major distinction in marginality theory—the idyllic warmth and cohesion of the rural village versus the isolated, impersonal, competitive nature of city life. This myth has long permeated the literature on the city and squatters in general.

To guard against the possibility that these answers were calculated to please the interviewer, or based in pure naivete, we also asked respondents if they felt there were any people in the favela who exploit others. Sixty-five percent said yes. Favelados are aware that they are exploited by a small minority of local people, but they still maintain that among residents at large there are positive bonds of trust and mutual

TABLE 18
Trust and Unity in the Favela
(N=600)

Questions	Percent
Q. How many of your friends and neighbors who live here can you count on when you need them?	
All	21
Most	22
A few	45
None	12
Q. Do you feel that the people who live here are united or do they lack unity among themselves?	
Highly united	52
More or less united	30
Lack unity	18
Q. In comparison with your home town, do you feel that there is more or less mutual help here among friends and neighbors?	
Much more help here	39
Little more help here	18
About the same	13
Little less help here	11
Much less help here	19

reliability. It is quite unlikely that communal help on a neighborhood basis is more prevalent anywhere else in Rio, whether on common floors of high-rise apartment buildings or on the more spacious streets of higher income districts.[6]

Although most migrants have made a complete and permanent transition to city life, it is interesting that this does not involve cutting all ties with their communities of origin. Not only is it false that they are isolated and lonely within the city, but also that they are cut off from friends and relatives at home. Half the migrants have returned to their villages for a visit at least once since arriving in Rio, and it is largely economic considerations, we were told, that kept more from doing so.

Favelas have a reputation as crime-ridden communities. The following excerpt from a *Time* magazine article is typical of the sensationalism that often accompanies this question: "Squeezed by belt-cinching inflation and an influx of some 3,700 newcomers a month, the favela gangsters have moved into the city streets, boosting the crime rate alarmingly. . . . In previously safe lovers' lanes girls were raped and their boyfriends robbed, beaten or murdered."[7] Our evidence on this question agrees with that of Portes on Santiago: "The number of delinquencies within the marginal population is insignificant compared with the total population."[8] Of favelados in our sample, including housewives, young girls (starting at 16) and the elderly (up to 65) only 16 percent regarded violence or "immorality" as an objection to life in the city. (Only 3 percent said they would try to end crime as one of their priorities if they were President.)

Evidently, crime and violence were indeed a problem in the favelas, at an earlier period, especially for the favelados themselves. Long-term residents of Jacarézinho, one of the largest favelas in Rio with a population of about 60,000, told how in the early years they were plagued by constant fights, robberies, and sometimes even murders. They said that often at night they would hear gunshots outside their shacks and were terrified to intercede for fear of getting killed themselves. This was the very first issue which brought the residents together. They joined forces to form a volunteer vigilante committee, with members rotating duty every night. This set the precedent for the gradual formation of strong norms of in-group cooperation and mutual security. By the end of the 1960s and early 1970s, most of the larger favelas—including Catacumba, Nova Brasília, and Jacarézinho—had official police posts staffed with regular city policemen. When I asked these policemen about the degree of crime in the favela, they generally said it was minimal, and that their largest problem was keeping rambunctious adolescents from "disturbing the peace." In each favela, however, they said that it was worse in the other favelas, and even within the same favela, it was common for the residents to say, "Up to here it's perfectly safe, but over there [higher on the hillside] it's really dangerous, and you'd better not go alone."

Of course, degree of crime is difficult to assess accurately. No one would declare "criminal" as a profession in an interview, and there are no statistics on the residential locations of arrested—or unarrested—criminals in the city at large. However, from my own observations, I can make two points about crime within the favela itself. First, many favelados have televisions, radios, and bicycles and leave their barracos relatively open during much of the time. Yet there is little complaint of robbery. Second, despite the fact that taxi drivers were afraid to drop me off even at the foot of the favela, and that most Cariocas could simply not believe I was living *in* the favelas, I felt safer walking around the favela at night, and living there, than I ever had in Cambridge or New York!

In sum, the lives of favelados are rich in associational experience, commonly imbued with friendship and cooperative spirit, and relatively free from crime and interpersonal violence. When we asked the favelados if they would want to leave the favela for a new public housing project where they could own their own residence, 74 percent said they would prefer to stay where they were. When the same people were asked if they wanted to return to their home towns, 74 percent said definitely not, and another 11 percent said probably not. Their home towns, they told us, were too *atrasado* (backward), *parado* (paralyzed), or *faltando movimento* (lacking activity, or not "where the action is").

EXTERNAL ISOLATION

The second major aspect of social marginality is the favelados' presumed lack of integration into the wider urban context. Since the favela is perceived as an isolated parochial enclave within the city, reaching out from it into the world of business and bureaucracy is considered too overwhelming for the favelados. Thus it is assumed that broadening contacts with city dwellers of diverse social roles is rare, that few favelados make use of the agencies and institutions available to urban residents, and that most favela residents are ignorant of the information available through the mass media. In short, favelados are seen as trying to recreate village life within the city, limiting their activities to the confines of the favela as much as possible, and never feeling fully at home in the broader urban context.

As we have already begun to see in the previous section, the favelado does not seem to be yearning for return to the countryside. Although half have gone back to visit, 85 percent said they would not want to live in the countryside. The two specific points of comparison we have—one social and one economic—help to explain why. Seventy percent found as much or more mutual help among neighbors in their Rio communities as in their home towns, and 71 percent said they were better off economically than their friends and relatives who stayed at home. Finally, when asked directly if they were satisfied with their lives in the city, our respondents answered almost unanimously in the affirmative. Ninety percent mentioned aspects of special appeal, the most frequent categories being economic and occupational opportunities (34 percent), and excitement, recreation, or diversion (28 percent). When pressed to describe an aspect of urban life they did not like, a quarter could not think of one.

The "isolated enclaves" of which marginality theory speaks simply do not exist. The majority of favelados make full use of the city context and gain exposure to a wide variety of urban experiences. This can be seen in Table 19 in terms of familiarity with different parts of the city, use of city facilities, contacts with people, exposure to media, and use of urban agencies and institutions. Although physically distinct from the rest of the city, the favela is by no means isolated in terms of human activity. Three-quarters of favelados feel they know their way around the city. This is partly because so many of their daily activities—marketing, work, and having fun—are carried on within the larger city. Medical care and schooling, for example, were sought outside the favela by 96 percent and 80 percent respectively. Also, nearly half (47 percent) of all favela and subúrbio residents work outside their communities, thereby gaining a multiplicity of daily contacts with the larger urban environment.

Lisa Peattie emphasizes the same points in her study of La Laja, a poor barrio in Ciudad Guayana, Venezuela. Residents dressed like other city dwellers, and women's hair styles were determined by the current New York fashion. Houses were constructed not in imitation of rural styles but in a kind of "poor people's urban." As we noted in Chapter Two, only the areas of Rio's favelas most distant from the main road are constructed in the wattle and daub characteristic of village architecture, and then not by preference but from economic necessity. Residents of La Laja will not be found in country clubs or expensive night spots, says Peattie, but they do shop in the city, go to movies, hospitals, and municipal offices, and they visit friends across town. The Guayana study revealed that lower-income groups are familiar with more of the city than the educated elite, who venture little beyond their own residential ghetto.[9]

It is quite consistent with our data to imagine that favelados are indeed more familiar with the city as a whole than upper-income residents who are isolated by their own "urbane" provincialism. In terms of contacts with different types of people, the few roles included in the questionnaire hardly do justice to the concept (see Table 19, Part III). However, despite relatively low percentages of favelados who had contacts with each of the different types of people mentioned, when all

TABLE 19
Use of the Urban Context
(N=600)

Indicators	Percent

I.   Familiarity with the environment

Q.   What area do you know well: only the part of the favela near your house, the entire favela, the areas around the favela, or mostly all of Rio?[a]

	Percent
Only the part of the favela near home	20
The entire favela	5
The surrounding areas	30
Most all of Rio	45

II. General use of the city

Q.   Where do you usually go to:

	Percent Going Outside Favela
Buy food	72
Buy clothing	92
Get help when someone is sick	96
Enjoy yourself, spend your leisure time	74
Take your children to school	80

III. Heterogeneity of contacts

Q.   Have you ever had the chance to speak with a:

	Percent Saying Yes
Foreigner	32
Industrialist	26
Army official	25
Political leader	14
Student leader	7

IV. Mass media exposure

Q.   To find out what's happening, or just for fun, how often do you usually listen to the

---

[a]In the Caxias questionnaire, "neighborhood" was substituted for "favela."

TABLE 19

Use of the Urban Context (Continued)

Indicators	Percent

radio, watch television, read a newspaper or a magazine, or go to the movies?

	Never	Few Times in Life	Few Times a Year	Few Times a Month	Few Times a Week	Every Day
Radio	10%	5%	2%	7%	19%	57%
Television	31	15	7	10	12	25
Newspaper	44	12	6	12	13	14
Magazine	52	13	7	13	10	6
Movies	42	26	14	14	3	0

V.   Use of urban agencies and institutions

　　Q.   Have you ever had occasion to:

	Percent Saying Yes
Consult a lawyer	19
Go to a government agency (such as a ministry, social security agency, or housing authority)	34
Borrow money from a bank, the "caixa economica," or a loan association outside the favela	2
Go to an employment agency or assistance bureau to find a job	4
Seek social security or illness compensation from the authorities	10

five items were analyzed together, over half (54 percent) had experienced some contact with at least one of the groups—an experience most unlikely in the Brazilian countryside.

　　Contact with new ideas and exposure to middle-class values and life styles are not only experienced through direct contact with different types of people or various districts of the city. Much of the experience is broadcast through the mass media. We interpret media exposure as one of the components of urban experience, or an "integrating" force. As Table 19 (Part IV) indicates, a great many favelados have had some exposure to the various forms of media: 90 percent to radio, 69 percent to television, 57 percent to newspapers, 58 percent to movies, and 48 percent to magazines. If we control for intensity by counting only those who participate a few times a week or daily, three-quarters of the favelados listen to radio, one-third watch television, and a quarter read newspapers. The percentages reading magazines and going to movies drop off more sharply because these are more costly diversions. The rate of newspaper reading, although not high in absolute terms, is impressive given literacy rates in the favela. It is not uncommon to see one person reading the news to a group of interested bystanders. High media exposure cannot be presumed to mean high interest in political matters, however. When asked "which type of program or news do you like best," the vast majority said "light entertainment." The newspapers most frequently read are *O Dia*, *Diário de Notíca*, and *A Luta*, all filled with stories of crime, scandal, sports, and favela news. Favelados listen most often to Rádio Globo, and watch "Chacrinha"—a kind of slapstick variety show—on television. Still, the media keep the favelados in touch with attitudes prevailing in the society as a whole. It gives them a great deal of "shared experience" with the middle classes.

We asked favela residents if they had any of a series of contacts with city institutions: lawyers, government agencies, banks, employment agencies, social security bureaus, and so forth. Over a third had visited a government agency and over half had at least one of these five kinds of contacts (see Table 19, Part V).

TERMS OF SOCIAL INTEGRATION

Having demonstrated, then, that the favelado is hardly socially marginal either by the criteria of internal cohesion or external city-use, we conclude that he must then be "integrated" in these respects. The terms of this integration, however, are not very favorable. For example, although favelados often know about and try to make use of urban services, they are often humiliated and defeated in the process. They find the system generally closed to their interests. The following vignette from the diary of one favelado is typical. Maria Carolina had been carrying scrap iron and had gotten severe kidney pains. She writes:

> So as not to see my children hungry, I went for help to the famous Bureau of Social Services. It was there that I saw . . . the coldness with which they treat the poor. . . . [After getting no response] I went straight to the Governor's Palace. The Palace sent me to an office [on the other side of town].

They in turn sent me to the Social Service Institute at the Santa Casa Charity Hospital. There I talked with a woman who listened to me, said many things, yet said nothing. I decided to go back to the Palace. . . . I said: "I came here to ask for help because I am ill. . . . Now I've spent all the money I have on transportation."[10]

When they said there was nothing they could do for her, she kept insisting, until they finally called a squad car. The policeman took her back to the favela and warned her that the next time she made a scene at the Welfare Agency, she'd be locked up. "Welfare agency!" she writes, "welfare for who???"

The Bureau of Social Services, an amalgam of 12 former institutes, consistently treats favelados and the poor in general in such a "slow, inefficient, punitive, brusque, and dehumanizing" manner that many favelados avoid using its facilities, and pay private institutions for the needed services.[11]

Furthermore, this type of treatment is not confined to the "institutes." Despite the fact that the favela fulfills the needs of its dwellers and offers them a desirable life style, it is still so stigmatized by the rest of society that favelados often have to give a false address to get a job, sometimes even to make a date. In the eyes of society, the marginal is not even within the system of class stratification—he is, to use Germani's term, an "outcast."[12]

The Boschi study concludes, "the social participation of [favelados] is not limited by the physical barriers of ecological separation, but participation *is* severely limited by the nature of class barriers. The fact that favelados have built a cohesive internal community and explore avidly the experiences of urban life means little in terms of opportunity to share in respect and well-being—the prerogatives of the upper sector."[13]

CULTURAL MARGINALITY

The major propositions of marginality theory contend that the favela is characterized by either of two related and sometimes contradictory subcultures. The first, the culture of traditionality, refers to the persistence of inappropriate rural ideas in the urban milieu. The second, the culture of poverty, refers to the self-defeating and self-perpetuating cycle of cynicism and passivity.

THE CULTURE OF TRADITIONALITY

Viewed as a culture of traditionality, the favela is dominated by mystic religiosity, low empathy, and little openness to innovation. Attitudes toward family are purportedly dysfunctional, allowing kinship ties to take precedence over rationality in associational membership, business enterprises, and political matters. In addition, deference to authority and long-term fatalism are considered maladaptive rural carry-overs into urban life.

Alex Inkeles and David Smith developed a scale of overall modernity (the OM Scale) which was refined and validated through work in six developing countries: Pakistan, India, Nigeria, Chile, Argentina, and Israel.[14] Because of the utility of comparative data, and the verified cross-cultural application of the items as indicators of modernity, I used some of the same measures in the favela study.

Several methodological provisos should be mentioned, however, regarding the discussion of cultural marginality. First, I will use modal responses to various attitudinal items to characterize the favelados as a whole. However useful this approach is in highlighting modal types, it should be noted that on many items there are large dissenting minorities. Second, *within* any individual there is a tremendous latitude for the coexistence of beliefs which might seem contradictory to a behavioral analyst but which are quite comfortably integrated by the individual. Many of the attitudinal items really did form interrelated clusters—in fact, some of them were quite strong—but in many cases also, items expected to co-vary were independent.

The categories I focus on as indicators of degree of traditionality-modernity are religiosity, openness to innovation, family orientation, and empathy. I deal with fatalism and deference to authority later in the chapter. Table 20 presents a summary of the findings.

Religious Orientation. All but 6 percent of favelados consider themselves members of some religion (72 percent Catholic, 10 percent Assembly of God, 5 percent Baptist, 4 percent Spiritists, and 4 percent others). However, only 58 percent say they belong to religious organizations (45 percent churches, 13 percent Spiritist centers), and only 31 percent attend regularly—once a week or more. Almost half (47 percent) go to church only a few times a year.

Marginality theorists predict both religious breakdowns, caused by the secularizing influences of cities, and increased religiosity caused by increased need for security in the unfamiliar and ambiguous urban setting. The empirical evidence shows that indeed a vast majority (84 percent) experienced a change in their religious values or practice after coming to the city. Of these, 65 percent said they had become less religious while the other 35 percent had become more religious—some embracing a new religion, other practicing more actively.

TABLE 20

The Culture of Traditionality in the Favela

(N=600)

Indicators	Percent
I. Religiosity	
Profess some religion (72 percent Catholic, 10 percent Assembly of God, 5 percent Baptist, 4 percent Spiritist, 4 percent other)	95
Think "a man can be truly good without having any religion at all"[a]	66
Have changed their degree of religiosity since coming to the city; of these:	84
65 percent became less religious	
35 percent became more religious	
II. Openness to innovation	
Think it is good that "scientists are studying such things as what determines whether a baby is a boy or a girl; or how a seed turns into a plant."[a]	62
Say that the first father is wiser in the following hypothetical situation: "Two boys took time out from their work in the fields to try and figure out a way to grow more corn with less hours of work. The first father said 'that is a good thing to think about,' and was interested in hearing their ideas. The second father said, 'the best way to grow corn is the way it has always been done and talking about it is a waste of time.' "[a]	52
III. Family orientation	
Agree that "it is necessary for a couple to limit the number of children they have so they can raise and educate them better."[a]	71
Think "young girls today should be free to choose their boyfriends without the advice of their family."	63
IV. Empathy	
Mentioned at least one measure they would take "if they were President of Brazil."	80

[a]Question taken from the OM scale.

In either case, few seemed dogmatic on the issue, and neither "breakdown" nor fanaticism was in evidence. In response to the classic OM item, "Do you think that a man can be truly good without having any religion at all," two-thirds said "yes." Thus, while most favelados identify with some religion and many are part of a religious network, there seems to be no indication that they are closing off rational modes of thinking or in any sense being maladaptively traditional.

Openness to Innovation. Using the two OM scale measures on this concept, we determined that the favelados are relatively open to science and technology as an enterprise but perhaps more hesitant about changing specific time-honored practices. Those who support the scientific study of such things as "what determines whether a baby is a boy or a girl" or "how a seed turns into a plant" outnumber those who oppose it two to one, and 42 percent feel such studies are "all very beneficial." On the second item, however, opinion is more equally divided. A hypothetical situation was presented of two fathers counseling young boys in their questioning attitude concerning new ways of growing corn. Respondents were split half and half, as seen in Table 20, Part II.

Of course, the true test of receptivity to innovation is whether or not in the real situation—as opposed to the hypothetical one—the favelados accept new ideas and ways of acting. From my observations, I found that they were astonishingly eager and receptive to anything that seemed new or modern, the constraints largely being economic, not attitudinal. The classic example of medicine, from the "diffusion of innovation" literature, illustrates the point. [15] The favelados were so receptive to new drugs on the market that the main problem became overspending, and the danger of too many antibiotics or injections too freely taken.

In terms of receptiveness to new styles of dress, music, and household appliances, the favelados were among the first to don "mod" clothes (or home-made versions thereof), listen to the latest popular music from the United States, and buy such new appliances as electric blenders whenever possible. Except perhaps for the elderly, favelados are all too eager to leave behind those traits which bear the stigma of rural backwardness.

Family Values. The attitude of the favelados toward family matters is an extension of their degree of flexibility and openness to new behavioral norms. Almost two-thirds feel that a young girl should be able to choose her boyfriend without the advice of her family, which is a sharp departure from traditional practice. Furthermore, a full 71 percent agree that "families should be limited in size" so children can be given more attention. This latter figure indicates a truly extraordinary change. Peasants and fishermen I interviewed in Bahia in 1963, for example, were almost unanimously opposed to limiting family size. Of a random sample of Belo Horizonte residents in 1966, including all classes, only about 30 percent (mostly women) would consider the idea.[16] The 72 percent of men and 70 percent of women who were sympathetic to the idea among favelados marks them as a modern group indeed, perhaps more modern than the middle-class who are usually the standard of comparison.

Accepting birth control means giving up a certain measure of machismo for the men, and in some cases it means going against religious doctrine for the women. There are no big campaigns in the favela for or against birth control, although it is controversial in many other circles. Practicality, economic necessity, and high aspirations for their children probably account for the favelados' receptivity to the idea. While they still have more children than they consider ideal, the birth rate is substantially lower than in the countryside.

Empathy. The concept of empathy, or "psychic mobility," was developed by Daniel Lerner in a study of modernization in Turkey. He used as one of his key questions, "What would you do if you were made President of the country?" The more traditional Turkish peasants could not even cope with the question: "My God! How can you say such a thing? . . . How can I? . . . I cannot . . . a poor villager . . . master of the whole world?"[17] When I asked this question in Rio, 80 percent of the favelados gave specific and generally quite sensible answers. These included "improve the living conditions of poor people" (40 percent), "lower the cost of living and provide more employment, better salaries, lower prices" (21 percent), "improve Brazil, make the country great, advance the progress of the nation" (19 percent).

In short, there is little evidence of maladaptive rural behavior among the favela population. Favelados, unlike hypothetical "traditionals," have a relatively high degree of secularism, cognitive flexibility, and empathy. Eighty percent are able to put themselves mentally into another role, two-thirds show an openness to religious unorthodoxy, about the same proportion to new ideas in family life, and only somewhat fewer to the ways of modern science. It would not be at all surprising, given these results, if this supposedly marginal and tradition-bound group was less rigid than most members of the Brazilian middle class.

THE CULTURE OF POVERTY

The major aspects of the culture of poverty define favela life as a cycle of despair for the migrant and the squatter. Oscar Lewis saw the members of the culture of poverty as removed and alienated, ignorant and uninterested, uninvolved and apathetic. According to the theory, the favelados would be characterized by mutual distrust and suspicion, criminality and violence, family breakdown, pessimism, low aspirations, and inability to plan for the future, with an overall fatalism paralyzing their actions. [18] I tested many of these characteristics, and applied the data gathered on social marginality where relevant. I found, as with the previous marginality propositions, that the contentions were largely unsupported. The above discussions on friendship, trust, and mutual help, and on crime and violence, speak directly to the first two concepts.

Family Breakdown. As for family life in the favela, it is relatively stable by any standard. Ninety percent of those we interviewed are members of a nuclear family (37 percent heads of household, 38 percent their spouses, and 15 percent their children). About 80 percent of households are headed by males, and two-thirds of residents are married or *conjuntado* (joined in informal but stable unions). Divorce is not common. Only five percent of all those we interviewed told us they were presently divorced. Importantly, divorce seems to be even less prevalent in the favela than in rural society. Among migrants at the time of arrival in the city, there was one divorce for every 8.3 marriages. Among favelados generally there is one divorce for every 13 marriages. Only 10 percent of favelados told us they had ever been separated or divorced. About the same proportion told us they had been married or *conjuntado* twice.

Pessimism and Frustration. Pessimism, cynicism, and frustration rank high in the marginality syndrome, supposedly prohibiting self-help and mobility. Favelados, however, despite the difficulties of their circumstances, show a strong sense of optimism, partly perhaps because it is a Brazilian characteristic in general, and partly perhaps because they need it to keep going. Table 21 documents the sense of optimism concerning the future of society and self that prevails in the favela.

In contrast with Bonilla's findings on these same items in Brazil in 1961, our data indicate that people now feel more optimistic about their own pasts and futures than about those of Brazil in general. [19] Over two-thirds feel their lives have improved in the past and are going to improve in the future. Somewhat fewer feel the same optimism for Brazil in general. Bonilla found that about one-fifth of the favelados said their

TABLE 21

Personal and General Optimism, Percentage Distribution

(N=600)

	Time-frame	Much Worse	Little Worse	About the Same	Little Better	Much Better
I.	Past					
	Q. Compared to 5 years ago, do you think life in Brazil now is:	23	18	9	31	18
	Q. Compared to 5 years ago, do you think your own life is:	10	14	7	39	30
II.	Future					
	Q. Do you think that 5 years from now life in Brazil will be:	19	16	15	34	21
	Q. Do you think that 5 years from now your own life will be:	8	8	16	33	35

lives had improved, but two-thirds said Brazil as a nation had improved. The discrepancy reflects the changing economic picture in Brazil. In the five years preceding the Bonilla study, 1955-1960, Brazil was experiencing growth at a record rate (4.2 percent annual average growth in GNP). By contrast, the years just following the military takeover were austere ones for everyone.

An intriguing finding that is consistent in Bonilla's study and in this one is that women are invariably *more* pessimistic and critical than men. Twice as many men as women in Bonilla's study felt their lives had improved. In our data, twice as many women as men said their lives had gotten "much worse," and twice as many women felt that five years from now life would be "much worse." Perhaps women have less need for "defensive optimism," feel they have less at stake in the system's success, or are subjected to less "brainwashing" because of their lower media exposure and more restricted contacts. Also, since women face more directly the daily problems of survival in the favela, it may be harder to convince them that things are getting better. We will return to this point in the next chapter in the discussion of radicalism.

More relevant than comparisons over time are comparisons between favelados and the rest of Brazilian society. The notion that favelados have a self-defeating pessimism and dissatisfaction which perpetuates their marginality is reflected by data collected by Kahl. On each of three separate indices of satisfaction—job, career, and general life—migrants (mostly favelados) consistently scored higher than metropolitans or provincials. This relationship held even when the occupational category was controlled; within each occupational category those who had migrated were the more satisfied.[20]

Aspirations. Along with the contention that pessimism perpetuates poverty is the corollary that low aspirations prevent marginals from striving to improve their own or their children's lot in life. The aspirations of favelados are supposedly typical of the culture of poverty in that people strive for intangible, traditional rewards rather than concrete goals that would help break the poverty syndrome. I found this to be entirely unsupported by the data. When asked the open-ended question, "What do you want most in your life?" 60 percent of the favelados gave rational, mobility-related answers such as money or material possessions (35 percent), education for themselves or their children (10 percent), and professional fulfillment (8 percent), as opposed to such intangible-type answers as "God's protection," "tranquility," or "family union." Of course, it is debatable whether the criteria are meaningful, since even if the entire sample had given more philosophical responses, it would not necessarily be true that favelados don't care about their job stability or their children's education, or that they were unmotivated regarding social mobility.

When asked what they wanted most for their children, 47 percent of the favelados said education and another 19 percent mentioned good jobs or improved living standards. Given the hypothetical assumptions that schools are free and there are places for everyone, a full 86 percent said the children of favelados should have more than grade school teaching, and almost half (46 percent) said education through the university level! Educational accomplishment is almost revered in the favela. A schoolteacher is often accorded more prestige than a doctor, priest, or businessman; and anyone with a college degree is respectfully called *doutor*.

The final indicator of aspirations is another classic measure: "What would you do if you won in the lottery?" To this there were unanimously future-oriented answers, the most frequent (68 percent) concerning housing—either buying a house or plot of land, or improving their present dwelling.

These are the responses of a people valuing modern forms of accomplishment, anxious to secure well-being for themselves and their children, striving to be integrated into the society at large. Kahl asked the "lottery" question of white- and blue-collar workers in Rio and two provincial towns to get a comparative base for judgment. The type, range, and distribution of responses were nearly identical in every group. In the country there was somewhat less concern for acquiring a better house, but this was still the most prevalent response.[21] As Portes concluded in his study of squatter settlements in Santiago, "in their totality, the aspirations of the 'marginals' do not differ from those of the middle class."[22]

TERMS OF CULTURAL INTEGRATION

Having seen that favelados have neither a subculture of traditionality nor a culture of poverty, we turn to the terms of their integration into society. In spite of the high value favelados place on education, for example, 31 percent remain illiterate and 99.8 percent without high school education. About half have had some elementary school education, but only 8 percent have progressed any further. One in ten has learned to read and write without formal schooling (see Table 22). Children have received somewhat more education, but much less than their parents had hoped for them. Among eldest offspring (those over 16) more than half had to drop out of primary school and only 5 percent completed junior high school.

The favelado is systematically excluded from educational opportunity at every level. As we mentioned earlier, the government does not locate schools in the favela. The occasional attempt by a concerned parent to take in a few school-age children and give them some instruction—however admirable as a community endeavor—is no substitute for regular schooling.

Schools outside the favela can only be attended by those living

TABLE 22

Educational Levels of Favelados and Eldest Children

Level of Education	Random Sample[a] (N=600)	Eldest Child of Interviewee[b] (N=176)
Never attended school and illiterate	30%	7%
Attended school but illiterate	1	3
No school but literate	9	1
Elementary school incomplete	44	40
Elementary school complete	7	34
Junior high incomplete	7	10
Junior high complete	2	1
High school incomplete	0	2
High school complete	0	1
University incomplete	0	1
University complete	0	0

[a]Includes 16-65-year-old range.
[b]Only asked if they had a child over 16.

within official school districts. These almost never include squatter settlements within their boundaries. If favelados are not gerrymandered out of an education, they are likely to be priced out of one. Entry fees and the conformity of required supplies and dress weigh heavily on favelados earning only minimal incomes. Even those who have the skill to maneuver themselves into school, using hand-me-down books or pretending residence where their mothers work as maids, often face the prospect of having to quit to support their families.

The terms of integration in other realms are equally harsh. Efforts to improve favela homes are not only discouraged but have often been outlawed on the justification that squatter shacks should not become integrated into the city.

FATALISM AND DEFERENCE TO AUTHORITY

One result of these terms of integration has been to reinforce a fatalistic and deferential outlook among favelados in general (see Table 23). Both the traditionality and poverty culture literatures claim that marginals are fatalistic; only the former deals directly with deference to authority. In these areas the issue is more the inappropriate nature of

TABLE 23

Fatalism and Deference to Authority

(N=600)

I. Fatalism

66 percent say that God's help or good luck is the most important thing for the progress of Brazil, not good government or the hard work of the people.

57 percent believe that "everything that happens in a person's life is because somehow it had to happen," rather than "it depends on what a person does to get what he wants."

II. Deference to authority

84 percent believe that older people are always or almost always right.

60 percent believe the world could be divided into two groups; the strong and the weak.

57 percent feel it is not right for an employee ever to argue with his boss.

the two traits as indicators of traditionalism or a culture of poverty in the Brazilian favela than their absolute truth or falsity. The point here is not merely the presence or absence of the syndrome, but the manner in which it is interpreted.

The fatalism of the favelados appears to contradict their optimism, but fatalism must be viewed in part as a protective rationale for the high chances of disappointment. It is not surprising that people in Brazil's lower sector have a fatalistic view of things. The attitude is less a rural artifact and more an accurate reflection of the lack of power a favelado has over his life. The arguments at the end of the following chapter, concerning the sense of powerlessness among the poor, are highly relevant to the phenomenon of fatalism. For a poor person, the feeling that "what happens in a person's life depends little on what a person does" is not necessarily an irrational belief in fate or in the "gods." It is a rational disbelief in the openness of the society he inhabits. When the favelados say *o pobre não tem vez* (the poor don't have a chance), or trying something *não adianta* (that won't get you anywhere, isn't worth it), they are not reflecting inborn resignation and fatalism so much as a realistic assessment of their situation. If the actual constraints on their "getting ahead" were altered, they might respond quite differently.[23]

Our data also indicate a marked deference to authority, but this concept as well must be interpreted with care. Egalitarian norms are the exception, not the rule, in Brazilian social and political life. Passivity and respect for authority among the "masses" is functional for the system and is encouraged in many ways. As Linz says, it is in the nature of authoritarian regimes to need a population which is quiescent and obedient.[24] In the Brazilian case, the favelados meet this need perfectly. A closer look at the precise questions we included which were purported to measure deference to authority clarifies the nature of the problem. What does it mean to feel "It is not right for an employee ever to argue with his boss" in a system where this would almost certainly mean loss of employment? What does it mean to feel that "the world could be divided into two groups, the strong and the weak" in a country with an elite and a "torturable" sector? Deference to authority and fatalism do indeed exist among favelados. Because of the realism of these attitudes, however, it would be unwise to attribute them to either the culture of traditionality or the culture of poverty. They are grounded in a political reality. It is an open question whether or not they would simply evaporate were political reality to change.

One classic experiment has indicated powerfully that they would. In 1952 the Cornell-Peru project, under the directorship of Allan Holmberg, leased a hacienda in Vicos, Peru, and totally changed the institutional setting by turning responsibility over to the Indians. Former attitudinal studies had revealed the deferential, fatalistic, static view of life, which Doughty refers to as the "servant syndrome," and which many of the favelados seem to subscribe to. Once the political and economic realities had been changed, however, these supposedly immutable and self-defeating predispositions were replaced by "high individual initiative, self-reliance, and 'ebullient optimism.' "[25]

ECONOMIC MARGINALITY

The propositions of marginality theory contend that the favelados are both a drain on the urban economy—parasitically siphoning off scarce resources for city services and infrastructure—and economically parochial with neither the values nor the credentials to be productive members of the labor force. This is an interesting and important issue on which more has been written speculatively than documented.

ECONOMIC PARASITISM

The contention that favelados contribute little to the economy in terms of labor or consumption is not supported by our data (see Table 24). We found that almost everyone who is able works. A third of the men are employed in industry, construction, or transportation, and many more would be if the jobs existed. Only one-tenth work on jobs within the local community, while all the others contribute their labor directly to the "external city economy." Favelados not only built the high-rise buildings in which Rio takes such pride, but they also are the ones who maintain and clean those buildings.

About one-third of the favela women are employed in the domestic services which the middle class find so essential. The favelados represent a constant supply of cheap household labor, relieving the upper-class women of the tasks of washing, cleaning, cooking, and child care.[26]

Thirty-two percent of male favelados are categorized as unskilled. Although some do unskilled factory labor or construction work, most are employed in the service sector as street vendors, garbage men, bus fare collectors, doormen, watchmen, streetcleaners, service station attendants, car washers, street repairmen, or janitors. These service-sector jobs, although their product is less visible, are in no sense a "drain" on the urban economy, nor are they—for the most part—artificially created. They are jobs which need to be done, and which generate income that recirculates throughout the economy.

TABLE 24

Employment Status by Sex and Leadership,
Percentage Distribution

Job Category	Random Sample			Elite Sample		
	Men (N=244)	Women (N=356)	Total (N=600)	Men (N=137)	Women (N=13)	Total (N=150)
White-collar	7	2	4	9	23	10
Security	3	0	1	9	0	8
Merchant	6	2	4	22	15	21
Skilled labor	5	4	5	5	0	5
Construction	15	0	6	14	0	14
Semi-skilled	9	1	4	14	15	14
Domestic	4	29	19	2	8	2
Unskilled	32	3	15	10	8	10
Primary	0	0	0	0	0	0
Unemployed	16	39	29	14	23	15
Never worked	3	20	13	1	8	1

Favelados contribute to the economy in terms of consumption as well. We have seen that 92 percent buy their clothing and 72 percent buy their food outside the favela. In spite of their meager incomes, favelados constitute a major market for consumer goods: 76 percent have radios, 69 percent have electric irons, 53 percent have sewing machines, 31 percent have refrigerators, and 26 percent have television.

A rough estimate of the purchasing power of the favelados of Rio, assuming that the income distributions of families in the three favelas studied is representative of the 200,000 favela families in the city, would be U.S. $14,720,000 per month, or almost 180 million dollars per year (by 1969 conversion rates). Estimates for the purchasing power of the barrios of Caracas run as high as $200,000,000 per year. [27]

The economy benefits doubly from purchases by lower sector residents because they must often buy on credit. If all payments are met on time, the final outlay is about twice the market value of a given item. If a payment is defaulted, the article is confiscated with no remuneration for the portion already paid. At the time of our study, 35 percent of favelados were paying installments—24 percent on household appliances or furniture, 11 percent on clothing or shoes. Some borrow money for food and clothing so they will not miss payments and forfeit hard-earned money already invested in larger items.

Favelados also contribute economically through individual entrepreneurial activities within the favela. Four in ten build their own homes. Fifty to 60 percent have put time, money, and effort into making improvements on their present dwellings. Five to 10 percent build little shops, stores, or bars on which taxes are paid to the city government. Furthermore, most improvements in infrastructure—water pipes, sewage lines, electricity networks, walkways, cement steps—are the result of investments of labor by favelados themselves. This is a primary kind of future investment in the favela. [28]

The value of the housing stock in Rio's favelas is approximately $110,000,000, assuming 200,000 dwelling units in the favelas and extrapolating from the best estimates of the favelados in my sample on the question: "What is your house worth today?" Michael Bamberger estimates that urban squatters have invested over one hundred million dollars in the construction of 125,000 dwellings over the last twenty years. He points out that these same individuals have built roads and water systems for their neighborhoods, installed electric networks, and constructed their own schools. [29]

ECONOMIC PAROCHIALISM

Having seen that the favelados contribute substantially to the economy, as builders of their own environment and as workers and consumers, we turn to those contentions of marginality theory regarding work-related values and attitudes. According to the "ideal type," the favelados do not place a high value on work, are not achievement-oriented, and lack the education and training to acquire the institutional norms of precision, promptness, and consistency. They supposedly have few of the attitudinal prerequisites for economic entrepreneurship, such as a belief in scientific technology and respect for impersonal bureaucratic relationships. Hence by preserving the traits of economic traditionality, migrants and squatters are reputedly—at least in part—the cause of their own urban poverty.

Our evidence does not support these contentions. When we asked respondents what qualities they most admired in people, "being a hard worker" was one of the most frequent answers. Leeds found that favelados consider "work as a proper state of being, whereas idleness, or inactivity, especially if enforced . . . produce expressions of discomfort, denigration, impatience, or anger. Work—the activity of doing something productive—is often used to evaluate the worth of others."[30] This "Protestant ethic" is found all over Latin America. Its rules are: "Work hard, save your money . . . outwit the state, vote conservatively if possible but always in your own economic self-interest; educate your children for their future and as old age insurance for yourself."[31]

We have already discussed the strength of the favelado's aspirations for education and self-betterment, his respect for science, and his general openness to innovation. The evidence is more confusing concerning familiarity with impersonal, bureaucratic norms of interaction characteristic of modern business enterprise. For example, preferences are split between hiring a "relative" or a "stranger who is more efficient" (47 percent of favelados say the former, 49 percent the latter). It is not completely clear which attitude represents the greatest economic acumen, however. Loyalties must be developed within any business firm to prevent cheating, to inspire people to work to capacity, and to keep employees from divulging information detrimental to the company's interest. Nepotism can be an effective transfer of loyalties from kinship to the economic realm.

On the other hand, favelados chose a job "in which you earned less but had more freedom" over one in which "you earned a lot but had a very demanding boss" by a margin of two to one. This preference probably runs counter to the needs of modern businesses, which often count on employees to place economic interests above personal happiness. The fatalism of favelados—whether rooted in rural cultural values or in a long history of subjugation—is likewise dysfunctional in modern, future-oriented organizations.

The favelado is not highly skilled in intellectual and technical tasks. Only 2 percent of favela residents have completed junior high school; one in 500 has completed high school. But the favelado has many of the attitudinal prerequisites for full participation in modern economy—especially in those areas where his or her own initiative counts most. These include openness to change, aspiration to educational and occupational improvement, valuing hard work, and accepting modern science. From the viewpoint of economic development, these attitudes are vital national resources. It is not our purpose to analyze fully why these resources are presently underutilized. Our study indicates clearly, however, that it is deceptive to include marginal economic attitudes of the favelado himself in the explanation.

TERMS OF ECONOMIC INTEGRATION

We have argued that the favelados are not economically marginal, either as a drain on the economy or as economic "parochials" who do not value work or aspire to improve themselves materially. Despite their high motivations and energy for work, however, they are often excluded from the economic rewards the system has to offer and used to the system's ultimate advantage rather than their own. Many who want jobs cannot get them. Those who do, get the least desirable jobs, with the least security, the fewest workers' compensation benefits, and the lowest pay. Because there are so many favelados, there is an ever-willing labor pool which enables wages to remain at low levels and employers to avoid workers' benefit requirements.

Nearly half the adult men (15 percent unemployed and 30 percent unskilled) could be considered members of a loosely defined "reserve army"—willing to accept work in the industrial sector if it were available.[32]

It is even more difficult to assess the degree of enforced unemployment or underemployment among women. Thirty-nine percent were unemployed as of 1969, another 20 percent had never worked, and most of the rest (29 percent) were domestics. Clearly such constraints as caring for families, arranging for child care, and spouse disapproval hinder the labor force participation of women, but since most family budgets in the favela need as many sources of income as possible, it is likely that more women would join the ranks of the productively employed if the opportunities existed.[33] The jobs that favelados succeed in getting are the least desirable ones in the economy. Three in ten favelados work at *biscate* (odd jobs) always precarious and often demeaning.

There has been little change in the occupational distribution of the favelados between 1959 and 1969, and, as can be seen in Table 25, what change did occur has been for the worse. The percentage of workers in unskilled positions has actually increased, as have the numbers of the unemployed. Moreover, since we concluded in Chapter Three that neither farm background nor recency of arrival in Rio was associated with lower status occupations, these declines cannot be attributed to larger percentages of migrants in the later period. It is much more likely that structural changes in occupational opportunities in the demand for low-skilled labor have caused this deterioration rather than changes in the characteristics of favela workers. In fact, according to all our calcu-

TABLE 25

Occupational Distributions Compared Over Time (1959-1969),
Calculated from Life-History Matrix for Random Sample
(N=600)

Job Category	1959		1969	
	Number	Percent	Number	Percent
White-collar	16	3	22	4
Security	5	1	8	1
Merchant	5	1	21	4
Skilled	24	4	28	5
Construction	37	6	37	6
Semi-skilled	34	6	26	4
Domestic	112	18	112	19
Unskilled	50	8	88	15
Unemployed	62	10	174	29
Primary	64	11	0	0
Never worked	191	32	80	13
Total	600	100	600	100

lations, favelado characteristics that would enhance their employability have been steadily improving over time.

Furthermore, favela workers are for the most part denied the benefits and guarantees won by other workers in the labor legislation passed under Vargas in the 1930s and 1940s. They are not guaranteed a minimum wage and do not have social security benefits, illness compensation, or retirement pensions. Of all favelados, only 5 percent receive social security benefits and 5 percent compensation for illness.

One reason favelados cannot claim these benefits or qualify for better jobs is that they do not have a work card (*carteira de trabalho*). To receive a *carteira*, Brazilians must have a birth certificate to prove they are recognized citizens. In most of the countryside, births are performed by midwives and birth certificates are not available. Even for those whose *documentos* are in order (documents, Brazilian style, means an enormous pile of obscure, frayed, and yellowed papers with assorted seals and signatures) there is an incredible mass of red tape requiring visits to bureau after bureau. Thus, many migrants are defeated before they start. The final blow, described to me by a sixty-year-old man who persevered for six months to obtain his *carteira*, is to be told by a manager that a job is available only on condition that the work card *not* be signed, so that the firm will not have to pay social security benefits, pensions, sick-leave, and overtime rates. Since he received his card this man has been working a twelve-hour shift for half the minimum wage, without any worker protection. To his firm he is unregistered, a non-entity.

The situation is even worse for those who have no documents at all. Periodically the military police raid the favelas—usually in the middle of the night—and arrest all those without documents for vagrancy. Once an arrest is on one's record it is almost impossible to get employment anywhere, thus completing a vicious circle.

Even those favelados who hold jobs have the least job security of all workers. Forty-five percent of favela workers say losing their job is their major worry and another 24 percent ranked it as a "considerable" worry. Only 35 percent of the men are paid by the month. Payment in more frequent intervals—by the day, task, or hour—is often an indicator of temporary employment which must be constantly reestablished.

Economic deprivation and exploitation is further reflected in the favelado's paycheck. For 1969, as shown in Table 26, 17 percent of individuals in the random sample were unemployed, 26 percent were earning half the minimum wage or less, and another 30 percent earned

TABLE 26

Individual and Household Incomes, Percentage Distribution,

Random Sample

(N=600)

Income Level[a]	Individual's Principal Job	Total Household Income
Nothing	17	0
½ minimum salary or less	26	3
½-1 minimum salary	30	19
1-1½ minimum salaries	16	26
1½-2 minimum salaries	8	19
2-2½ minimum salaries	3	15
2½-3 minimum salaries	0	7
3-4 minimum salaries	1	6
4-5 minimum salaries	9	2
5 minimum salaries or more	0	3

[a]One minimum salary equals 160 cruzeiros per month or U.S. $40 in 1969.

less than one minimum wage (the U.S. equivalent of the minimum wage at the time was $40 per month). In sum, three-quarters of those gainfully employed were receiving $40 a month or less—a maximum of $10 per week.

One of the critical questions that arises in assessing the economic life of the favelados is that of occupational mobility. Whether or not the favelados are rising in occupational status and income with successive job changes makes a big difference in how their economic situation is interpreted. In order to examine this, I treated each job change in the work history of each individual as a separate event or unit of analysis, and then looked at these together. Since the great majority of the upper-level and middle-level occupations are excluded, I opted for a simple three-part classification: unskilled, semi-skilled, and skilled jobs. Including only those males who had held at least two jobs in Rio as of 1969, and drawing upon the elite as well as random samples to include the potentially more mobile sub-section of the population, there were 269 individuals and a total of 650 job changes. As shown in Table 27, horizontal changes were by far the most common (55 percent of all job changes), and there were an approximately equal number of upward and

TABLE 27

Occupational Mobility, Using Job Changes as
Unit of Analysis*
(N=650)

| | After Job Change | | | |
Before Job Change	Unskilled	Semi-skilled	Skilled	Total
Unskilled	45%	23%	29%	100% (N=176)
Semi-skilled	12%	62%	26%	100 (N=210)
Skilled	25%	21%	55%	100% (N=264)

Summary: Total horizontal changes = 357 = 54.92%
Total upward changes = 147 = 22.61%
Total downward changes = 146 = 22.47%

*Includes only those males who, as of 1969, had changed jobs at least once while living in Rio de Janeiro, and draws upon both elite and random samples. Incorporates 269 individuals.

downward moves (22.6 percent and 22.4 percent, respectively). The high degree of downward mobility seems to indicate that even if favelados manage to escape unskilled positions at one time in their working lives, they are as likely to fall back as to move up. The job prospects appear to be highly unstable and discouraging.[34]

How, then, does the favelado survive? In the majority of the households (67 percent), both husband and wife work. Fifteen percent of families supplement their income with biscate. Total household income is thus somewhat higher than job income, but still painfully low, as seen in Table 26. One out of five families subsists on a total income less than $40 per month; half live on $60 per month or less. The average household, it must be remembered, consists of six persons.

The favelado, like slum dwellers everywhere, is exploited by the neighborhood economic system as well. Local store owners, for example, charge higher prices than those prevailing in other districts. The systems of control over electricity and water can push the costs of these services to ten times the standard rates. Slum landlordism, although fairly rare, is nevertheless a growing problem in the areas where a few men own a number of barracos.

To the extent that the favelado has little education, a poor job, and a low income, he is economically "marginal." But this is a marginality of exclusion and exploitation rather than one of low motivation and parochialism. He is deeply integrated into the economic system, not only in action and attitudes but in the even more fundamental sense that his fate depends on such macroeconomic factors as policies of industrial protection, subsidies to agriculture, and publicly created jobs. During the immediate postwar period, Brazil's economy was able to provide as many new manufacturing jobs as there were migrants to the cities. But by the mid-1950s the growth of manufacturing employment was slowing down and the influx of migrants accelerating.[35] This continuous imbalance affects a favelado's economic situation more than any factors within his own control.

The favelados, then, are not marginal to the national economy; they are integrated into it on terms detrimental to them. Favela workers appear condemned to failure in the labor market—plagued by a continual cycle of job changes which involve downturns, demotions, and frequent intervals of unemployment. There is little evidence that the fundamental terms of this economic integration/exploitation are likely to change in the near future.

Chapter Six
Political Marginality:
Participation and Radicalism

The propositions of marginality theory contend that favelados are not integrated into city and national political life. The favela supposedly lacks internal political organization, resulting in the effective impotence of favelados in relation to external government agencies. Squatters and migrants are thought to have little interest in politics, and little awareness of political events. The ideal type we have derived predicts that favelados rarely participate in electoral politics, avoid direct action politics, and only infrequently attempt to pursue individual goals through administrative channels.

A corollary to the proposition of political non-participation is the contention that favelados are so alienated from the social, cultural, economic, and political structures of the city they represent a potential revolutionary force. Squatters and migrants supposedly channel their frustrations into political aggression, withholding legitimacy from the regime and demanding basic structural changes in the system.

In this chapter we will take a careful look at the propositions and assumptions about favela politics in an attempt to go beyond the surface appearances and examine the reality in its various manifestations. I will examine first the contention that favelas have no internal political organization. Next I will look at the favelados' interest in and awareness of politics and assess their political participation at the city and national level. This examination will provide the background for an analysis of the prospects for radicalism in the favela. Finally, I will test the powerlessness and dependency experienced by favela residents and attempt to relate my findings to the realities of Brazilian politics.

POLITICAL AND SOCIAL ORGANIZATION WITHIN THE FAVELA

In Chapters Two and Five I described briefly the abundant social, political, and religious associations within the favelas. From both direct observation of the activities of these organizations and statistical analysis of the type of membership, I have concluded that the social and political organizations serve very similar functions and draw upon a similar constituency. Both are of critical importance in understanding the politics of the favela. Both train members in the ritual of election of officers, rules of procedure, formation of charters, constitutions, and by-laws, and the process of collective decision-making. But the critical dimension which determines their political nature is that participation in either type confers broad experience in bargaining for benefits from the outside world.

These associations maintain a wide variety of contacts with public and private institutions—as well as individual "patrons"—to secure individual financial support, permits, authorizations, and documents. The local leaders who serve the brokerage function between their members and outside contacts are a continual source of information on the aspects of city bureaucracy most relevant to the daily lives of the favelados.

Religious organizations, on the other hand, do not serve these same "political" functions, even in the broadest sense of the word. Beyond the obvious fact that they are oriented toward the sacred rather than the secular level of problem-solving, they do not have the form of a politiciz-ing association. Their leaders are appointed, not elected; decisions are made without collective input from the members; and contacts with external agencies are restricted to those within the religious heirarchy. Because they vary so much, from spiritist to Pentacostal to Catholic, it is difficult to generalize about any predisposition they may create toward other sorts of participation, or to predict what might politicize the insti-tutions themselves. For our present purpose, then, we will focus on those organizations that are explicitly or implicitly political in nature.

Of the 68 percent of favelados who belong to some voluntary associ-ation, just under half belong solely to a religious group, leaving 35 per-cent who belong to social or political organizations. Fourteen percent belong to two or more such organizations. As would be expected, among elites the membership rates are substantially higher; 88 percent belong to at least one social or political group and almost half belong to two or more.

The most important political organization in the favela is the Residents' Association. It typically serves as the official spokesman for the community in dealings with outsiders and has the important job within the favela of handling the extension of urban services to the area. Also, as we have noted, Residents' Associations often try to provide basic welfare services for their constituents—such as medical and dental care—and adult literacy courses. Association headquarters frequently serve as meeting and recreation places and are the points of mail delivery for the entire community. Although membership strength varies from area to area, the average in the three areas we investigated was over 15 percent of the adult population.

Electricity commissions were first established by the C.E.E. (State Commission of Energy) as a part of a plan to distribute electric power within the favela. The local commissions organize and run the local *cabine* or distribution point, charging residents more than what they must pay back to the C.E.E. and "pocketing" the difference. Commission members receive service directly from the *cabine* at a price higher than that paid by other city residents but generally lower than that for the other alternative—hooking up an extension wire from another individual. The electricity commission's control over a scarce resource and its ability to accumulate funds makes it a strong political force in every favela where one exists. It is regularly embroiled in struggles over all sorts of issues in the local area, and often is led by a splinter group hostile to the directors of the Residents' Association. Fourteen percent of our sample said they belonged to such a commission.

Most local social functions within the favela—dances, festivals, picnics, and outings—are organized by recreation clubs. Five percent of our respondents said they belonged to such groups. While wealthier clubs have their own headquarters, less fortunate ones often borrow the facilities of the Residents' Association. Funds come mainly from dues and admission fees at club-sponsored events.

An elaborate network of sports clubs, mainly soccer teams, also exists in the favela. Members (8 percent of the population) play not only against each other but also in numerous inter-favela matches which are well-attended by the rest of the favela population. Buses are hired to transport teams to competitions around the city. Some sports clubs, because they have outside "patrons" or are unusually successful in competition, have their own local headquarters which members use as a place to talk, drink, play cards, or hold parties on weekends.

The major social event of the year—and one in which the favelados play the principal roles while the rest of the city looks on admiringly—is Carnival. The carnival groups (called *escolas de samba,* literally, "samba schools") begin their preparation in late August, at least five months in advance of the event itself. Rehearsals are held weekly at the beginning but increase in frequency (and frenzy) until they take place almost daily with publicly open parties on weekend evenings. Only 5 percent of residents in the eight favelas studied said they belonged to samba schools, but these communities were not among the famous favelas whose dancers and drummers parade down the main avenue of Rio in a blaze of color on the main night of Carnival. In some of Rio's other favelas, as many as 50 to 85 percent of the residents can be found participating in the activities. Local samba schools are linked with a citywide network tied to the Ministry of Tourism, national beer companies, and many other supra-local governmental and private groups. Many of these institutions contribute to the cost of preparation—the government to underwrite a tourist attraction, others to gain concession rights at the many events. [1]

Local favela groups, while based in and drawing membership from the favela proper, have strong ties to the outside. It is these ties that allow the Residents' Association to bargain for benefits for their community, [2] and the samba school to finance the elaborate preparations for Carnival. As Pearse has indicated, even sports clubs and social organizations are "closely linked to, and often funded by, patrons interested in building up a political constituency in the favela." [3]

It is not only the funding that is important, but also the contacts to be made with "upper-sector" sponsors. Such contacts are often invaluable for finding a better job or getting medical or educational advantages. And more often than not, the relationship is reciprocal: if, for example, the "sponsor" has a friend or relative running for local elective office, he can count on a large ready-made constituency.

The network of sociopolitical organizations in the favelas is clear evidence of an internal political framework in the squatter settlements rather than the presumed atomization and isolation. Contrary to the assumptions of our ideal type, the favelados participate actively in local organizations and seek continually to establish links with the outer society.

LEADERSHIP WITHIN THE FAVELAS

In many squatter settlements in Latin America, local leadership is rigorously dominated by one powerful ruler, the *cacique* or boss. Often by organizing the "invasion" of land, he obtains de facto power over a neighborhood and rules it thereafter with an unlimited mandate. A retinue of friends, relatives, and dependents who can be called upon for assistance allows the cacique to threaten—and use if necessary—strongarm tactics to get his way. [4]

The pattern of local leadership in Rio's favelas is considerably more diffuse than this. Each organization elects not only a president but often a seemingly endless slate of vice-presidents, secretaries, first and second treasurers, and so on. Although memberships often overlap, it is unusual for a person to be an officer in more than one group. All members of an organization are eligible to participate in its elections. Those acquiring office are bound by the rules and duties outlined in the charter or "constitution" which each organization draws up and regards with much pride. In many cases a president and some of his associates will be reelected, but there are usually serious challengers to any incumbent. The openness of favela leadership is further maintained by the absence of appointed party or government officials in the neighborhood, the modal pattern in squatter settlements of Mexico and Venezuela. Furthermore, none of the established political parties court favela support as they did in Chile before the 1973 coup.

Yet in other respects there are many similarities between the situation of favela leaders and that of caciques. Both are local residents, not outsiders; both are concerned with all matters in their areas, not single issues. Although the favela does not have a single leader who has exclusive control over linkages to external authority, a group of leaders does assume the "role of the political broker or middleman standing guard over the crucial junctures or synapses of relationships which connect the local system to the larger whole."[5] As Lisa Peattie found in Cuidad Guayana, this "access to higher levels of authority" often makes a critical difference in defending local interests.[6]

Like the caciques, it is the favela elites who have the contacts with supra-local agencies, the bureaucrats, politicians, architects, lawyers, and other high-status individuals possessing skills or resources relevant to the satisfaction of local needs. While useful, as Adams points out, the "derivative power" flowing from sources outside the domain of the local leader can be "used effectively within the settlement to maintain control and discourage serious challenges to authority."[7] Like the caciques, favela leaders often use their privileged positions in pursuit of personal wealth and prestige and thus have strong vested interests in maintaining the status quo.[8]

If the squatter settlements were to achieve legal rights to their lands and full urban services and facilities, in many cases the usefulness, power, and importance of these leaders would be severely reduced. The control they have over internal resources would be dissolved and their bargaining power deflated. In order to survive, they must persuade residents to be content with token change and slow progress, and to trust that local leadership is doing its best to deal with the difficult problems of infrastructure and tenure. This may sound Machiavellian, but it is generally true. As the Brazilian sociologist Machado explains: "In the case, for example, of the networks of water and electricity and internal commerce, these can only function as resources for the *bourgesia favelada* [favela bourgeois] insofar as the status quo is preserved, and the favela doesn't undergo profound changes which would transform it into a regular working-class neighborhood."[9]

POLITICAL INVOLVEMENT OUTSIDE THE FAVELA

Theoretically, it might be argued that while the favelados are indeed participants within their own communities, they are nonetheless marginal in terms of their interest and involvement in the wider political sphere outside the favela. It has been assumed, for example, that lack of leisure time and resources conspires against the active involvement of the favelado in city and national politics and to some extent that is true. Their hour-by-hour existence presents them with a nearly unsuperable burden of immediate concerns. Politics attains high salience for them only insofar as it directly touches their lives.

POLITICAL AWARENESS

In the pre-test interviews we asked favelados how often they talked about political matters and with whom. Five out of 41 said they discussed political matters occasionally, but not a single person said this was a frequent practice and the vast majority said "never." Political discussion that did occur took place not with family, friends, or neighbors, but with politicians or government functionaries, usually in conjunction with obtaining some political favor. Bonilla found a similar pattern in an earlier study in Rio; only about 12 percent of favelados had discussed politics with a friend over the six-month period prior to his study.[10]

The meaning of "talking about politics" as well as the sense of what is political clearly varies from person to person and culture to culture. For the purposes of looking at political interest and awareness in this study, we used the following four criteria: perceived relevance of politics; degree of interest in political matters; level of political information; and degree of opinion-holding about matters at each of three political levels—local, state, and national.

The components of each of these dimensions and the distributions for men, women, and leaders can be seen in Figure 9. As shown, the closer to home, the more relevant politics appears to the favelados, with leaders recognizing more clearly the relevance at all levels.

Prevailing levels of political awareness among the other favelados seemed inadequate to the leaders, who often complained that their constituents were *apáticos, desinteressados,* or *ignorantes,* or that they *não querem nada, não se esforçam* (apathetic, uninterested, or ignorant, they don't want to get involved, don't want to make any effort).[11]

The same relationships hold for political interest and information: levels are relatively low for the favelado in general and substantially higher for leaders. About half of the favelados mentioned a "preferred source" of political information, most often the media, as opposed to local "opinion leaders," friends, or family; and only 11 percent said they "had ever become so involved (angered or enthused) over some political issue that they really wanted to do something about it." Leaders, as expected, are more highly politicized: 80 percent expressed a preferred source of political information, and about a third had grown sufficiently involved to want to do something.

As to be expected, degree of interest in politics and perceptions of its relevance co-vary with levels of political information. Data on levels of political information are also presented in Figure 9. The composite scales, however, obscure the important point that levels of political information tend to decrease as events grow distant from the favela.

Finally, contrary to the idea that favelados are too apolitical even to formulate opinions, we found that 92 percent of those interviewed held definite opinions on at least half of a series of eight controversial issues, and almost half held an opinion on all eight.

Comparisons with studies of attitudes in rural areas indicate that the favelado is much more knowledgeable about political affairs than his rural counterpart. Philippe Schmitter found only one-third of people in rural areas able to name the President of Brazil[12]—in comparison with 59 percent of the favelados and 95 percent of their leaders in my study.[a] Further, I had observed during a stay in a Bahian fishing village several years earlier that although everyone knew that "Pedro Alvares Cabral discovered Brazil in 1500," students and teachers alike were ignorant of the contemporary President of their country.

---

[a]It should be noted that knowledge of the President was reduced somewhat by the fact that at the time of the study Costa y Silva was seriously ill and leadership had passed somewhat ambiguously into the hands of a temporary junta.

Percentage

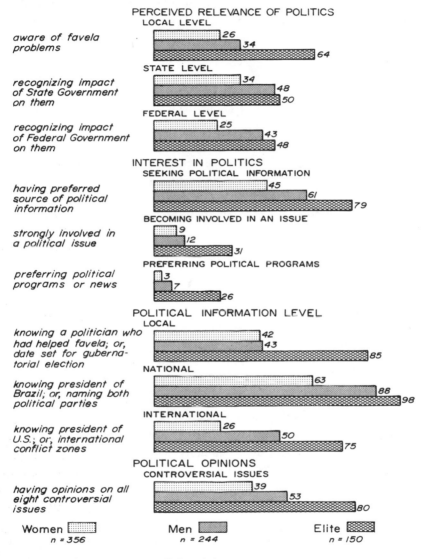

9. Political Awareness.

The political marginality concept does not do justice to the nuances of political awareness in the favela. The amount of information the favelados have about international politics may not be great, nor is political discussion valued over other topics of conversation. However, the favelados are led by persons who are more keenly aware of politics and its ramifications than they are, and their attention is astutely selective, focusing on the local arena where their concern is more likely to produce results.[13] It is in the realm of political participation that the degree of awareness and interest can be actualized.

POLITICAL PARTICIPATION

We measured political involvement in three areas: electoral participation, including voting and working for a candidate in an election; direct-action politics, including demonstrating, petitioning, and attending political meetings; and administrative participation, including the "use of urban agencies" such as governmental bureaus, social welfare institutions, banks, lawyers, employment agencies or labor unions. In an authoritarian regime where many channels of political expression are blocked or available only in symbolic form, "making use of the political process" becomes very important.

Electoral Politics. The degree of participation of the favelados in each of these three realms is shown in Figure 10. Roughly 60 to 70 percent of favelados who are eligible have voted at least once.[14] This figure is a bit misleading, however, because voting is supposed to be compulsory in Brazil. Ironically, a more precise measure of meaningful participation is the act of not voting, that is, casting a blank ballot. This moderate but expressive form of protest was followed by 55 percent of the voters in the November 1970 Guanabara elections.[15]

The second measure of electoral participation, open to anyone regardless of age, literacy, or work status, is working for a political candidate as a *cabo eleitoral,* a type of local ward healer. One in ten favelados has canvassed and done publicity work for a candidate in this manner, and 10 percent is a rather high figure for a population that is supposedly nonactive and apathetic. One Brazilian observer describes their role as follows: "While the great topics are being discussed, each voter looks for a personal benefactor and each politico strives to guarantee his constituency. This is where the most important figure in Brazilian elections appears: the *cabo eleitoral.* . . . He fills the gap between what the candidate proclaims and what he will perform. Politics is thus imbued with a highly demographic content. The candidate presents the voter with a program of action, but to the individual he promises his personal attention. It is this which counts."[16]

The *cabo eleitoral* is a broker operating between voter and candidate. In return for the votes he delivers, the *cabo eleitoral* receives

Percentage

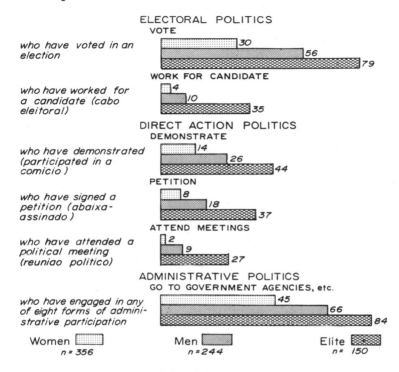

ELECTORAL POLITICS
VOTE

who have voted in an election   30 / 56 / 79

WORK FOR CANDIDATE

who have worked for a candidate (cabo eleitoral)   4 / 10 / 35

DIRECT ACTION POLITICS
DEMONSTRATE

who have demonstrated (participated in a comicio)   14 / 26 / 44

PETITION

who have signed a petition (abaixa-assinado)   8 / 18 / 37

ATTEND MEETINGS

who have attended a political meeting (reuniao politico)   2 / 9 / 27

ADMINISTRATIVE POLITICS
GO TO GOVERNMENT AGENCIES, etc.

who have engaged in any of eight forms of admini-strative participation   45 / 66 / 84

Women n = 356   Men n = 244   Elite n = 150

10. Political Participation.

promises of favors from the candidate. Sometimes these are collective benefits such as sewer pipes or cement steps; and sometimes the "favors" are last-minute payoffs that can be distributed around to individuals, such as clothes, shoes, or food. Often, the reward is personal. One *cabo eleitoral* who boasted 2,000 committed votes is said to have held out for a Chevrolet Impala, another for someone who would get the bigamy charges against him cleared. The system takes people with purely local influence and ties them into a larger system of power relations, but always on a pragmatic basis. There is little room for ideology or even loyalty to abstract collectivities.

Direct-Action Politics. Electoral politics is not the only way favelados can express themselves politically. They can work outside these channels altogether—in direct actions such as signing petitions, going to meetings, or demonstrating. Twelve percent of the favelados have signed their name to a petition (*abaixo-assinado*), usually to support some community-level demand: a local school, legal title to favela land, or linkage into urban networks of water or electricity. Only 5 percent said they had attended meetings, although the question may have been interpreted to exclude the general assemblies of the Residents' Associations, and to include only explicitly political meetings. To admit participating in meetings organized by a labor union, a political party, or a specific pressure group outside the favela would be somewhat risky. Likewise, only 19 percent of the favelados said they had participated in a demonstration. Those who did mentioned such diverse activities as the hunger strikes in Caxias, labor union walkouts, sit-ins at the Governor's Palace, or, in the past, rallies against removal.

In numbers of participants, direct-action politics is clearly the realm of least involvement. It is interesting to note, however, that these figures correspond closely to those for participation in direct action by poor people in the United States. A sample of over 1000 persons in five neighborhoods (three black, one white, one Chicano), indicated that 14 percent of the rank and file had complained to a manager and 12 percent to a government official. Nineteen percent had participated in a picket line; the same porportion of favelados have participated in demonstrations.[17]

Administrative Politics. Turning from the high-risk activities of direct action to the low risk, individually oriented arena of administrative participation, we find impressive increases in involvement. Administrative participation is by far the most frequent form of political activity undertaken by favelados. On one component of our scale alone, "going to a government agency," we find participation by 28 percent of women, 42 percent of men, and 63 percent of leaders. Not counting the leaders, 54 percent have either gone to a government agency about a problem, consulted a lawyer, sought out employment counseling, used a bank, obtained social security, or belonged to a labor union.

Administrative participation is a viable way to make use of the political process and is a clearly "integrated" form of involvement. Many of the favelas' problems are played out in the administrative realm, and the contribution of many local leaders consists primarily in slogging through endless administrative channels on the community's behalf. Nevertheless, this is playing the political game by the rules of the system. If the government creates another agency to be consulted or another requirement to be met, there is generally no recourse but to accept the added, and perhaps definitive, delay. At the unsuccessful end of administrative outcomes is the instance, cited earlier, of Maria

Carolina's humiliating defeat in trying to receive disability compensation from the government.

On the other end, however, is the astute political gaming that takes place between favela leaders and politicians or bureaucrats one step up the ladder. A remark by one favela leader about a call he had received from the director of an important government agency captures the intricacies well: "The Director said that he wanted to warn me that 'I was being used by the Deputy.' . . . I responded that no, on the contrary, 'it was I that was using the Deputy.' The only thing I didn't tell him was that who was really being used by the Deputy was himself, the Director."[18]

Political participation by the favela elites is similar in distribution to that of other favelados, but much higher in overall amount. Eighty percent have voted; one in three has worked for a political candidate. A great many indeed have demonstrated (44 percent) and petitioned for favela causes (37 percent). Again we note that these rates of involvement correspond to those prevailing among leaders in poor neighborhoods of the United States. A study of 630 leaders chosen by the poor in 100 neighborhoods across the country revealed that 47 percent had complained to a government official and the same number to a local proprietor, and that 35 percent had participated in picket lines.[19]

Administrative participation among favela leaders, as among the rank and file, is the most frequent kind of political involvement. Eighty-four percent have engaged in one of the forms of it we measured. Access to administrative contacts is one of the main sources of power they hold in the squatter settlements and is critical in understanding the politics of the favela.

We can conclude, from this evidence, that while politics is not the dominant interest in the lives of favelados, they are far from apathetic and inactive. They are sensibly concerned with those issues that affect their lives most directly and wisely participate in ways which disrupt the system least while still offering hope of advancing their partisan interests. The leaders take a more active role in all realms of activity but abide by the same strategy of minimizing risks and maximizing gains. Given Brazilian political realities, this amounts to the opposite of marginality—a smooth, non-disruptive integration into the national political system. Nonetheless, the governing classes' fear of disruption and antisocial behavior has led to widespread stereotypes regarding radicalism in the favelas.

RADICALISM AND CONFORMISM IN THE FAVELA

In the years preceding the Brazilian military coup of 1964, there was great fervor on the part of students, intellectuals, journalists, young professionals, and even some labor leaders concerning the inevitability of a social revolution. The Goulart government spoke of structural reforms (*reformas de base*); the National Student Union (U.N.E.) led a nationwide student strike; Francisco Julião organized peasant leagues (*ligas camponesas*) in the Northeast, and leftist Miguel Arraes, as Governor of Pernambuco, was instituting a wide range of reforms. The revolution seemed just around the corner. The left presumed that its evaluation of the Brazilian reality (*a realidade Brasileira*) was widely shared by other segments of the population, particularly the masses (*o povo*). Surely the favelado, of all Brazilians, would be supportive of movements for radical change. Newspapers chimed in as well with dire predictions of hoards of angry favelados descending from their hillsides upon the city, rioting, looting, and threatening the lives of respectable citizens. On April 1 the "revolution came"—not from the left, but from the right— in the form of a military coup. The favelados did indeed come down from the hills, but in support of the reestablishment of law and order and the sanctioning of "God, family, and private property." Bearing this experience in mind, it will be useful to put to empirical test the two conflicting theories espoused in Chapter Four—one regarding squatters as radicals, the other regarding them as conformists.

The literature on squatter settlement radicalism raises a series of challenging questions. What is really meant by "radical" in terms of the favelas? How is it possible to determine whether or not favelados are "radical"? The term radical has been used in a very loose and imprecise way in the literature on marginality. It often carries the connotation of alienation or frustration, which supposedly leads the squatters to disruptive acts, riots, and the creation of general social instability. Because of the great differences in living standards between the favelados and the rest of the urban population, many observers on both the right and the left have assumed a basis of resentment and hostility among favelados that would make them receptive to a "radical" ideological perspective. This perspective, in the Brazilian context of the late 1960s, meant such things as a disaffection with the government and the political system, a belief in basic structural change, a degree of class consciousness, and a nationalist, anti-imperialist outlook. It is these four sets of perceptions which many Brazilian social scientists used as indicators of radical ideology, and which I have used to measure its presence or absence. [20] However, before examining the data, it should be pointed out that these indicators do not tell the whole story.

First of all, many of the indicators apply more directly to the ideological perceptions of students or professionals than they do to the relevant features in the lives of favelados. Structural change or nationalism, for example, are abstract concepts which the favelados may never have considered. The threat of favela removal, however, has a great deal of meaning to the favelados and has catalyzed their collective action numerous times in the past, as we shall see in the next chapter.

Furthermore, as with all attitudinal questions, there is no certainty that actions can be predicted by attitudes, or that a change in the objective situation will not completely reverse both the attitudes and the behavior of the people involved.

I will examine the responses of the favelados, then, with a good deal of caution, but also with the recognition that belief in favela radicalism is a strongly held stereotype upon which policy is based. There is something to be learned about how closely the political beliefs of the favelados approximate an ideology, how true the frustration-aggression theory is, and what internal differences exist between leaders and followers, men and women, and the favela sub-classes. Using specific behavioral and attitudinal tests for radicalism, I have attempted to establish how favelados acted and thought at a given time in Brazilian history.

MEASURES OF RADICALISM

The first measure of the radicalism to be explored is disaffection with the government and unwillingness to concede its legitimacy. When we asked in our pre-test "Do you think, in general, the present government is good or bad for the country?", only 3 of 41 responded "bad." The remaining 80 percent varied in opinion, but all favored the government to some degree. This finding is confirmed by two similar items we wrote for the standardized questionnaire which we felt were less threatening and thus less likely to evoke evasive responses (see Figure 11). When asked if "the people in the government really try to understand and solve your problems," 60 percent said "yes." On a second item, 82 percent said the government provides the masses (o povo) with the things they need, either in the normal process of things (38 percent) or when the people demand them (44 percent). Only 8 percent said the government doesn't provide in either case. In this respect, favelados are much less alienated than the American poor. When asked, "How do you think

Percentage

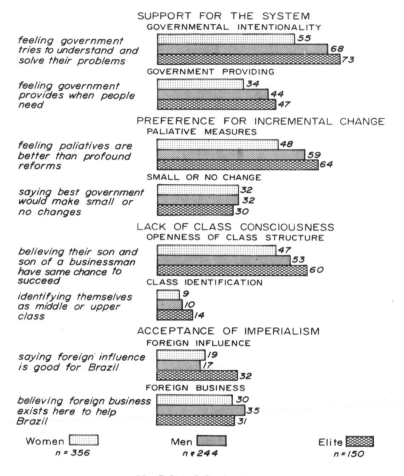

11. Political Conformism.

the American government feels about poor people?", 43 percent of poor Americans maintain it is doing "very little" to help, and another 12 percent say that it is trying to "keep the poor down."[21] Perhaps they have higher expectations than favelados.

Conformism also dominates the picture of the scope of changes the favelado perceives as desirable. The pre-test question, "Do you agree that some basic changes should be made even if they cause some disorder?" was eliminated because no one, not one person, said yes. Given the sensitive political climate at the time, and the clear uncertainties in an interview situation, that was not surprising. Two milder forms of the same question were used instead. On the first, only 28 percent said they would prefer "profound change going to the root of problems" as opposed to 53 percent who opted for "small modifications" and 18 percent who said they "didn't know." When asked later in the interview what kind of changes would be best for the development of Brazil, 59 percent said "big changes," 22 percent "small changes," and 9 percent "no changes." A comparison of the responses to these questions indicates that while a majority of favelados might be in favor of large changes in policy, fewer favor changes in the social order and almost no one favors changes which might involve violence.

Class consciousness appears to be rather low in the favela, despite arguments that "the world view of migrants is characterized by intense hatred of the rich."[22] To begin testing this notion we asked in the pretest, "In Brazil there are the rich and the poor. How do you explain this?" The responses were exceedingly varied in style, but most revolved around the themes "it is natural because they complement each other," "since the beginning of the world it has always been that way," and "that's just the way it is." Five of 41 said that being poor depended on the amount of effort a person put into his work and studies—a different answer, but hardly one reflective of a class-based outlook. Seven percent stated that wealth depended on family name and inheritance, but even this response was devoid of a sense of class antagonism, domination, or exploitation.

Soares found that migrants, when they first arrived in the city, continued to call themselves "the poor" (pobre), as they had been known in the country, but that slowly they began to call themselves members of the working class. The most mobilized and class-conscious elements, however, called themselves the proletariat.[23]

We included a standard measure of perception of class barriers in the final questionnaire. The result: fully half of the population feels "their son and the son of a businessman have the same chance to succeed in life." Although favelados believe there will always be rich and poor, many feel little frustration, apparently because they have real hopes that their children will succeed in life.

When asked directly what class they belonged to, 10 percent said lower-middle or above, and about one-quarter said "proletariat." In fact, it is the heartfelt aspiration of many of the favelados to emulate and someday become—perhaps through their children—the middle class. Others take a certain pride in being a favelado, having accomplished the things they did on their own, and through working together. This was especially true in Nova Brasília. The favelados did aspire to raise the level of their living conditions in the direction of the middle class and to acquire land tenure for their favela, but they were proud to be in the squatter community and wouldn't have moved out even if economic circumstances permitted.

While the favelados do not have contacts ordinarily through their place of work—since most of them work on their own and in unstable conditions rather than in factories— they *do* have these contacts through their place of residence. They tend to interact with each other daily in their communities, raising the issue of another kind of group organized on another basis than that of labor. This point came to the fore in the United States with the Alinsky approach to community organizing,[25] and it was, in fact, one of the reasons that the Brazilian government was so interested in breaking up these communities. As in the lower-class U.S. communities, however, the residents were very suspicious of "outside agitators," and of rhetoric that didn't lead to tangible results.

The final component of the radicalism measure is nationalism. In Brazil, being nationalistic and anti-imperialistic (especially anti-American) has always been associated with the world-view of the left. When we asked in the pre-test questionnaire, "What is nationalism?", 33 of 38 had never heard of the word; the remainder thought it was "some sort of national policy."

Anticipating ignorance of "nationalism" as a concept, we asked several questions about the content of nationalism and national pride in the pre-test. The first was, "In your opinion are there some peoples (nations) who are more capable and intelligent than others?" Fifty percent responded "yes," but when prodded to say which peoples, almost no one answered "Brazilians." The overwhelming vote of confidence went instead to Americans. When asked what they felt the most striking characteristics of the Brazilian people were, they said: "happiness, gaiety, kindness, friendliness, and style"—not very "politicized" answers.

In keeping with the interests of the upper sector, favelados, although not nationalistic, are in fact "patriotic" in the traditional sense. About 75 percent think that national holidays such as Independence Day (September 7) should be commemorated, mostly because "it is an established tradition and should be perpetuated." Since the time of our study the present regime has undertaken an elaborate publicity campaign of moral and civil education (*educação moral e cívica*) to encourage exactly these sentiments of patriotism. Aside from compulsory courses at all levels of the educational system, one of the elements of the campaign is widespread distribution of banners, flags, and bumper stickers saying "Security," "Brazil, Love It or Leave It," "Brazil, Love It or Die," or simply, "You can count on me." There are also frequent radio, television, and newspaper commercials about the nation's glory and progress. The most sophisticated media experts from all over the world have been hired to devise these media spots.

For the final questionnaire, two measures of nationalism were used: On the first, "Do you think there is any foreign influence on what happens here in Brazil, and if so, is it good or bad for the country?", only 23 percent produced the nationalistic response—that it existed and was bad for the country. (Of those recognizing foreign influence, 70 percent identified the United States as its major source.) Similarly, on a question concerning the purpose of foreign business in Brazil, only 22 percent gave the anti-imperialist response, "to exploit the Brazilian people," whereas 64 percent said such businesses were there to help the Brazilian people or just to take care of their own affairs.

IDEOLOGICAL SYNDROMES

In addition to examining the individual items, I searched carefully for syndromes of radical ideas. Nothing approaching an ideology, either of the left or the right, could be found. The situation is typical of a general Brazilian political style which tends to be pragmatic, not ideological. As one high-ranking Brazilian politician announced concerning an important problem of the day, "Eu não sou nem a favor, nem contra: muito pelo contrário." ("I am neither for, nor against; quite the contrary.")[26]

Table 28 indicates the interrelationships between the measures of radicalism used in this study. Knowing how a person has responded to any one measure is almost no help in predicting how he will respond to any other. Included in Table 28 are all the interrelationships (Rank Order Correlations) between the eight indicators of radicalism reported in Figure 11. Only two of the 28 pairs attain meaningful levels of covariance, these being the two indicators of "nationalism" and the two on "evaluation of the government." We found, furthermore, no relationship between any of four "composite" indicators ("government evaluation," "nationalism," "preference for big changes," and "class identification"). We decided to include in the table three additional measures concerning attitudes toward popular participation (whether all Brazilians should participate in politics, whether the vote should be given to

TABLE 28

Lack of Radicalism Syndrome, Spearman Rank Order
Correlation Coefficients*

	1	2	3	4	5	6	7	8	9	10	11
1. Government tries to understand and solve problems	+	.28	.03	.01	.05	.00	.07	**.14**	.00	.04	.06
2. Government provides		+	.04	.00	.03	.04	**.14**	**.16**	.00	.02	.03
3. Palliatives preferred			+	.03	.06	.03	.06	.01	.11	.07	.03
4. No change or small change preferred				+	.09	**.13**	.03	.03	.08	.06	.06
5. Favelado same chance for success					+	.04	.01	.00	.08	.08	.00
6. Class identification						+	.11	.07	.05	.03	.03
7. Foreign influence good							+	**.26**	.01	.00	.00
8. Foreign business good								+	.02	.01	.03
9. Politics left in hands of politicians									+	.02	.04
10. Illiterate should not have vote										+	.06
11. Brazilian people lack capacity to vote well											+

*Entries with significance at the .001 level are in bold face.

the illiterate, and whether the Brazilian population has the capacity to vote wisely). Again no relationship existed, either between them, or between them and the other "radicalism" measures.

Even though the numbers of persons giving the radical answers to these questions were few in absolute terms, we could have spoken of them as a group if they were more or less the same people on each item.

It would have made sense to speak of radicalism as a phenomenon, to compare the radical with more conformist groups, and to see what factors conditioned the formation of a radical point of view. This kind of analysis was obviously inappropriate because no syndrome could be found.

One might object, of course, that this failure to find syndromes of radical attitudes and behavior in the favela is due to faulty measurement or analytical technique. However, it was precisely our success in isolating syndromes of political awareness and political participation that encouraged us in our search for a radical ideology. The matrices are shown in Table 29.

SECOND-GENERATION HYPOTHESIS

We tested as well the "second generation" hypothesis that radicalism should be expected not among those newly arrived in the city but among those who have lived there longer. Two measures were constructed to measure length of time in the city, one categorizing people from "native of Rio" to "first year in Rio," the other from "native of big

TABLE 29

Awareness and Participation Syndromes*

| | I. Awareness | | |
	Interest	Saliency	Information	Opinions
Interests	.43	.51	.54
Saliency		.38	.44
Opinion-holding			.48

| | II. Participation | | |
	Electoral	Direct/Action	Administrative/ Participation
Electoral			
Direct action		.52	.38
Administrative participation			.34

*Statistics are Gammas; all entries are in bold face because all tables were significant well above. 001 levels. (An examination of the Spearman R's produces the same results.)

city" to "first year in big city." None of the eight indicators of radicalism in Figure 11 was significantly related to either of the two measures.[b]

FRUSTRATION-AGGRESSION THEORY AND RADICALISM

Although holding serious reservations about the pseudo-psychological nature of the frustration-aggression approach, I felt that since it is so widely accepted among social scientists studying the urban poor, it would be more useful to test the concept than to ignore it.

Our findings are consistent with the frustration-aggression theory of radicalism in one sense, for if frustration may be seen as contributing to disaffection, then it must be granted as well that satisfaction promotes conformism. Contrary to radical expectation for the squatter settlement, favelados told us they were reasonably satisfied with their lives and prospects for the future. More than eight in ten said they do not want to return to the places they came from, although half had returned at some time for a visit. Four-fifths felt their economic situation was better than that of their friends who had remained home. Nine out of ten mentioned aspects of their present lives in the city they especially liked; and 70 percent said there was as much or more mutual help in the favela as there was in their home areas; and half felt their children had as much of a chance to "make it" in life as the children of the typical businessman. There is little evidence in this picture of the "want-get" disparities or thwarted hopes of the frustration-aggression hypothesis. Despite the favelados' existence in a city which openly invites invidious comparisons of social class, the favelados were comparing themselves with each other or with their rural counterparts and coming out ahead.

We tested the frustration theory further by checking to see if measures of radicalism varied with indicators of frustration and satisfaction, using as measures of frustration: (1) wanting to return to one's home town; (2) feeling one was better off before migrating; (3) believing there was more mutual help in one's home town; (4) having few people to count on; (5) wanting to leave the favela; (6) disliking Rio; (7) preferring to be relocated; (8) being pessimistic about Brazil's and one's own future. These variables cover a wide variety of dissatisfactions and disappointments, but more disappointment or frustration in any of these

---

[b]The average absolute gamma between "Rio-born" and the eight measures was .03; the average between "city-born" and the eight measures was .06; and the highest single gamma among all was only .13. Not one table was statistically significant, even at the minimal .05 level.

ways was not related to any of the radicalism measures (see Table 30). The result is striking in face of the large body of theoretical literature premised on this relationship.

We also looked closely at two kinds of persons experiencing great disparities of aspiration and attainment in their own lives: those who

TABLE 30

Radicalism-Conformism and Frustration-Satisfaction

(Matrix of Spearman's R's)

Measures of Radicalism-Conformism[a]	Measures of Frustration-Satisfaction[b]							
	A	B	C	D	E	F	G	H
1	.000	-.069	.086	.049	-.087	-.047	.000	.101
2	.063	.055	-.067	-.070	-.007	.101	.024	-.156
3	-.021	-.032	-.050	-.014	-.005	.068	.053	.016
4	.052	.043	.000	.016	.054	.076	.121	.002
5	.038	-.084	.052	.037	-.051	-.042	-.047	.138
6	.057	.077	-.106	-.034	.091	.050	-.041	.018
7	-.044	-.048	-.039	-.009	-.069	-.017	-.028	.166
8	.032	.014	.055	.053	-.051	-.019	.017	-.099

NOTE: Relationships significant at .001 level are in italics. Out of the entire table, there are only three significant relationships; all are extremely low, and the one which is highest is in the opposite direction from the predicted one.

[a]The measures of Radicalism-Conformism are:
1. Government not trying to help people like us
2. Government does *not* provide
3. Want palliative measures
4. Want small or no changes
5. Their son has same chance as businessman's son
6. Vague class identity
7. Foreign influence good
8. Foreign business good.

[b]The measures of Frustration-Satisfaction are:
A. Want to stay in city
B. Better off economically
C. More mutual help in city
D. Can count on people in neighborhood
E. Want to stay in favela
F. Like something special about the city
G. Dislike nothing about city
H. Have good prospects for past and future of both self and Brazil.

would work for better pay under a more demanding boss and still had the lowest level of income, and those especially concerned about the education of their children but whose children had been conspicuously unsuccessful in getting through school. Neither of these two measures of personal frustration was related to radicalism. The frustration-aggression theory, then, is doubly useless in seeking to understand radicalism in the favela. First, no matter how downtrodden and frustrated the favelados appear from the outside, the external view varies with their self-image; and second, what frustration does exist is not channeled into political nonconformism.

LEADERSHIP AND RADICALISM

In any political system the attitudes and orientation of the most active and powerful members are of particular importance. Though a minority, their views weigh heavily on the political scales since they oversee the conversion of attitudes into action. They also receive the majority of communications from the broader political matrix and interpret them to the rest of the population. Finally, they serve as models for the rest of the community. It is important, then, to note that favela leaders, on every available measure, are more conformist and more conservative than the people they represent. Not only are they failing to stir their followers into a "frenzy of radical activity," as many have feared, but they are not even catalyzing the small degree of discontent that does exist. On most measures they are roughly 10 percent more system-supportive than the random sample. In short, it is precisely those elements of favela society that have the most political interest, knowledge, and political participation—those who can assert themselves most effectively in the outer world—that are least likely to challenge that world to change its repressive policies toward the favela. As Machado has pointed out, favela leaders have a high stake in maintaining the system that has brought them relative power and status, and their outlook is correspondingly determined much more by supra-local groups and politicians—all extremely conservative—than by the masses of favelados.[27]

It is possible that the favela elites have risen to their positions of power and leadership in part precisely because their own political outlook was more akin to that of the establishment than those of others. As they became active within their local communities and had to deal increasingly with supra-local agencies in bargaining for benefits, many may have developed an increasing stake in maintaining the status quo.

If the favelas were legalized and provided with the full array of urban services, for example, the leaders would be deprived of the political bargains which are presently so lucrative and rewarding for them.[28]

WOMEN AND RADICALISM

Exclusion of women from power roles is deeply rooted in the Brazilian political style; it is the political reflection in the mirror of machismo. Consistent with the argument I have been developing, the least powerful favelados—women—turn out to be the least conformist. Only one neighborhood leader in ten is a woman. Women are more likely to be illiterate, jobless, underpaid, and more isolated from urban life than men. They are also lower on all indicators of political awareness and involvement. Correspondingly, according to our measures, they are less conformist than men (see Figure 11). Women are more doubtful that the government is doing its best by the favelado, more skeptical that palliative measures can solve their problems, and more cynical about their children having the same chance for success as businessmen's children. On all these measures they are about 10 percent less conformist than men, which seems to indicate that they perceive the true position of the favela more clearly than men. This follows the notion, turned into a general theory by Gunder Frank, that persons least closely linked to the established order have the greatest likelihood of developing an autonomous sense of self and a clear definition of self-interest.[29]

In the specific case of favela women, their relatively lower degree of conformism may result from a combination of factors: they may simply not be as savvy as the men, or the leaders, about the potential dangers of being critical and saying how they really see things; they may have had less exposure to the middle-class myths of "equal opportunity" and "governmental good-will" because of their lower media exposure and more restricted contacts with other groups; and they may be more realistic about their own and their family's position since they are the ones most in touch with the daily problems of survival. It is the women of the favela who most often have to stretch a sub-minimum wage to feed a six-member family or confront the disappointment of their children having to leave school to go to work.

The issue of the "revolutionary" potential of favela women, however, should be approached with caution. To say that women are less conformist does not necessarily mean they are more radical. While their readiness to criticize is greater than that of men or elites, in absolute terms it is still very low. Women in Latin America are not a very realistic source of radical change. Past experience has shown that as women acquire more political know-how and move from their peripheral location in the society, they will adopt the more acquiescent stands of men and leaders. It would be interesting to compare women leaders with women followers, but the actual number of women leaders—13 out of all 150—is too small to make the analysis meaningful.

CLASS AND RADICALISM

There is an important perspective which unifies many of the observations we have been making so far. Leaders are undeniably the highest status group within the limited-class spectrum of the favela. It is this privileged position that accounts in part for the leaders' greater familiarity with events and personages in the city, and for their self-confidence in assuming initiative on local issues. Concomitantly, the lower socioeconomic position of women in part underwrites their modest political nonconformism.

Some local leaders undoubtedly have the economic means to leave the favela and live elsewhere but remain to enjoy the prerogatives of "big fish in little ponds." This desire for prestige and power, however limited, is the foundation for the contention that leaders do not want to solve the problems of the favela so much as they want to maintain a series of short-term victories which they can work on one at a time, always increasing their own status and wealth.[30]

A secondary analysis of the present data and two similar studies in other favelas by Cardoso and Martins, confirm these points:

> The greatest concentrations of anti-conservative and anti-system attitudes and values tend to occur precisely in the lowest strata on the scale of socioeconomic stratification. . . . The socioeconomic determinants tend to focus the anti-conservative or opposition attitudes in those sectors in which there is the greatest concentration of apathy and political inactivity; and conversely tend to accumulate in the most mobile, informed, and active sectors exactly the attitudes and values which predispose the most conformist forms of intervention in the political process.[31]

These conclusions were reached after a composite indicator of socioeconomic status was matched against the awareness, participation, and evaluative items we have been discussing.[32] In every instance the higher the sub-class of the respondent within the favela, the greater his political awareness, participation, and conformism.

Some would interpret the discovery of a class or quasi-class basis for political alienation as a sign of the revolutionary potential of the most deprived favelado. We should emphasize, along with Cardoso and Martins, however, that although the lower stratum within the favela is numerically the most important, it is probably misleading to conceive of it as a "concentration of revolutionary potential."[33] Several factors enter into this judgment. First, the level of alienation among the lowest sectors is high not in absolute terms, but only in comparison with the other favelados. A 10 percent differential from utter acquiescence is a tenuous purchase on revolutionary fervor. Second, the fact that the most frustrated favelados are not the most radical ones discredits the postulated dynamic—that increasing deprivation or oppression will lead to increasingly revolutionary activity. Third, since there is no evidence for any radical symptoms, although lower-status persons have a more critical perspective in general, few have linked their ideas into a framework capable of explaining new phenomena or supporting political action. Finally, although there is heightened alienation from government within the lower strata, they are also the least politically efficacious. While one could interpret the lack of involvement in traditional political activities by this group as an expression of disdain for establishment procedures, this explanation does not account for the lack of belief that actions of the federal government affect them, or for their non-involvement in demonstrating and petitioning.

Overall, given the limitations of this type of inquiry and analysis, I would conclude that the favelados showed few signs of rebellion, leftist radicalism, or propensity to disruption. They also did not seem particularly vulnerable to the appeals of "radical rhetoric." Favela residents were very suspicious of *isquerdistas* (leftists) coming into the favela with their pamphlets. ("These outsiders all have relatives who are lawyers or have connections in the military, so they can afford to take risks, while we have no protection at all.") This shows neither apathy-ignorance nor radicalism-disruptiveness, but a keen understanding of the existing reality. The very recognition of their vulnerability is itself a sign of the favelados' political astuteness and pragmatism. Also, simply trying to survive as favelados has given them experience in collective action, and often positive reinforcement along with it. Favelados give their collective attention and allegiance to those issues and individuals that can bring them material improvement and a degree of security. Under different circumstances, I have no doubt that the favelados would be quite capable of perceiving their self-interest and acting accordingly.

The point is simply that under the circumstances in 1968-1969 they were not about to assume any dead-end risk or harbor any ideological illusions.

POWERLESSNESS AND DEPENDENCY

Having seen that the favelados are not politically marginal—that they participate actively within their own communities and moderately but wisely in the external arena—and that they are neither radical nor disruptive, we can ask in what way they are integrated. Just as socially, culturally, and economically the terms of the favelados' integration were defined by stigma, exclusion, and exploitation, so in the political realm they are marked by manipulation and repression. We will see a clear example of this in the following chapter, and examine in the conclusion how this has been played out throughout Brazilian history. Over time, this has resulted in the feelings of vulnerability discussed above, and in a sense of powerlessness and dependency.

This was clearly shown in the pre-test stage, when we asked several questions from the Almond and Verba study dealing with the feelings of "perceived efficacy."[34] In response to the query, "If the government does something harmful to you is there something you can do about it?", 36 out of 41 people said "no," half giving as explanation the idea that "the government is always right," the rest mentioning fear of repressive reactions the government might take. The same high proportion answered negatively to the parallel question, "If you want the government to do something in your interest, is there something you can do?" All but two of the 41 agreed on a third standard item, that "politics and government are so complicated that you really can't understand what is going on." Most revealing of all, however, were the responses to an item stating that "all Brazilian citizens have certain rights," and asking "Which in your opinion are the most important?" The most frequent responses were: "the right to support the government," "the right to respect the authorities," and "the right to obey the laws." The critical distinction between rights and duties, privileges and obligations seems to have no meaning in the experience of this group. Most of these questions were so obviously inappropriate to the Brazilian favela context that they were eliminated in the final version of the questionnaire.

Powerlessness and dependency were important concepts to measure, however, and a number of items regarding them were asked of all respondents. Emerging from Figure 12 is a striking portrait of political reality seen from the favelado's point of view. Only 16 percent of those we interviewed thought they could "do something to influence the government," and only 26 percent thought that they "could really have a say in what the government does." Even on a very local and personal level, lack of perceived political influence was abundant: only 3 percent said that "people often ask their opinions about elections, candidates, or political problems in general," with another 5 percent saying that this occurred sometimes.

Multiple experiences of political impotence have left an even deeper mark on the consciousness of the favelado. We discovered a normative orientation that actually legitimizes this lack of participation in molding one's own destiny. When asked whether "every Brazilian should participate in political life" or whether "politics should be left in the hands of politicians," only 30 percent chose the former. Further evidence comes from two questions dealing with the capacity of people in general, and illiterates in specific, to take a responsible role in political life. Only 31 percent felt strongly that "in general the Brazilian people have the capacity to vote wisely," and only 41 percent were in favor of giving illiterates the vote. This was, incidentally, *independent* of whether or not one was illiterate oneself, and was still further evidence

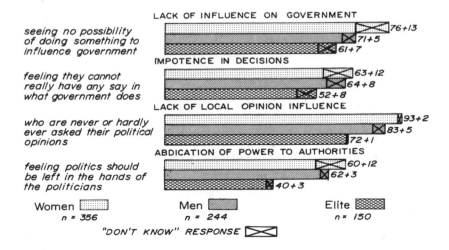

Percentage

LACK OF INFLUENCE ON GOVERNMENT

seeing no possibility
of doing something to
influence government
76+13
71+5
61+7

IMPOTENCE IN DECISIONS

feeling they cannot
really have any say in
what government does
63+12
64+8
52+8

LACK OF LOCAL OPINION INFLUENCE

who are never or hardly
ever asked their political
opinions
93+2
83+5
72+1

ABDICATION OF POWER TO AUTHORITIES

feeling politics should
be left in the hands of
the politicians
60+12
62+3
40+3

Women n = 356   Men n = 244   Elite n = 150

"DON'T KNOW" RESPONSE

12. Political Powerlessness.

of the lack of radicalism, since giving the vote to illiterates was one of the major leftist platforms of the time.

This combination of recognized and sanctioned powerlessness casts light on the evidence presented earlier in this chapter indicating that most favelados agree that "the government provides things when the people need them," and "people in the government try to understand and solve our problems." As Schmitter has stated, in Brazil "expectations are that power will be exercised from without by others for one's benefit but without one's participation."[35]

A point must be made here, however, about the validity of the concepts "political efficacy," "political modernity," and "civil competence" in the Brazilian context. The favelado who says he "has a voice in government decisions" or can "do something to influence the government" is not more efficacious, more modern, or more competent as a citizen; he is simply more of a fool, more effectively blinded by the rhetoric of the government and less in touch with his own reality. It is a tribute to the favelados' common sense that this group is a tiny minority.

Let us look for a moment at who the most naive elements are, and conversely, which groups seem most aware of their actual situation. Differences in residential district have little relevance. In Catacumba, Nova Brasília, and Caxias, the responses were almost identical. Favelados saying either there was no possibility of doing something to influence the government, or that they "don't know," for example, were 83 percent, 80 percent, and 86 percent in the three communities respectively. Although Catacumba was facing an immediate threat of removal at the time and the legal neighborhoods of Caxias were completely safe in this regard, the message of vulnerability had reached everyone and feelings of powerlessness were equally great in each case.

Differences in perception of powerlessness do occur, however, between the regulars and leaders and between men and women. The same monotonic relationship we observed in terms of awareness, participation, and conformism appear again concerning powerlessness. On every measure, the general population feels more powerless than the elites, and women feel more powerless than men. In relative terms, elites and men are more active, efficacious, and influential within the favela and it is thus natural that this fact should gain expression in their world view. From a perspective taking into account the actual powerlessness of all favelados vis-à-vis the global system, however, these groups must be judged as simply more deluded and more deceived by the occasional symbolic gestures of concession granted favelados. We should remember here the discussion of political conformism in which the elites more than the rank and file, and men more than women, were convinced of the openness of Brazilian society, the beneficence of government, and the benign nature of foreign influence.

Although the leaders show more efficacy than the favelados at large, even in this group, powerlessness is the major sentiment. Forty percent of local leadership feels that politics should be left in the hands of politicians (the professionals), and that Brazilians generally, presumably including themselves, cannot be trusted with it.

TERMS OF INTEGRATION

One of the most compelling conclusions that we can make concerning the nature of the favela as a political subculture is how perfectly suited it is for manipulation and exploitation from above. There is an almost perfect congruence between political beliefs and activities in the favela and the needs of the larger system. The profile of the favelados we have drawn in terms of awareness, involvement, conformism, and powerlessness-dependency, portrays a social group readily accessible to control and manipulation from above. Although the favelados do take an interest, and have participated in each political era to the extent demanded of them, they have never wielded any real power or had autonomy over their own lives. The political subculture of the favela cannot be understood outside of the context of political repression.

Perhaps the most striking recent example of this is to be seen in the massive favela removal programs which struck at the very core of the favelados' survival. It is to this program and its effect that we now turn our attention.

PART III
THE POWER OF AN
IDEOLOGY

Chapter Seven
Favela Removal:
The Eradication of a Life Style

T he preceding two chapters have demonstrated that the prevailing stereotypes regarding social, cultural, economic, and political marginality are clearly contradicted by reality. The evidence strongly indicates that the favelados are not *marginal* but in fact *integrated* into the society, albeit in a manner detrimental to their own interests. They are certainly not separate from, or on the margin of the system, but are tightly bound into it in a severely asymmetrical form. They contribute their hard work, their high hopes, and their loyalties, but they do not benefit from the goods and services of the system. *It is my contention that the favela residents are not economically and politically marginal, but are exploited and repressed; that they are not socially and culturally marginal, but are stigmatized and excluded from a closed social system.* Rather than being passively marginal in terms of their own attitudes and behavior, they are being actively marginalized by the system and by public policy.

The data presented here suggest that favela eradication expresses basic and sometimes calculated misunderstandings of the favelados, and is best understood as a specific instance of upper-sector policy carried out at the expense of lower sectors using the ideology of the myths of marginality for justification.

Ironically, the ideology of marginality has been so powerful in Brazil that it has become a self-fulfilling prophecy. Favela removal is perversely creating the marginalized population that it was designed to eliminate. Although the favelados were regarded as living outside the middle-class mainstream, they identified very strongly with it. After removal, however, the favelados found themselves literally cast out of the city—rejected and punished for being poor, and geographically isolated from the myriad opportunities of urban life that had initially attracted them. In the city, they had achieved a measure of integration, and had gradually been developing their communities into working-class neighborhoods. Favela removal, motivated by land-use interests and justified by the myths of marginality, in a sense de-integrated the favelados, stressing many of the symptoms of breakdown that had been previously and erroneously ascribed to them.

Of course, favela removal is not the only reflection of the myths of marginality in practice. It is, however, a clear expression of the general phenomenon of the ideology of marginality, which acts as a material force to diminish the bargaining power of certain popular sectors by isolating them from the rest of the people.

THE FUNCTIONALITY OF THE FAVELA

The possibility of being expelled from their homes and communities fills most favela residents with dread. Their attitude toward removal can only be understood if it is realized that, given the economic constraints under which they operate, the favela is an extremely functional solution to most, if not all, of their major problems.[1] The location of the favela (especially in the South Zone) puts its residents within close range of the best job markets and affords multiple opportunities for biscate in times of unemployment or financial stress. It also places them at the very center of a wide variety of urban services and benefits: free medical clinics, social services, sometimes even schools. It gives them a sense of "being where the action is" (movimento), which figures highly both in their motivations for migration and in their satisfaction with urban life.

The favela provides a community where friends and neighbors can be counted on for mutual favors: there is always someone to leave the children with; an accommodating neighbor with a refrigerator where the baby's milk can be kept fresh in the summer heat; someone whose sewing machine can be borrowed for repair work. Also, food and staples can be purchased on credit from local merchants (albeit at higher prices) so that even when there is no income, families can be fed.

This level of sharing may seem trivial, but it is of absolute importance to those living on the margin of subsistence. Lacking government attention, it provides a minimal, community sponsored, social security and family welfare system.

Furthermore, because it is the outcome of many incremental decisions based on human needs, the favela is well-designed. Friends and families live close together; walkways are distributed where the need requires; public spaces emerge and recede according to use; and tacit agreements not to develop certain areas are obeyed. A certain degree of pride is derived from the fact that most of the families built the homes they live in and that most public amenities are the result of communal efforts. Despite the insecurity of tenure on the favela lands, many families have invested in their homes, creating spacious, solid, and well-serviced houses from what were once simple shacks.[2]

Most critical of all, the favela is *free*. No monthly rents must be taken out of meager family incomes.[a] Although in the older favelas, like Catacumba, residents often have to pay the former tenant for the privilege of succeeding him, once this is paid there are no further expenses. Some purchase price was paid by 55 percent of the present residents of Catacumba, by 50 percent of Nova Brasília residents, and by 19 percent of Caxias residents. Most of the remainder in each case built their own shacks (barracos). This self-built housing, along with cooperatively built community facilities, represents the creation of significant capital through the use of labor. It was estimated in 1966 that the value of houses, schools, churches, and cooperatively built electricity and water networks in 185 Rio favelas was fifty million dollars.[3]

With all these benefits, it is small wonder the favelados resist efforts to relocate them in government housing projects. Hostility to relocation emerged strongly in our interviews. In spite of the image the authorities give to relocation in the mass media—the advantages of "modern living," legal home ownership, and a healthy new environment for children—less than a quarter of the favelados saw removal as desirable (see Table 31).

It is interesting to note that the residents of Catacumba, who are more directly threatened with removal than the people in Nova Brasília and Caxias, seem to have adapted somewhat more to it—or perhaps were more afraid to take a stand against it. Even in Catacumba, however, about twice as many are opposed to removal as are in favor of it. Almost 50 percent (more than in any other place) gave distance from work as the main reason for not wanting to leave. In Caxias, where most residents already work far from their homes, this factor is less important than responsiveness of the community to personal needs and the social factors of proximity to friends and relatives. The figures for Nova Brasília on these specifics fall in between, but the level of general opposition is greater there than anywhere else.

Among individuals in the favelas, those with housing of relatively high quality (where housing quality is measured by the number of rooms, the quality of construction material, the number of stories, and

---

[a]About 10 percent rent their barracos but the rates are very low, about $10 per month.

TABLE 31

Attitudes Toward Favela Removal, Percentage Distribution

Opinion on Removal	Catacumba (N=200)	Nova Brasilia (N=200)	Caxias[b] (N=100)
In favor of relocation[a]			
Yes, because it is urbanized there, the houses are better, and they will be legally ours.	24	14	23
Yes, because the atmosphere is better.	8	7	5
Total favoring relocation	32	21	28
No opinion			
If it's obligatory you have to go, there's no use having an opinion if it's a government order.	6	1	5
Against relocation			
No, because I've become accustomed to where I am, I have everything here that I like and need including my friends and relatives.	6	21	30
No, because it will simply become an urbanized favela worse than this one; and without any of the activity or diversity.	2	4	4
No, because you have to pay rent.	5	8	10
No, because there are no schools, hospitals, stores, churches, and other conveniences.	3	7	5
No, because it's too far from work and transportation is too expensive and inconvenient.	47	38	18
Total against relocation	63	78	67
Total	100	100	100

[a]The actual question was: "Would you like to leave here to live in Cidade de Deus, Vila Kennedy, Cordivil, etc.? Why? or Why not?"

[b]This refers only to the 100 favelados of Caxias; homeowners in the five neighborhoods were *not* asked the question.

TABLE 32

Relationship Between Housing Quality and Attitude to Relocation

Housing Quality	Percent Wanting to Relocate	Percent Not Wanting to Relocate	Number
Poor	33	67	231
Good	23	77	216

TABLE 33

Relationship Between Community Integration and
Attitude to Relocation

Community Integration[a]	Percent Wanting to Relocate	Percent Not Wanting to Relocate	Number
Not integrated	34	66	102
Somewhat integrated	28	72	223
Very integrated	23	77	141

[a]Index of integration includes the location of friends and family, the frequency of visiting them, to whom they go in times of need, and their feelings about the unity of their community.

the standard of water, sewage, electrical, and bathroom services) are more likely to be against relocation than those with housing of lower quality (see Table 32). Further, residents who are more highly integrated into the favela show a greater reluctance to leave than those who are less integrated (see Table 33).[b]

While there are obviously many features of favela life which could be improved, the data indicate that from the point of view of the favelados, the advantages of favela life far outweigh the disadvantages of removal to publicly provided housing.[4]

GOVERNMENT POLICY TOWARD THE FAVELA

From the government's point of view, however, the favelas have always been seen as the *problem* rather than the *solution*. From the very first appearance of favelas in the 1930s and early 1940s, official policy

[b]Although good housing quality and high level of integration correlate with opposition to removal, other potential factors, such as income level and the exact amount of time presently traveled to work, did *not* show significant relationships.

has been ill-disguised repression of migrants, and prevention of favela improvement or expansion.

Motivations underlying these policies are complex and difficult to isolate. Both "do-goodism" and calculating self-interest have been involved. Although the motives of church agencies and real estate brokers are relatively easy to discuss, those of politicians attempting to respond to multiple interests on the matter are inevitably less easily categorized. Some have no doubt believed that the "humanistic" policy was to save the "poor dears" (*pobre coitados*) from their squalid existence by giving them a chance to live a decent life in a healthy atmosphere. On the other hand, the fight for turf, the crude economic interests, and the desire to preserve the city as the citadel of the privileged—keeping out the "riff-raff" along with their unsightly settlements—undoubtedly played a large role as well.

Even under Vargas, the erstwhile hero of the underclass, there was an official call to eradicate the favelas in the *Código do Obras* of 1937.[5] The Brazilian "red scare," beginning in 1947 when the National Communist Party won its first big vote, added a new dimension to fear of the favela. An imagined threat to the entire political and social order capped the upper sector's traditional abhorrence of visible poverty and the fundamental affront that squatting represents to the ethic of private property.

In 1947 an official Commission for the Eradication of the Favelas was created. Its intent, according to Mendes de Morais, who helped establish its policies, included "returning favela residents to their states of origin, committing favela residents over the age of 60 to State Institutions, and expelling from the favela all families whose incomes exceeded a set minimum."[6]

The main reason these measures were not fully implemented was lack of sufficient power and resources to do so. Official policy toward the favelas was humanized only briefly, from 1960 to 1962, when José Artur Rios was the Director of Guanabara's Coordinated Social Services. Most of the Residents' Associations were created with strong encouragement from the government during that time—71 new associations in 1961 alone. In 1962 Rios was removed by Carlos Lacerda, then Governor of Guanabara, thus ending the only period of open dialogue between the favelados and the government.

Although official opposition to squatters has existed throughout Brazilian history, only since the military takeover in 1964 has the government had the power, centralization, and resources to implement full-scale eradication. The main body through which the government has channeled this power is the National Housing Bank (BNH). It was created in August 1964 to "direct, discipline, and control the financing of a housing system aimed at promoting home ownership for Brazilian families, especially among low income groups."[7]

Financing for the National Housing Bank comes equally from two sources—one forced and one voluntary. The first is the Guaranteed Employment Fund, a form of mandatory savings to which all employers contribute 8 percent of the wages earned by their employees.[c] The accounts may be drawn upon in times of illness, disability, unemployment, or for the purchase of a BNH house. The second is voluntary savings from the sale of housing bonds and from the savings deposited through passbook accounts (cadernetas de poupança) in the savings and loan system.[8] From these sources, BNH has control over assets estimated at approximately $1.5 billion in 1970 and $5.7 billion in 1973, roughly 5 to 6 percent of the gross domestic product. This is expected to double in the period 1974-1976, reaching $10 billion, which will be 25 percent of the total investment in the Brazilian economy.[9] In applying its resources the bank uses, according to its own account, the following list of priorities: (a) the building of housing projects aimed at eradicating shanty-towns and other subhuman dwellings; (b) state or municipal projects which through the use of sites already provided with basic facilities could permit the immediate start of construction; (c) cooperative projects and other forms of association aimed at promoting home ownership among its members; (d) private projects that may help solve the housing problem; and (e) home building in rural areas.[10]

The BNH acts through various state agencies to finance housing construction according to the economic level of the housing. The agency concerned with housing low income families (those earning from one to three minimum salaries) is COHAB, which is responsible for the planning, building, and administration of low cost housing.[d] Funds for this are lent by BNH, to be repaid later by the monthly payments of purchasers of COHAB housing. For families in the next income level (three to six minimum salaries) the same function is performed by the cooperatives. For the upper-income brackets, the savings and loan associations perform this function.

In the case of Rio, a special agency, CHISAM, was created in 1968

---

[c]This is the FGTS, or Fundo de Guarantia de Tempo de Serviço.
[d]COHAB, or Companhia de Habitação Popular (Company of Popular Housing).

specifically to deal with the lack of coordination that existed between the
COHABs of the states of Guanabara and Rio.[e] CHISAM was charged with
ensuring that there would be "no more people living in the slums of Rio
de Janeiro by 1976.[11] Although CHISAM could choose to upgrade and
urbanize favelas or remove them, it concentrated only on removal. With
funding from the National Housing Bank, COHAB began a massive building program in Rio which allowed CHISAM to begin eradicating favelas in
earnest. It set itself the goal of removing 100 families a day. By the
summer of 1973, CHISAM had destroyed a total of 62 favelas or parts of
favelas, and moved 35,157 families (comprised of 175,785 people) into
public housing projects.[12] According to income level, families were sent
to five-story walk-up apartment blocks, minimal "core" houses, or—in
the poorest cases—into provisional housing, called *triagem*. Plates 15
and 16 are taken from CHISAM's report.

CHISAM's public rationale for this massive removal effort was that
human "recuperation" would follow physical rehabilitation (along the
lines of the ecological school of marginality outlined in Chapter Four).
One of its major publications states that the slum-dweller is "seen by the
community as an outsider because of his barraco."[13] CHISAM never
acknowledged that the threat of favela removal is in itself a strong disincentive for upgrading either housing or infrastructure, or that the lack
of services is due at least as much to the refusal of urban authorities to
supply them as to the physical and technical difficulties.

Using a simplistic model of environmental determinism, CHISAM
and BNH justified removal as integrating the favelado into society: "The
first objective is the economic, social, moral, and hygienic reclaiming of
the slum families. Likewise, the program aims at changing the slum-
dwelling family's position as squatters on other people's property with
all of the insecurity that goes with it, to that of owners of their own home.
These families then become completely integrated in the community,
especially in the way that they live and think."[14]

They also concede that the program benefits the larger society. One
frequent justification, for example, is concerned with beauty and
rational urban planning. As an American university professor once
commented to me upon returning from Rio, "The favelas are like syphil-
itic sores marring the body of a beautiful woman." In CHISAM's words,

[e]CHISAM stands for Coordenação de Habitação de Interesse Social da Area Metropolitana do Grande Rio (Coordination of Social Interest Housing of the Greater Rio
Metropolitan Area).

PLATES 15 AND 16.   Public Housing in Rio. These pictures, taken from CHISAM's official report show their best examples of the apartment blocks and core houses that are the relocation sites for former favelados. In contrast to the spontaneity and individuality of the favela dwellings as shown in plates 3 to 5 and 10 to 12, they are lifeless and monotonous at best.

"The urban landscape, at present marred by conglomerations of sub-dwellings, would be reclaimed by replacing the shacks with worthy housing, public works, and parks."[15]

Undoubtedly, however, one of the strongest motivations for favela removal is freeing the valuable inner-city land for more "profitable" uses, such as hotels or high-rise apartment buildings. Also, new housing provides a boost for the private construction industry: legislation founding the National Housing Bank, enacted shortly after the military coup in 1964, stated that one of the major aspects of the new government's housing policy would be "stimulus to the activities of the private sector."

The creation of BNH with its vast sources of funds for the improvement of housing in Brazil was lauded by the United Nations Committee on Housing, Building, and Planning as "the most advanced system of housing finance in Latin America at the present time."[16] In the first eight years of its operations, from 1964 until the end of 1972, a total of 875,000 housing units had been financed by the bank throughout Brazil, providing a considerable stimulus to the construction industry, to employment, and hence to Brazil's economic development. The cost of relocation from favelas was $80 to $100 million, and it was estimated that the entire project would cost $350 million. Theoretically, this cost was to have been borne at least in part by the former favelados as they paid off the cost of their new apartments or houses. Thus far, however, the default rates are startingly high, so the removal has not paid for itself. Worse still, the social-welfare goal of creating housing for low-income groups has not been achieved and a disproportionate share of the resources has been used to benefit others. As Clark Reynolds and Robert Carpenter conclude, "Our study indicates that the majority of funds in the program to date is used to finance middle and upper income housing, other urban construction, and works of infrastructure, rather than subsidizing housing for the poor, and that this trend has been increasing."[17]

The first reason for the failure of the bank to create better housing conditions for the low income groups is that the bank is interested in profits to increase the future supply of housing finances. It therefore has a strong disincentive to provide low-interest funding for low-income housing. While it is increasingly becoming a source of funds for middle-income and upper-income housing, BNH draws 80 percent of its capital from the working class through the guaranteed employment fund and from the savings of low-income workers.[18] The second reason for the failure is that the housing which has been financed by BNH for low-income people has been built in such a way that it actually *decreases* the welfare of those forced to live there after being driven from their homes.

Both BNH and CHISAM have been rather insensitive to the needs of the favelados; they have instead served their own interests as a bank and a removal agency respectively, and have provided benefits mainly to already privileged groups. As expressed by the Leeds: "The creation of CHISAM . . . reflects an institutionalization on a national level of economic and social policies and an ideology operating to intensify control by the elites, to serve their economic and political interests, to concentrate wealth in fewer hands—and to control and repress any agent seeking to prevent these developments. Favela policy is a mirror of all these institutionalizations, operations, controllings, and repressions; in the Rio area, CHISAM is the agent of the national hierarchy as the BNH is for the country at large."[19]

RESISTANCE TO REMOVAL

With the threat of mass favela eradication and forced removal to housing projects constantly hanging over them, the Residents' Associations in several favelas joined to form FAFEG (the Federation of Favela Associations in Guanabara) in March 1963.[f] The aim of FAFEG was to represent the interests of all favelados, to make known their reasons for opposing eradication, to take a strong political stance on the issue, and at the same time to help organize the favela dwellers for mutual aid.[20] The first action of FAFEG members to receive public attention was their support of the residents of the Morro do Pasmado favela in resisting removal in 1964. As reported in newspapers at the time, this resistance was met by soldiers armed with machine guns, who forced the residents to abandon their homes.[21]

In the following year, 1965, strong political opposition to removal was demonstrated electorally in the gubernatorial race. Lacerda, the Governor of Guanabara until 1965 and a committed supporter of favela eradication, put forward his son-in-law, Flexa Ribeiro, as a candidate. Ribeiro was defeated, largely by the votes of the working-class districts including favelas and relocated favelados. As the *Jornal do Brasil* reported:

[f]Federação das Associações de Favelas do Estado da Guanabara.

At the closing of yesterday's work (in tallying up the votes) in Maracanã, the *urnas* of Vilas Kennedy, Aliance, and Jacqueline totaled 4,734 votes for Negrão de Lima and only 408 for Flexa Ribeiro. . . . The population of the three vilas was brutally transferred from Botafogo last year, against the will of the majority of families. ["A Resposta de Vila Kennedy," April 14, 1965.]

All those who had lived in the favela Pasmado, and had been moved to Vila Kennedy, had to return to vote in *urn* #128 of the Third Electoral District of Botafogo. It was in this district that Lacerda's candidate supposedly had the best chance of winning, but he was totally crushed—getting only 12 votes out of the entire *urn*. . . . Thus, Vila Kennedy is not the golden dream of the favelado. ["Por Que Os Favelados de Vila Kennedy Derrotaram Carlos Lacerda," April 16, 1965.]

In another issue, an unnamed editor wrote an "Ode to the Vila Kennedy Urn," recreating in the style of Keats the entire story of the forced displacement of the favelados and how secret elections had given them one chance to reveal their true feelings. The verse powerfully suggests the direction that spontaneous political action would take if it were freed from the shackles of official restraint.

Official restraint continued, however. On May 25, 1966, in Favela Jardim America, the police arrived at 7 A.M. to confront about 2,000 terrified individuals, many of them children, who had received word on the previous day that their homes were to be eradicated. To speed up the process and discourage any possible "protest" or "revolt," gunshots were fired randomly into the crowd, and those who seemed to resist were beaten.[22]

Then, in 1968, just after the creation of CHISAM, FAFEG (which by then had about 100 member favelas) held a congress which resolved to forcefully oppose the government's policy of eradication. The official report of the congress explicitly stated the FAFEG position as the "rejection of any removal, and the condemnation of the human and financial waste and of the social problems resulting from removal."[23] In accordance with their position, FAFEG immediately mobilized to prevent action against the very first favela CHISAM had designated for removal—Ilha das Dragas, on the other side of the lagoon from Catacumba. Almost immediately afterward, the FAFEG leaders were arrested by police, held incommunicado for days, and threatened with severe consequences if there should be any further attempt at opposition.[24] From then on, open protest by FAFEG was effectively ended.

The following year, however, the 7,000 residents of Praia do Pinto (a favela situated on a choice piece of level terrain in the middle of the upper-class neighborhood of Leblon as shown in Figure 2) refused—on their own initiative—to evacuate the favela and be relocated. During that night, the favela "accidentally" caught fire, and although many alarmed residents and neighbors called the fire department, orders had evidently been issued that no help was to come. By morning almost everything had been destroyed. Most families were unable to salvage the few meager possessions they had, and the leaders of the "passive resist-ance" disappeared altogether, leaving their families in desperation (see Plates 17, 18 and 19). Subsidized high-rise housing for the military was constructed in its place (see Plate 20).

This contrasts dramatically with the experiences many favelas had during the pre-coup period. Nova Brasília, for example, had been threatened with removal in 1962, and had proceeded, through its Resi-dents' Association, to rent eight buses, pack them with every man, woman, child, chicken, and pig in the favela, and stage a sit-in on the steps of the Governor's Palace. They also notified the major radio, tele-vision, and newspaper reporters and then presented the Governor with a petition demanding that they be allowed to stay on their territory. Since at that time elections were still held, the Governor was unwilling to alienate the hundreds of thousands of squatters in the city and signed the petition.[8]

With the end of most direct elections after the coup, the squatters lost the major bargaining power they had. The centralization of housing policy and authority through the National Housing Bank, COHAB, and CHISAM included the power to use the armed forces for implementing programs, and changed the situation entirely. The fact that the favelados recognize their increased vulnerability and powerlessness was clearly demonstrated in many ways.

At the time of the initial study in 1968-1969, most of the favelados interviewed had been confronted with threats of removal at one time or another and had struggled and bargained in an attempt to preserve their

[8]In a similar manner, the squatters were able to use their numbers for bargaining power at election time. When a candidate came around to campaign, the leaders of the Residents' Association would promise all of the favelas' votes if he would provide water pipes. Then he would tell the next contender that so-and-so had promised to supply water pipes, but if *he* would supply water pipes and cement for stairways as well, the favela's votes would go to him. Furthermore, they were astute enough at this bargaining procedure to say that they distrust politicians' promises and that they wanted the "goods" delivered *before* the election.

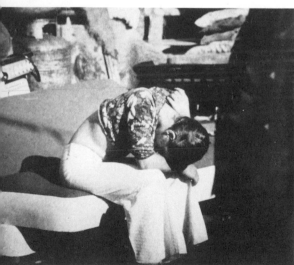

PLATES 17, 18, AND 19.   The Burning of Praia do Pinto, 1969. After residents
refused to leave, the favela was burned to the ground. These scenes are from the
following morning as people, despairing at the disaster, tried to salvage what they
could of their meager possessions or to seek relatives lost in the chaos. Police
piled people into garbage trucks and hauled them off to the outskirts of the city.

PLATE 20.   Site of Praia do Pinto, 1973. Subsidized high-rises for military personnel covers the site of the 1969 fire. Locally called "selva do pedra" or jungle of stone these buildings clash with the architectural style and diversity of the surrounding area. They are both more dense and more visually obtrusive than the favela had been.

existence. The threat was always more immediate in the South Zone than in the North, and was felt least of all in the Baixada Fluminense, following decreasing land values. In Catacumba, 81 percent of residents were aware that the favela had been threatened with removal, contrasted with only 52 percent in Nova Brasília and 32 percent in Caxias.

Two parallel, open-ended questions were asked at separate points in the interview, one regarding what was done in response to the past removal incident, the other what would be done in a similar situation today. Table 34 shows the responses for the random samples from Catacumba, Nova Brasília, the three favelas of Caxias, and for the leaders as

TABLE 34

Past and Present Responses to Removal Threats, in Percentages[a]

Type of Response	Catacumba (N=200)		Nova Brasília (N=200)		Favelas of Caxias (N=100)		Combined Leaders (N=150)	
	Then	Now	Then	Now	Then	Now	Then	Now
I. Active responses:								
Got all the residents together and protested, made up a petition, etc.	12	5	7	5	2	3	21	4
Went to the government and asked for intervention	17	16	21	17	8	17	40	18
Solved the problem through the "pull" (*pistalao*) of an influential friend	6	0	5	1	2	3	19	1
Total active	35	21	33	23	12	23	80	23
II. Passive responses:								
Did nothing due to lack of access to the government	16	11	9	10	14	15	9	14
Collaborated with the government	0	29	0	11	0	12	0	25
Don't know	39	29	57	51	64	46	8	31
Total passive	65	79	69	77	90	77	20	78

[a]Two questions were asked. (1) *Then:* What did the residents do when the favela was threatened with removal in the past? (2) *Now:* What do you think could be done *now* concerning the problem of removal?

a group. In each case, I have compared the responses to the question about past actions to those about contemplated future action, and divided responses into two general categories—active and passive responses.

While the modal response in each of the three places is a cautious "don't know," the main, systematic differences between responses referring to the past and those concerning the future is a general decrease in responses mentioning active, protest measures, especially the use of "pull" (*pistolão*), and an enormous increase in the proportion saying they would "collaborate with the government." This response did not even appear in the first set of responses, yet in relation to what would be done today it was the answer of 30 percent in Catacumba, and 10 percent in Nova Brasília and Caxias. The intensification of repression is evident in the decrease of active opposition measures and the large increase in the proportions spontaneously indicating they would collaborate were removal to become a reality.

Trends are even more visible among leaders, whose behavior is subject to closer scrutiny from above. Regarding past efforts, leaders appear to have been far more active than the residents at large, but all active responses declined substantially in this group from past to present: mobilizing collective protest from 21 percent to 4 percent, seeking governmental intervention from 40 percent to 10 percent, and using client-patron relationships from 19 percent to 1 percent. Concomitantly, all "passive" responses doubled, "don't knows" tripled, and "collaborate" responses moved from zero to the preferred alternative of a fourth of the sample.

RESULTS OF RELOCATION

According to CHISAM, the process of removing a favela is a very smooth operation. [25] The first notification about removal comes via public news media, later followed by official communication with the Residents' Association. Interviewers arrive in the favela seeking information on family size, income, and location of workplace. This survey forms the basis for the allocation of new housing units. Information about the new housing is made available and the favelados are invited to visit the projects. A few days before being removed, each family is told when it will leave and where it will be taken. On the morning of removal each family loads its possessions onto trucks, leaving behind all building materials, which are to be destroyed rather than risk their re-use in a future favela home. In CHISAM's words, when the moving trucks arrive: "He [the favelado] and his family show joy and confidence. This attitude on the auspicious start of a new life marks the moving from the slum to the Coordination offices apartment." [26] CHISAM aimed at moving 100 families each day in order to "empty" the favelas, destroy the houses and infrastructure, and hand over the cleared land as rapidly as possible to be developed for new uses.

When I returned in 1973, evidence indicated that the removal

program had been carried out in an impersonal, arbitrary, and bureaucratic manner which degraded the favelados and helped guarantee the
failure of the program. From direct conversations with some of the favelados who had been removed by CHISAM, a very different account of the
removal process emerged. Most people complained that although there
were several project types available, ranging from houses to apartments
and from no bedrooms to three, the choice was made by CHISAM and
forced upon the families without consulting them. No preparation was
offered, no meetings held, no information was available as to the total
cost and time-period involved; those few who were taken to visit new
housing projects were disappointed and angry because the places to
which they were finally sent were quite inferior to those they had been
shown. A notice would arrive a day before removal telling the family to
pack its possessions and be ready at dawn the following day for removal
to an unspecified destination.

When the families arrived at the project, they were assigned an
apartment or house (without regard to location near friends or relatives)
and keys were distributed which turned out to be the same for the entire
building. With the loss of home and community still fresh in their
minds, and with the feeling of having been cheated by the removal
agency, favela families began life in their new housing environment and
began to experience some of the consequences of their removal. The
present case reinforces a growing body of findings from Brazil and other
developing countries which have documented widespread dissatisfaction with such relocation efforts and devastating economic, social,
cultural, political, and physical repercussions.[27]

ECONOMIC REPERCUSSIONS

These fall into three categories: those relating to the time and
expense of travel to work; those relating to the changed availability of
jobs, especially biscate and jobs for women; and those relating to the
need to make monthly payments of the mortgage for the housing.

A consistent finding of relocation studies in Brazil and elsewhere is
that the time taken by the journey to work for the ex-squatter increases
significantly and causes severe hardship. Low-income people, who can
ill afford the cost of transportation, generally locate by preference close
to their labor market near the city center.[28] Relocation areas, however,
tend to be placed on the outskirts of the city where land is relatively
cheap. The first effect of removal, then, is a long and expensive journey
to work on a usually unreliable transportation system. The existing

intraurban lines by 1974 were having 700,000 passengers a day in crowded, unreliable, and dangerous coaches.[29]

In his 1966 study of Vila Kennedy, Salmen found that people travelling to the Center of Rio would have to travel two hours each way and spend about one-third of the minimum salary on fares. Several men reported to him that because of the unreliability of the service, they had lost their jobs for coming to work late.[30] The CENPHA study of Cidade Alta and Cidade de Deus in 1970 reported that only about 20 percent of the people took half an hour or less to go to work and that about 50 percent had to travel more than an hour and a half each way.[31] Rush found in a 1973 study of 300 people in five Rio *conjuntos* (housing projects) that before removal, 79 percent of favelados from the South Zone took less than half an hour to reach work and only 4 percent took an hour or more; after removal, fully 65 percent had to travel for over an hour each way. He also found that over half of favela families had to spend one-tenth of their income or more on transportation for the head of the household, and many spent as much as one-fourth.[32]

Apart from cost in time and in money, the isolation of the conjuntos leads to a feeling of separation from the center of urban life and activities, and to a very acute isolation from the job market. This has seriously affected working women who depend on service jobs for the upper classes such as washing clothes, sewing, or working as babysitters or maids. The pay from these jobs is barely enough to cover transportation costs, and since they can no longer be done at home, arrangements must be made for child care (which is even more difficult with the dissolution of mutual favor networks after removal). Because the conjuntos are generally located in peripheral low-value land far from wealthy families, many women are forced to give up their jobs entirely after removal. Rush found that, whereas 46 percent of women from South Zone favelas and 30 percent of women from North Zone favelas had worked before removal, only 32 percent and 20 percent from the two areas respectively were still able to work after removal.[33] And a similar decline is evidenced for children whose odd-jobs after school and on weekends were a welcomed contribution to family incomes.

The *Jornal do Brasil*, reporting the tenth year of "great failure" of Vila Kennedy, stated: "The first consequence of removal was a severe drop in family income because wives and children are located a long way from their former employment in homes and apartments and doing odd jobs in middle-class areas."[34]

For men, there is a strong tendency to continue working at the same

job, and to learn to tolerate the long daily commute. Salmen relates the
not uncommon story of men who find the cost and time of the daily
commute so burdensome that they arrange for a place to stay in the city,
returning to their families only on weekends. Eventually they stop
returning home at all, meet other women in the city and begin second
families, thus creating the social disintegration and family breakdown
they were accused of in the favela.[35]

In spite of the inconvenience of the traveling, Rush found that even
three years after removal, 60 percent of household heads retained their
former jobs, and many of those who changed jobs still worked in the
section of the city where they had formerly lived and worked. He
believes this is caused by the lack of jobs for low-skilled workers
throughout Rio, especially in the less populated areas near the
conjuntos, and by the tendency of the favelados to develop contacts only
in their own section of the city. Over half of the relocated favelados felt
that job opportunities were worse for them after removal.[36]

The possibility of finding lucrative biscate is also reduced by the
location of the conjuntos. One man I spoke to, who had found work near
his conjunto, said that "in the South Zone I would make twice as much
because there people have more money to spend—here, even the rich
are poor." Rush found that the percentage of favelado household heads
engaged in doing biscate dropped from 35 percent to 20 percent after
removal because they no longer had the time, contacts, or customers
they had before.[37]

One group whose livelihood is critically affected by removal is
favela merchants, who are almost universally bankrupted by loss of
clientele, costs of new licenses, prohibitions against using part of their
new homes for business, or exorbitant rent for new store premises. Sr.
Joya, one of the foremost merchants of Catacumba, was one of the
hardest hit. On hearing about removal, Sr. Joya united with the other
merchants to demand that they be given stores to rent in the new conjuntos with monthly payments of 65 to 95 cruzeiros. Besides not being
given any assistance in moving their stores or compensation for trade
lost during the process of removal, the merchants were provided stores
located at the back of the conjuntos, away from the main thoroughfare,
at a cost of 3,000 cruzeiros downpayment and monthly payments of 300
cruzeiros. Nobody took the new stores, which still remain empty. Most
of Catacumba's storekeepers were simply forced out of business. Sr.
Joya is still running a store, but in Ramos, not in the conjunto.

Besides the financial cost of transportation, and the income lost because of inaccessibility to jobs, the favelados must accept the loss of all their investment in their favela homes and pay a high proportion of their monthly income as mortgage repayment for their new housing. CHISAM guidelines state that monthly payments should not exceed 25 percent of the family income.[38] Considering that favela housing was virtually free and favelados still had to struggle to adequately feed and clothe their children, the demand of one-quarter of the family income is a change of disastrous dimensions. Additional charges must also be met for water, gas, and electricity, and "condominium" (an amount paid for the upkeep of the conjunto), as well as for the bus or train fares, which are indirect housing costs. In many cases, these costs are well above one-quarter of family earnings; often they are 75 to 80 percent of total family income.[h]

It has been shown in many studies that people who have been moved to projects express resentment over the payments for the new housing because they never wanted to incur the payments, because the cost keeps rising because of adjustments for inflation (monetary correction), and because the length of time for repayment of the loan is continually being extended. While expenses for food, clothes, transportation, and services cannot be delayed, inhabitants of the new housing have defaulted on their mortgages in vast numbers. In 1966, Salmen reported that Vilas Kennedy and Esperanca had 60 percent and 40 percent of their families, respectively, behind in payments,[39] and BNH figures four years later show that the same vilas have default rates of 74 percent and 85 percent.[40] For 1970, BNH figures for eight different conjuntos show an average default rate of 77 percent.[41] The Rush study found the average default rate in five conjuntos to be 74 percent, due largely to the residents' shrunken incomes and to their lack of desire to pay.[42]

Once in the position of defaulting, the inhabitants of conjuntos worry that they will soon be evicted from their new homes and be given an even less desirable home, or simply be forced to begin life again in some other favela. Some people, finding the situation intolerable, have left the conjuntos of their own accord,[43] leaving the vacant apartments and houses prone to invasion, or to takeover by moderate income

[h]To make matters worse, in attempting to be relocated in a better or closer project, many families reported their incomes as higher than they actually were, while others included income from grown children who subsequently moved into their own homes or were relocated elsewhere, and still others were counting on earnings of the wives and younger children, along with the husband's extra jobs.

families. Others have been forced to move to the "triage" houses (*casa de triagem*), long barrack-like buildings with one family per room, located even further from the center of the city. The triagem are, in effect, a type of punishment for poverty, like debtors' prison, in which the indigent is supposed to remain until he mends his ways and becomes affluent enough to move out. However, the triagem provide no opportunity for moving out.

As of September 1973, CHISAM has been dissolved and the state Secretary of Planning and Coordination along with COHAB-Guanabara had devised a new scheme for dealing with the massive defaults. They embarked on a process of *escritura* (sign-ups) by which inhabitants of the conjuntos had their former debt cancelled and were re-interviewed to assess their actual ability to pay. If the monthly mortgage payments were over 25 percent (later reduced to 18 percent) of their total income, or if they still defaulted, they would be removed immediately to triagem in Paciencia—in the Santa Cruz area, in the far western part of the State of Guanabara, as shown in Figure 2, at least twice as far away as any of the former relocation sites (see Plates 21 and 22). Arrangements were underway to construct 250,000 units there to receive both conjunto defaulters and the lower-income families from the remaining favelas as they were removed.

SOCIAL AND CULTURAL REPERCUSSIONS

The sociocultural effects of removal can best be understood in relation to the advantages of the favela as a functional community. Because individuals are scattered throughout new districts on the basis of income level rather than on the basis of their social and familial ties, the support structure of the favela does not survive relocation.

In their new setting, the favelados are separated from the urban services on which they had relied in the favelas. Shops are less convenient and more expensive, and do not provide the informal social welfare services of allowing purchases on credit or in very small quantities; and schools and medical services are often inaccessible and of lower quality. Conjunto residents are also cut off from most of the "urban use" factors which enriched their lives, gave them experience with a diverse range of peoples and institutions, and integrated them into the city at large. It was often for just such advantages that people migrated to the city in the first place. Movies, beaches, markets, spectator sports, hang-outs, even newspapers and magazines are all inaccessible, or nearly so, from the new districts. Even religious organizations

PLATES 21 AND 22.   Old and new Triagem Houses in Paciencia, at the far western part of Guanabara. The older triagem have sloped roofs which allow the construction of sleeping lofts for extra space; the newer ones have flat cement roofs not only making them smaller but creating intolerable internal heat; 250,000 of such units are being built.

are unavailable as yet in most places. In the words of Jacqueline, a young woman who had been living in a conjunto for three years: "At first I missed the beach, the lagoon, the shops, everything—I still miss them. . . . Here there is nothing to do so I'll have to get married. . . . There's no night life at all so I just watch television."

Suspicion and distrust seem to rise in some of the new districts, as does the crime rate. While this varies from place to place, aspirations remain high for a time but with decreased probabilities for fulfillment, people grow more passive, fatalistic, and resigned. Although there has been little empirical research on these issues, popular opinion is unanimous. People who live in the projects repeatedly say there is more violence there than in the favela, more street fights, more maltreatment of children, and less concern for others. They say they are afraid to go out on the streets at night, and meanwhile the government procrastinates in installing street lights.[44]

The *Jornal do Brasil*, for example, reports that the conjunto of Cruzada São Sebastião is "considered to be a center of delinquency" and that some of its residents who think of themselves as upright and moral are resentful of the "marginal element" who also lives there.[45] Whether or not the crime rate in conjuntos is actually higher than in the favelas remains to be documented. However, the widespread feeling of residents attests to their own unease in living in that environment, and it seems likely that high unemployment, difficult living circumstances, and lack of recreational outlets contribute to antisocial expressions of inner frustration.

In this atmosphere of distrust and lack of satisfaction with the housing conditions, the organization of communal activities—such as sports associations, youth clubs, samba schools, and even church groups—seems doomed to failure. In the words of a three-year resident of a conjunto: "Here I know my neighbors by name but we are not friends—my old friends are far away. . . . Here we don't have any more outings like taking the ferry to Paquetá, making picnics, or going to the beach. Everyone stays to themselves. There's no youth athletic club, no more soccer teams, no more samba or Carnival here. They once showed two films, and never again. . . . There's no meeting of people together—each one looks on their own."

POLITICAL REPERCUSSIONS

The political consequences of removal follow a similar trend. The local favela leaders, who initially formed Residents' Associations for the specific purpose of fighting against removal and coordinating efforts toward favela improvement, were the first to be removed and most have either disappeared or been sent to housing projects distant from one another and their constituencies. Those who have tried to create new Residents' Associations or organizations find apathy and distrust among their neighbors, and such great overall fear and despair that it is impossible even to get people to come to a meeting.

Sr. Souza, founder of SOMAC (the Residents' Association in Catacumba), lived for 22 years in Catacumba until being moved to the Quitungo conjunto in 1970. He admitted that even though nobody wanted to leave the favela, he and other SOMAC leaders eventually were co-opted into helping the government carry out the removal. They distributed evacuation notices and helped with the house-to-house census. He said that SOMAC couldn't fight the state order, and in any case there was always a government agent in the organization. Souza tried to set up an association of residents when he got to Quitungo; he even registered the association and worked out a written constitution for it. However, hardly anyone came to the meetings. Even within his own building, he said, the people wouldn't get together. "We're totally abandoned here—no one has the energy to try to better the situation. Here it's difficult to get together, not like in the favela where everyone was used to working with each other." In addition, there were some misunderstandings within the leadership over whether or not the directors should be paid, and then the people would not join for fear that their money would go into the pockets of the directors.

The one time when the people did join together to protest was over an unprecedented and dramatic rise in their housing installment payments. All the residents of Quitungo signed a petition which a delegation presented at the Governor's Palace. But nothing ever came of it.

The other kinds of political involvement which link the favela to the larger system suffered as well. The process of gerrymandering the new settlements out of independent representation is already under way. Now that the "dangerous elements" are concentrated in isolated districts, all-important local officials are appointed, not elected. Direct-action politics such as petitioning and demonstrating have diminished, partly because of reduced access to authorities and partly because of increased fear of repression. In addition, the implicit threat of violence to the upper classes is less real now with the favelados removed to distant locales. They can no longer play upon the fear of those in the city that they would—if pushed too far—*descer do morro* (come down from the hills) to loot and riot.

Finally, the most immediately detrimental political consequence of removal has been the disruption of administrative political activity. In the absence of effective action on the favela's behalf by interest groups, it has always been possible for the favelados to pursue their interests on their own through the labyrinthine bureaucracy of government. Although they have never been highly successful in these efforts, the potential of such action is even further reduced in the relocated settlements. Of major importance is the sheer physical difficulty of getting to agencies in the center of the city. The traditional bureaucratic "run around" is even more devastating when sandwiched between long, expensive trips to and from home.

These factors may have serious effects on the favelados' political orientation. All of our indicators of conformism were positively related to socioeconomic status and power within the system—that is, to the degree of integration. It is reasonable to expect, therefore, that if this integration is seriously disrupted, increasing disaffection from the system might be the result. It is my impression that this is going on. The normally optimistic favelados—perhaps "defensively optimistic in times of stress"—are now voicing strong discontent with their situation, and for the first time their anger is linked directly to actions the government imposed on them. After their experience of removal, it is no longer so easy to see the system as benign.

PHYSICAL REPERCUSSIONS

While the economic, social, and political ramifications of removal have tended to be mostly negative, the physical effects of the new housing have been mixed. Water, bathrooms, and sewage services in the conjuntos are major improvements over those in the favelas, and this reportedly results in improved health of children, as well as greater convenience.[46] Electricity services are usually cheaper than in the favelas, and for some people the new housing is more spacious than where they formerly resided. There is also less fear of disastrous consequences from fire or landslide. However, despite potential gains in comfort, the poor quality of construction in the new housing is the subject of numerous complaints. In Quitungo, for instance, after only a few years the apartments are extremely run down, the walls are badly chipped, and there are constant leaks in the plumbing system, leaving all apartments damp except for those on the top floor (see Plate 23). Maintenance by COHAB is blatantly inadequate; for example, *Jornal do Brasil* reports that the Conjunto de Realango was without water for five months, and had backed up sewage drains and frequent blackouts.[47]

PLATE 23.   The Conjunto of Quitungo, 1973. It already looks old after only four
years, especially since the plumbing and water leakages stain through the walls.

Many complaints are also voiced over the spatial organization of the
new apartments and houses. They are often cramped closely together in
monotonous, simplistic rows as shown in Plate 15. The buildings themselves are identical, and the favelados miss the variety of their former
owner-built houses. In contrast to the favelas, where doors were always
open during the day, the doors of the new apartment units are always
kept closed. The layout and scale of the housing projects is not conducive to the sense of spatial and social intimacy that is so much a part of
favela life.

Finally, while the new units were intended as permanent and
secure homes owned by the favelados, the inability or unwillingness of
the residents to pay for them has made the people as insecure in the new
housing as they were in the old. In the new housing they await the day of
eviction to an even less satisfactory environment.

OVERALL OUTCOME

A consistent finding in studies of relocated families is the widespread desire to return to the favela if given the opportunity to do so. Salmen found in Vila Kennedy that 36 percent of the people would like to return to their former homes. Among the women, 49 percent wished to do so.[48] Rush found that 53 percent of his favela sample would like to return to the favelas, and that this figure rose to 70 percent when given the option of returning to an urbanized favela.[49]

CHISAM's allocation of favelados to different conjuntos on the basis of family income alone rather than a combination of economic, social, and geographical criteria is the source of many problems. As CHISAM itself recognizes, even allocating dwellings by ensuring that monthly repayments do not exceed 25 percent of the family income is precarious because the income level of favela families is variable in the unstable labor market they occupy.[50] Further, CHISAM adopted the arbitrary figure of 25 percent of income without regard to the income per capita, or the expenditures of the family for education, medical services, or for debts previously incurred. The result is a high level of incompatibility between the needs of the favela family and the home in which it is placed.[51]

Confirmation of the importance of personal choice in housing comes from both the CENPHA study and the Rush study. Each examined conjunto housing of forcibly relocated favelados and families who had sought out the apartments voluntarily. Those who had come voluntarily tended to have higher occupational status and to have higher incomes than the favelados, and were more satisfied with their housing than the favelado group.[52] Rush found that 46 percent of non-favelados kept up with their mortgage repayments, while only 26 percent of favelados were up to date.[53]

While the policy of removal has been ruinous for the favelados, the original aim of BNH to stimulate the construction industry has been partially fulfilled. In addition, the visual scars of the favelas have been removed from the landscape, especially in the elite South section of the city. However, the original intention of reinvesting the monthly mortgage payments into still further housing has had to be altered because of the massive default rates. The aim of providing housing for low-income people has also been shifting slightly as low-income people abandon the new housing because it is too expensive, leaving it open to those in a higher income bracket who are delighted with the low interest terms of BNH.[54] However, as of 1974-1975, many conjuntos had been totally abandoned and others had to be destroyed or totally remodeled to attract any population at all.[55]

The aim of integrating the favelado into middle-class life has not been achieved. Rather, alienation and despair have taken over. As Sr. Joya, the storekeeper, said, many of his friends have actually died from sadness at leaving their homes. "Everyone who had a little sickness got worse and died."[i] Using misguided notions about the favelados, the government has unwittingly been *creating* exactly the sort of marginalized, unintegrated people it wrongly presumed to reside in the squatter settlements in the first place.

THE CASE OF CATACUMBA

A clear demonstration of what favela destruction and forced relocation means for the individuals involved can be seen in the case of Catacumba. As of 1973, Catacumba was the only one of the favelas I had studied to have been eradicated, and its story illustrates well the points I have made.

THE PROCESS OF REMOVAL

As early as 1968, Waldevino, the President of the Catacuma Residents' Association, and his fellow members were so disturbed by rumors of eradication that they drew up a plan for the "urbanization" of the favela on the local site. This is shown in Figure 13.

The plan was presented to various state agencies and it appeared in the September 15, 1969, edition of *O Dia*, a Rio newspaper, bearing the caption, "The Project of Urbanization presented by the residents of Catacumba and for which they ask the attention of the authorities." It consisted of two rows of high-rise apartment buildings and a row of two-family houses on the top of the hill. The favelados hoped to build it and pay for it themselves if permitted to remain in their locations. In an accompanying article, the residents made a plea for the attention of the authorities: "There isn't a single resident of Catacumba in agreement with the possible forced move to 'Cidade de Deus' or any other place far from the site of our jobs where we work to support our families. . . . This favela can be sanitized and urbanized. We do not want alms, charity, or handouts. With the approval of the public powers, we will construct and pay for our own houses."

---

[i]I found that many people I had known and inquired after had suffered fatal illnesses, or had been in fatal bus or work accidents; this inordinate rise in fatalities is a well-known concomitant of high stress.

WALDEVINO'S PLAN FOR
THE URBANIZATION OF CATACUMBA

13. Residents' Plan for Urbanizing Catacumba. This plan appeared in the September 15, 1969 edition of *O Dia*, a Rio newspaper. The caption was "The project of urbanization presented by the residents of Catacumba and for which they ask the attention of the authorities." It shows two rows of highrise apartment buildings and a row of two family houses on the hilltop. The favelados said they would build it and pay for it themselves if permitted to remain there.

When I interviewed Waldevino in early 1968, he told me, "At the hour of removal everyone suffers, especially the old people, the very poor people, and the owners of shops and bars." He went on to say that the situation had become increasingly serious in recent times since none of the former recourses to action were open. He cited the examples of the Favela de Providencia and the Isla das Dragas and the fate of the FAFEG leaders. The Fifth Institutional Act "did not stop at the foot of the favela," he said.[j]

Our study confirmed that these threats were felt by people at large. The vast majority of residents said that although they did not want to leave, fear of reprisal would make them cooperate with government orders. Waldevino went to great lengths to describe the disadvantages of

[j]The Fifth Institutional Act, instituted on December 13, 1968, was the turning point in the government's move toward a hard-line position. It was considered "a revolution within the revolution," because of the centralization of authority and the ultimate repression of all civil liberties. It closed the National Congress and Legislative Assemblies, authorized the executive to legislate in all matters of national policy and to intervene in the states and in the municipalities, suspended individual political rights, forced many politicians to retire from public office, and mounted a series of investigations which led to imprisonment, torture, and sometimes death.

the government sponsored housing, much of it two and a half hours away. He showed me the urbanization plan for Catacumba, adding regretfully that he no longer hoped to accomplish much, since favelados were generally too apathetic and their leaders too mindful of the risk of "being sent to jail, deprived of their political rights, or even tortured." He also pointed out the paucity of channels of influence now that FAFEG had been disbanded, direct elections suspended, the state powers removed to the federal level, and the President inaccessible and probably unsympathetic to the favelados.

In August 1969, shortly after the burning of nearby Praia do Pinto and the disappearance of its leaders, the Secretary of Social Services started to organize a house-to-house census in Catacumba. It was evidently next on CHISAM's removal list. Newspapers were full of stories about plans for eradication,[56] and the people quickly learned that the purpose of the census was to determine who would be sent where: Ability to pay was to be the sole criterion of the decision. Few could believe what was happening. Many told me it would never be carried off: "They've threatened us so many times before with this same sort of thing, but we are still here." "It's just another rumor to give people something to gossip about." "There are too many of us; they could never afford to build new houses for so many families." "Just wait and see—after all this studying and everything is done, nothing will happen."

Soon, however, the situation grew serious. Groups of friends and families began to take Sunday excursions to Cidade de Deus in Jacarepaguá (two and a half hours away by unreliable public transportation), to Cidade Alta (a district of closely packed apartment buildings, distant but more accessible), and the dismal triagem where those unable to pay are sent. They returned exhausted and discouraged, saying they "didn't know what to do." An old woman told us she had never seen any of those places but she was sure she would go crazy if she had to leave Catacumba. When we asked her why she and all the others who agreed with her did not take action, she said, "If we try to defend ourselves they will say we are Communists. . . . I'm not sure what that means, but I know it's very, very bad and that they will kill me and my children if they think we are that."

Meanwhile, favela leadership in Catacumba had been completely co-opted. Waldevino, who had drawn up and presented the plan for urbanization of the area just one year before, surrendered the Residents' Association headquarters to the Social Service agents, donned the uniform of a State Guardsman, and assumed leadership of the local vigilante committee mandated to "maintain order in the favela." He and his fellow association officers, as well as many who had figured prominently in previous battles against removal, were "appointed" to positions of leadership and status by the Social Service Authorities. Leadership was thus completely denatured in a classic example of co-optation. Selznick defines the process as "absorbing new elements into the leadership or policy-determining structure of an organization as a means of averting threats to its stability or existence."[57]

The government's action in renewal was thus legitimized by local leadership, which provided the "vehicle of administrative accessibility" for the removal agencies. By September 1969, Waldevino and other leaders would no longer talk with me, saying they were "too busy with administrative duties." Indeed, they had been organized into a tight unit of control which had men on duty 24 hours a day making sure that nothing "irregular" happened in the favela. "Through these techniques of anticipatory paternalism and co-optation," says Schmitter, "newly emergent representative associations have been converted from potentially aggressive promoters of new demands . . . to protectors of already acquired special interest. . . . In short, they have been incorporated before they could learn the skills of opposition."[58]

Some families who wanted to stay together tried to combine households or move furniture between them to give the appearance of being in the same economic bracket. These attempts to *dar jeitinhos* (get around the rules) were generally discovered and controlled—the blessing of communality turning to a curse when local leadership changed sides. These leaders had been told in no uncertain terms that they were to be held personally responsible for any disturbances.

The days of actual removal were dismal ones indeed, according to Margarida (who had been born and raised in Catacumba). People were given less than 24 hours notice as to when they would have to vacate their homes, and they were not told where they would be going. Her family was all worried that it would be separated, and in fact one of her brothers, Manuel, was relocated in Nova Hollandia, while the rest of the family was sent to Quitungo. On the day of removal, she said, it was chilly and pouring rain and all her possessions got soaked while out in the open waiting for the removal trucks. Her treasured mattress, for which she had saved many years, was totally destroyed. Some of her things could not be taken down the steep hillside in all the rain, and had to be left behind. Then, too, many of her possessions were cracked and broken as they were carelessly thrown onto the trucks. To Margarida it seemed as though the reason it rained so hard was that "the skies were crying for our sorrow."

According to the newspapers, the removal of Catacumba was peaceful and orderly.[59] As reported by CHISAM:

> The press, not only Brazilian but foreign, noted the change of mentality of the people of this slum; everybody wanted to move, from the oldest inhabitant to the youngest. . . . In general, the dwellers of Catacumba had waited anxiously for the day of their moving. Only some with brick houses in better locations were contrary to leaving the place. A few did not like the idea of leaving the banks of the lagoon to live in another area, even though they knew that the new dwellings would have piped water, light, and human, livable conditions. But, after they went to the new complex, even *they* accepted the move calmly and praised the housing plan.[60]

CHISAM reportedly removed 2,158 dwellings from Catacumba. Of these, 1,420 families were sent to the newly completed conjunto of Guaporé-Quitungo, 350 to the older and cheaper housing of Cidade de Deus, 87 to Vila Kennedy, and 350 to triagem.[61]

Shortly after removal, negative reports began to appear. As the newspaper *Correio da Manhã* reported on January 21, 1971, under the heading "Not Even in Catacumba Did they Have So Many Problems:"

> They were 2,230 families occupying 98,000 square meters of the Morro do Catacumba. They did not pay rent, nor condominium, nor fees (various fees, rates and excises for land use and for urban services), nor for water which they transported in big cans on their heads. They did not pay for transportation either. Many had three jobs and still studied at night to be able to improve their lives. Then along came CHISAM and did away with the favela, promising their own homes to those who could pay monthly payments of about 100 cruzeiros [now a little over U.S. $20 per month] for 18 years. And in the first three months, the fees would be paid by the state. Now, four months having passed, the majority cannot manage to pay: aside from the monthly installment, there is the 60 cruzeiros [about $12] for light; 95 cruzeiros [about $18] for fees; 10 cruzeiros [about $2] for condominium, water, the prorated shares for building repairs, plus a number of other expenses, not to speak of transportation costs to work. Added up, it is more expensive than the rent of an average apartment located in Ipanema [an elite section of Rio's South Zone] near the beach. He who cannot pay will have to clear out, and no one can say where to. For those who manage to stay, it will be a lousy deal; the apartments are worth nothing; they lack finishing; there is no area for the children to play. The building at the Guaporé Project was built

hurriedly and is already cracked. For the residents, the only difference between the new building and the old shacks is that they no longer have to carry water. Now they have water galore: when it rains, everything is flooded, and if they wash the floor, the ceiling of the apartment below becomes a showerbath.[62]

THE HOUSING PROJECTS

When I returned to Rio in 1973, three years after the removal, I visited the projects to which the people of Catacumba had been sent (see locations in Figure 2 above). Guaporé-Quitungo, in the North Zone of the city about an hour away from downtown, consists of 2,880 apartments pressed closely together into 72 blocks. Its location can be found in Figure 2. The streets were unpaved and unlit, the complex lacked recreation areas, had no medical clinic, church, or club and no job training program. There was one elementary school for the whole conjunto, and few shops nearby. The buildings already seemed old and deteriorating and supposed play areas have become muddy dumps.

Cidade de Deus is a mixture of triagem, core houses, and five-story walkups (see Plates 24 and 25). Built over a period of several years from 1965 to 1970, it is located in Jacarepaguá (see Figure 2) even further from the center of Rio than Quitungo, and in the opposite direction so that friends and relatives are separated by almost four hours of uncomfortable bus rides. The triagem area is crowded and demoralized. Even among the residents of Cidade de Deus it is considered to be a dangerous, high-crime area. The apartments are poorly constructed and disliked by some residents for being multi-story. As one woman so poignantly told me: "Ay dona, I was born on the ground, raised from the earth, and lived my life on flat land. How do they expect me to put up with living four stories high in the sky? It just gives me goose-flesh. . . . I have to leave the apartment as much as possible." The streets of Cidade de Deus are pure mud in the rainy season, and in the dry season the whole area is covered in billowing dust. The shops which opened after many years have small stocks and charge high prices. There is a medical clinic staffed for only a few hours each week, and the one movie theater has ironically been converted into a police station.

Vila Kennedy, one of the first housing projects, was completed in 1964 and now houses 25,000 people. It is located on the extreme outskirts of the city where land is cheap, and it received help in its planning, execution, and financing ($3.5 million) from USAID.[63] The buildings have a boxy sameness, stretching as far as the eye can see on

PLATES 24 AND 25. "Cidade de Deus," the City of God, in remote Jacarepaguá, has high-rises, core houses, and triagem as shown in the aerial photo (Pl. 24) and seen from closer-up (Pl. 25). People dread going there because it is so far removed from the city and access is so difficult.

the flat and barren land. During the first years after construction, it lacked many of the urban services, and the residents suffered from the effects of isolation and poor transportation. However, there has been a considerable change-over in tenancy over the ten-year life of the project, so that many of the current residents are self-selected. Many homes have been improved, painted, and landscaped, and as the city has expanded, the location has become relatively less remote. Nevertheless, on the occasion of its tenth anniversary, the *Jornal do Brasil* carried a telling article entitled "Vila Kennedy Celebrates Ten Years of Great Failure."[64]

THE CONSEQUENCES FOR CATACUMBANS

Comparisons between the data from Catacumba in 1968-1969, my own post-removal follow-up, and the Rush study further illuminate the effects of relocation. My original study had shown that the vast majority of Catacumba residents (79 percent) took only a half hour or less to arrive at their jobs. Follow-up studies in the relocation projects found that only 13 percent had this ease of access, while almost three-fourths (71 percent) traveled over an hour each way. Apart from the waste of time, an obvious concomitant to these long journeys is the increased cost: 64 percent of former Catacumbans now pay two cruzeiros or more for transportation each way, and more than half are required to pay 10 percent or more of the total family income on transportation for the head of household alone.

Part of the reason for the increased time and cost of travel is that three years after relocation, 59 percent of the people from Catacumba still work either in Rio's South Zone or in the city center. They are tied to that area of the labor market where they have lived and developed contacts over many years. Compounding this problem is the general difficulty of finding any job in the competitive Rio economy. BNH and COHAB had assumed an open and flexible job market whereby the favelados could quickly find new jobs nearer to their homes. Quite to the contrary, the 1973 Rush study found that most people believed job opportunities in the new area to be worse than before, and that the number of people doing odd jobs and the number of working wives dropped considerably.

The 1973 study also revealed that for about one-third of the people, the conjunto seemed a less united community than the favela. For example, residents found that they spoke with their neighbors less often. Both Margarida and Geraldo, lifelong Catacumbans, were among those who felt their old community had broken up entirely. "Only the children manage to make new friends," they said, "while the adults stick with the few people they know from before. People don't care about the place the way they used to. When a kid breaks something now, it stays broken."

One of the clearest manifestations of the unsuitability of the conjuntos for the people of Catacumba is the high default rate. Only 20 percent of the people from Catacumba were up to date with their mortgage payments, and at least 46 percent were more than six months behind. Many people, faced with severely reduced incomes and higher expenses caused by the move, had a choice between feeding their families or making their payment. Although they feared reprisal and dreaded being expelled to the triagem, they had no choice but to default.

Margarida said, "I got very angry at the government. . . . I had real hatred and rage for them because of their badness. There are people here who can't even earn one minimum salary—they can't even manage to feed themselves. How are they going to pay 300 cruzeiros a month for an apartment? Her husband, Geraldo, was bitter because they were never told how much the apartment would really cost, or how long the payment would continue before they owned it. For the first three months they were paying 140 contos per month. After that, they were informed every few months of an increase in payments, until at the time I saw them they were paying nearly twice the original amount plus payments for water, sewage, electricity, and condominium.

Geraldo said that he wouldn't mind paying for the apartment at the original price. "If we came here and it was nice, we'd even go hungry to pay the installments." He was willing to pay the originally quoted price of 140 contos per month for 15 years, but they have now been told they will have to pay a total of 60,000 contos even though they know the apartments only cost half that much. Geraldo has found the current price impossible on his salary, for which he works twelve hours a day.[k] He believes the buildings are constructed so cheaply that they will fall down within 15 years: "They used more sand than cement. If you knock

[k]Although monetary correction is supposed to correct for inflation by keeping pace with rises in the minimum salary, in fact there are significant lags in salary scales, especially at this level. Also, while monetary correction applies to the FGTS and savings and loans, it does not have direct and immediate effects on the conjunto residents (most of whom have no passbook accounts and receive their pensions much later), as opposed to the continual rise in housing payments which affects them both directly and immediately.

hard on the wall, it falls in. The people have to plaster over the walls if they want to preserve them. Also, the plastic water and sewage pipes are always leaking. When they break, each family is taxed to fix them."

Geraldo estimated that it would cost about 5,000 cruzeiros to get the apartment into "decent living condition." The 1973 study found that 69 percent of the people said their apartments required major repairs. Geraldo also wanted to know what assurance he had that he wouldn't be removed from his new home—just as he was removed from Catacumba—if land values rose before all his payments were made.

For Felix, a Catacumban relocated in Quitungo, the move was a total economic and personal disaster.[65] The increased cost of transportation and distance from work made it impossible for Felix's wife to work and take care of the children as well. Felix is trying to compensate for the loss of her income by working the equivalent of two full-time jobs— his regular one at a bakery, and an informal job selling refreshments on the beach. He is home only a few hours a day.

Even with all this effort, Felix's family faces an impossible financial situation. With a total income of about 700 cruzeiros per month (U.S. $120), Felix faces expenses of 500 cruzeiros for food, plus substantial transportation, clothing, and home repair costs. He has had little choice but to default on the payments for the apartment, and had paid nothing for the last 18 months. Whatever money Felix can manage to save is now kept for the expected eviction of his family by COHAB, the administrator of the conjunto.

Strong overall dissatisfaction with the conjunto is evident from the response of the people of Catacumba to a question on whether if given the opportunity they would choose to remain in the conjunto or return to their former homes. Sixty-nine percent answered that they would return to the favela. This figure increased to an overwhelming 82 percent for the opportunity to choose between the conjunto and an urbanized favela. Common opinions expressed by the former Catacumbans were: "I'd go back and build a new shack the same day if they'd let me"; "if I could go to any favela in the South Zone, I would"; "we were fooled—they told us that we'd come to beautiful places with direct and cheap transportation, and that the payments would be minimal"; "they only removed the favelas so that the rich could earn more money."

The official justifications for the removal of the Catacumbans and the destruction of their homes were put forward in 1972 by the State Secretary of General Planning and Coordination (*Secretaria de Planajamento e Coordinação Geral do Estado da Guanabara*). The report cited the "unstability of the soil and pollution of the nearby Rodrigo Freitas lagoon."[66] CHISAM further stated that a tunnel through the Catacumba hill was planned to connect the lagoon area with the Botofogo district, facilitating the commute of businessmen to their offices.[67]

The favela's removal, however, unleashed such bitter legal disputes over land ownership that absolutely no action could be taken to begin *any* project. As of 1973, the uninhabited hills were overgrown with vegetation. Enormous billboards advertising Kodak cameras, Ben-Gay, automatic dishwasher detergents, and American cosmetics surround the area, bordered with barbed wire to keep out potential squatters (see Plate 26).

For the former residents of Catacumba, this is a source of immense bitterness. They said they would have accepted leaving their homes if the hill had really been put to good use for public benefit. But seeing it deserted and grown over makes them feel like "crying with pain" at the needless loss of their homes and community.

By 1974-1975, building had begun on luxury high-rise apartments which were to sell for as much as $125,000 each, and land values in the area were reportedly up to $300 per square meter.[68]

ALTERNATIVES AND PROSPECTS FOR THE FUTURE

We have shown that the Rio housing experience, which was the first and most massive housing program in Brazil, has been a disaster in almost every way. By comparison, when I revisited those favelas that had been left to develop on their own, striking dynamism, progress, and good spirits were in evidence. I reexamined the favela of Nova Brasília and the favelas in Duque de Caxias with particular attention to see how they had changed over the four years since I had conducted my original studies.

Nova Brasília showed a tremendous amount of improvement. There were many more two-story houses; almost all construction had been transformed into brick; a new school had been built; the central plaza had been leveled and covered with asphalt; the principal internal roads had been paved; concrete steps put in; sewage, water, and electrical services extended to reach almost all the population; medical, dental and optical care was available inside the favela; and internal commerce had quadrupled (see Plates 27-31). There was an impressive feeling of vitality and productivity, mitigated only by the ever present fear and uncertainty about removal.

Unfortunately, unless there is an unexpected change in policy,

PLATE 26.   Former site of Catacumba, 1973. The uninhabited hillside had become overgrown with vegetation in the four years since the favela's removal. Billboards advertising luxury products for the rich and laced with barbed wire are used to keep potential squatters from returning.

Nova Brasília will soon go the way of Catacumba. From what I could ascertain, it has been slated for removal, since its name did not appear on the list of favelas that were under study for urbanization or already being urbanized.

The favelas of Duque de Caxias had also shown incredible improvement over the intervening four years. There were many more brick houses, several new schools, more stores and services of all sorts, and new public lighting on the streets. The various Residents' Associations had made plans to pave internal streets and were considering a number of long-term improvement projects. Most of the people I had known were still there. They had no wish to incur rents or be separated from their

PLATE 27.   Leaders of Nova Brasília Residents' Association supervise the asphalting of the Praça do Terço. Sr. Levi (front left) and Sr. Francisco (front right) are two of the major figures involved in organizing this effort.

communities even if they were able to move out, and they were eager to show me all of the improvements they had made. Likewise, the neighborhoods I had studied were gradually becoming more developed and better provided for.

The Codesco Solution. The one group of favelas that had fared even better over the years of my absence was the group that had been legalized and urbanized on the site.[69] This is a major alternative to that of eradication. In Rio itself a number of experimental favela urbanization projects had been tried and were flourishing.

Only a few months before the National Housing Bank set up CHISAM to eradicate Rio's favelas, the state government of Guanabara authorized a group of young architects, planners, economists, and sociologists to form an organization called CODESCO (Companhia de Desenvolvimento de Communidades). It was charged with the responsibility of deciding how to use USAID (United States Agency for International Development) resources of 250,000 cruzeiros which had been earmarked for innovative work on "slum clearance and urban planning.[70] The guidelines formulated by CODESCO demonstrate a philosophy diametrically opposed to that of CHISAM. Rather than demolishing

PLATES 28, 29, 30, AND 31. Commerce thrives in Nova Brasília—it has quadrupled between 1969 and 1973. Shown are a shoe store along Avenida Nova Brasília, a cultist shop for Umbanda the African spiritist cult, a clothing and hardware store, and—on top of the hill—a family-run grocery store.

the favelas, CODESCO sought to upgrade and legalize them, purchasing the land as a public entity and providing the best possible terms for resale to the favelados. Their philosophy stressed the importance of security of land ownership for the favelados, the necessity of allowing the favelados to stay near their jobs, and the positive value of including the favelados in the improvement of community public services and in the design and building of their own homes.

Three favelas—Brás de Pina and Morro União in the North Zone and Mata Machado in the South Zone—were selected for urbanization programs. These programs included demarcating, paving, and lighting the main streets, installing water, sewers, and electricity, helping to finance the rebuilding of homes by self-help construction (with free technical assistance provided by architecture students and long-term low-interest loans for building materials), and administering the resale of the land to which CODESCO had acquired title. To execute the program CODESCO has received some loans from the National Housing Bank. These are miniscule, however, in comparison with the funds for the eradication and housing project programs of the COHABs. In the CODESCO case, rather than awaiting the evolutionary process of home improvement which the favelas normally undergo over a period of many years, the BNH funds are loaned directly to the favelados for immediate home improvements at low interest rates and with repayments spread over a long term. Economic comparisons between CODESCO and COHAB show that houses financed by the former cost only half that of the latter to construct[71] and have the additional benefits of utilizing former investment in favela homes, preserving existing survival networks, and avoiding the disruption and trauma of removal.

The CODESCO process of development was based on a detailed preliminary study, which first categorized all the favelas of Rio into "urbanizable," "semi-urbanizable," or "non-urbanizable" according to such characteristics as terrain, density, and location. The three favelas that were chosen represented three points on the continuum, one on flat marsh land, one on a rather steep hillside and the third on rolling terrain. They ranged in population from fairly sparse to extremely dense, and they were located at varying distances from downtown.

The next stage of the process involved a careful study of the location and condition of each barraco (favela dwelling). Meanwhile, CODESCO negotiated to acquire not only the land upon which the favelas themselves were located but also adjacent lands. In the areas where the housing was too dense for agreed-upon minimum standards of space per dwelling, the residents decided among themselves who would move to adjacent land, and who would remain. In addition, those families who were located where paths were to be widened into principal roadways also moved to the new areas.

In some places a "remanagement" process was experimented with to facilitate development by clearing areas to avoid the expense of installing infrastructure around and under standing shacks. An entire subsection of the favela moved together to an area which had already been serviced, thus vacating the area they had occupied to ease the installation of infrastructure there.

As for work on the houses themselves, each family was encouraged to design its own home according to its particular needs and preferences. Members of the CODESCO staff and volunteer architecture students from the university worked with each family individually to insure that the plans were viable, and to help them estimate the type and quantities of building materials needed and the costs involved. Later, after considerable experience with the design, three basic housing plans were posted in the Residents' Association to facilitate the process. Since the building materials were acquired by CODESCO in bulk and distributed as a cooperative, prices were considerably lower than market rates. Credit was made easily and cheaply available on very long-term repayment schedules.

The three pilot projects were quite successful. An evaluation study of Brás de Pina made only two years after the initiation of the project showed that significant upgrading of the houses had already taken place. Many of the houses had been converted from wood to brick, and had doubled in size (thus substantially reducing overcrowding). The people were secure and enthusiastic about their land and their community.[72]

When I returned in 1973, the change was even more striking (see Plates 32-34). Much of Brás de Pina had originally been constructed on stilts over muddy, infested swamps. These had all been filled in, and in the worst area a soccer field and open plaza had been constructed with benches and trees around the periphery. The houses were delightful. Each demonstrated a strong individual flair, reflecting the tastes, preferences, and priorities of the family. Some had second stories, some porches or verandas of various design, some little fences or gardens around them. Almost all were of plaster-covered brick, brightly painted and creatively adorned with plants and flowers.

The favela of Morro União was similarly transformed. Located on a hillside, the favela had various physical levels of construction and

PLATES 32, 33, AND 34.   Bras de Pina 1969 and 1973. The favela was situated in a muddy swamp. Rebuilt houses (see example below) were designed by each family—with the help of architecture students through CODESCO—and reflect the individuality of the residents.

activity coordinated from a field center. Commerce was flourishing, a central plaza had been defined and paved, a water tower had been built on the hilltop, services had been extended to reach all areas, and in some sections small-scale multi-family dwellings for higher density and lower cost had been constructed.

Despite the success of these pilot projects, by 1973 CODESCO's funds had been severely reduced and the original director and staff had been replaced by a much less active group. The Mata Machado project had apparently been dropped, and although there was talk of some new projects, none had been undertaken. Clearly the new CODESCO is continuing the organization in name only.

Across the rest of Brazil, BNH has given limited support to a number of experiments in low-income housing. A notable example is their recent approval of an urbanization plan for 90,000 units in the Alagados over the bay in Salvador Bahia (see Plates 35 and 36). The Rio de Janeiro experience I have described was by far the greatest failure, both in terms of meeting the needs of the people and of being economically viable. This occurred partly because the project was done hurriedly and on a massive scale so that it could be used as a "showcase" for national and international prestige.

Despite all of the evidence against favela removal and in favor of on-site urbanization, the government still intends to eliminate the favelas of Rio by the new target date of 1983.[73] Given the facts that the new housing policies have not, thus far, resulted in decreased migration to Rio, that new squatter settlements continue to grow while existing ones expand, and that construction costs are rising daily, it is not at all clear whether this goal will be met. If some of the disastrous consequences of the initial government policy could be attributed to naive altruism, it now should be evident that favela removal is essentially intended to further improve the condition of the upper sector in Brazil at the expense of the poor. As the government policies persist, it is increasingly difficult to see the startling default rates on public housing as a result only of economic pressures on the poor. Even now, defaulting on payments is partly a political expression of deep frustration and resentment.

Since it seems that the present military regime in Brazil is unlikely to be overthrown from without, or undergo radical changes from within, the poor will doubtless continue to be subjected to policies which sacrifice their own interests in protecting the power, wealth, and

PLATES 35 AND 36.   The Alagados in Salvador Bahia; 90,000 people live in stilt houses over the bay. Land is gradually built up by packed garbage and finally asphalted. Plate 36 shows the people and vultures fighting over the newly dumped garbage. The writing on the truck reads "Povo Desenvolvido é Povo Limpo" (a developed people is a clean people).

privilege of the upper sectors. Although their discontent and bitterness may grow, their position of powerlessness is sufficiently evident that it is unlikely they will take any futile risks.

Chapter Eight
Marginality and
Urban Poverty

Marginality is both a myth and a description of social reality. As a myth it supports personal beliefs and social interests, and is anchored in people's minds by roots that will remain unshaken by any theoretical criticism. As a description of social reality, it concerns a set of specific problems that must be treated in an alternative theoretical way in order to be correctly understood.

The purpose of this study so far has been to delineate popular and scholarly stereotypes of the urban poor, to contrast these stereotypes with the existing reality in Rio's favelas, and to show how they continue to mold the policies affecting the lives of this ever-growing sector of the population. By way of conclusion, this chapter will attempt to do several things: (1) assess the overall validity of the myths of marginality, both as a series of propositions and as a set of fundamental assumptions about the nature of society; (2) account for the persistence and appeal of the myths; (3) point out the functions and political implications of the myths; (4) show how objective social conditions account for the persistence of what has been described as marginality; (5) propose an alternative theoretical explanation of marginality, as an expression of conditions of dependency; and (6) show how the favelados as a group perform functions that are accepted and even required by the rest of society.

THE VALIDITY OF THE MYTHS

The myths of marginality can be evaluated in two ways: according to their degree of accuracy in defining the attitudes and behavior of those populations considered marginal (of whom Rio's favelados are a prime example), and according to the soundness of their underlying assumptions and analytical scheme.

In terms of accuracy of definition, I have found the prevailing wisdom completely wrong: the favelados and suburbanos do *not* have the attitudes or behavior supposedly associated with marginal groups. Socially, they are well organized and cohesive and make wide use of the urban milieu and its institutions. Culturally, they are highly optimistic and aspire to better education for their children and to improving the condition of their houses. The small piles of bricks purchased one by one and stored in backyards for the day they can be used is eloquent testimony to how favelados strive to fulfill their goals. Economically, they work hard, they consume their share of the products of others (often paying more since they have to buy where they can get credit), and they build—not only their own houses but also much of the overall community and urban infrastructure. They also place a high value on hard work, and take great pride in a job well done. Politically, they are neither apathetic nor radical. They are aware of and keenly involved in those aspects of politics that most directly affect their lives, both within and outside the favela. They are responsive to the changing parameters in which they operate (bargaining with candidates astutely in the populist period and keeping wisely apolitical in the authoritarian period), and they are generally aware of their vulnerable position. As for any signs of radical ideology, or propensity for revolutionary action, these are completely absent. Favelados are generally system-supportive and see the government not as evil but as doing its best to understand and help people like themselves. Though this benign attitude may have changed with their forced relocation to public housing, they remain unwilling to take political risks.

In short, *they have the aspirations of the bourgeoisie, the perseverance of pioneers, and the values of patriots.* What they do *not* have is an opportunity to fulfill their aspirations. When they go to public agencies, for example, they are often humiliated and mistreated (as strikingly documented in Maria Carolina's diary, quoted in Chapter Five).[1] And despite their high educational aspirations, their children are zoned or priced out of schools. The closed nature of the Latin American class structure makes it extremely difficult to achieve the social mobility they hope for. Favelados get the worst jobs with the lowest pay, under the most arduous conditions and with the least security. Since many of those born in remote villages do not have birth certificates, they cannot get official work permits and therefore are excluded from all the benefits gained by the past forty years of labor legislation. Because of this lack of protection, they are employed for less than the minimum wage, receive no social security, no illness compensation, no retirement benefits, and no protection under the law. Likewise, they are politically intimidated and manipulated in order to maintain the status quo. When squatters try to organize to defend themselves, as they did attempting to prevent favela removal, they have been fired upon, jailed, and burned out of their homes.

These conclusions are not limited in their application to the case of Rio de Janeiro, or to the present study alone. All over Latin America where empirical research has been conducted, the data simply do not support the propositions of marginality. Findings from Rio de Janeiro (Leeds), Salvador and São Paulo (Berlinck), Santiago (Castells, CIDU, Kuznetzoff), Buenos Aires (Margúlis), Lima (Turner), Bogota (Cardona), Mexico City (Munoz, Oliveira, and Stein), and Monterrey (Balan, Browning, and Jelin) all seem to show clearly the opposite. Review articles by Mangin and Morse had already started to disprove the prevailing wisdom by the late 1960s, and the more recent research has been quite clear.[2]

But this is not the only level on which marginality "theory" has been misleading. It is based on a number of fundamental assumptions about the nature of society which are not necessarily true. First of all, its analytical scheme has posited not only a series of ecological, economic, social, cultural, and political characteristics of "marginal" populations, but it has taken as a basic assumption the covariation of each of these dimensions; thus, it has diverted attention from the independence which exists between these spheres. For example, some people choose to live in a squatter settlement as a matter of life style, or as an economic preference, even though they have stable employment as workers in the capitalist sector. A person may also be earning little, yet have quite a sophisticated and urbane set of cultural values, social practices, and political activites. Many such cases were evident from our research.

The second misleading assumption is that poverty is a consequence of individual characteristics of the poor rather than a condition of society itself. Without looking at the societal institutions which provide the basic parameters of the life of the poor—that is, at labor markets, social class divisions, and the state itself—it is difficult to go beyond a self-determined posture of blaming the poor for their own poverty. As we have seen, this is a fruitless line of reasoning which leads to completely distorted policy recommendations that worsen rather than alleviate the conditions they are attacking.

But perhaps most fundamental of all, the marginality paradigm is based on an equilibrium or integration model of society. Not only are the myths untrue; the model is invalid as well. Marginality theory assumes that in a functioning system the interconnections between sub-portions tend to be mutually satisfactory and beneficial to all. It is perfectly possible, however, to have a stable system which is balanced to the advantage of some precisely through the explicit or implicit exploitation of others. Exploited groups in such a situation are not marginal but very much integrated into the system, functioning as a vital part of it. In short, integration does not necessarily imply reciprocity.

The functionalist or integration model of society is founded on the premise that every functioning social structure is based on a set of shared values among its members. It sees society as an integrated social system defined by a shared set of values which are differently allocated through the different subsystems. Society is a whole, and the question is how the parts are integrated into it. The "marginals" in this case are defined as permanently outside of the society since they do not participate in the shared values which are the definition of society itself. This entire set of assumptions (which can be traced in sociology through Durkheim, Simmel, Merton, and Parsons) can be contrasted with the conflict model, which does not assume shared values or interests and sees every society as based on *coercion* of some of its members by others.[3] In this sense the "marginal" sector is just one of many competing and conflicting groups—specifically, a powerless group subject to a good deal of coercion and doing very little coercing.

Marginality theory seems to assume, whether naively or by calculation, that the adoption of middle-class culture (attitudinal consensus) will be rewarded by access to middle-class privileges. Its proponents do not recognize the fundamental antagonisms between the interests of the privileged and non-privileged in the society, and the inherent asymmetry of the relationship. What they cannot see is precisely what José Artur Rios, the one-time Secretary of Social Services for Guanabara State, concluded after many years of working in the favelas: "The favela is a necessity of the Brazilian social structure. It demands relations of economic dependence which result in the temporary or permanent misery of the dependent element for the benefits of the society."[4] In such a situation the only consensus can be a forced one, and that is precisely what we observe in Brazil today.

WHY THE MYTHS PERSIST

If the myths of marginality are both empirically false and analytically misleading, why have they gained such wide and continued acceptance? Partial answers lie in the ethnocentrism and class bias of those who make both theory and policy. Misunderstanding and misperception can also be the result of useful perceptual screens, designed to help filter out evidence that contradicts convenient and comfortable belief systems.

We have already mentioned Lisa Peattie's contention that because Latin American cities have been enclaves of Europeanized culture for so long, their inhabitants have been bound to consider new arrivals as unwanted intruders. This snobbery undoubtedly helps sustain popular images of migrants as bucolic and backward. Moralizing plays a part as well. There is no mistaking the tone of the Foundação Leão XIII's description of the "moral level" of the favela—its concern, for example, that young girls feel no shame at being pregnant out of wedlock, or its horror that children in the favela witness the sexual act.

Middle-class ethnocentrism is present also. While some middle-class Brazilians look on favelas as barbaric, filthy, and dangerous, and others see them more as "unfortunate" places filled with helpless, pitiable folk, all are offended by the favelados' supposed nonconformism with middle-class norms. For example, they take the favelado to task for the enormous economic frivolity of Carnival costs—the expensive parties, the hundred-dollar costumes, the endless hours "wasted" on preparations. It is the kind of behavior one would expect from people without any motivation, they say, people who would rather dance than plan for the future. Yet listen to the lyrics of the Carnival song in the film *Black Orpheus* ("A Felicidade" by Vinicius de Morais):

> A gente trabalha o ano enteiro
> Por um momento do sonho
> Para fazer a fantasia
> De rei ou de pirata ou jardineira
> P'ra tudo se acabar na quarta-feira.

"We poor people work the whole year through for a moment of dreaming," they sing, "to costume ourselves as kings, pirates, and gardeners; and all is over on Wednesday" (Ash Wednesday, the last day of Carnival's four-day celebration). It is only middle-class bias that fails to see samba schools as the complex social invention they are, or to recognize the careful budgeting behind favela expenditures on Carnival as a pure form of "deferred gratification."

What we are talking about here is *class bias*. On the most fundamental level, the myths thrive not because of snobbery, moralizing, or ethnocentrism, but because they fulfill the ideological-political function of preserving the social order which generated them.

Ironically, the myth of marginality is itself a real material force—
an ideology which informs the practice of the dominant classes and has
deep historic roots in the history of Latin American cities. It is a vehicle
for interpreting the social reality in a form which serves the social
interests of those in power. A myth is merely a strongly organized and
widespread ideology which, to use Karl Mannheim's definition, develops from the "collective unconscious" of a group or class and is rooted in
a class-based interest in maintaining the status quo. It involves a belief
system, a systematic distortion of reality reflected in this system, and a
specific function for those ideas in serving the interests of a specific
group.[5] The myths of marginality fit the definition on all these counts.

This raises the question of the social and political function of
theory. When social scientists give academic respectability to a world
view which conforms with prevailing prejudices and gives policy makers
confidence and legitimacy, it is extremely difficult to introduce a contradictory set of understandings into that closed circle. The correspon-
dence between popular notions and intellectual theories of marginality
is no coincidence. Social science theory has always mirrored our social
ideology, or what we call "common sense."

Inequalities in society pre-date by far the specific problems related
to hyperurbanization and squatter settlements. Sociology only began to
gain popularity as a discipline when the prevailing social order and
stability was widely threatened by these inequalities at the beginning of
the twentieth century. Marginality theory as such was the social scientists' way of combining the old ideologies with the new social realities in
the period between the world wars, and especially in Latin America after
World War II, when the threat of disruption in the cities seemed to take
on crisis proportions. The myths of marginality are in part an ideological
expression of the sociologists' concern with the integration of masses of
people.

There are three interacting components to be dealt with here. There
is a set of existing conditions and social practices, which in this case is
the condition of urban poverty in shantytowns; there is the common
sense reaction to this reality, in this case the ideology of marginality as a
dangerously disruptive condition arising from the lack of certain
attributes or characteristics of the individuals in the situation; and there
is the intellectual theory, which is both derived from common sense
ideology and then verified by it. Thus there is a closed circle.

Like the evil queen in the story of *Snow White*, the upper sector of
Brazilian society looks into the mirror of social theory, which reassures

it of its perfection and beauty, affirming that it is the fault of the marginal population that it does nothing to overcome its marginality. In fact, the mirror of social theory might even imply that the marginal people live in filth and squalor because they prefer it that way. Since this corresponds with the society's own image of itself, the theory is verified and given legitimacy as an excellent theory (a very perceptive mirror indeed), and the common sense stereotypes are given intellectual credibility. The theory reflects not only the ideological expression of society's concern about integration but also the spontaneous reactions of the people. This can be called a "specular" relationship.[6]

The reasons for the persistence of the myths of marginality can be seen even more clearly in the specific ways they function to preserve the status quo.

POLITICAL IMPLICATIONS AND FUNCTIONS OF THE MYTHS

Five political implications or functions of the marginality myths are immediately apparent.

1. The myths function in such a way as to isolate one fraction of the working class from the rest, so that the two groups fight against each other rather than uniting.

2. Insofar as the myths reinforce the idea of the popular sectors as dependent, isolated, and powerless, they also reinforce the idea that these sectors can be integrated by populist policies, coming either from the state apparatus or from competing political parties. As we contended when discussing the "terms of political integration" in Chapter Six, such populist policies are attempts to gain support through palliative concessions while at the same time avoiding basic changes and avoiding giving any real power or autonomy to the popular groups themselves.

3. The marginality myths justify the existence of extreme inequality and the inabiity of the system to supply even minimal standards of living for vast portions of its population. By blaming these conditions on the lack of certain attributes of the squatter population, the myths preserve the legitimacy and credibility of the structural rules of the game.

4. The myths of marginality facilitate the acceptance of and justify the implementation of *any* public policy directly or indirectly concerning the popular sectors of urban society. Favela removal was permitted as part of the restructuring of the urban system precisely because the favelados were considered marginal and therefore dispensable. If they had been regarded as "normal" working-class citizens with their own

rights, they would have been treated in quite a different manner. Insofar as they were considered "marginal," however, they had no rights or claims on the system and were therefore easier to manipulate.

The specific urban policies flowing from the myths of marginality are only the symptoms of even larger political implications. Urban policy made under the pretext of "integrating" the favelados disregards the extent to which they were already integrated—integrated through their own initiative and efforts and in spite of "social policy." It was the favelados who scrabbled after schooling for their children and biscate to fill the family purse, *not* the society which offered the family good schooling or employment. It was the favelados who saved their pennies and trusted that their children would have the same chances for success as do those of a businessman, *not* the system that offered them good reason to hold on to such hopes. Because of the removal-relocation policies, the few small chances favelados did have to stretch the fabric of society toward their own ends have now been eliminated. The lack of support from other sectors is now starkly evident, and the disproportional effort the favelados contributed to their own integration is clear. They are no longer physically able to actualize their desire for integration. The system, unable to see that the favelados thought they were doing all right, has taken from them even the pretense of participation in society. As if to spite itself, it dammed up a spring of seemingly cost-free allegiance and cut the favelados off from their only real hope of advancement— their own enthusiasm and enterprise.

Take, for example, the question of political conformism. All our indicators of political conformism (preference for incremental changes, lack of class consciousness, allegiance to the state, and welcoming of foreign influence) were positively related to socioeconomic status and power within the system—that is, they reflected a degree of integration. It is therefore reasonable to expect that if this integration is seriously disrupted, increasing disaffection with the system will be the result. It is our impression that this is what is happening. The normally optimistic favelados—"defensively optimistic in times of stress"—are now voicing strong discontent with their situation in the relocation communities. On the other hand, the relocated favelados are even more at the mercy of a repressive regime than ever before. Their existence, which is on the periphery of national concern, is now being lived out on the periphery of the citys. In some ways Brazilian officials have accomplished their age-old dream of sending the favelados back to the country where they came from. It is easier to exert police control over a distant ghetto, and easier to treat the needs of the poor in a perfunctory manner when they are no longer a visible part of the urban scene. The completion of one massive public gesture toward the favelado makes it easier to neglect his true needs.

5. Finally, the myths of marginality shape the self-image of those labeled as marginal in a way that is useful for the rest of society. Favelados more often than not absorb and internalize the negative definition ascribed to them, blaming their own ignorance, laziness, or worthlessness for their lack of "success."

Their real economic and political powerlessness helps reinforce this world view. (It is clear, however, from the case of the *campamentos* under Allende's regime in Chile, that any change in the objective situation leads to a rapid and complete alteration of this negative self-image.) This sense of inferiority in turn makes the squatter population even more manipulable and even less able to organize itself in an autonomous manner, either in unions or in political parties.

Since the political left is also influenced to some extent by the myths of marginality, it too is ineffective in providing alternate channels. In fact, the Fanon-inspired view of "marginals" as revolutionary because they are so "desperate and despairing" merely reinforces their marginality. It is merely the radical version of the populist client-and-leader relationship. In both cases, the political leaders claim to speak for the marginals, deriving their own legitimacy from that role and distributing in return some form of spoils. The same problem needs to be dealt with in both cases—that is, to destroy the view that the "marginals" are a separate entity and begin to see them as part of the same reality as the working class. Ultimately, favelados must be dealt with in terms of all the existing political, social, and economic relationships in the society.

THE PERSISTENCE OF THE SOCIAL REALITY

It is critically important for us to recognize that the *objective conditions* of the popular sectors persist as tenaciously as the myths of marginality themselves. There is a concrete set of ecological, economic, social, cultural, and political circumstances which continue to exist regardless of any theory of mythology, and which places most residents of squatter settlements at a severe disadvantage in trying to fulfill their own goals and aspirations. While all of these dimensions are combined and labeled "marginal" in the myth, the favelados continue to live out their lives—despite their efforts—at the bottom of the various scales of wealth, power, and prestige.

Having shown that the causes and continuation of this condition are not rooted in the attributes of the individuals concerned, and that their own attitudes, values, and behavior do *not* comprise a self-defeating and mobility-inhibiting syndrome, we must look to some set of circumstances outside individual control. This logic leads us to examine the structural factors or societal institutions—the nature of labor and capital markets, social stratification and the class system, and the role of the state in modern capitalistic societies, as well as the international setting, all of which have a strong bearing on the urban inequalities we have been discussing.

It is precisely along these lines that the recent work on marginality by Latin American scholars has developed. Their critique of the marginality theories, focusing on the historical situation of dependency, as well as on capitalism itself, is of critical importance in taking the next step in our understanding.

MARGINALITY AS A REFLECTION OF DEPENDENT DEVELOPMENT

It is precisely because of the political significance of the marginality statements, and their functionality for the system as discussed above, that such strong criticism has developed among Latin American scholars in recent years. Their basic position recognizes the condition of the reality referred to as "marginal," but it explains these conditions as expressions of the social structure and the historical process of development and industrialization in Latin America. The critique refutes the idea of covariance of the different dimensions of marginality and seeks rather to examine the specificity of their interaction in each instance. It also refutes the theory of modernization implicit in marginality theory and poses an alternate framework for the analysis of underdevelopment.

According to this critique, the traits defined as characterizing marginality are seen as only the external symptoms, as merely the tip of the iceberg. The key point here is that marginality is not caused by poor housing conditions or by characteristics of individuals or groups, but by a form of society rooted in the historical process of industrialization and economic growth in the developing nations, particularly Latin American nations. "Marginalization" is the consequence of a new model of development (or underdevelopment) that has a basic characteristic the exclusion of vast sectors of the population from its main productive apparatus.

In contrast to the general notion of European and North American experience during the Industrial Revolution, Latin American economic growth has failed to generate a sufficient number of manufacturing jobs to absorb the rapid expansion of the urban labor force. Basically the factors contributing to this situation are: (1) the centrality of production of raw materials because of the asymmetric international division of labor; (2) unprecedented rates of rural-urban migration coupled with high rates of natural growth in the cities; (3) limited outlet for the labor force in terms of foreign outmigration due to the relative lateness of the modernizing surge with respect to the rest of the world; (4) the diffusion—if not the imposition—of advanced capital-intensive technologies to countries which are labor-rich and capital-poor; (5) the use of locally accumulated capital for both conspicuous consumption by local elites and for investment in central capitalist countries; and (6) the narrow internal market which is unable to provide a self-sustained process of investment in capitalist terms.[7]

As an early report by the United Nations Economic Commission for Latin America pointed out: "In the previous century, the development of factory industry all over the world was inevitably accompanied by a substantial increase in factory employment. . . . Such no longer is the case. Industrial development in the less developed countries means in large measure the adaptation of advanced techniques. . . . Under these circumstances, the rapid growth of industrial production does not necessarily imply a substantial increase in industrial employment."[8]

The outcome of this process is a disproportionate number of underemployed people who are not wage-earners, have no particular credentials, no job stability, no social security, no protection of labor legislation, and who live in a state of constant uncertainty.[9]

The issue is not merely one of new terminology, of whether or not the present urban proletariat and sub-proletariat are "poorer" or more "pampered" than that of the classical industrial period. As Anibal Quijano has stated, "In all modern societies and in every moment there has been observed the existence of a category of persons excluded more or less permanently from the dominant nucleus of work that, by reason of their insufficient incomes, had no access to the consumption of goods and services. . . . But they were isolated individuals, or united into small groups, dispersed, atomized, and disconnected from all the economic sectors of society."[10]

He points out, however, that today in Latin America "the process compromises vast sectors of the population that, because of this, have ceased to be isolated and dispersed. It is now a problem that concerns the whole of society, and not exclusively the marginals."[11]

In contrast to the approach characteristic of the early sociological literature—with its emphasis on the individual's lack of integration *in* society—the question of marginality now becomes that of the integration *of* society itself: how certain groups in society are integrated into the productive and distributive spheres.[12]

These problems are severely intensified by the fact that historically the development of Latin America has taken place as part of a wider process of capitalist expansion throughout the world. Whereas the first Industrial Revolution occurred with the new emergence of capitalistic forms of market organization, the present industrial surge is taking place in the context of already dominated markets and industrial spheres of influence. The very formation of the social structures within under-development has been conditioned by external dominance, first felt in the colonial ties to the European metropolis. It is this historical reality which makes the theme of dependency central to discussions of Latin American marginalization. As Theotonio dos Santos has pointed out, the productive system under dependent capitalism expands not through the elimination of outmoded or archaic subsistence sectors, but rather through the transference of the surplus generated within it to the modern advanced sectors.[13]

The notion of dependency does not imply simply a situation of economic dominance from one country to another. Although this element is crucial, dependency implies a whole system of social, political, *and* economic relations, tying together groups of people, or better, entire social classes, across countries as well as within them. As Bodenheimer explains, dependency means that the development alternatives open to the dependent nation "are defined and limited by its integration into and functions within the world market."[14]

Thus, the difference between development and underdevelopment is not simply one of stages in growth but also of a position and a function in a single dominant international structure of production and distribution. External, or for that matter internal, market forces alone are not sufficient to explain the continuity or direction of development. To quote from Cardoso and Faletto:

> In considering the "situation of dependency" in the analysis of Latin American development, what is intended is to show that the mode of inter-action between the national economies and the international market produces definite and distinct forms of interrelationships of the social groups

within each country, between countries and with external groups . . . and
that, in the extreme cases, the decisions that affect production or consumption in a given economy are taken in function of the interests in the
developed economies.[15]

Historically, one can delineate at least three major phases or "situations of dependency" in the course of Latin American development
since the sixteenth century. The first was colonial domination, characterized by the direct administration of intensive resource extraction and
by the political sovereignty of the colonial power that made territorial
possession the key point in its expansion. The second was capitalist-
commercial domination, which was manifested principally through the
terms of trade, purchasing raw materials beneath their value and opening new markets for manufactured products at prices above their value.
The third was, and is, imperialist or industrial-financial domination,
marked by speculative investment and the creation of industries in the
dependent countries that tend to control the movement of import substitution according to a strategy of benefit directed by multinational corporations in the entire world market.[16]

These three stages of development are not only historical moments,
but also specific forms of economic and social organization which are
now combined in each society. They correspond to the three forms of
domination exerted during the formation of the capitalist mode of
production on a world scale: primitive accumulation, competitive
capitalism, and imperialist-monopoly capitalism.[17]

Between the second and third stages there was a brief deviation in
the dependency structure, linked to the crisis in world capitalism that
began in 1929. The national bourgeosie of the Latin American countries
embarked on a policy of import substitution, building industrial equip-
ment and producing goods for their own internal markets which,
because of the worldwide depression, were no longer being supplied.
This attempt collapsed abruptly in the 1950s, when the new expansion
of foreign investment by the central capitalist countries easily overtook
the national capital enterprises, absorbing them without resistance.[18]

The situation in Latin America today is a new form of dependency
within the third stage of world monopoly capitalism. It is characterized
by the internationalization of the process of production, of the distribution of products, and of the circulation of capital. Among its effects on
the class structure in the dependent countries are the following: (1) The
creation of factions within social classes depending on the strength of

their links to the sectors directly involved in the world economy. (2) The existence of a growing part of the labor force whose reproduction is not economically required by the system, which means that their reproduction will be treated through the social and political processes. (3) The instability of class alliances underlying established power relationships, and consequently the growing instability of the entire political system. And (4) the reorganization of the process of divsion of labor, including some recent attempts at industrialization in peripheral countries which are rapidly changing the traditional class structure, causing breakdown particularly in the handicraft and agricultural sectors. [19]

The size and importance of the marginalized sectors, although existing throughout these various stages, only reach massive proportions in the present mode and structure of production. With the pre-eminence of monopolistic forms of organization, large segments of the labor force are excluded from the main process of accumulation and attached to subordinate and archaic forms of production, whether subsistence farming, mercantilistic agriculture, competitive industrial capitalism, or urban services. It is precisely the superimposing of the new hegemonic or dominant forms of production on previously existing archaic economic structures, and the simultaneous coexistence of these, that creates marginalization.

According to Quijano, two types of marginal workers are produced by this final stage of dependency: first, the "marginalized bourgeoise," which consists of self-employed craftsmen, small independent businessmen, and shopowners or even managers in the now peripheral competitive capitalist sector; and second, the "marginal proletariat," which consists mainly of migrants expelled from agriculture and—if working at all—employees in low-echelon jobs, such as domestic servants or messenger boys. [20]

In the first case, certain economic functions lose their significance with respect to the dominant new mode of production. They become inefficient in relation to the new productivity levels (as in the case of the crafts industry), or unnecessary (such as small industrial enterprises), or lose their market (as was traditionally the case in the involution of the export sector during the colonial period). All these activities, and the individuals affected by them, do not disappear; they become marginalized with respect to the dominant forms of production.

The second group is marginalized salaried workers who are mostly landless peasants, expelled from the agricultural sector and unable to find work within the dynamic sector of production in the city. Thus they are forced to accept temporary work in the marginalized sector of the economy or settle for careers restricted to the very lowest ranges of the modern industrial sector.

The marginal sector does not, however, constitute a new entity with respect to the advanced monopolistic means of production. As we have attempted to demonstrate, the two sectors are the result of a single historical process which gave rise to the poles of Latin American society. Furthermore, an extensive chain of exploitation links marginalized labor to the productive processes in the new dominant sector, and there may even be some movement from one to the other.

One of the questions that arises, then, is what function this large marginal population serves, and whether it is the equivalent of the classical "industrial reserve army" or the relative "surplus population" mentioned in Marxist literature. There is some debate on this among scholars, but many see the marginal population as an overflow beyond the reserve army itself. The reserve army is generally seen as serving the function of keeping wages down and serving capital in its moments of expansion or cyclical recuperation. Its members are typically the last to be hired in periods of expansion and the first to be fired in periods of economic depression. Some argue that the migrants are not even a part of this reserve army but comprise an "excess population" or "super-population" which is *never* hired by the advanced industrial sector, even in its boom periods, and is not even eligible for such employment because of its lack of skills and credentials. In fact, the mode of production of which the large multinational and monopoly corporations are a part requires a highly skilled, educated, and adaptable labor force. Thus these corporations are willing to hire workers at excellent, non-competitive wages, and to train and retrain them if necessary in order to reduce turnover and secure the type of work force needed. This group is not only well paid and well protected but also benefits from selective recruitment into these jobs. The function, then, that the rest of the population serves is to provide services and home-made goods at costs below those that would be incurred if these goods were produced in the dominant sector. In this way, they contribute to the process of capital accumulation by lowering the reproduction cost of labor in the dominant sector.

According to this analysis, the introduction of the multinational corporations leads to a dual or segmented labor market: one part exists among the competitive capitalistic enterprises, established in a previous phase of dependency, and the other applies to the new and hegemonic sphere of monopoly capital. In the words of José Nun:

> [There is] a superimposition and combination of two qualitatively distinct processes of accumulaion that introduce increasing differences in the labor market and with respect to which the functionality of the surplus population varies. In this manner, the unemployed can be, at the same time, a reserve labor army for the competitive sector and a marginal mass for the monopolistic sector. Furthermore, the redundant labor force can be occupied in the other [competitive] sector. . . . In this way, [the] functionality [of the marginal mass] will depend on the extent of satellization of the competitive sector that, in many cases, can be working for the large corporations . . . and, in fact, the small and medium enterprises would be contributing to reduce the wage costs of the monopoly sector.[21]

The coexistence of the monopolistic mode of production and the competitive capitalist one produces an extreme case of marginalization, going even beyond that situation characterized by the coexistence of surviving archaic modes of production in a single market economy.[22]

The question raised by this kind of analysis is whether the structurally permanent unemployment is functional or dysfunctional. In fact, as Cardoso has pointed out, the distinction between the two sides of the unemployed sector of the population—between the marginal group and the reserve army of the hegemonic sector—is dubious insofar as the two are aspects of one and the same process.[23] Because capital accumulation is a contradictory process when it expands at the world scale, it simultaneously produces new profits and new poverty. Thus marginality as a specific characteristic of the relationship between the labor market and the population is not a dysfunctional aspect of the new productive system of dependent capitalist societies. It is simply the inevitable reverse side of new capital accumulation, because multinational monopoly investment is increasingly separating the places where the surplus value is produced and the markets where people are able to absorb products because their income has expanded.

Finally, according to Castells, the specific conditions in the social structure lead to the political use of marginality. To the extent that the nation-states of dependent societies need a new source of legitimization in order to find a particular place in the new chain of dependency being forged at the top level of the system, there is a generally growing trend, especially in Latin America, for the state to expand popular participation. That means mobilizing people to support not their own views but the views of the state apparatus. One of the sectors most needed for this type of popular support is the "marginal" sector, and one of the chief ways for the state to mobilize its support is to propose reforms concerning "urban issues," since these have immediate appeal and at the same time pose no threat to the overall pattern of dependent economic development. Thus, marginality becomes a political issue not because some people are "outside the system" but because the ruling class is trying to use the absence of organization and consciousness of a particular sector in order to obtain political support for its own objectives, offering in exchange a clientelistic or patronage relationship. [24]

To summarize, from the structural-historical perspective prevalent in the Latin American literature, the situation of marginality arises from a peculiar form of integration of certain segments of the labor force into the main productive apparatus. Hence the defining characteristic of the marginalized sector is its role in the accumulation process characteristic of dependent nations. It is from this condition that the other expressions of marginality arise, be they ecological manifestations in the emergence of squatter settlements, psychological characteristics of the "marginal" personality, sociocultural characteristics of "marginal" behavior, or political processes characteristic of the relationship between the state and the popular sectors.

HOW THE FAVELADOS SERVE THE SYSTEM

Beyond the discussion and criticism of marginality theory lies another fundamental issue. There is a great difference between the uses of the "myths of marginality" and the utility of having a large portion of the population in a "marginalized situation." The popular sectors, in this case the favelados, help in many fundamental ways to perpetuate the system and facilitate its reproduction. It is therefore essential to understand their usefulness to the system in order to comprehend their persistence as a group. [25]

Economically, the favelados accept very low wages for long hours of work, frequently in precisely those jobs that no one else is willing to perform. The cheap labor that they provide in services, crafts, and inputs to the competitive sector serves to lower the reproduction costs of all economic sectors, either directly or indirectly. For example, by doing repair work as part of their odd-jobbing, and by charging substantially less than an "institutionally certified" electrician or plumber, favelados directly lower the living costs of those outside the favela as well as within it. By providing cheap inputs to certain stages of the manufacturing or assembly activities of the competitive capitalist sector—by making buttons or sewing upholstery at home, for example—favelados reduce reproduction costs indirectly as well. Furthermore, whether or not they function as a reserve army in the classical sense of the term, their very presence and numbers puts pressure on the working classes and serves to reduce their economic and political bargaining power.

Also, insofar as favelados purchase goods and services that the rest of society rejects, they prolong their usefulness. For example, they will buy second-hand clothes and furniture, stale bread, or imperfect manufactured products, and they will use the services of outdated professionals, or trainees—such as new doctors, who traditionally learn by experimenting on those unable to choose where they go for their medical care and how they get it. Finally, the favelados serve in the creation of jobs for diverse sorts of professionals and quasi-professionals, especially social workers, social scientists, and urban planners.

The existence of "those at the bottom" is useful on a social level as well. First of all, favelados provide a scapegoat for a wide array of societal problems, legitimating the dominant norms. They can be considered the source of all forms of deviance, perversity, and criminality, and because they lack the means to defend their own actions or image, the self-image of the rest of society can thus be constantly repurified. In addition, favelados provide a measuring rod, or bottom baseline, for the social status of all other groups—especially the working class, which feels privileged in comparison. Culturally, the favelados provide much of the vitality for bourgeois culture even while they are disdained by it. Their slang, their music, their soccer, their sambas—all these become part of the life and entertainment of the middle class.

Politically as well, the functions of the favela population are multiple and system-maintaining. First, its existence allows for the division of the popular sectors, thereby preventing them from being a strongly organized political force. Even internally they are divided, with leaders even more system-supportive than their less-active constituencies. Martins and Cardoso have summed up the point: "The socioeconomic factors within the favela population divide it internally and permit its incorporation into the global system with minimal effort or cost to that system. . . . The favela helps maintain the status quo by immobilizing the less conservative factors and dynamizing the more conservative ones."[26]

Second, because they are so non-demanding politically, and so willing to leave politics to the professionals, they are accustomed to justifying the general political exclusion of all popular classes in

society. At the same time, however, they provide the symbolic constituencies for diverse political actors, from conservatives who need them to
blame for societal ills to radicals who claim to speak on their behalf and
who need them to justify their actions.

Above all, the masses of favelados can be easily and conveniently
manipulated to serve the fluctuating and varying needs of the system. In
each era they have obligingly played the role assigned them. This can be
seen in a brief comparison of the populist and modern periods.

In the populist era, especially in the 1950s and early 1960s, when
the system asked for votes, the favelados voted, and when populist
politicians wanted local organization, they formed Residents' Associations. Under the authoritarian regime since the 1964 military coup, the
system has demanded acquiescence and apathy, and the favelados have
been quiescent and apathetic. In each period they had a definite role to
play. But in all instances this role has been determined by "the essentially elitist nature of the Brazilian polity, which even in the most
populist eras of Brazilian history has always involved firm control over
the lower classes through a government basically representative of the
propertied and moneyed elite classes of society."[27]

During the populist period, the favela participated in the power
game between competing segments of the national elite. In Weffort's
words, the masses "conferred legitimacy upon a Populist leader—and
through him on the state—insofar as they served as an instrument which
was particularly useful when no one of the dominant groups had
hegemony over the rest."[28] The underlying dynamic constructed by
populist politicians consisted of playing off the masses' desire for
mobility against the oligarchy's fear of revolution. To the oligarchy, they
could promise to keep the masses in check; to the masses they could
claim the ability to win concessions from the elite. Manipulation of this
basic conflict made populist politicians "mediators" and left them free
to "wheel-and-deal," consolidate power, and "line their own pockets."

At no point did the masses achieve any autonomous power in the
system, however. "It proved impossible," says Ianni, "to legitimize the
political participation of the masses in a bourgeois and traditional
society without profound changes in the society itself, which none of the
upper sectors was ready to tolerate."[29] Brazilian populism was an
attempt to reconcile the paternalistic and authoritarian elements of
traditional domination with the increasing need for social and political
participation of the masses. The essential incompatibility of these two

elements, the growing fear of the oligarchy that populism was getting too "popular," were both factors in the coup of 1964.

According to Juarez Brandão Lopez, a foremost goal of the military takeover was to get rid of populist leaders—especially those pushing to increase participation of the masses in government—and to "slow down the dissolution of the patriarchal order."[30] The submissive and acquiescent posture of the favelados is a major legitimizing and stabilizing force for the present military regime. Malori Pompermayer, a Brazilian political scientist, places the present situation in the context of needs of authoritarian regimes in general:

> After a certain amount of time in power, the authoritarian regime tends to be characterized by low mobilization of the population. The ordinary citizen expresses little or no enthusiasm for elections and the regime itself hopes for passive acceptance and utilizes apathy to consolidate its power. . . . Depoliticization can be a means of reducing social tensions after intense political participation in the previous regime. To achieve integration dissidents are suppressed, and the career of politics is discouraged.[31]

How did the military regime gain legitimacy from favelados so easily, given its propensity to ignore the interests of the under-class? In part because the situation of the favelados was not, in fact, much altered by the takeover—they were not deprived of any major mode of political involvement to which they might have grown accustomed.[32] The net result, in Cardoso and Martins' words, is that "the effective behavior of the less favored classes is characterized without doubt by passive acceptance of the new rules imposed in the play of social forces, and by their adaptive capacity."[33]

Thus the favelados have played, and are playing, critical roles in the maintenance of the economic, sociocultural, and political system in Brazil. Concomitantly, what happens to them is almost entirely dependent on the global economic and political trends in the country. They can in no sense be regarded as the agents of their own destinies. Their fate depends in great measure on developments in the larger Brazilian society to which they are so closely tied. If they are offered any option permitting them to minimize their risks and maximize their material gains, they will surely embrace it wholeheartedly. But the recent political evolution of the Brazilian regime hardly supports that hope.

Marginality theory, then, can be criticized not only as a false statement about the nature of a social group but also as a myth in the full sense of the word—a manner of telling the history of humanity in such a way as to serve the interests of a particular class.

The material force of the myths of marginality is to allow the perpetuation of the role of favelados and squatters in general in the social, economic, and political forms spelled out above. Clearly the use of these myths is not specific to Rio de Janeiro, or to Brazil, but relates to all societies. Thus the foregoing analysis of how these myths are applied as instruments of social control, despite their total lack of confirmation in empirical reality, is relevant for all countries which have large populations of urban poor. This situation exists for a large majority of the people everywhere in the world. Rejecting the way these problems have been interpreted according to the marginality vision by no means implies rejecting their social significance or the urgent need for more adequate theoretical conceptualizations. Thus, our final word should serve not to close this topic but to open it to the search for a new perspective—one that will combine both theory and reality and bring social research closer to the real social issues.

Appendix
Research Methodology

This is the methodological foundation of a study of migrants and squatters in Rio de Janeiro. Conducted in 1968-1969, the study focused on a series of stereotypes regarding the nature of these squatters and poor suburban residents. Squatters are illegal invaders of the land they live on; the "suburban" dwellers own their own lots, although these are merely small pieces of land without benefit of public services. Despite the legal distinction, the socioeconomic levels of the two groups are comparable. I have called the prevailing stereotypes of these groups the "myths of marginality."

What follows is a detailed description of the methods used to conduct this study. The specific design and content of the questionnaire operationalizes many of the concepts of marginality for the first time. The sampling procedures were devised for a shantytown environment lacking phone directories, registration lists, maps, or even street addresses. The techniques used in gathering and coding the life-history data enabled us to examine process rather than static states, and hopefully will be useful to other investigators.

This supplement briefly describes (1) site selection, (2) initial questionnaire construction, (3) development of a longitudinal life history matrix, (4) formulation of the final survey instrument, (5) sampling procedures, (6) the interviewing process, and (7) coding, editing, and processing the data.

SITE SELECTION

Rio de Janeiro, with approximately one million of its people or one-seventh of its total metropolitan population living in some 300 favelas across the city, was a natural choice for this study. While the city itself was growing at 2.7 percent per year, these favelas and the surrounding subúrbios were growing at an astounding 7.5 percent per year. The vast proportion of this growth can be accounted for by the rapid cityward migration of the past decades.

One of the first steps of the study was to wait at the truck stops, depots, and crossroads around Rio and trace the routes of the migrants (newcomers) in their search for shelter, jobs, companionship, and social amenities. I began talking (in Portuguese) with the families as they arrived and followed them to their destinations. People who knew someone already living in the city embarked on the tedious process of discovering where that particular favela or subúrbio was—not an easy task—and I went with them, gradually becoming more familiar with the range of possibilities. Those who knew no one usually "camped out" on the site of a construction project if they were single men, tried to find a position as a housemaid if they were single women, or ended up in Albergue, a state-run "hostel" for families picked up sleeping on the streets.

After a number of weeks at this informal procedure, and combining my observations with what scarce documentation existed at public and private agencies, I was able to identify three distinct "urban environments"—three separate social and geographic areas in which most first- and second-generation migrants lived. These were favelas on the hillsides in the midst of the commercial and wealthy residential area of the South Zone; the favelas in the more peripheral industrial North Zone; and the remote subúrbios—or satellite towns in the Baixada Fluminense (Fluminense Lowlands) which offer a choice of very low-cost unserviced lots or illegal squatting. For the purposes of the study, I selected one favela typical of those in the South Zone, Catacumba; one favela to represent those in the North Zone, Nova Brasília; and one municipality in the dormitory city area, Duque de Caxias, where I chose three favelas and five small legal neighborhoods of equal socioeconomic level with the favelas for the study.

FORMULATING THE QUESTIONNAIRE

During my first contacts with the three communities in September and October, I tried to find out as much as possible about the local culture: how the social system was structured, what was important to people, how the political universe was perceived. At every point, I tried to keep from imposing my own thoughts on those of the favelados. A long period of participant observation and non-structured interviewing proved most valuable. After open-ended discussions with various types of people, including long-time residents, leaders, and newcomers, I was ready to make a list of items which were emerging as especially interesting or important. By the end of February this had become the full-fledged, pre-test version of the questionnaire.

The pre-test questionnaire was designed to minimize the effect of my own preconceptions and maximize the consideration of issues as self-defined by the favelados. The intent was to allow the manner in which the favelados structure their own world to determine the structuring of the final questionnaire.

The pre-test was extensive and every question was open-ended. (There were 66 items on general background, 77 on urban experience, 43 on values, attitudes, and aspirations, and 80 on political attitudes and behavior.) It took from two to six hours to administer and often demanded two or even three sessions.

During the second and third weeks of March 1969, 41 of the pre-test questionnaires were administered—21 in Catacumba, 10 in Nova Brasília, and 10 in Caxias. A simultaneous quota-sampling method was used to obtain the widest variation in length of time in the city (plus urban born), type of job, age, sex, and position within the community. For each question, the answers were gathered on separate sheets and then classified into mutually exclusive categories derived from the entire range of obtained responses. This was a crucial step to insure that the terms of reference for the study were an appropriate blend of local reality and scholarly concerns.

I next returned to the pre-test questionnaires and applied the newly derived coding categories to each item. I had the results keypunched and ran a simple analysis to see which items seemed to be "working." Those questions which were ambiguous, hard to understand, too politically sensitive, or which did not discriminate among the population were revised or dropped, as were those that seemed most distant from measuring the underlying concepts being sought.

The final product of this analysis was a revised questionnaire with most items in closed form. Devising the final instrument took the better part of April and May 1969, during which time I also began sampling procedures and interviewer training.

There were two major changes in the instrument by this time. First, many political questions were dropped. Although innocuous by ordinary standards, many items such as direct questions on the 1964 coup, the Fifth Institutional Act, or the present military regime had to be omitted; it was senseless to jeopardize the entire study over a few items, however interesting. The second major change was that a Life History Matrix was developed and added to the questionnaire.

LIFE HISTORY MATRIX

As the pre-test was being analyzed it became apparent that conventional techniques were sadly inadequate for tracing the migratory and occupational paths of respondents. Using only three touchpoints on location, for example (place of birth, place lived most of life, and present location), did great disservice to the complexities of people's lives and grouped together people with quite different experiences. Furthermore, three or four of these questions became boring and repetitious within the standard interview format.

A technique for analyzing the life histories of large samples—designed by Balan, Browning, and Jelin—then came to our attention.[a] After further testing and experimentation this became the first portion of the final questionnaire. It consisted of a large matrix including year-by-year migration, occupation, education, and family histories. Interestingly, it helped a great deal in creating interview rapport. Filling out the matrix was a joining task, and nonthreatening. Reliability was excellent because memory could be aided by moving back and forth among the several areas of the respondent's life. Omissions and inconsistencies showed up easily and could be corrected immediately before proceeding to the next items.

During the interview, data were recorded in longhand on a series of pages which had the years 1904 to 1969 printed along the left-hand margin and eleven major variables along the top, as shown in Appendix Table 1. Each variable had a set of codes. The matrices were first transformed into numerical coded form on specially printed sheets arranged so that in each cell the respondent's age and code number of the variables were already printed in, leaving just enough space for two additional digits for the variable content, as shown in Appendix Table 2.

After recording the data about place of birth, only *changes* in any of the variables were entered. The rest of the cells were left blank. In the next step, only those cells which had been completed (those which represented changes) were transferred onto the standard IBM coding sheets for keypunching. For each person, then, there was a set of chronologically ordered six-digit fields (of varying lengths) affixed to the standardized data from his questionnaire.[b]

[a]Jorge Balan *et al.* "A Computerized Approach to the Processing and Analysis of Life Histories Obtained in Sample Surveys." *Behavioral Science*, vol. 14 (1969): 105-120.

[b]To be precise, in each six-digit field, the first two digits represented the respondents' age, the second two the variable number in which the change had occurred, and the final two the coded content of that change. For example, the series 160108 would mean that at the age of 16 the person had moved his residence (variable 01) to the south zone of Rio (content code 08).

APPENDIX TABLE 1
Life History Matrix

Year	Age	Migrational History						Occupational History				Educational History	Family History
		(1)	(2)	(3)	(4)	(5)	(6)	(7)	(8)	(9)	(10)	(11)
		Name of Place	Municipality	State	Size Classification	Type Residence	Reason for Move	Type of Work	Job Classification	Job Location	Reason for Job Change	Schooling	Marriages, Separations, Births, Deaths, etc.
1969													
1968													
1967													
1966													
.													
.													
1904													

APPENDIX TABLE 2
Life History Coding Sheet

	Variable Number				
Age	01	02	03	04	05 (etc.)
01	0101--	0102--	0103--	0104--	0105--
02	0201--	0202--	0203--	0204--	0205--
03	0301--	0302--	0303--	0304--	0305--
.	.	.	.	.	.
.	.	.	.	.	.
65	6501--	6502--	6503--	6504--	6505--

FINAL SURVEY INSTRUMENT

The final survey instrument which appears with the frequency distributions below began with the Life History Matrix and included a revised version of the original four sections. Under General Background were included demographic information not covered in the Life History Matrix: details about job, household and living standards, and education, migration, and occupation data on spouse, parents, and eldest children. The Urban Experience section covered pre-migration contacts with the city, initial adaptation to the urban environment, interpersonal relations and integration into the community of the favela, voluntary association membership, type and degree of use of the wider urban context, heterogeneity of contacts, and mass media exposure. The Attitudinal and Value section included aspirations, secularism, fatalism, family traditionalism, trust, universalism, propensity to accept innovations, optimism, achievement motivation, empathy, and authoritarianism. The Political section included cognitive measures (interests in politics, saliency of politics, degree of political information, and opinion holding); behavioral measures of all types of participation, local and general; and evaluative measures (such as perceptions of the system, passivism, paternalism, efficacy, alienation, legitimacy, class consciousness, party affiliation, and ideology).

An attempt was made to include items from similar studies of other areas for comparative purposes. Questions from Almond and Verba's *Civic Culture*, Kahl's *The Measurement of Modernism*, Inkeles' "overall modernity" scale, the Belo Horizonte Political Science Group's radicalism index, Fried's study of black migration to Boston, and others, were used. I discovered, however, that questions which grew from my field experience worked best and made the most sense. Many of the standardized items, especially those of the "civic culture" variety, had to be eliminated altogether.

In addition to the individual questionnaire, a Contextual Data Interview Schedule was devised. This was given to a handful of what anthropologists call "key informants," people especially well-informed about the history of the community and its present activities. Questions dealt with the size and growth rates of the community in past and present; the location of regional groups within the favela; the general problems that newcomers face in adapting to the city; origins and history of the favela; extent of urban services, commercial enterprises, schools and medical services; membership, history, and leadership of voluntary associations; the history of removal as it affected the local area;

politicians who had helped the favela in the past; and political events that had affected the community. This contextual questionnaire, with dozens of nonstructured interviews, formed the basis of the descriptions of the three communities.

DRAWING THE SAMPLE

A total of 750 persons were interviewed for the present study: in each of the three locations, we interviewed 200 persons selected at random and 50 leaders chosen by reputational and positional techniques. The sample included men and women from 16 to 65 years old rather than the conventional "heads of household." This decision resulted from my conviction that urban and political life are not experienced in the same way by men and women, young and old. (Through sampling, I hoped to increase analytical leverage on these convictions.)

Two hundred originally seemed a minimum sample size from each location, given the kinds of multivariate analysis I wished to pursue. By the time sampling decisions were made, however, it became clear that a random sample of 200 would yield only a tiny fraction of the really active elements in each area. I was interested in examining what kinds of urban experience were typical for these "deviant" men and women, and so I decided to undertake an additional purposive sampling of community leadership. Lists of all the leaders of the various groups, clubs, associations, and organizations in each place were compiled. These persons, and others at random, were then asked the names of other present or former leaders, people who had taken an especially active role in favela life, were particularly well-informed about local events, had been active in fights against removal, had taken part in election campaigns, or had launched petitions (for school or medical care, for example). As a result, 58 names emerged in Catacumba, 61 in Nova Brasília, and 73 in Caxias. In each case I listed the suggested elites in order of the frequency of their mention and the importance of their position and began interviewing from the top of the list until the quota of 50 was filled.

SELECTION OF DWELLING UNITS

I settled on a cluster sampling procedure based on 200 dwelling units in each location. My first problem was constructing sampling frames for each area, that is, compiling a comprehensive list of either individuals or households in the three locations. Weeks were spent between agencies in search of maps, census data or aerial photographs which could serve the purpose.[c] I finally obtained a series of aerial photographs from the Ministry of Mines and Energies. Since the exact process of sample selection differed according to the nature of the area, I will discuss them separately.

Catacumba. Because of its steep slope, Catacumba appeared on the Ministry photographs as one row of roofs and a series of blurry, overlapping shapes beneath. I therefore had to rent a paddle boat on the lagoon from which I took a series of front-view photographs with a telephoto lens. When these were blown up and spliced together they permitted identification of almost every residence in the favela; the result is shown on the cover of this volume. The houses later chosen by the random sampling technique were numbered and colored in red dots, and those which were reserves (in case of substitutions) were shown in green. The major social institutions were labeled.

Transparent paper was placed over the photographs and each shack sketched in and given a number. In a series of extensive walks, starting at each of the 15 entry points, those houses that had been hidden from view by other buildings, trees, or rocks were filled in. In this manner a total of 1457 houses were identified and numbered on our maps. Using a random numbers table, I chose 200 of these to enter the sample with 50 more in reserve for substitution.[d] A simple random sample was done in Catacumba because it seemed fairly homogeneous and those areas of better homes near the road were impossible to delineate with any degree of confidence.

Nova Brasília. The aerial photographs of Nova Brasília proved ideal for constructing a sampling frame. The favela was clearly distinguishable from the air, and when the photograph was enlarged, each individual dwelling unit was also quite distinct. Transparent paper was superimposed on the enlarged photograph and maps drawn accordingly. Two

---

[c]In this process I visited the Fundação Leão XIII, CODESCO, the Cooperativa Central de Abastecimento, the Secretary of Education of the State of Guanabara, IBGE (Brazilian Institute of Geography and Statistics), the Department of Engineering and Urbanism of the State of Guanabara, the Ministry of Mines and Energies, the Ministry of War, and the Geotechnique Institute, to mention only a few.

[d]Substitutions were to be made in case the chosen dwelling unit was vacant, or if the specific individual to be interviewed was unavailable due to illness, military service, travel, or other reasons. After five unsuccessful attempts to locate the designated individual, we picked out a substitute household (in order of appearance on the list) and began the procedure again.

thousand one hundred and twelve residences were identified, and follow-up walks were made along each of the paths to insure that every house had been counted.

Nova Brasília is clearly divided into three subregions (corresponding to socioeconomic status and length of residence, and visible in the construction types from brick to wood to wattle and daub). I therefore decided to improve our sample reliability by taking a stratified, rather than a simple, random sample.

Of the 2112 dwelling units in the favela, 671 fell into the highest SES category (the "good zone"), 952 into the intermediary classification (the "medium zone"), and 489 into the newest (or "poor zone"). Choosing proportionately, again with the aid of a random numbers table, 64, 98, and 46 units were chosen in the good, medium, and poor zones respectively, with the necessary reserves for substitution.

Caxias. In Caxias I decided to take advantage of the municipality's complete census data and detailed maps of residence locations to sample precisely according to my interests. The result was a multi-stage sample carried out as follows:

Stage 1. I decided to sample only from the First District of the city. Other areas were deemed semi-rural and not part of the metropolitan area. All five sectors of the First District were given a chance to be included in the sample.

Stage 2. The five sectors were in turn divided into 32 neighborhoods. Of these, five were chosen on a purposive basis because they were known to be areas of great migratory influx, past and present, and because they had a socioeconomic level comparable to that of the favelas. For this selection I used the huge "service maps" available in the Prefectura. Each one showed the range of extension of a different service. I chose those neighborhoods that had the least number of paved roads, the poorest extent of light, water, sewage, and drainage. I was familiar with most of the area from earlier visits so these decisions were relatively easy. A lifelong resident of Caxias also advised us throughout the entire process.

In addition to the five legal neighborhoods, I selected the three principal favelas in Caxias. This choice was facilitated by the availability of other special maps showing the location and size of each favela.

Stage 3. Each of the neighborhoods and favelas is divided into large, often irregularly shaped blocks called *quadras*, composed of 10 to

350 houses. In this stage, ten of these blocks were chosen at random from each neighborhood and favela and the number of dwellings on the block recorded. This was done for convenience in interviewing, because the neighborhoods cover vast expanses and it would have been difficult within time and money constraints to have sampled from dwellings spread out in every block.

Stage 4. The total number of dwellings from each of the ten blocks in the selected neighborhoods and favelas was calculated. The size of the sample from each neighborhood and the number of dwellings to be sampled from each block was determined proportionally in such a manner as to total 100 dwellings from all neighborhoods together and 100 from all dwellings from all the favelas. This gave equal numbers of persons with secure and insecure tenure for comparative purposes. Because the favelas are more dense than the neighborhoods, this gave about equal numbers of dwellings in the five neighborhoods as in the three favelas.[e]

Stage 5. Once the numbers of dwellings to be chosen from each block had been determined, a random numbers table, along with census notebooks, maps, and aerial photographs, was used to select and identify the 200 locations. Each number drawn was checked in the notebook from the corresponding neighborhood to verify that it represented a dwelling and that the dwelling was occupied. If two families lived there, a coin flip determined the one to be interviewed.

SELECTION OF INDIVIDUALS WITHIN DWELLING UNITS

The selection of residence was only an intermediate stage in the process since we were sampling individual adults, not households. To us, households were merely convenient subclusters. We ascertained that the average number of adults age 16 to 65 per household was 2.5.[f]

[e]The breakdown of the 200 dwellings was as follows:

Neighborhoods		Favelas	
1. Vila Leopoldina	26	1. Vila Operária	50
2. Sao Sebastiao	20	2. Favela do Mangue	15
3. Vila Sarapui	11	3. Favela Central	35
4. Centenário	26	Total	100
5. Olavo Bilac	17		
Total	100		

[f]This figure is based on the Caxias census data, the 1960 Guanabara census which included data for the favelas, and our own investigations in each locale.

A continuous-list sampling frame was devised to pick the persons to be interviewed within each household. For each household chosen, the first step was to obtain the names of all adult residents. By rearranging their first names in alphabetical order, the list could be conveniently randomized and then every second or third person alternately chosen, with the list continuing from household to household. The frame was set up as shown in Appendix Table 3.

Upon arrival at the residence, the interviewer stated his purpose briefly. Most residents were already aware of the study so little explanation was needed. The interviewer then said that to pick the person(s) to be interviewed he needed the names of all adults in the household. He listed these in order of age and after the last one drew a distinct wavy line across the page. The residence identification was indicated in the center column. Then the names were alphabetized and transcribed into the right column. Check marks were indicated beforehand by every second and third entry alternately to keep the ratio of 2.5. The person whose name appeared next to the check was the one to be interviewed. Sometimes the name of the one or two adults in a small household would

APPENDIX TABLE 3

Continuous List Sampling Frame

List of Adults by First Name in Order of Age Starting with Eldest			Identification of the Residence	Relisting of Adults in Alphabetical Order by First Name		
First Name	Age	Sex	House Number	First Name	No.	Chosen Person
Carlinhos	50	M	186	Carlinhos	1	x
Nadir	34	F	186	Nadir	2	
Jose	47	M	275	Antonio	3	x
Maria	38	F	275	Jose	4	
Antonio	16	M	275	Maria	5	
Joao	28	M	586	Cecelia	6	x
Cecelia	24	F	586	Joao	7	
Miriam	17	F	586	Miriam	8	x
Rafael	38	M	1407	Odete	9	
Odete	35	F	1407	Rafael	10	
Edgar	60	M	883	Edgar	11	x

fall *between* check marks. In these homes, only an abbreviated questionnaire concerning demographic data was administered. When more than one person in a household was indicated, both were interviewed separately but preferably on the same day to minimize contamination.[g]

INTERVIEWING

Recruitment and Training of Interviewers. It was evident from the start that I could not administer 750 questionnaries without help. Some had warned me against using students as interviewers, but I wished to have as much participation in the study as possible at every phase, which meant avoiding commercial "market research" types of interviewers. I visited all the Social Science Departments in the major universities of Rio and held open meetings or recruitment sessions in which I explained my research interests in detail and indicated that those who wished were encouraged to contribute to the study at all levels. At that time, the last week in January, the only major decision already taken had been the choice of the three locations. With my limited budget, I could pay only a minimal fee for each interview. In these meetings, then, it was stressed that payment would be primarily in the experience itself. This tended to reduce the numbers of interested students by half, but self-selection is often the best type.

Over 100 students were trained in the course of six months. The formal part of the training was an intensive "theory and methods" course which took about two months. Those who remained interested at its conclusion, again about half, participated in the formulation of the pre-test, its application, coding and analysis, and the development of the final survey instrument. For practice, each trainee administered one questionnaire to a colleague and two or three to favela residents in locales not included in our study.[h]

Keeping the momentum of the research going so that students did not lose interest was a major problem at this stage. There was a fairly

[g]Sampling procedures were initiated in mid-February 1969, when I hired two young architects, with experience in favelas through CODESCO, to help me with the mapping of the favelas. We worked through July, when final interviewing began, thus covering a time span of six months on the task.

[h]Most difficult for the interviewers to master was the Life History Matrix, but with sufficient practice it began to go smoothly. I went over each practice questionnaire in detail with the interviewer and we discussed problems and difficulties at length. Training was also given in the use of the Continuous List Sampling Frame.

high turnover rate throughout the study as the novelty wore off and it was discovered how difficult the task was going to be. Particular discouragements were the long climbs up the hillsides and the necessity of weekend and evening interviewing to catch working men at home. New interviewees were constantly recruited and trained, necessitating the repetition of the entire process described above several times over.[i]

The final interviewing was carried out in July, August, and September of 1969.[j] Catacumba took three weeks, Nova Brasília four, and Caxias five, because of the progressively greater distances, sizes of the communities, and complexities of the samples.

Receptivity and Comprehension. Great care was taken to prepare the communities for the influx of researchers (limited to no more than a dozen at any one time). Partly because of my own many prior conversations with local residents, but mostly because of their native friendliness, the interviewers were very well received and the interviewing went even better than was hoped. Eighty-two percent of the random sample were judged receptive and enthusiastic, either from the start or after some initial reluctance. Only 9 percent remained suspicious or reluctant throughout, and only one interview had to be terminated because of blatant hostility. The figures for the elite sample are almost identical on these points. Furthermore, a full 91 percent of random samples and 87 percent of elite samples were judged to have responded "openly and honestly to all of the questions."

Comprehension, however, varied greatly between the random and the elite samples. Just over half of the random sample "seemed to understand all the questions," compared with 86 percent of elite. One in five of the general populace "failed to understand many questions," whereas *none* of the elite did.

[i]From the checks we have run in the analysis (where we control for specific interviewers and their lengths of tenure, etc.), there did not seem to be any biasing of the data or loss in quality accruing from the high turnover rate.

[j]In order to protect the interviewers we took the precaution of providing each one with a printed "Declaration," bearing his or her name, and stating that he was cooperating on a "study of the Impact of Urban Experience under the direction of Janice Perlman, with the collaboration of IBAM (the Brazilian Institute of Municipal Administration) and the Getúlio Vargas Foundation Research Center." These were signed by Lordello de Mello, the Executive Director of IBAM, and by Aluizio Pinto, the Director of the Research Center of the Getúlio Vargas Foundation. As it turned out these were very seldom needed, but they were a useful precaution given the conditions under which we were working. They gave the interviewers a sense of legitimacy and security.

Duration and Location. Interview time ranged from a half hour to three hours, with an hour and a half the average. Interviews with those in the elite sample took consistently more time because they had more to say on each item and demanded fuller explanations. Locations varied between the two samples as well. Whereas 91 percent of random interviews were conducted in the respondent's home, only 61 percent of elite interviews were. The remaining elite interviews were distributed equally between place of work and public places, Residents' Association headquarters, bars, and so on.

It was considerably easier to locate the individuals in the random sample. Three quarters of them were found at home and interviewed on the first attempt, and most others on the second visit. In contrast, less than two-thirds of the leaders were located on the first try. Some required as many as six or seven attempts. It is an interesting comment on life in the favela that although interviewers tried to be alone with the respondent, this was found to be impossible in 80 percent of cases among the general population, and in 70 percent of cases among elites.

Completion Rates. Refusal rates were remarkably low: 0.5 percent, 2.5 percent, and 1.5 percent for Catacumba, Nova Brasília, and Caxias respectively. The leadership sample in each area refused at modestly higher rates: 4 percent, 6 percent, and 4 percent, respectively. Leaders were more likely to be busy or feel they had something better to do with their time. They were somewhat more wary of giving information on their beliefs and behavior as well. Those most eager to cooperate may well have been the more conformist and system-supportive types; and perhaps the more anti-establishment and critical leaders, few though they may be, were among the ones choosing not to be interviewed. Although this is interesting to note in passing, the refusal rates were so small that it could hardly have made a difference statistically.

More common than refusal was finding an indicated dwelling closed up or having no one at home, usually because of traveling, hospitalization, army service, or evening work patterns. Combining these failures to locate subjects with refusals and the occasional interrupted interviews gives overall substitution rates of 5 percent and 16 percent for random and elite samples in Catacumba, 15 percent and 22 percent for Nova Brasília, and 18 percent and 40 percent for Caxias. The last figure is high because time was short, and since we had compiled a long list of leaders we could afford the liberty of not returning for multiple tries without reducing the number of elites in the sample. The higher substitution rate among elite samples was mirrored in the three stratified areas of Nova Brasília where those rates increased proportional to distance from the center of Rio, partly because of difficulty of access for repeated visits, especially in evenings. No systematic bias seems to have been caused by this, however.

A final comment should be made on the numbers of households with no persons interviewed and those with two or three. If the sampling ratio of 2.5 adults per household was correct, the number of cases of each kind would balance out exactly. This was almost the case, but the estimate turned out to be a little on the low side, perhaps because a few more non-interviews than multiple interviews were reported.

INTERVIEWER CHECKS

The first precaution against interviewer bias was taken during the training course when I discussed the various—usually inadvertent—tendencies to impute consistency where there is none, to fulfill stereotypic expectations, and to "correct" for apparent skewedness in the overall population distributions. I also discussed how to avoid the more blatant forms of bias—body signals, verbal approval, and so on—and finally the problem of outright cheating. It was decided that interviewers should be dispersed randomly throughout the favela instead of being assigned to one area or to a specific type of person so that coded interview numbers could be used in later analysis to catch systematic bias.

I also made it clear that at least 10 percent of the people interviewed would be revisited, ostensibly to thank them for their help, but actually to see if the interviewer had really located the house and spoken with the persons indicated by the randomization procedure.

Finally, in each community I set up some sort of headquarters from which interviewers were assigned houses and to which each set of three interviews was returned upon completion. This gave me a chance to look over each one as it came in and catch any gross errors while there was still time to return for corrections.[k]

[k]In Nova Brasília and Caxias we discovered a series of houses which were clearly indicated in the sample but which no one had visited. They were mostly in high inaccessible places. We finally traced them all to one young woman who had entered the group late. She admitted to completing the interviews with any person conveniently at hand, saying she didn't see what difference it made. She was dismissed from the project, the interviews she had done discarded, and the correct respondents located and interviewed—a depressing incident.

CODING, EDITING, AND PROCESSING

There were only a few open-ended questions and occupational or residential items that had to be coded. Two of the items had to be totally *re*coded when the original codes proved an unsatisfactory match to the type and range of responses. This was possible because for all important items we had taken the precaution of writing the answers verbatim into the questionnaire before checking one of the pre-specified coding categories. When codes did not work it was thus possible to return to the individual responses, formulate a more appropriate set of categories, and apply them.

Coding and editing began in August, when the full set of interviews from Catacumba had been completed. It then proceeded simultaneously with the interviewing. Three persons worked on it full time through mid-October, when the questionnaires were taken to a local IBM office to be keypunched and verified. By then I had two full-time research assistants. We checked each interview for coding and editing once again before they were sent to be keypunched.

The data were eventually transferred onto a small magnetic tape in which form it was transported back to the United States. For each of the 750 respondents there were five cards in standard format corresponding to the questionnaire and an additional two to 22 free fields corresponding to the Life History Matrix.

The cards had to be reverified in the United States when a number of errors were discovered. They were further "cleaned" using the interactive systems ADMINS and programs written to check consistency in the life-history information. When the data were ready for use, some five months later, they were input into the Statistical Package for the Social Sciences program (SPSS) for analysis. More than 170 new variables were created according to specifications on the life-history strings, which were input as well. Reliability and validity checks were highly satisfactory.

Notes

1. Gideon Sjoberg, "The Origin and Evolution of Cities," *Scientific American* 213, no. 3 (September 1965): 55-63.
2. Kingsley Davis and H. H. Golden, "Urbanization and the Development of Pre-Industrial Areas," *Economic Development and Cultural Change* 3, no. 1 (October 1954): 120-141.
3. The figures in this paragraph are based on Philip M. Hauser and Leo F. Schnore, *The Study of Urbanization* (New York: John Wiley and Sons, Inc., 1966).
4. Kingsley Davis, "The Origin and Growth of Urbanization in the World," *American Journal of Sociology* 60 (March 1955): 434.
5. Charles Abrams, *The City is the Frontier* (New York: Harper Colophon Books, 1965), p. *v.*
6. Davis and Golden, "Development of Pre-Industrial Areas," p. 120.
7. Abrams, *The City is the Frontier*, p. 3.
8. Joan Nelson, *Migrants, Urban Poverty, and Instability in Developing Nations*, Center for International Affairs, Occasional Papers in International Affairs No. 22 (Cambridge, Mass.: Harvard University, 1969), p. 1.
9. John Friedmann, "The Phenomenon of Urbanization in Latin America," mimeographed, n.d., p. 1.
10. Richard M. Morse, "Recent Research on Latin American Urbanization: A Selective Survey with Commentary," *Latin American Research Review* 1, no. 1 (Fall 1965): 42.
11. Kingsley Davis, "The Urbanization of the Human Population," *Scientific American* 213, no. 3 (September 1965): 10-12.
12. E. Arriaga, "Components of City Growth in Selected Latin American Countries," *Milbank Memorial Fund Quarterly* 46, no. 2, part 1 (April 1968): 241-243.
13. G. Vernez, "El Processo de Urbanización en Colombia," *Revista de la Sociedad Interamericana de Planificación* 5 (September 1971): 24-26.
14. Unless otherwise stated, the figures in this section are based on G. Edward Schuh and Morris Whitaker, "Migration, Mobility, and Some Problems of the Labor Market in Brazil," mimeographed (Latin American Seminar on Development in Agriculture, Bogota, Colombia, November 6-8, 1968).
15. The definition used for "urban" is an administrative one and includes all municipal and district seats.
16. Growth Sinopse. Preliminar de Censo Demográfico de 1970; growth rate of favelas from Estado da Guanabara, *Area Prioritária 1*. Richard M. Morse, "Recent Research on Latin American Urbanization," p. 56, points out that in general "if urban growth rates are two to three times rural rates, we must remember that 'marginal' growth rates in the city may be three to four times the general urban rate."
17. John Friedmann and Thomas Lackington, "Hyperurbanization and National Development in Chile: Some Hypotheses," *Urban Affairs Quarterly* 2, no. 4 (June

1967): 3. Friedmann and Lackington define "hyperurbanization" as a "relation of disequilibrium between levels of a country's urbanization and economic development . . . [a] concentration of workers in the cities *in excess* of steady remunerative employment in the modern sector of the economy." See also Friedmann, "Phenomenon of Urbanization," p. 5. Morse, "Recent Research on Latin American Urbanization," p. 43, says: "The flow of people to large cities is out of proportion to fresh opportunities for stable urban employment, especially industrial." He argues that the city has insufficient capacity, governmental and private, to absorb the growing urban population.

18. Glenn H. Beyer, ed., *The Urban Explosion in Latin America* (Ithaca, N. Y.: Cornell University Press, 1967), p. 191.

19. Although it is not our purpose in this book to go into the specifics of the economic growth of Brazil and the form of capitalism that is developing there at present, the interested reader may want some background references on the topic. Among the classic works are Celso Furtado, *A Formação Econômica do Brasil* (Rio de Janeiro: Fundo de Cultura, 1959), translated into English as *The Economic Growth of Brazil* (Berkeley: University of California Press, 1963); Caio Prado, Jr., *História Econômica do Brasil*, 7th ed. (São Paulo: Editora Brasiliense, 1962); and Fernando Henrique Cardoso, "The Brazilian Political Model" (Paper presented for the Workshop on Brazilian Development, Yale University, April 1971).

Good historical interpretations, through the notion of dependency, the development of underdevelopment, and the nature of labor markets, are F. H. Cardoso and E. Falleto, *Dependência e Desenvolvimento na América Latina*, 2nd ed. (Rio de Janeiro; Zahar, 1973); André Gunder Frank, *Capitalism and Underdevelopment in Latin America*, part 3 (New York: Monthly Review Press, 1969); F. Oliveira, "A Economia Brasileira: Crítica a Razão Dualista," *Estudos CEBRAP*, no. 2 (October 1972): 3-82, translated into Spanish as "La Economia Brasileña: Crítica a la Razon Dualista," *El Trimestre Económico* 40: 441-484; M. C. Tavares and J. Serra, "Una Discusión Sobre el Estilo del Desarrollo Recente de Brasil," *El Trimestre Económico*, no. 152 (November-December 1971); and Theotonio dos Santos, "Brazil, the Origins of a Crisis," in *Latin America: The Struggle with Dependency and Beyond*, eds. Ronald Chilcote and Joel Edelstein (New York: Schenkman Publishing Co., 1974), pp. 415-490.

On import substitutes, see M. C. Tavares, *Da Substituição de Importações ao Capitalismo Financeiro* (Rio de Janeiro: Zahar, 1973); and "The Growth and Decline of Import Substitution in Brazil," in *Economic Bulletin for Latin America* 9, no. 1, U. N. Economic Commission for Latin America (New York and Santiago: March 1964).

For an excellent image of contemporary Brazil, see A. Stepan, ed., *Authoritarian Brazil: Origins, Policies, and Future* (New Haven: Yale University Press, 1973). Also, recent issues of *El Trimestre Económico* (Mexico, D. F.: Fondo de Cultural Economica) carries many articles on the Brazilian economy.

20. Schuh and Whitaker, "Migration, Mobility," p. 23.

21. *Ibid.*, p. 4.

22. Quoted in Bertram Hutchinson, "The Migrant Population of Urban Brazil," *América Latina* 6, no. 2 (April-June 1963): 47. Using the methodology employed by A. J. Jaffe and J. N. Froomkin for Panama and Japan in "Economic Development and Jobs: A Comparison of Japan and Panama, 1950 to 1960," *Estadística* 24, no. 92 (September 1966): 577-593, to estimate the rate of growth of the non-agricultural sector that would maintain the number of workers in the agricultural sector constant, we obtain figures of 12 percent per year for the same decade in the case of Brazil. The high rate of growth is a

consequence of the pattern of change of the Brazilian labor force, where new entries is the important component in its change.

23. Friedmann, "Phenomenon of Urbanization," p. 1.

24. *Ibid.*, p. 5.

25. Louis Wirth, "Urbanism as a Way of Life," *American Journal of Sociology* 44 (July 1938).

26. Robert Redfield, *The Folk Culture of Yucatan* (Chicago: University of Chicago Press, 1941); *idem*, "The Folk Society," *American Journal of Sociology* 52 (1947): 293-308. Redfield develops the idea that the transformation from folk to urban society is accompanied by the assertion of the technical over the moral order in *The Primitive World and its Transformations* (Ithaca, N. Y.: Cornell University Press, 1953).

27. Oscar Lewis, "Urbanization Without Breakdown," *Scientific Monthly* 75 (1952): 31-41.

28. These findings have since been substantiated by a variety of research: William P. Mangin, "Latin American Squatter Settlements: A Problem and a Solution," *Latin America Research Review* 2, no. 3 (Summer 1967): 65-90; John Turner, *Uncontrolled Urban Settlements: Problems and Policies* (Pittsburgh: University of Pittsburgh Press, 1966); Frank Bonilla and José Silva Michelena, eds., *Studying the Venezuelan Polity: Explorations in Analysis and Synthesis* (Cambridge, Mass.: M. I. T. Press, 1966); José Matos Mar, "The Barriadas of Lima," in *Urbanization in Latin America*, ed. Philip Hauser (New York: International Document Service, 1961), pp. 170-190; Gino Germani, "The City as an Integrating Mechanism: The Concept of Social Integration," in *The Urban Explosion in Latin America*, ed. Glenn H. Beyer (Ithaca, N. Y.: Cornell University Press, 1967); Daniel Goldrich, Raymond Pratt, and C. R. Schuller, "The Political Integration of Lower Class Urban Settlements in Chile and Peru," *Studies in Comparative International Development* 3, no. 1 (St. Louis: Social Science Institute, Washington University, 1967-1968).

29. On the concept of the "city as a fortress of high culture" and the policy implications of this, see Lisa Peattie, "Some Notes on the Problems of Urbanization," mimeographed (Cambridge, Mass.: Massachusetts Institute of Technology, Department of Urban Planning [1967]).

30. Richard M. Morse, "Internal Migrants and the Urban Ethos in Latin America," mimeographed (paper for the 7th World Congress of Sociology, Varna, Bulgaria, September 1970), p. 6. Morse calls the first two of these "hand-wringers" and "positive thinkers."

31. Prime examples of this mentality are Lambert and Mattelhart, "L'urbanisation Acceleréé de l'Amerique Latine et la Formation d'un Secteur Tertiare Refuge," *Civilisations* 15 (1965): 2-4, and Armand Mattelhart and Manuel A. Garreton, *Integración y Marginalidad: Ensayo de Regionalización Social de Chile* (Santiago: 1965).

32. Barbara Ward, "The Uses of Prosperity," *Saturday Review*, August 29, 1964, p. 191.

33. See Bert F. Hoselitz, "The City, The Factory, and Economic Growth," *American Economic Review* 45, no. 2 (May 1955): 177-184. This is also the point of view of Philip M. Hauser, "On the Impact of Urbanism on Social Organization, Human Nature, and the Political Order," *Confluence* 7, no. 1 (Spring 1958): 57-69, and Davis and Golden, "Development of Pre-Industrial Areas," p. 137.

34. Friedmann, "Phenomenon of Urbanization," p. 3; Benjamin Higgins, "The

Scope and Objectives of Planning for Underdeveloped Regions," *Documentación del l Seminario Sôbre Regionalización* (Rio de Janeiro: Instituto Panamericano de Geografia y História, Comisión de Geografia, 1969); Harley L. Browning and Waltrout Keint, "Selectivity of Migrants to a Metropolis in a Developing Country: A Mexican Case Study," *Demography* 6, no. 4 (November 1969): 347-357; Albert O. Hirschman, *Journeys Toward Progress* (New York: Twentieth Century Fund, 1963); and *idem.*, *A Strategy for Economic Development* (New Haven, Conn.: Yale University Press, 1961).

35. Harley L. Browning, "Recent Trends in Latin American Urbanization," *Annals of the American Academy of Political and Social Science* 316 (March 1958): 111-120.

36. E. J. Hobsbawn, "Peasants and Rural Migrants in Politics," in *The Politics of Conformity in Latin America*, ed. Claudio Veliz (New York: Oxford University Press, 1970), p. 64.

37. Gideon Sjoberg, "Cities in Developing and Industrial Societies: A Cross-Cultural Analysis," in *The Study of Urbanization*, eds. Hauser and Schnore, p. 233. Sjoberg goes on to say that misery in the countryside, though often greater, is inevitably more diffuse and less transparent.

38. Bert F. Hoselitz, "The Role of Urbanization in Economic Development," in *India's Urban Future*, ed. R. Turner (Berkeley and Los Angeles: University of California Press, 1962), p. 157.

39. Report of the Secretariat of the Economic Commission for Latin America on the Social Development of Latin America (May 1963).

40. Daniel Lerner, *The Passing of Traditional Society* (New York: The Free Press of Glencoe, 1964). Further analysis of this paradigm from the empirical point of view of various causal models has been carried out by Hayward Alker in "Causal Inference and Political Analysis," in *Mathematical Applications in Political Science*, ed. Joseph Bernd (Dallas, Texas: Southern Methodist University Press, 1970).

41. Alex Inkeles, "The Modernization of Man," in *Modernization: The Dynamics of Growth*, ed. Myron Weiner (New York: Basic Books, Inc., 1966), pp. 138-153, and *idem*, "Making Men Modern: On the Causes and Consequences of Individual Change in Six Developing Countries," *American Journal of Sociology* 75, no. 2 (1969): 208-225.

This argument is almost tautological since education and factory experience are inherently part of the urban experience. One wonders with a certain uneasiness what is left of the urban experience if education and factory work are taken out, assuming that methodologically and conceptually such a thing is possible. Other institutions or orders, such as the religious one, tend to be more national in character than local, so their impact on the migrant is obviously limited within an urban context.

42. Morse, "Internal Migrants and the Urban Ethos," p. 3.

43. Anibal Quijano, "Dependencia, Cambio Social y Urbanización en Latino-america," Social Affairs Division, Economic Commission for Latin America (ECLA), 1967. The writings of André Gunder Frank develop the argument more fully. See Frank, "The Development of Underdevelopment in Brazil," in *Capitalism and Underdevelopment in Latin America*, ed. A. G. Frank (New York: Monthly Review Press, 1967), and *idem*, *Latin America: Underdevelopment or Revolution* (New York: Monthly Review Press, 1967).

44. Jorgé Balan, "Migrant-Native Socioeconomic Differences in Latin American Cities: A Structural Analysis," *Latin American Research Review* 4, no. 1 (Winter 1969): 4.

45. Morse, "Internal Migrants and the Urban Ethos," p. 2.

46. Beyer, *The Urban Explosion*, p. 98. Beyer goes on to make the interesting point that existing conditions of rural poverty prevent those remaining from benefitting from this out-migration through rural integration and land reform while the talent that goes to the cities is generally dissipated in slum life.

47. Germani, "The City as an Integrating Mechanism," pp. 175-189.

48. N. V. Sovani, "The Analysis of Over-Urbanization," *Economic Development and Cultural Change* 12, no. 2 (January 1964): 27.

49. Werner Baer and Michael E. A. Herve, "Employment and Industrialization in Developing Countries," *Quarterly Journal of Economics* (February 1966), and Werner Baer in *Economic Development and Cultural Change* 12 (April 1964). See also Ben Cohen and Nat Leff, "Comment," *Quarterly Journal of Economics* (February 1967). Similarly, Bazzanella divided Brazil into three regions: retarded, intermediate and advanced, by socioeconomic status and found urbanization and income from the tertiary sector about equal in each area. See Waldermiro Bazzanella, "Industrializacão e Urbanizacão no Brasil," *America Latina* 6, no. 1 (January-March 1963): 3-26. This finding was confirmed and elaborated by Douglas Graham, "Divergent and Convergent Regional Economic Growth and Internal Migration in Brazil, 1940-1960," *Economic Development and Cultural Change* 18, no. 3 (April 1970): 366ff. Beyer, *The Urban Explosion*, p. 97, complains that "There is no solid body of tested quantitative data describing the reasons for such a large-scale movement towards the cities," and refuses to decide between the push and pull theories.

50. For example, see Douglas B. Butterworth, "A Study of the Urbanization Process Among Mixtec Migrants from Tilantongo in Mexico City," in *Peasants in Cities*, ed. William P. Mangin (Boston: Houghton Mifflin Co., 1970); A. L. Epstein, "Urbanization and Social Change in Africa," *Current Anthropology* (October 1967): 275-298; Colin Leys, "Politics in Kenya: The Development of Peasant Society," mimeographed, Institute for Development Studies, Discussion Paper no. 102 (Nairobi: University of Nairobi, 1970); and Oya Ozurelli, "Dynamics of Urban Family and Rural Kin Relations in a Transitional Setting: A Study of Two Turkish Communities," mimeographed (May 1973).

51. Lucian W. Pye, "The Political Implications of Urbanization and the Development Process," U. N. Conference on Applications of Science and Technology for the Benefit of Less Developed Areas, U. S. Papers (Washington, D. C.: U. S. Government Printing Office, 1962).

52. Wayne A. Cornelius, Jr., "The Political Sociology of Cityward Migration in Latin America: Toward Empirical Theory," mimeographed for *Latin American Urban Annual*, eds. Francine F. Rabinowitz and Felicity M. Trueblood (Beverly Hills, Calif.: Sage Publications, forthcoming); also see Anthony and Elizabeth Leeds, "Brazil and the Myth of Urban Rurality: Urban Experience, Work, and Values in 'Squatments' of Rio de Janeiro and Lima," (Paper delivered at Conference on Urbanization and Work in Modernizing Countries, St. Thomas, November 1967).

53. Charles Abrams, *City is the Frontier*, p. 13; Herbert Friedmann, "Squatter Assimilation in Buenos Aires" (draft of Ph.D. dissertation, Massachusetts Institute of Technology, December 1967), p. 21; Nelson, *Migrants, Urban Poverty, and Instability*, p. 3. For general work on the subject, see Charles Abrams, *Man's Struggle for Shelter in an Urbanizing World* (Cambridge, Mass.: MIT Press, 1964).

54. Morse, "Recent Research on Latin American Urbanization," p. 56.

55. Quoted in Maria Lúcia de Paula Petiz, "A Utilização do Método de P.O.C. Em Um Programa de Melhoramentos Físicos na Favela," Pontífica Universidade Católica, Instituto Social (Rio de Janeiro: November 1963), p. 3. Author's translation. Note: all translations from the Portuguese or Spanish are the author's.

56. *Jornal do Brasil* (Rio de Janeiro), May 10, 1971, p. 9. See also "Aspectos Humanos das Favelas Cariocas," *O Estado de Paulo*, April 13, 1960.

57. This discussion is based primarily on Andrew Pearse, "Some Characteristics of Urbanization in the City of Rio de Janeiro," in *Urbanization in Latin America*, ed. Philip M. Hauser (New York: Columbia University Press, 1961), pp. 192-193, and José Artur Rios, "Social Transformation and Urbanization—The Case of Rio de Janeiro" (Catholic University, Rio de Janeiro, Brazil, 1970, mimeographed).

58. Data from Anthony Leeds and Frank Bonilla.

59. Friedmann, "Urbanization in Latin America," p. 10.

60. Mangin, "Latin American Squatter Settlements," p. 66. For an example from another setting, see Granville Hardwick Sewell, "Squatter Settlements in Turkey: Analysis of a Social, Political, and Economic Problem," (Ph.D. dissertation for Massachusetts Institute of Technology, June 1964).

61. John R. Seeley, "The Slum: Its Nature, Use, and Uses," *Journal of the American Institute of Planners* 25, no. 1 (February 1959). Fried and Gleicher also mention convenience, variety, mutual self-help networks, sense of community, and "localism"; see Marc Fried and Peggy Gleicher, "Some Sources of Residential Satisfaction in an Urban Slum," *Journal of the American Institute of Planners* 28, no. 4 (November 1961). See Marc Fried, "Grieving for a Lost Home," in *The Urban Condition*, ed. Leonard Duhl (New York: Basic Books, 1963); Jane Jacobs, *The Death and Life of Great American Cities* (New York: Vintage Books, 1961); and John Turner's work for the U. N. on "uncontrolled urban settlements."

62. Machado da Silva, *et al.*, "Sociólogos São Contra Solução Paternalista Para As Favelas," *Jornal do Brasil*, August 26, 1968.

Chapter Two

1. John Turner, "Four Autonomous Settlements in Lima, Peru" (draft, May 1967); *idem, Uncontrolled Urban Settlement: Problems and Policies* (Pittsburgh: University of Pittsburgh Press, 1966); William P. Mangin, "Latin American Squatter Settlements: A Problem and a Solution," *Latin American Research Review* 2, no. 3 (Summer 1967): 70; Richard M. Morse, "Trends and Issues in Latin American Urban Research, 1965-1970, Part I," *Latin American Research Review* 7, no. 1 (Spring 1971).

2. Lawrence F. Salmen, "Housing Alternatives for the Carioca Working Class: A Comparison Between Favelas and Casas de Cômodos," *América Latina* (1970).

3. Data for the following derives from contextual interviews, standardized questionnaires, field notes, and documents.

4. Maria Lucia de Paula Petiz, "A Utilização do Método de P.O.C. Em Um Programa de Melhoramentos Físicos na Favela," Pontífica Universidade Católica, Instituto Social (Rio de Janeiro: November 1963), p. 3.

5. The first figure comes from Fundação Leão XIII, Divisão de Serviços Sociais e

Estatística, *1967 Report on Favelas of Guanabara*. Other estimates are 1,823 units, 2,230 families, and 9,000 people reported in the *Jornal do Brasil* (Rio de Janeiro), May 10, 1971; 12,000 people estimated by Anthony and Elizabeth Leeds, "Brazil in the 1960's: Favelas and Polity, the Continuity of Social Control," unpublished manuscript to appear in Riordon Roett, ed., *Brazil in the 1960's* (Nashville, Tenn.: Vanderbilt University Press), p. 46; and 4,500 residences with 20,000 people estimated by CODESCO, 1963. The large estimate quoted above comes from the President of the Association of Residents as quoted in *O Dia* (Rio de Janeiro), September 15, 1968, and is purposely high because he was stressing the costliness of relocating the favela.

6. *Correio da Manhã* (Rio de Janeiro), January 21, 1971.

7. This and all other statistics presented without specific reference in this chapter come directly from the administered questionnaire in each community.

8. João Rath, *Ultima Hora* (Rio de Janeiro), October 18, 1969, estimates membership at 3,000.

9. *Ibid.*

10. *Jornal do Brasil*, August 7, 1967.

11. Observations from general field work, confirmed by interview of January 16, 1969 with Carlos Nelson dos Santos and Sylvia Wanderley, two Brazilian architects who have worked intensively in Rio's favelas.

12. There are a number of favelas as well as plots (*loteamentos*) in the first district, permitting a control group analysis since the education, occupation, and income levels of these persons are about the same as those of favelados and yet they own their own land. We can thus test for the effect of security of tenure, an influence stressed by Turner and other students of the favela.

13. The figures are from the Instituto Brasileiro de Geografia e Estatística and are for 1968.

14. All of the above discussion on history is based on Mauricio Roberto, "Plano de Desenvolvimento Local Integrado," section 1.3, "Historical Evolution," and "Relatório Para O IBAM Sôbre Duque de Caxias," (1969).

15. Heraldo Dias, "Desníveis Sociais Na Baixada Fluminense São Cada Vez Maiores," *Jornal do Brasil*, 25 August 1968, p. 16.

16. This arrangement is part of the Fifth Institutional Act.

17. The following is based on an interview with José Barbosa, President of the Residents' Association, September 4, 1969.

Chapter Three

1. Joseph Kotta, in an unpublished paper for the Cornell-Columbia-Harvard-Illinois Summer Field Studies Program in Anthropology, Columbia University (1963), revealed over 40 racial terms in current usage with little agreement as to how to apply them.

2. This figure provides a cross-check on the reliability of the data. The *Estudos Cariocas* (Rio de Janeiro: Estado da Guanabara, 1965) found 19 percent of the favelados were Rio-born. See also Andrew Pearse, "Some Characteristics of Urbanization in the City of Rio de Janeiro," in *Urbanization in Latin America*, ed. Philip M. Hauser (New York: Columbia University Press, 1961), and Anthony and Elizabeth Leeds, "Brazil and the Myth of Urban Rurality: Urban Experience, Work, and Values in 'Squatments' of

Rio de Janeiro and Lima" (Paper delivered at the Conference on Urbanization and Work in Modernizing Countries, St. Thomas, November 1967). William P. Mangin, "Latin American Squatter Settlements: A Problem and a Solution," *Latin American Research Review* 2, no. 3 (Summer 1967), lists the conception of favelados as migrants as the first among commonly held myths concerning the favela.

3. Leeds and Leeds, "Brazil and the Myth of Urban Rurality," p. 8, found in one of the older favelas they studied that "perhaps 40 percent or more were Carioca . . . quite a number of these were second and third generation in the favela itself."

4. For some good background reading on the history of internal migration in Brazil, see: (1) Manuel T. Berlinck and Daniel J. Hogan, "O Desenvolvimento Econômico do Brasil e as Migrações Internas para São Paulo: Uma Análise Histórica," mimeographed (Escola de Administração de Empresas da Fundação Getúlio Vargas, São Paulo, 1972). (2) Manuel Augusto Costa, ed. "Migrações Internas no Brasil," monograph no. 5 (Rio de Janeiro: Instituto de Planejamento Econômico e Social [IPEA] and Instituto de Pesquisas [INPES], 1971). (3) Douglas H. Graham, "Divergent and Convergent Regional Economic Growth and Internal Migration in Brazil, 1940-1960" mimeographed (Vanderbilt University and Instituto de Pesquisas Econômicas, Universidade de São Paulo, n. d.); *idem*, "Migration, Regional and Urban Growth and Development in Brazil: A Selective Analysis of the Historical Record, 1872-1970" mimeographed (Instituto de Pesquisas Econômicas, Universidade de São Paulo, 1971). (4) Douglas H. Graham and Sergio Buarque de Hollanda Filho, "Interregional and Urban Migration and Economic Growth in Brazil," mimeographed, n. d. (5) "Macro-economia da Urbanização Brasileira," *Pesquisa e Planejamento Economico* 3, no. 3 (October 1973): 585-644. (6) Milton da Mata, "Urbanização e Migrações Internas," *Pesquisa e Planejamento Econômico* 3, no. 3 (October 1973): 714-746. (7) Milton da Mata, Eduardo Werneck R. de Carvalho, and Maria Tereza I. I. de Castro e Silva, *Migraçoes Internas no Brasil: Aspectos Econqmicos e Demográficos* (Rio de Janeiro: Instituto de Planajamento Econômico e Social (IPEA), 1973). (8) John Redwood III, "Internal Migration, Urbanization, and Frontier Region Development in Brazil since 1940" (Honor's thesis, Harvard University, 1968). (9) Paulo Singer, "Migrações Internas: Considerações Teóricas Sôbre O Seu Estudo," mimeographed, n.d.

5. Richard M. Morse, "Internal Migration and the Urban Ethos in Latin America" (paper delivered at the 7th World Congress of Sociology, Varna, Bulgaria, September 1970, p. 2).

6. *Ibid.*; Glenn H. Beyer, *The Urban Explosion in Latin America: A Continent in Process of Urbanization* (Ithaca, N. Y.: Cornell University Press, 1967), p. 98; Jorge Balan, "Migrant-Native Socioeconomic Differences in Latin American Cities: A Structural Analysis," *Latin American Research Review* 4, no. 1 (Winter 1969): 4; Gideon Sjoberg, "Rural Urban Balance and Models of Economic Development," in *Social Structure and Mobility in Economic Development*, eds. Smelser and Lipset (Chicago: University of Chicago Press, 1966); and Gino Germani, "Social and Political Consequences of Mobility," in *ibid.*

7. Octavio Ianni, *Crisis in Brazil* (New York: Columbia University Press, 1970), p. 52. E. J. Hobsbawm also makes this point in "Peasants and Rural Migrants in Politics," in *The Politics of Conformity in Latin America*, ed. Claudio Veliz (New York: Oxford University Press, 1967).

8. Balan, "Migrant-Native Socioeconomic Differences," p. 4.

9. Frank Bonilla, "Rio's Favelas: The Rural Slum Within the City," American Universities Field Staff Report, East Coast South America Series, vol. 8, no. 3 (Brazil: August 1961).

10. Leeds and Leeds, "Brazil and the Myth of Urban Rurality," p. 6.

11. The Instituto Universitário study found that about 20 percent of the population was second generation (that is, the city-born), but the study used the figure of 44 percent as rural origin. Leeds discusses the problem of the definition of "rural." I assume that in this case the authors have combined what I have called *roça* with *vila* and *povoado*. This would account for the discrepancies between this study and ours. See Renato Raul Boschi and Rose Ingrid Goldschmidt, "Populações Favelados do Estado da Guanabara" (Rio de Janeiro: Edições DADOS, 1970), p. 6.

12. See, for example, "Northeast Brazil," *Realities*, no. 161 (April 1964): 60-67, and Maria Carolina de Jesus, *Child of the Dark* (New York: Signet Books, 1962).

13. According to the *Estudos Cariocas*, a total of 64 percent came from Rio and the East, which is *exactly* the same as our combined figures for the two areas.

14. One of the most compelling presentations of this type of "push" migration—fleeing the droughts of the "sertão"—is the Graciliano Ramos novel, *Vidas Sécas* (*Barren Lives*), and the film based on it.

15. Marvin Harris, *Town and Country in Brazil* (New York: Columbia University Press, 1966).

16. Leeds and Leeds, "Brazil and the Myth of Urban Rurality," p. 6.

17. N. V. Sovani, "The Analysis of Over-Urbanization," *Economic Development and Cultural Change* 7, no. 2 (January 1964): 27.

18. Ianni, *Crisis in Brazil*, pp. 32, 52.

19. Gino Germani, "Emigración del Campo a la Ciudad y sus Causas," in *Sociedad, Economia y Reforma Agraria*, eds. Horatio Gilberti *et al.* (Buenos Aires: 1965), p. 74.

20. Werner Baer and Michael E. A. Herve, "Employment and Industrialization in Developing Countries," *Quarterly Journal of Economics* 80, no. 1 (February 1966), and Baer, "Regional Inequality and Economic Growth in Brazil," *Economic Development and Cultural Change* 13, no. 3 (April 1964). See also Ben Cohen and Nat Leff, "Comment," *Quarterly Journal of Economics* 81, no. 1 (February 1967). Similarly, Bazzanella divided Brazil into three regions—retarded, intermediate, and advanced—by socio-economic status and found urbanization and income from the tertiary sector about equal in each area. See Waldemiro Bazzanella, "Industrializaçao e Urbanização no Brasil," *América Latina* 6, no. 1 (January-March 1963): 3-26. This finding was confirmed and elaborated by Douglas Graham, "Divergent and Convergent Regional Economic Growth and Internal Migration in Brazil, 1940-1960," *Economic Development and Cultural Change* 18, no. 3 (April 1970): 366ff. Beyer, *Urban Explosion in Latin America*; p. 97, complains that "There is no solid body of tested quantitative data describing the reasons for such a large-scale movement towards the cities," and refuses to decide between the push and pull theories.

21. Leeds and Leeds, "Brazil and the Myth of Urban Rurality," pp. 14-15. Two individuals mentioned earlier, Waldevino (president of the Catacumba Residents' Association) and José Barbosa (founder of Nova Brasília's Residents' Association) fall into this category. It is my impression that the discrepancies between the Leeds' findings and my own are attributable to the fact that working as anthropologists, rather than talking with a representative sample, they consistently spoke with more articulate and

interesting informants—usually leaders or those in special circumstances (such as having Peace Corps members living in their homes).

22. Ianni, *Crisis in Brasil*, p. 55, has demonstrated that migrants are indeed likely to be better off in the city than in their local areas. In salaries, doctors per 1,000 persons, educational opportunities, radios, movies, and so forth, the advantage clearly goes to the city. Hobsbawm, "Peasants and Rural Migrants," p. 60, has written that nowhere is the gap between rural and urban levels greater than in Latin America.

23. See José Pastore, "Satisfaction Among Migrants to Brasilia, Brazil: A Sociological Interpretation" (Ph.D. dissertation, University of Wisconsin, Madison, 1968); E. A. Wilkening, "The Role of the Extended Family in Migration and Adaptation to Brazil" (paper delivered at the Annual Meeting of the Rural Sociological Society, San Francisco, August 1967); Richard M. Morse, "Recent Research on Latin American Urbanization: A Selective Survey with Commentary," *Latin American Research Review* 1, no. 1 (Fall 1965); and Leeds and Leeds, "Brazil and the Myth of Urban Rurality;" Mangin, "Latin American Squatter Settlements."

24. Lucian W. Pye, "The Political Implications of Urbanization and the Development Process," U. N. Conference on Applications of Science and Technology for the Benefit of Less Developed Areas, U. S. Papers (Washington, D. C.: U. S. Government Printing Office, 1962), p. 85.

25. See, for example, John Turner, *Uncontrolled Urban Settlement: Problems and Policies* (Pittsburgh: Pittsburgh University Press, 1967); *idem.*, "Four Autonomous Settlements in Lima, Peru" (draft, May 1967); and Mangin, "Latin American Squatter Settlements."

26. Leeds and Leeds, "Brazil and the Myth of Urban Rurality," p. 12.

27. Bertram Hutchinson found, ten years earlier in Rio, that 84 percent of male migrants seeking employment immediately upon arrival found it within a month. His sample was not drawn, however, entirely from the lower sector, so the comparison is not precise. See Hutchinson, "The Migrant Population of Urban Brazil," *América Latina* 6, no. 2 (April-June 1963); 68.

28. Celso Furtado, "Political Obstacles to Economic Growth in Brazil," *International Affairs* (April 1965); *idem.*, *Economic Growth of Brazil* (Berkeley: University of California Press, 1963); *idem*, *Diagnosis of the Brazilian Crisis* (Berkeley: University of California Press, 1965); and Thomas E. Skidmore, *Politics in Brazil* (New York: Oxford University Press, 1967).

29. Balan, "Migrant-Native Socioeconomic Differences," pp. 3-29.

30. José Silva Michelena, "Conflict and Consensus in Venezuela" (Ph.D. dissertation, Dept. of Political Science, Massachusetts Institute of Technology, 1968), p. 201.

Chapter Four

1. Lisa R. Peattie, "Some Notes on the Conceptualization of Problems of Urbanization" mimeographed (Massachusetts Institute of Technology, n. d.); and Alejandro Portes, "Urbanization and Politics in Latin America," *Social Science Quarterly* (December 1971): 697-720.

2. Walter Miller commented similarly on anti-poverty strategies in the United States, comparing the PTA and playing the numbers. Quoted in Lisa Peattie, "The Concept of 'Marginality' as Applied to Squatter Settlements" (mimeographed, Dept. of Urban Studies and Planning, Massachusetts Institute of Technology, n. d.), p. 8.

3. "Favelas of Guanabara" (mimeographed, Rio de Janeiro: Fundação Leão XIII, 1968).

4. Ibid.

5. Quoted by Anthony Leeds, "The Culture of Poverty," in Eleanor Burke Leacock, ed., The Culture of Poverty (New York: Simon and Schuster, 1971), p. 255, fn 18.

6. Everett V. Stonequist, "The Problem of the Marginal Man," American Journal of Sociology 41, no. 1 (July 1935): 4.

7. See Everett Cherington Hughes and Helen MacGill Hughes, Where People Meet: Racial and Ethnic Frontiers (Glencoe, Ill.: The Free Press, 1952), pp. 189-199.

8. See Stonequist, "Problem of the Marginal Man," p. 9.

9. Rudolfo Stavenhagen, "Seven Fallacies about Latin America," in Latin America: Reform or Revolution?, eds. James Petras and Maurice Zeitlin (Greenwich, Conn.: Fawcett Publications, 1968); and Pablo Gonzales Casanova, Democracy in Mexico (New York: Oxford University Press, 1970).

10. Gino Germani, "Aspectos Teóricos de la Marginalidad," Revista Paraguaya de Sociologia 9, no. 30 (January-April 1972).

11. Milton Myron Gordon, Assimilation in American Life: The Role of Race, Religion, and National Origins (New York: Oxford University Press, 1964).

12. Robert E. Park, "Human Migration and the Marginal Man," American Journal of Sociology 33, no. 6 (May 1928): 892.

13. Ibid., p. 893.

14. Stonequist, "Problem of the Marginal Man," p. 7. Stonequist does not consider gypsies, hobos, or hotel dwellers to be migrants in the social sense but only in the geographic sense, since they do not change loyalties or break home ties. His main examples are the Jews of Eastern Europe, migrating in waves and producing the intelligensia of their era.

15. Ibid., p. 10.

16. Kerckhoff and Mann, for example, used it as the basis for their scales of marginality. See A. C. Kerckhoff, "An Investigation of Factors Operative in the Development of the Personality Characteristics of Marginality" (Ph.D. dissertation, University of Wisconsin, 1953); and J. W. Mann, "The Problem of the Marginal Personality" (Ph.D. dissertation, University of Natal, 1957).

17. Quoted in H. F. Dickie-Clark, The Marginal Situation (London: Routledge and Kegan Paul, 1966), p. 9.

18. Stonequist, "The Problem of the Marginal Man," pp. 10-12, discusses the life-cycle stages.

19. Ibid., p. 12.

20. Robert Merton, Social Theory and Social Structure (New York: The Free Press, 1957), p. 266.

21. Ibid., p. 265.

22. Milton M. Goldberg, "A Qualification of the Marginal Man Theory," American Sociological Review 6, no. 1 (1941): 52-58.

23. Ibid.; J. S. Slotkin, "The Status of the Marginal Man," Sociology and Social

Research 28, no. 1 (1943): 47-54; Golovensky, "Marginal Man Concept"; and Aaron Antonovsky, "Toward a Refinement of the 'Marginal Man' Concept," *Social Forces* 36, no. 1 (1956): 57-62.

24. Irvin L. Child, *Italian or American? The Second Generation in Conflict* (New Haven: Yale University Press, 1943).

25. Alan C. Kerckhoff and Thomas C. McCormick, "Marginal Status and the Marginal Personality," *Social Forces* 34, no. 1 (October 1955): 48-55.

26. Mann, "Problem of the Marginal Personality."

27. See Kerckhoff and McCormick, "Marginal Status," and Mann, "Problem of the Marginal Personality."

28. Dickie-Clark, *Marginal Situation*, p. 37.

29. A. Solow and L. Vera, *Panorama del Problema de la Vivienda en América Latina* (Washington, D. C.: Pan American Union, 1952).

30. Josephina R. Albano, *El Factor Humano en los Programas de Rehabilitación de Tugurios* (Bogota: Centro Interamericano de Vivienda, 1955).

31. Ramiro Cardona, "Los Asentamientos Espontaneos de Vivienda," in *Las Migraciones Internas*, ed. R. Cardona (Bogota: ACOFAME, 1973).

32. See *Proyecto de Evaluación de los Superbloques* (Caracas: Banco Obrero, 1962).

33. See William P. Mangin, ed., *Peasants in Cities* (Boston: Houghton Mifflin Co., 1970).

34. José Matos Mar, "Migration and Urbanization—The Barriadas of Lima: An Example of Integration into Urban Life," in *Urbanization in Latin America*, ed. Philip M. Hauser (New York: Columbia University Press, 1961), p. 174.

35. José Matos Mar, "Urbanización y Barriadas en América del Sur" (Lima: Instituto de Estudios Peruanos, 1968).

36. Juarez Brandão Lopez, "Aspects of the Adjustment of Rural Migrants to Urban Industrial Conditions in São Paulo, Brazil," in *Urbanization in Latin America*, ed. Philip M. Hauser (New York: Columbia University Press, 1961), p. 247.

37. Gino Germani, "Inquiry into the Social Effects of Urbanization in a Working Class Sector of Greater Buenos Aires," in *Urbanization in Latin America*, ed. Philip M. Hauser (New York: Columbia University Press, 1961), p. 232.

38. Andrew Pearse, "Some Characteristics of Urbanization in the City of Rio de Janeiro," in *Urbanization in Latin America*, ed. Philip M. Hauser (New York: Columbia University Press, 1961), p. 204.

39. *Ibid.*, p. 200.

40. Robert Redfield, *The Folk Culture of Yucatan* (Chicago: University of Chicago Press, 1959).

41. Talcott Parsons and Edward A. Shils, *Toward a General Theory of Action* (Cambridge, Mass.: Harvard University Press, 1954).

42. Max Weber, *The Protestant Ethic and the Spirit of Capitalism*, 1958, ed. (New York: Charles Scribner's Sons, 1904-1905).

43. Max F. Millikan and Donald L. M. Blackmer, *The Emerging Nations* (Boston: Little, Brown and Co., 1961).

44. For example, see Lucian W. Pye, *Politics, Personality, and Nation Building: Burma's Search for Identity* (New Haven: Yale University Press, 1962); *idem.*, *Aspects of Political Development* (Boston: Little, Brown and Co., 1966); Gabriel A. Almond and G.

Bingham Powell, Jr., *Comparative Politics: A Developmental Approach* (Boston: Little, Brown and Co., 1966); G. A. Almond and James S. Coleman, eds., *The Politics of Developing Areas* (Princeton, N. J.: Princeton University Press, 1961); and Thomas H. Marshall, *Class, Citizenship and Social Development* (Garden City, N. Y.: Doubleday Books, 1963).

45. On mobilization and participation, see Alex Inkeles, "Participant Citizenship in Six Developing Countries," *American Political Science Review* 63, no. 4 (December 1966); and Karl Deutsch, "Social Mobilization and Political Development," *American Political Science Review* 55, no. 3 (September 1961); 493-505. Deutsch's basic idea is that social mobilization is both a consequence and a cause of modernization. It involves a stage of uprooting and a stage of introduction into new patterns which, in the process, expands the size of the politically relevant strata of the population, multiplies demand for government services, and thus stimulates an increase in governmental capabilities, a broadening of the elite, an increase in political participation, and a shift of attention from the local to the national level.

46. Cyril E. Black, *The Dynamics of Modernization* (New York: Harper and Row, 1966).

47. W. W. Rostow, *The Stages of Economic Growth* (Cambridge: University Press, 1963).

48. On fatalism, see Florence Kluckhohn *et al.*, *Variations in Value Orientations* (Evanston, Ill.: Row, Peterson and Co., 1961); Barbara Ward, *The Rich Nations and the Poor Nations* (New York: W. W. Norton and Co., 1962); Robert Redfield, *The Primitive World and its Transformations* (Ithaca, N. Y.: Great Seals Books, 1953); and Rostow, *Stages of Economic Growth*. Both Redfield and Millikan and Blackmer, *Emerging Nations*, have sections on the sacred-secular dimension.

49. Redfield, *Primitive World and its Transformations*.

50. For further discussion on this point, see Alex Inkeles, "The Modernization of Man," in *Modernization: The Dynamics of Growth*, ed. Myron Weiner (New York: Basic Books, Inc., 1966); Millikan and Blackmer, *Emerging Nations*; Ward, *Rich Nations and Poor Nations*; and others.

51. Milton Rokeach, *The Open and Closed Mind* (New York: Basic Books, Inc., 1960); and Daniel Lerner, *The Passing of Traditional Society* (New York: The Free Press, 1958).

52. Lerner, *ibid.*

53. Everett E. Hagen, *On the Theory of Social Change* (Homewood, Ill.: Dorsey Press, 1962). Millikan and Blackmer, *Emerging Nations*, also discusses the importance of prestige for manual labor.

54. David Clarence McClelland, *The Achievement Motive* (New York: Appleton-Century-Crofts, 1953).

55. Among those that develop this point are Rostow, *Stages of Economic Growth*, Millikan and Blackmer, *Emerging Nations*, Kluckhohn *et al.*, *Variations in Value Orientations*, and Talcott Parsons, *The Social System* (Glencoe, Ill.: The Free Press, 1951).

56. Alex Inkeles, "The Modernization of Man," in *Modernization: The Dynamics of Growth*, ed. Myron Weiner (New York: Basic Books, 1966).

57. See the earlier discussion by Oscar Lewis, "Urbanization Without Breakdown,"

Scientific Monthly 75 (1952): 31-41. In this article, Lewis attacks Redfield's folk-urban continuum and a number of prevailing stereotypes about family breakdown, seculariza-tion, and social disorganization in the city.

58. Many of Lewis' critics, among them Valentine and Leeds, take exception to this claim and contend that the culture of poverty does *not* fit any of the accepted definitions of culture. See Charles A. Valentine, *Culture and Poverty: Critique and Counter-Proposals* (Chicago and London: University of Chicago Press, 1968); and Anthony Leeds, "The Concept of the 'Culture of Poverty': Conceptual, Logical, and Empirical Problems, with Perspectives from Brazil and Peru," in *The Culture of Poverty*, ed. Eleanor Burke Leacock.

59. Oscar Lewis, *Five Families* (New York: Random House, 1958), p. 2.

60. Oscar Lewis, *La Vida: Studies in the Culture of Poverty in San Juan and New York* (New York: Random House, 1969), pp. *xiv-xivii*.

61. *Ibid.*

62. Valentine paraphrases E. Franklin Frazier, *The Negro Family in the United States*, in Charles A. Valentine, *Culture and Poverty* (Chicago: University of Chicago Press, 1968), p. 20.

63. Leacock, ed. *The Culture of Poverty*, p. 9.

64. John Bartky, *Social Issues in Public Education* (Boston: Houghton Mifflin, 1963), pp. 135-141.

65. William Ryan, *Blaming the Victim* (New York: Pantheon Books, 1971).

66. Lewis, *La Vida*, p. xiv.

67. Jerome Kagen, for example, points out that in our society many critical developments take place for children between the ages of 6 and 10; among these developments are the formation of attitudes about peer relationships, intellectual mastery and rationality, sex identification, and sex-role behavior. Kagen's work is discussed in Leacock, *Culture of Poverty*, p. 13.

68. Lewis, *La Vida*, p. *lii*.

69. Oscar Lewis, "The Culture of Poverty," *Scientific American* (1966): 21.

70. *Ibid.*

71. Lewis, *La Vida*, p. *xlix*.

72. Ibid., p. *li*.

73. Ibid., p. *lii*.

74. Roger Vekemans and I. Silva F., *Marginalidad en América Latina: Un Ensayo Diagnóstico* (Barcelona: Herder, 1969), p. 44, quoted in R. Stavenhagen, "Marginality, Participation and Agrarian Structure in Latin America," *Bulletin*, IILS, vol. 7 (June 1970): 70.

75. Roger Vekemans, "Una Estrategia para la Miseria," Centro para el Desarrollo Económico y Social de América Latina (Santiago: DESAL, 1967), p. 7.

76. Roger Vekemans and I. Silva F., *Marginalidad, Promoción Popular e Integra-ción Latinoamericana* (Buenos Aires: Ediciones Troquel, 1970).

77. J. Giusti, "El Programa de Promoción Popular en Chile. Un Entento de Organización Política de los Sectores Populares," *Revista Latinoamericana de Ciencias Sociales* (April 1972).

78. Fernando Kuznetzoff, "Housing Policies or Housing Politics: An Evaluation of

the Chilean Experience" (draft, Department of City and Regional Planning, University of California, Berkeley, 1974).

79. Roger Vekemans, "Marginalidad, Incorporación y Integración," Boletin no. 37 (Santiago: DESAL, May 1967), p. 8.

80. Barbara Ward, "The Uses of Prosperity," *Saturday Review*, August 29, 1964. Lucian W. Pye, in the same vein, speaks of "teeming urban populations . . . so highly politicized that they have become in a sense loaded revolvers pointed at the responsible governments and on the verge of being triggered off at the slightest provocation." See Pye, "The Political Implications of Urbanization and the Development Process," in *The City in Newly Developing Countries: Readings on Urbanism and Urbanization*, ed. Gerald Breese (Englewood Cliffs, N. J.: Prentice-Hall, Inc., 1969), p. 87.

81. Neal Miller and John Dollard, *Social Learning and Imitation* (New Haven: Yale University Press, 1941).

82. Glaucio Soares, "The Politics of Uneven Development: The Case of Brazil," in *Party Systems and Voter Alignments: Cross-National Perspectives*, eds. Seymour M. Lipset and Stein Rokkan (New York: The Free Press of Glencoe, 1967), p. 470.

83. Karl Deutsch defines "mobilization" more completely in "Social Mobilization and Political Development," *American Political Review* 55, no. 3 (September 1961): 403-505, and in "The Growth of Nations: Some Recurrent Patterns of Political and Social Integration," *World Politics* (January 1953). The concept of "mass man" comes from William Kornhauser, *The Politics of Mass Society* (New York: The Free Press, 1959).

84. Gino Germani, "Sobre Algunos Aspectos Teóricos de la Marginalidad," unpublished paper (Harvard University: Center for Population Studies, November 1970), p. 11.

85. Karl Marx, *The Eighteenth Brumaire of Louis Bonaparte* (New York: International Publishers, fourth printing 1968).

86. Franz Fanon, *The Wretched of the Earth* (London: MacGildoon and Kee, 1965), p. 104.

87. Samuel P. Huntington, *Political Order in Changing Societies* (New Haven: Yale University Press, 1968), p. 282.

88. Charles Tilly, "Race and Migration to the American City," in *The Metropolitan Enigma*, ed. James Q. Wilson (Cambridge, Mass.: Harvard University Press, 1968); Myron Weiner, "Urbanization and Political Extremism: An Hypothesis Tested," mimeographed (Massachusetts Institute of Technology, n. d.); *idem*, "Violence and Politics in Calcutta," *Journal of Asian Studies* 20, no. 3 (1961): 277; and Glaucio Soares, "The Political Sociology of Uneven Development in Brazil," in *Revolution in Brazil*, ed. Irving Louis Horowitz (New York: Dutton, 1964), pp. 192, 195.

89. E. J. Hobsbawm, "Peasants and Rural Migrants in Politics," in *The Politics of Conformity in Latin America*, ed. Claudio Veliz (New York: Oxford University Press, 1967), p. 60.

90. Ernst Halperin, "The Decline of Communism in Latin America," *Atlantic Monthly* 215 (May 1965): 65.

91. William P. Mangin, "Latin American Squatter Settlements: A Problem and a Solution," *Latin American Research Review* 2, no. 3 (Summer 1967): 83.

92. Frank Bonilla and José Silva Michelena, eds. *Studying the Venezuelan Polity: Explorations in Analysis and Synthesis* (Cambridge, Mass.: MIT Press, 1966), p. 87.

93. Frank Bonilla, "Rio's Favelas: The Rural Slum Within the City," American Universities Field Staff Report, East Coast South America Series, vol. 8, no. 3 (Brazil: August 1961), p. 11.

94. Hobsbawm, "Peasants and Rural Migrants," pp. 60-61.

95. "Aspectos Humanos das Favelas Cariocas," in *O Estado de S. Paulo.*

96. Anthony and Elizabeth Leeds, "Brazil and the Myth of Urban Rurality: Urban Experience, Work, and Values in 'Squatments' of Rio de Janeiro and Lima" (Paper delivered at the Conference on Urbanization and Work in Modernizing Countries, St. Thomas, November 1967), p. 34.

97. Germani, "Aspectos Teóricos de la Marginalidad," makes this point quite well.

Chapter Five

1. Samuel P. Huntington, *Political Order in Changing Societies* (New Haven: Yale University Press, 1968), p. 280.

2. Lamb found that only 21 percent of the 4,000 residents said they "had anything to do with any neighborhood or community organization." See Curt Lamb, "The New Group Life of the Poor" mimeographed (Yale University, n. d.), p. 21.

3. The question listed 13 different possible groups. It included unions and church-related organizations but excluded church affiliation. See Gabriel A. Almond and Sidney Verba, *The Civic Culture* (Boston: Little, Brown and Co., 1963), p. 247.

4. Renato Raul Boschi and Rose Ingrid Goldschmidt, "Populações Faveladas do Estado da Guanabara" (Rio de Janeiro: Edições Dados, 1970), p. 109.

5. Bonilla found similar levels of trust in his 1961 study of Rio. To the question regarding unity (Table 18), he found that 72 percent said "very united" or "more or less united". See Frank Bonilla, "Rio's Favelas: The Rural Slum Within the City," American Universities Field Staff Report, East Coast South America Series, vol. 8, no. 3 (August 1961), p. 13.

6. Mutual help networks have been noted in lower-class neighborhoods in the United States. See, for example, Marc Fried, "Grieving for a Lost Home," in *The Urban Condition: People and Policy in the Metropolis*, ed. Leonard J. Duhl (New York: Basic Books, 1963); and Herbert Gans, *The Urban Villagers* (New York: The Free Press, 1962).

7. *Time*, September 23, 1957, p. 38.

8. Alejandro Portes quoted in Maria Elena Hurtado, "Marginalidad Sorpresa," *Revista del Domingo*, October 5, 1968, p. 8.

9. These observations and the reference to the planners' study come from Lisa R. Peattie, "The Concept of 'Marginality' as Applied to Squatter Settlements," mimeographed (Department of Urban Studies and Planning, Massachusetts Institute of Technology, n. d.), pp. 5-7. See also Peattie's more extensive reflections in *The View from the Barrio* (Ann Arbor: University of Michigan Press, 1968).

10. Maria Carolina de Jesus, *Child of the Dark* (New York: Signet Books, 1926), pp. 42-43.

11. For further discussion of this point, see Anthony Leeds, "The Concept of the

'Culture of Poverty': Conceptual, Logical, and Empirical Problems, with Perspectives from Brazil and Peru," in *The Culture of Poverty*, ed. Eleanor Burke Leacock (New York: Simon and Schuster, 1971), p. 250.

12. Gino Germani, "Sobre Algunos Aspectos Teóricos de la Marginalidad," Center for Population Studies, Harvard University (November 1970), p. 5. Bonilla, "Rio's Favelas," p. 12, reached a similar conclusion, that the favelado is part of a cohesive community but feels bypassed, forgotten, and excluded only vis-à-vis the outside.

13. Boschi and Goldschmidt, "Populações Faveladas," p. 109.

14. David Smith and Alex Inkeles, "The OM Scale: A Comparative Socio-Psychological Measure of Individual Modernity," *Sociometry* 29, no. 4 (December 1966).

15. Everett M. Rogers, *Diffusion of Innovations* (New York: Free Press of Glencoe, 1962).

16. Janice E. Perlman, "Dimensões de Modernidade Numa Cidade em Franco Desenvolvimento: Estudo do Caso de Belo Horizonte," *Revista Brasileira de Estudos Políticos*, no. 30 (1971); 158.

17. Daniel Lerner, *The Passing of Traditional Society* (New York: The Free Press, 1964), p. 24.

18. For an excellent critique of the culture of poverty, and some good examples from Rio's favelas, see Leeds, "Concept of the 'Culture of Poverty,'"pp. 226-281.

19. Bonilla, "Rio's Favelas," pp. 8-9.

20. Joseph A. Kahl, *The Measurement of Modernism: A Study of Values in Brazil and Mexico* (Austin: University of Texas Press, 1968), p. 96.

21. *Ibid.*, p. 126. Although Kahl used many of the same measures as the present study, he rarely presents marginals on individual questions. His statistical presentations do not allow for easy comparisons.

22. Alejandro Portes, "Los Grupos Urbanos Marginados" mimeographed (June 1969), p. 11.

23. Leeds, "Concept of the 'Culture of Poverty,' " p. 256, makes this point and offers two excellent examples.

24. See Juan J. Linz, "An Authoritarian Regime: Spain," in *Cleavages, Ideologies, and Party Systems*, eds. Allardt and Littunen (Helsinki: Transactions of the Westermark Society, 1964), pp. 291-341; and Malori Pompermayer, "Authoritarianism in Brazil" (paper presented at the Workshop Conference on Brazil Since 1969: Political and Economic Theories Re-examined, sponsored by the Latin American Studies Center, Yale University, New Haven, April 1971).

25. See Paul Doughty, "The Interrelationship of Power, Respect, Affection, and Rectitude in Vicos," *American Behavioral Scientist* 8, no. 7 (March 1965); Allan Holmberg, "The Changing Values and Institutions of Vicos in the Context of National Development," in *ibid.*; and Henry F. Dobyns, "The Strategic Importance of Enlightenment and Skill for Power," in *ibid.*

26. In this regard, Lisa Peattie, in Puerto Rico with a group of people discussing Papa Doc's illness (which was eventually fatal but at the time not definitive), heard one woman mutter, "I hope he doesn't die; I'll *never* get a good maid then." Personal communication, July 1970.

27. Quoted in Peattie, "Concept of 'Marginality'," p. 3.

28. Judith Hoenack and Anthony Leeds, "Marketing Supply and Social Ties in Rio Favelas" mimeographed (1966); and Leeds, "Future Orientation: The Investment Climate in Rio Favelas" (mimeographed, n. d.) p. 3.

29. Peattie, "Concept of 'Marginality,'" p. 3.

30. Anthony and Elizabeth Leeds, "Brazil and the Myth of Urban Rurality: Urban Experience, Work, and Values in 'Squatments' of Rio de Janeiro and Lima" (Paper presented at St. Thomas Conference, November 1967).

31. William P. Mangin, "Latin American Squatter Settlements: A Problem and a Solution," *Latin American Research Review* 2, no. 3, (Summer 1967): 84. Peattie, "Concept of 'Marginality,'" p. 4, reports that her neighbors told her, "industry is the future of the worker."

32. For more detailed descriptions of the concept of reserve army, especially as applied to the Latin American context, and to the concept of marginality, see José Nun, "La Marginalidad en América Latina" and "Superpoblación Relativa, Ejército Industrial de Reserva, y Masa Marginal," mimeographs (Santiago: DESAL, n. d.). On the point about preference for the informal sector, see Lisa R. Peattie, "'Tercialization,' 'Marginality,' and Urban Poverty in Latin America" (draft, MIT, [1974]), and *idem*, "The Informal Sector: A Few Facts from Bogota, Some Comments and a List of Issues" (draft, MIT [1974]).

33. Further work on this topic is underway. See Laura Schlichtmann and Janice E. Perlman, "Labor Force Participation Among Lower-Class Women in Brazil" (draft, University of California, Berkeley, 1974).

34. Further work on the issue of occupational mobility is in progress, using regression analysis to explore more fully the determinants of different patterns of mobility. See Paulo Vieira da Cunha and Janice E. Perlman, "An Empirical Verification of Occupational Mobility of Low Income Workers in Rio de Janeiro (draft, University of California, Berkeley, 1974).

35. The percentage figures on the increase in population and employment in Brazil in the period 1940-1960 are shown below:

Increase in Population and Employment in Brazil

	Total Population	Urban Population	Manufacturing Employment	Second Sector Employment
1940-1956	26%	39%	41%	49%
1950-1960	37%	54%	29%	28%

Along with the decline in secondary employment as shown in this tabulation, the proportion of the labor force in the tertiary sector slowly rose to absorb the "overflow." According to Singer, tertiary sector employment increased from 21 percent of all employment in 1950 to 38 percent in 1969. See Paulo Singer, "Força de Trabalho e Emprêgo no Brasil: 1920-1969," mimeographed (Santiago, 1970), p. 16. These politico-economic forces, more than any others, determine the economic situation of the favelado. As an ECLA bulletin issued in 1967 summarized the situation: "For the country as a whole there was little or no increase in industrial employment in 1965-1966. Nearly all increases in the urban labor force—which in two years would have amounted to 1.5–2.0 million persons—have been forced into the urban services sectors that are characterized by low productivity and income and high levels of hidden unemployment or underemployment." See Economic Commission for Latin America (ECLA), *Statistical Bulletin on Latin America* (1967), p. 20.

Chapter Six

1. See David Morocco, "Carnival Groups: Maintainers and Intensifiers of the Favela Phenomenon in Rio de Janeiro," mimeographed (Austin: University of Texas, Department of Anthropology, n. d.).

2. See Alejandro Portes, "Urbanization and Politics in Latin America," *Social Science Quarterly* (December 1971): 697-720.

3. Andrew Pearse, "Some Characteristics of Urbanization in the City of Rio," in *Urbanization in Latin America*, ed. Philip M. Hauser (New York: Columbia University Press, 1961).

4. For further details on local political leadership styles and *cacquismo*, see Talton Ray, *The Politics of the Barrios of Venezuela* (Berkeley: University of California Press, 1969); Paul Friedrich, "The Legitimacy of the 'Cacique,'" in *Local-Level Politics: Social and Cultural Perspectives*, ed. Marc Swartz (Chicago: Aldine, 1968), pp. 243-269; Eric R. Wolf and Edward Hansen, "Caudillo Politics: A Structural Analysis," *Comparative Studies in Society and History* 9 (1967): 168-179; Wayne A. Cornelius, Jr., "Local-Level Political Leadership in Latin American Urban Environments: A Structural Analysis of Urban Caciquismo in Mexico" (paper prepared for delivery at the Annual Meeting of the American Political Science Association, Chicago, 1971); Richard N. Adams, *The Second Sowing: Power and Secondary Development in Latin America* (San Francisco: Chandler, 1967).

5. See Wolf and Hansen, "Caudillo Politics," p. 9.

6. Lisa Peattie, *View from the Barrio* (Ann Arbor: University of Michigan Press, 1968), pp. 88-89.

7. Adams, "Second Sowing," p. 250ff; Vaughn, "Links Between Lower Income Residential Areas and Political Parties"; Toness, "Power Relations;" and Ray, *Politics of the Barrios.*

8. Cornelius, "Local-Level Political Leadership," p. 12. See also, L. A. Machado da Silva, "A Política Na Favela," *Cadernos Brasileiros* 3: 35-47.

9. Machado, *ibid.*, p. 41.

10. Frank Bonilla, "Rio's Favelas: The Rural Slum Within the City," American Universities Field Staff Report, East Coast South America Series, vol. 8, no. 3 (Brazil: August 1961), p. 12.

11. Machado, "A Política Na Favela," p. 41, confirms my own observations on this point.

12. Philippe C. Schmitter, *Interest Conflict and Political Change in Brazil* (Stanford, Calif.: Stanford University Press, 1971), pp. 47-78.

13. The case was recently overstated by Geraldo Targino of CENPHA to a reporter for *Correio da Manhã* (Rio de Janeiro), January 28, 1971: "The favelado is a politicized element. He is aware of the global political phenomenon, and has high interest in the political regime of the country . . . especially as it relates to his survival. He is informed of any and all types of government action relevant to his own life or that of the community in which he lives. He even knows the legal mechanisms relating to land

ownership, and is always preinformed when the State Government intervenes directly and announces the plans for eradication." We found that only 21 percent of the favelados in general knew who owned the land on which they lived, and only 3 percent knew the agency responsible for favela removal.

14. This calculation is adjusted for those who cannot vote because they are illiterate (30 percent), too young to vote (15 percent), or unable to vote for other reasons: chronic illness, police records, or residency requirements (5-10 percent). In the 1970 national elections, 70 percent of the total eligible electorate voted. See "Too Large a Victory," *The Nation* 211, December 14, 1970, p. 613.

15. *Ibid.* The way the compulsory voting is enforced is through stamping—and thus validating—the work permits (*carteiras de trabalho*) at the voting booth. Thus, those who are not formally employed are not really affected, which explains why 100 percent of the eligibles do not vote even though it is supposedly compulsory.

16. Carlos Alberto de Medina, *A Favela e o Demagogo* (São Paulo: Imprensa Livre, 1964), pp. 97-98.

17. See Curt Lamb, *Political Power in Poor Neighborhoods* (Cambridge, Mass.: Schenkman Publishers, 1975).

18. Machado, "A Política Na Favela," p. 45.

19. Lamb, *Political Power in Poor Neighborhoods.*

20. Janice E. Perlman, "Dimensoes de Modernidade Numa Cidade em Franco Desenvolvimento," *Revista Brasilera de Estudos Políticos,* no. 30 (1971).

21. Lamb, *Political Power in Poor Neighborhoods.*

22. E. J. Hobsbawm, "Peasants and Rural Migrants in Politics," in *The Politics of Conformity in Latin America,* ed. Claudio Veliz (New York: Oxford University Press, 1967), p. 60.

23. See Glaucio Soares, "The Politics of Uneven Development: The Case of Brazil," in *Party Systems and Voter Alignments: Cross National Perspectives,* eds. Stein Rokkan and Seymour M. Lipset (New York: The Free Press, 1967), p. 491.

24. Karl Marx, *The Eighteenth Brumaire of Louis Bonaparte* (New York: International Publishers, 1963).

25. Saul David Alinsky, *Reveille for Radicals* (Chicago: University of Chicago Press, 1946); and *idem, Rules for Radicals: A Practical Primer for Realistic Radicals* (New York: Random House, 1971).

26. Quoted in Schmitter, *Interest Conflict and Political Change,* p. 72.

27. Machado, "A Política Na Favela," pp. 39-42. See also Cornelius, "Local-Level Leadership in Latin American Urban Environments."

28. Eckstein has made a similar point concerning Mexican local elites: "Local elites tend not to publicly challenge the status quo because they are dependent on higher ranking officials for their positions and future promotions." See Susan Eckstein, "Theory and Methods in the Study of Poverty and Politics and Poverty: The Substitution of a Social-Economic Structural Approach for an Individualistic Cultural Approach" (paper prepared for the Annual Meeting of the American Political Science Association, Chicago, 1971).

29. André Gunder Frank, "The Development of Underdevelopment in Brazil," in *Capitalism and Underdevelopment in Latin America* (New York: Monthly Review Press, 1967), pp. 50-62. Frank's idea is that the more "peripheral areas" are also more aware of reality, more "autonomously developed." He found that those areas of a country least

in touch with modern sectors, those seemingly less "integrated," were in fact less subject to the exploitive nature of that form of integration and more able to develop on their own. He uses extensive economic analysis to document the theory both for peripheral countries in relation to central ones (Latin America vis-à-vis the United States) and for peripheral regions within a country vis-à-vis those more closely integrated into the world capitalist market.

30. See Machado, "A Política Na Favela," p. 39.

31. Fernando Henrique Cardoso and Carlos Estevan Martins, "La Favela: Estratificación Interna y Participación Política" (paper delivered at the conference on La Marginalidad en América Latina, Santiago, Chile, November 1970).

32. *Ibid.*, pp. 29, 32, 34, 37, 39, 41.

33. Joseph A. Kahl, *The Measurement of Modernism: A Study of Values in Brazil and Mexico* (Austin: University of Texas Press, 1968), p. 38.

34. Gabriel A. Almond and Sidney Verba, *The Civic Culture* (Boston: Little, Brown and Co., 1965).

35. Schmitter, "Political Enculturation," *Interest Conflict and Political Change.*

Chapter Seven

1. Over the last ten years, an increasing number of works have appeared pointing out the rationality of life in squatter settlements for the poorer sectors of the urban society in developing countries. See, for example: Charles Abrams, *Man's Struggle for Shelter in an Urbanizing World* (Cambridge, Mass.: MIT Press, 1964), Abrams, *Squatter Settlements: The Problem and the Opportunity*, Ideas and Exchange No. 63 (Washington, D. C.: Department of Housing and Urban Development, April 1966), and the works of John C. Turner.

2. Using an index of housing quality (measuring the number of rooms in the house, the quality of the construction material, the number of stories, and the standard of water, sewage, electrical, and plumbing services), it was found that the percentage of houses of "high" quality was 13 percent, 42 percent, and 23 percent in Catacumba, Nova Brasília, and Caxias respectively, and the percentage of houses of "medium" quality was 23 percent, 21 percent, and 30 percent. Thus, the percentage of houses of "low" or "very low" quality was 64 percent in Catacumba, 37 percent in Nova Brasília, and 47 percent in Caxias.

3. *New York Times*, August 12, 1966, p. 12.

4. Turner discusses at length the misplaced priorities among urban planners. See John C. Turner, "Barriers and Channels for Housing Development in Modernizing Countries," *Journal of the American Institute of Planners* 33, no. 3 (May 1967): 167-181.

5. The following discussion is based largely on Anthony and Elizabeth Leeds, "Brazil in the 1960's; Favela and Policy, the Continuity of the Structure of Social Control," in *Brazil in the Sixties*, ed. Riordan Roett (Nashville, Tenn.: Vanderbilt University Press, 1972).

6. Translated by Leeds and Leeds, "Brazil in the Sixties," p. 12, from *O Globo* (Rio de Janeiro).

7. National Housing Bank, *National Housing Bank—A Brazilian Solution to Brazilian Problems*, n. d.

8. National Housing Bank, *Economic Development and Urban Growth in Brazil* (Rio de Janeiro: 1972), p. 39.

9. National Housing Bank, *Orçamento Plurianual: 1974-76* (Rio de Janeiro: 1974) pp. 33-34. For earlier figures, see Lawrence Salmen, "Urbanization and Development," in *Contemporary Brazil: Issues in Economic and Political Development*, eds. H. Rosenbaum and W. Tyler (New York: Praeger, 1972), p. 428.

10. National Housing Bank, *A Brazilian Solution*, pp. 14, 15.

11. *CHISAM: Coordenação de Habitação de Interesse Social da Area Metropolitana do Grande Rio* (Rio de Janeiro: Ministry of the Interior, 1971), p. 78. CHISAM was created partly in response to a call for a coordinating agency to deal with the favelas made in an AID report in 1966. See Bernard Wagner, David McVoy, and Gordon Edwards, *Guanabara Housing and Urban Development Program*, AID Housing and Urban Development Team, mimeographed, July 18, 1966. The AID recommendation was made with the idea that the coordinating agency would organize for improvements on the favela sites, but CHISAM has on the contrary dealt almost exclusively with eradication.

12. *Ibid.*, p. 103.

13. CHISAM, p. 78.

14. *Ibid.*, p. 79.

15. *Ibid.*, p. 79.

16. United Nations Committee on Housing, Building, and Planning, *World Housing Survey*, January 31, 1974, p. 186.

17. Clark W. Reynolds and Robert T. Carpenter, "Housing Finance in Brazil: Towards a New Distribution of Wealth," mimeograph (Palo Alto, Calif.: Stanford Food Research Institute, 1974), p. 30.

18. Robert T. Carpenter, "Brazil's Housing Finance System: Social Inequity in a Dynamic Mechanism of Savings Mobilization," working copy (Palo Alto, Calif.: Stanford University Food Research Institute, 1974). Carpenter concludes that Brazil's Housing Finance System views low income groups as "an excellent place to seek funds, but not a particularly desirable place to apply them," p. 22.

19. Leeds and Leeds, "Brazil in the Sixties," p. 48.

20. Information on FAFEG comes from *ibid.*, pp. 48-49, and from a personal interview with Sr. Souza, president of FAFEG, on August 10 and 17, 1973.

21. Leeds and Leeds, "Brazil in the Sixties," p. 49.

22. *Jornal do Brasil* (Rio de Janeiro), May 26, 1966.

23. Quoted in Leeds and Leeds, "Brazil in the Sixties," p. 49, from FAFEG, "Relatório final do 11° Congresso Estadual das Associaçoas de Moradores das Favelas e Morros do Estado da Guanabara," mimeographed (Rio de Janeiro).

24. *Jornal do Brasil*, March 14, 1969.

25. CHISAM, pp. 85ff.

26. *Ibid.*, p. 95.

27. *For studies of the effects of relocation in Brazil, see*: (1) Centro Nacional de Pesquisas Habitacionais (CENPHA), "Condições de vida em conjuntos habitacionais de interesse social. Cidade de Deus e Cidade Alta" (Rio de Janeiro: Banco Nacional de Habitação, 1970). (2) Afonso de Aragão Peixoto Fortuna, *et al.*, "Habitação Popular: O Caso da Cidade Alta" (Rio de Janeiro: March 1973). (3) Barney S. Rush, "From Favela to Conjunto: The Experience of Squatters Removed to Low-Cost Housing in Rio de

Janeiro, Brazil" (Thesis presented to the Committee in Degrees in Social Studies, Harvard College, March 1974). (4) Lawrence F. Salmen, "A Perspective in the Resettlement of Squatters in Brazil," *América Latina*, ano 12, no. 1 (January-March 1969).

For studies of the effects of relocation in other Third World countries, see: (1) Roy Simon Bryce-Laport, "Urban Relocation and Family Adaptation in Puerto Rico: A Case Study in Urban Ethnography," in *Peasants in Cities*, ed. William P. Mangin (Boston: Houghton and Mifflin, 1970), pp. 85-97. (2) Mary R. Hollnsteiner, "The People versus Urbano Planner y Administrador," in *Development in the 70's*, 5th Annual Seminar for Student Leaders, March 19-24, 1973 (The Philippines). (3) Mary R. Hollnsteiner, "Urban Planning: A Curbside View" (paper prepared for the SEDAG Urban Development Panel on "Urban and Regional Planning: Southeast Asian Experience," Bali, Indonesia, April 15-18, 1974). (4) Keith Hopkins, "Housing the Poor," in *Hong Kong: The Industrial Colony*, ed. Hopkins (London: Oxford University Press, 1971), pp. 271-335. (5) Oscar Lewis, "Cruz Moves to a Housing Project," *La Vida* (New York: Vintage Books, 1968), pp. 661-669. (6) Alejandro Portes, "The Urban Slum in Chile: Types and Correlates," *Ekistics* 202 (September 1972): 175-180. (7) Helen Icken Safa, "Puerto Rican Adaptation in the Urban Milieu," in *Race, Change, and Society*, eds. P. Orleans and W. R. Ellis, Jr. (Beverly Hills, Calif.: Sage Publications, 1971), pp. 153-190. (8) Robert M. Worth, "Urbanization and Squatter Resettlement as Related to Child Health in Hong Kong" *American Journal of Hygiene* 78 (1963); 338-348. (9) Stephen H. K. Yeh, *Homes for the People* (Singapore: Statistics and Research Department, Housing and Development Board, 1972).

28. Turner develops the idea that people of different income levels or at different stages in the life cycle have different sets of preferences for the three following attributes of housing: (1) being located close to work and urban facilities; (2) having the security of owning the land on which the house is built; and (3) having modern amenities such as running hot and cold water in the house. See John F. C. Turner, "Housing as a Verb," in *Freedom to Build*, eds. Turner and Robert Fichter (New York: The Macmillan Company, 1972), pp. 148-175.

29. David Vetter, "Low Income Housing Policy as Part of an Urban Development Strategy: Alternatives for Brazil," mimeographed (Los Angeles, Calif.: University of California at Los Angeles, January 1975).

30. Salmen, "Resettlement of Squatters in Brazil," p. 86.

31. CENPHA, "Condições de Vida," pp. 33, 38.

32. Rush, "From Favela to Conjunto," pp. 44-48. In addition to the essay, Rush also made available special data on the 45 former Catacumba residents and 99 South Zone residents out of his sample of 300, and much of the following information is based upon that data. His research was carried out jointly with Antonio Carlos dos santos.

33. *Ibid.*, p. 53.

34. *Jornal do Brasil*, January 20, 1974.

35. Salmen, "Resettlement of Squatters in Brazil," pp. 82-83.

36. Rush, "From Favela to Conjunto," pp. 48-50.

37. *Ibid.*, p. 52.

38. CHISAM, p. 95.

39. Salmen, "Resettlement of Squatters in Brazil," p. 79.

40. CENPHA, "Condições de vida," p. 78.

41. *Ibid.*, pp. 76, 78.

42. Rush, "From Favela to Conjunto," pp. 60-63.

43. Ray Langsten, "Remoção: A Study of the Rehousing of Urban Squatters in Rio de Janeiro" (preliminary draft, June 1973).

44. Salmen reports that even after three years, Vila Kennedy still has no street lights, and I found the same to be true of Quitungo in August 1973. See Salmen, "Resettlement of Squatters in Brazil," p. 82.

45. *Jornal do Brasil* December 16, 1973, reports that "Cruzado São Sebastião is responsible for 70 percent of crimes in the South Zone."

46. Rush found that 43 percent of favelados felt that their children's health had improved, 43 percent felt it was the same as before, and 14 percent felt it was worse. See Rush, "From Favela to Conjunto," p. 68. Worth, in his comparative study of health in a Hong Kong squatter settlement and in a resettlement estate, found that, while rates of parasitic disease decreased in the new sanitary housing, rates of respiratory disease increased, possibly caused by the crowded conditions of the new apartments. See Worth, "Urbanization and Squatter Resettlement as Related to Child Health."

47. *Jornal do Brasil*, January 1, 1974, reports, "Conjunto de Realengo is without water for five months and has clogged drains."

48. Salmen, "Resettlement of Squatters in Brazil," pp. 74-82.

49. Rush, "From Favela to Conjunto," p. 84.

50. CHISAM, pp. 86, 87, 93, 94.

51. Hollnsteiner, in "People versus Urbano Planner," and in "Urban Planning," emphasizes one aspect of the conflict between the choices made by the people and the choices made for the people: middle-class professionals and poor people have different perceptions of things. Hopkins, in "Housing the Poor," writes that in Hong Kong a survey showed that there was a size discrepancy between the needs of the rehoused squatters and the size of the housing units allocated to them by the resettlement department, which relied only on an index of overcrowding. Hopkins emphasizes the need for giving the people greater choice over their housing in the future, pp. 304-314.

52. CENPHA, "Condições de vida," p. 66.

53. Rush, "From Favela to Conjunto," p. 60. Yeh, *Homes for the People*, p. 195, reports consistent findings for housing in Singapore. Twice as many people living on housing estates not of their own choice wished to move, as compared to those living where they had chosen to live.

54. The *Jornal do Brasil* frequently carries stories about abandoned apartments, about bribes given to the manager by middle-income people to be allowed to "invade," about relatives of residents moving in when an apartment is abandoned, and about poorly attended auctions held by COHAB to sell off vacant apartments. See, for example, *Jornal do Brasil*, September 19, 1973, December 12, 1973, February 15, 1974, and April 13, 1974.

55. *Jornal do Brasil*, November-December 1974, January 1975.

56. See the *Jornal do Brasil*, September-December 1969.

57. Phillip Selznick, *TVA and the Grass Roots: A Study in the Sociology of Formal Organizations* (Berkeley: University of California Press, 1949), pp. 259-260. Selznick continues: "To develop the needed sense of legitimacy, it may not be necessary to actually share power; the creation of a 'front' or the open incorporation of accepted elements into the structure of the organization may suffice. . . . In this way, an aura of

respectability will be gradually transferred from the co-opted elements to the organization as a whole, and at the same time a vehicle of administrative accessibility may be established."

58. Phillipe C. Schmitter, *Interest Conflict and Political Change in Brazil* (Stanford, Calif.: Stanford University Press, 1971), p. 815.

59. *Jornal do Brasil*, May 3, 1969.

60. CHISAM, p. 90.

61. Data comes from "Favelas Removidas e Respectivos Conjuntos," mimeographed (Rio de Janeiro: Secretaria de Planejamento e Coordenação Geral do Estado da Guanabara, 1973).

62. *Correio da Manhã* (Rio de Janeiro), January 21, 1971.

63. Salmen, "Resettlement of the Squatters in Brazil," p. 78.

64. *Jornal do Brasil*, January 20, 1974.

65. The interview with Felix was made by Barney Rush in 1973.

66. "Programa Desenvolvido Pela CHISAM" (Rio de Janeiro: Secretaria de Planejamento e Coordenação Geral do Estado da Guanabara, 1972), p. 5.

67. CHISAM, p. 96.

68. Cf. David Vetter, "Low Income Housing Policy as Part of an Urban Development Strategy."

69. This confirms studies of squatter settlements throughout the world which have shown that security of tenure releases individual and collective energy for investments in favela improvement. Abrams says: "If squatters know when they seize land that other squatter groups in the same city have been given running water or electricity or have been allowed to remain in possession without serious challenge, they are apt to put up more durable buildings from the start and are likely, as soon as circumstances permit, to improve their makeshift structures." Charles Abrams, "Squatter Settlements: The Problem and the Opportunity," Department of HUD, Washington, D. C.: *Ideas and Methods Exchange*, No. 63, April 1966, p. 21.) Also, the United Nations recently recommended "that every effort be made to reduce or eliminate the cost of urban land for the poor of the developing countries," recognizing that "once security of land ownership is established, the path is clear for infrastructure and housing development by a process of community action." (*Improvement of Slums and Uncontrolled Settlements*, UN, New York, 1971.)

70. The following account of CODESCO is based on my own observations, an article by José Arthur Rios entitled "Social Transformation and Urbanization—The Case of Rio de Janeiro" (Catholic University, Rio de Janeiro, Brazil, 1970, mimeo), and Leeds and Leeds, "Brazil in the Sixties", particularly pp. 38-42.

71. Leeds and Leeds, "Brazil in the Sixties," p. 40.

72. See Carlos Nelson, "The Brás de Pina Experience," mimeographed (Cambridge, Mass.: MIT, December 1971). This report also indicates some of the problems of urbanization such as the lengthy rebuilding process, the need for much professional supervision, and the fact that about 20 percent of the families sold their rights to participation in the urbanization in order to use the cash for more immediate priorities.

73. See *Jornal do Brasil*, December 23, 1973, "Plano elimina em 10 anos as favelas da Guanabara."

Chapter Eight

1. Maria Carolina de Jesus, *Child of the Dark* (New York: Signet Books, 1962), pp. 42-43.

2. See Bibliography for full citations.

3. For a good discussion of the difference between the conflict and integration models, see Ralf Dahrendorf, *Class and Class Conflict in Industrial Society* (Stanford, Calif.: Stanford University Press, 1959).

4. José Arthur Rios, "Aspectos Sociais dos Grupamentos Subnormais," (Rio de Janeiro: CENPHA, May 1967).

5. Karl Mannheim, *Ideology and Utopia* (New York: Harcourt, Brace and World, Inc., 1936).

6. For a precise epistemological discussion of the nature of specular relationships, see Manuel Castells and Emilio de Ipola, "Pratique Epistemologique et Sciences Sociales ou Comment Developper la Lutte de Classes sur le Plan Theorique san Sombrer dans le Metaphysique" (Paris, 1967).

7. For an elaboration of these factors, see Lucio Kowarick, "Capitalismo, Dependência, e Marginalidade Urbana na América Latina: Uma Contribuição Teórica," *Estudos Cebrap*, no. 8 (Abril-Junho 1974): 79-96.

8. Economic Commission for Latin America (ECLA), "Structural Changes in Employment Within the Context of Latin America's Economic Development," *Economic Bulletin for Latin America* 10, no. 2 (October 1965): 163-187.

9. See M. Murmis, "Tipos de Marginalidad y Posición en el Proces Productivo," *Revista Latinomericana de Sociologia* 5, no. 2 (July 1969), and L. A. Machado, "Labor Markets and Political Propensities of Marginal Groups: A Tentative Theory of Marginality Theory," unpublished manuscript (November 1971).

10. Anibal Quijano, "La Formación de un Universo Marginal en las Ciudades de América Latina," in *Imperialismo y Urbanización en América Latina*, ed. M. Castells (Barcelona: Gustavo Gili, 1973), p. 141.

11. *Ibid.*, p. 142.

12. Anibal Quijano, "Notas Sobre el Concepto de Marginalidad Social" (Santiago: CEPAL, Division de Asuntos Sociales, October 1966).

13. Theotonio dos Santos, "The Structure of Dependence," in *Readings in U. S. Imperialism*, eds. K. T. Fann and D. C. Hodges (Boston: Porter Sarges Publications, 1971), p. 233.

14. S. Bodenheimer, "Dependency and Imperialism: The Roots of Latin American Underdevelopment," in *Readings in U. S. Imperialism*, eds. Fann and Hodges, p. 158.

15. F. H. Cardoso and E. Faletto, *Dependencia y Desarrollo en América Latina* (Mexico: Siglo XXI, 1969), pp. 24, 28.

16. See Manuel Castells, "La Nueva Estructura de la Dependencia y los Procesos Políticos de Cambio Social en América Latina," Paper presented at the 10th Congreso Interamericano de Planificación, Panama, September 1974; and Fernando H. Cardoso, "Participación Social y Desarrollo: La Clase Obrera y los 'Grupos Marginales'," *Boletin ELAS* 4, no. 6 (December 1970): 52-61.

17. See Manuel Castells, *Imperialismo y Urbanizacion en América Latina* (Barcelona: Gustavo Gili, 1973), p. 17.

18. *Ibid.*, pp. 16, 17, 21.

19. For further elaboration of these effects, see Castells, "La Nueva Estructura de la Dependencia."

20. Quijano, "Formación de un Universo Marginal," p. 143.

21. José Nun, "Superpoblación Relativa, Ejército Industrial de Reserva y Masa Marginal," *Revista Latinoamerica na de Sociologia* 69, no. 2: 202.

22. It should be pointed out, however, that the factual veracity of this model has been challenged on numerous occasions. For example, see Kowarick, "Capitalismo, Dependência e Marginalidade Urbana," pp. 88-90.

23. Fernando H. Cardoso, "Comentário Sôbre Os Conceitos de Superpopulação e Marginalidade" (paper presented at the 2nd Seminario Latina América para el Desarrollo, Santiago, 1970).

24. Manuel Castells, "Clase, Estado, y Marginalidad Urbana," *Estructura de Clase y Política Urbana en América Latina* (Buenos Aires: Ediciones SIAP, 1974).

25. For a general discussion of the functions of urban poverty, see Howard M. Wachtel, "Looking at Poverty from a Radical Perspective," *Review of Radical Political Economics* 3, no. 3 (Summer 1971): 1-19; and Herbert J. Gans, "The Positive Functions of Poverty and Inequality," *More Equality* (New York: Pantheon Books, 1973).

26. Carlos Estevan Martins and Fernando Henrique Cardoso, "La Favela: Estratificación Interna y Participación Política" mimeographed (Santiago, November 1970), pp. 14, 16.

27. Anthony and Elizabeth Leeds, "Brazil in the 1960s," in *Brazil in the Sixties*, ed. Riordan Roett (Nashville, Tenn.: Vanderbilt University Press, 1972).

28. Francisco Weffort, "State and Mass in Brazil," in *Masses in Latin America*, ed. Irving Louis Horowitz (New York: Oxford University Press, 1970), p. 403.

29. Octavio Ianni, "O Colapso do Populismo no Brasil," *Estado e Capitalismo* (Rio de Janeiro: Editora Civilização Brasileira, 1965), p. 219.

30. Juarez R. B. Lopez, "Some Basic Developments in Brazilian Politics and Society," in *New Perspectives of Brazil*, ed. Eric Baklanoff (Nashville, Tenn.: Vanderbilt University Press, 1966), p. 59.

31. Malori J. Pompermayer, "Authoritarianism in Brazil," paper prepared for Brazil Workshop, Yale University, April 1971, p. 4.

32. As Leeds points out, "All attempts made within the past 30 years to grant a degree of freedom and responsibility to favela residents have been met with simple neglect, lack of continuity, or direct opposition in the form of counter-policies and actions." See Leeds and Leeds, "Brazil in the 1960s," p. 51.

33. Martins and Cardoso, "La Favela."

Bibliography

Aaron, H. J., and G. M. Van Furstenberg. "The Inefficiency of Transfers in Kind: The Case of Housing Assistance." *Western Economic Journal* (June 1971): 184-190.

Abrams, Charles. *The City is the Frontier.* New York: Harper, Colophon Books, 1965.

———. *Man's Struggle for Shelter in an Urbanizing World.* Cambridge, Mass.: MIT Press, 1964.

———. *Squatter Settlements: The Problem and the Opportunity.* Ideas and Exchange, no. 63. Washington, D. C.: Department of Housing and Urban Development, 1966.

Ackerman, Frank. "Industry and Imperialism in Brazil." Mimeographed. August 1969.

Albano, Josephina R. *El Factor Humano en los Programs de Rehabilitacion de Tugurios.* Bogota: Centro Interamericano de Vivienda, 1955.

Alinsky, Saul David. *Reveille for Radicals.* Chicago: University of Chicago Press, 1946.

———. *Rules for Radicals: A Practical Primer for Realistic Radicals.* New York: Random House, 1971.

———. "The War on Poverty—Political Pornography." *Social Issues* 21, no. 1 (1965).

Almond, Gabriel A., and James S. Coleman, eds. *The Politics of Developing Areas.* Princeton, N. J.: Princeton University Press, 1961.

Almond, Gabriel A., and G. Bingham Powell, Jr. *Comparative Politics: A Developmental Approach.* Boston: Little, Brown and Co., 1966.

Almond, Gabriel A., and Sidney Verba. *The Civic Culture.* Boston: Little, Brown and Company, 1965.

Alonso, William. "Theory of the Urban Land Market." In *Readings in Urban Economics,* edited by M. Edel and J. Rothenberg, pp. 16-36. New York: Macmillan, 1972.

Anderson, Nels, ed. *Urbanism and Urbanization.* The Netherlands: E. J. Brill, 1964.

Antonovsky, Aaron. "Toward a Refinement of the 'Marginal Man' Concept." *Social Forces* 35, no. 1 (1956), pp. 57-62.

Araud, G., G. Boon, V. Urquidi, and P. Strassman. *Studies on Employment in the Mexican Housing Industry.* Paris: OECD, 1973.

Arnold, David O. "Subcultural Marginality." In *The Sociology of Subculture,* edited by David O. Arnold. Berkeley: The Glendessary Press, 1970.

Arriaga, E. "Components of City Growth in Selected Latin American Countries." *Milbank Memorial Fund Quarterly* 46, no. 2 (1968).

Baer, Werner. "A Recente Experiência Brasileira de Desenvolvimento: Uma Interpretação." *Pesquisa e Planejamento Econômico* 3, no. 2 (1973): 265-302.

———. "Regional Inequality and Economic Growth in Brazil." *Economic Development and Cultural Change* 12, no. 3 (1964).

Baer, Werner, and Michael E. A. Hervé. "Employment and Industrialization in Developing Countries." *Quarterly Journal of Economics* 80, no. 1 (1966).

Baklanoff, Eric N., ed. *New Perspectives of Brazil.* Nashville, Tenn.: Vanderbilt University Press, 1966.

Balan, Jorge. "Are Farmers' Sons Handicapped In the City?" *Rural Sociology* 33, no. 2 (1968).

———. "Migrant-Native Socioeconomic Differences in Latin American Cities: A Structural Analysis." *Latin American Research Review* 4, no. 1 (1969).

————. "Un Siglo de Corrientes Migratorias en el Brasil: Ensayo de Interpretación Histórico-Comparativa." Department of Political Science, Universidade Federal de Minas Gerais, 1973. Mimeographed. n. d.

Balan, Jorge, Harley L. Browning, Elizabeth Jelin, and Lee Litzler. "A Computerized Approach to the Processing and Analysis of Life Histories Obtained in Sample Surveys." *Behavioral Science* 14, no. 2 (1969): 105-120.

Bartky, John. *Social Issues in Public Education.* Boston: Houghton Mifflin, 1963.

Bazzanella, Waldemiro. "Industrialização e Urbanização no Brasil." *América Latina* 6, no. 1 (1963).

Beals, Ralph L. "Urbanism, Urbanization, and Acculturation." *American Anthropologist* 53 (1951).

Bender, Richard. "Incremental Infrastructure." Draft of paper. Department of Architecture, University of California, Berkeley, 1974.

Berlinck, Manuel T. "Algumas Definições Populares de Marginalidade." Escola de Administração de Empresas de São Paulo. São Paulo: Fundação Getúlio Vargas, 1972.

————. "Relações de Classe Numa Sociedade Neo-capitalista Dependente: Marginalidade e Poder em São Paulo." São Paulo, n. d. Mimeographed.

Berlinck, Manuel T., and Youssef Cohen. "Desenvolvimento Econômico, Crescimento Econômico e Modernização na Cidade de São Paulo." *Revista de Administração de Empresa* 10, no. 1 (Rio de Janeiro: 1970).

Berlinck, Manuel T., and Daniel J. Hogan. "Associações Voluntárias, Canais de Comunicação de Massa, Informação e Adaptação Urbana Entre Classes Populares na Cidade de São Paulo." São Paulo, n. d. Mimeographed.

————. "O Desenvolvimento Econômico do Brasil e as Migrações Internas para São Paulo: Uma Análise Histórica." São Paulo, 1972.

Beyer, Glenn H., ed. *The Urban Explosion in Latin America: A Continent in Process of Modernization.* Ithaca, N. Y.: Cornell University Press, 1967.

Black, Cyril E. *The Dynamics of Modernization.* New York: Harper and Row, 1966.

Bodenheimer, S. "Dependency and Imperialism: The Roots of Latin American Underdevelopment." In *Readings in U. S. Imperialism,* edited by K. T. Fann and D. C. Hodges. Boston: Porter Sarges Publications, 1971.

Bolaffi, Gabriel. "Aspectos Socio-econômicos do Plano Nacional de Habitação." Ph.D. dissertation, Universidade de São Paulo, 1972.

Bonilla, Frank. "A National Ideology for Development: Brazil." In *Expectant Peoples,* edited by K. H. Silvert. New York: Random House, 1963.

————. "Rio's Favelas: The Rural Slum within the City." American Universities Field Staff Report. *East Coast South America Series* 8, no. 3 (Rio de Janeiro: August 1961).

————. "Rural Reform in Brazil, Diminishing Prospects for a Democratic Solution." American University Field Staff Reports Service. *East Coast South America Series* 8, no. 4 (Rio de Janeiro: October 1961).

————. "The Urban Worker." In *Continuity and Change in Latin America,* edited by John J. Johnson. Stanford, Calif.: Stanford University Press, 1964.

Bonilla, Frank, and Jose Silva Michelena, eds. *Studying the Venezuelan Polity: Explorations in Analysis and Synthesis.* Cambridge, Mass.: MIT Press, 1966.

Boschi, Renato, and Rose Goldschmidt. *Populações Faveladas do Estado da*

Guanabara. Rio de Janeiro: Instituto Universitário de Pesquisas do Rio de Janeiro, 1970.

Breese, Gerald. *Urbanization in Newly Developing Countries.* Modernization of Traditional Societies Series. Englewood Cliffs, N. J.: Prentice-Hall, 1966.

Brigg, Pamela. "Migration to Urban Areas." Bank Staff Working Paper, no. 151. Washington, D. C.: International Bank for Reconstruction and Development, June 1971.

Brody, Eugene B. *The Lost Ones: Social Forces and Mental Illness in Rio de Janeiro.* New York: International Universities Press, 1973.

Brown, Diana. "Macumba and Umbanda in Brazil." Ph.D. dissertation, Columbia University, 1972.

Browning, Harley L. "Recent Trends in Latin American Urbanization." *Annals of the American Academy of Political and Social Science* 316 (1958).

Browning, Harley L., and Waltrauz Feindt. "Selectivity of Migrants to a Metropolis in a Developing Country: A Mexican Case Study." *Demography* 6, no. 4 (1969).

Bryce-Laport, Roy Simon. "Urban Relocation and Family Adaptation in Puerto Rico: A Case Study in Urban Ethnography." In *Peasants in Cities,* edited by William P. Mangin, pp. 85-97. Boston: Houghton Mifflin, 1970.

Burgess, M. Elaine. "Poverty and Dependency: Some Selected Characteristics." *Journal of Social Issues* 21, no. 1 (1965).

Burns, E. B., ed. *A Documentary History of Brazil.* New York: Knopf, 1966.

Burns, L. S., and F. G. Mittelbach. "A House is a House is a House." *Industrial Relations* 11, no. 3 (1972).

Butterworth, Douglas B. "A Study of the Urbanization Process among Mixtec Migrants from Tilantongo in Mexico City." In *Peasants in Cities,* edited by William P. Mangin, pp. 98-113. Boston: Houghton Mifflin, 1970.

Camargo, Candido P. F. "Objetivos de Pesquisas de Fertilidade." *Estudos Cebrap* 3 (January 1973).

Camargo, José Francisco. *Exodo Rural no Brasil.* Faculty of Economics and Administration, Bulletin no. 1. University of São Paulo, 1957.

Cardona, R. "Los Asentamientos Espontaneos de Vivienda." In *Las Migraciones Internas,* edited by R. Cardona. Bogota: ACOFAME, 1973.

Cardoso, Fernando Henrique. "Althusserianismo ou Marxismo? A Propósito do Conceito de Classes em Poulantzas: Comentários." *Estudos Cebrap* 3 (January 1973).

————. "The Brazilian Political Model." Paper prepared for Workshop on Brazilian Development, April 1971, at Yale University.

————. "As Classes Sociais e a Crise Política da América Latina." Instituto de Investigaciones Sociales, Universidade do México, n. d.

————. "Comentário Sobre os Conceitos de Superpopulação Relativa e Marginalidade." Paper presented at the 2nd Seminario Latinoamericano para el Desarrollo, Santiago, November 1970. Mimeographed.

————. "Participación Social y Desarrollo: La Clase Obrera y los 'Grupos Marginales'." *Boletin ELAS,* ano 4, no. 6 (1970): 52-61.

————. *Sociologie du Developpement en Amerique Latine.* Paris: Editions Anthropos, 1969.

————. Unpublished bibliography on marginality. São Paulo: Centro Brasileiro de Análise e Planejamento (CEBRAP), n. d.

Cardoso, Fernando Henrique, and Enzo Falleto. *Dependencia e Desenvolvimento na América Latina: Ensaio de Interpretação Sociológica*. 2nd edition. Rio de Janeiro: Zahar, 1973.

————. *Dependencia y Desarrollo en América Latina*. México, D. F.: Siglo XXI, 1969.

Cardoso, Fernando Henrique, and Carlos Estevan Martins. "La Favela: Estratificación Interna y Participación Política." Paper delivered at the conference on "La Marginalidad en América Latina," Santiago, November 1970.

Carpenter, Robert T. *Brazil's Housing Finance System: Social Inequity in a Dynamic Mechanism of Savings Mobilization*. Working draft, Stanford University Food Research Institute, 1974.

————. "The National Housing Bank: An Oblique Approach to Low-cost Housing in Brazil." Latin American Studies Program, Stanford University, June 1973.

Casanova, Pablo Gonzales. *Democracy in Mexico*. New York: Oxford University Press, 1970.

Casasco, Juan A. "The Social Function of the Slum in Latin America: Some Positive Aspects." *América Latina* 12, no. 3 (1969).

Castells, Manuel. "Immigrant Workers and Class Struggles in Advanced Capitalism: The Western European Experience." Centre D'Etudes des Mouvements Sociaux, Ecole Pratique des Hautes Etudes, Paris, 1974. Mimeographed.

————, ed. *Imperialismo y Urbanización en América Latina*. Barcelona: Gustavo Gili, 1973.

————. "La Nueva Estructura de la Dependencia y los Procesos Políticos de Cambio Social en América Latina." Paper presented at the 10th Congreso Interamericano de Planificacion, Panama, September 1974.

————. "A Teoria Marxista das Classes Sociais e a Luta de Classes na América Latina." *Estudos Cebrap* 3 (January 1973).

————. "Urban Struggles and Political Power." Translated by B. Lynne Lord. Paris: Cahiers Libres, 1973. Mimeographed.

Castells, Manuel, and Emilio de Ipola. "Pratique Epistemologique et Sciences Sociales, ou Comment Developper la Lutte de Classes sur le Plan Theorique sans Sombrer dans la Metaphysique." Paris: École Pratique des Hautes Études, 1972. Mimeographed.

Centro Nacional de Pesquisas Habitacionais (CENPHA). "Condições de vida em conjuntos habitacionais de interesse social. Cidade de Deus e Cidade Alta." Rio de Janeiro: Banco Nacional de Habitação, 1970.

————. *Pesquisa Piloto: Estudo de Viabilidade para Recuperação de Areas Urbanas: Modelo Demonstração Vila Valqueire*. Volumes I and II. Rio de Janeiro: CENPHA, 1972.

Chilcote, Ronald H., and Joel C. Edelstein, eds. *Latin America: The Struggle with Dependency and Beyond*. New York: Schenkman Publishing Company, Inc., 1974.

Child, Irvin L. *Italian or American? The Second Generation in Conflict*. New Haven: Yale University Press, 1943.

CHISAM. *CHISAM: Coordenação de Habitação de Interesse Social da Area Metropolitana do Grande Rio*. Rio de Janeiro: Ministry of the Interior, 1971.

CIDU, Equipo de Estudios Poblacionales del. "Reindicacion Urbana y Lucha Política: Los Campamentos de Pobladores in Santiago de Chile, EURE 2, No. 6 (November 1972): 55-81.

Cloward, Richard A., and Frances Fox Piven. *The Politics of Turmoil: Essays on Poverty, Race, and the Urban Crisis.* New York: Pantheon Books, 1974.

————. *Regulating the Poor: The Functions of Public Welfare.* New York: Pantheon Books, 1971.

Cohen, Ben, and Nat Leff. "Comment." *Quarterly Journal of Economics* (February 1967).

Cohen, Michael. "Urban Policy and the Decline of the Machine: Cross Ethnic Politics in the Ivory Coast." Paper delivered at the Annual Meeting of the African Studies Association, Denver, Colorado, 1971.

Cole, H. J. "National Urban Development Policies: Brazilian Case Study." Paper presented at the Seminar on Social Sciences Urban Development in Latin America, Jahuell, Chile. April 1968.

Companhia de Desenvolvimento de Comunidades (CODESCO). "Critérios de Intervenção: Anexo I." Mimeographed, n. d.

————. *Estudo sobre Parque União.* Rio de Janeiro: CODESCO, n. d.

————. *Levantamento Sócio-Economico da Comunidade de Mata-Machado.* Rio de Janeiro: CODESCO, 1971/1972.

————. *Plano Setorial do Serviço Social.* Elaborado por Maria Lucia de Paulo Petiz. Rio de Janeiro: CODESCO, n. d.

Cornelius, Wayne A., Jr. "Local-Level Political Leadership in Latin American Urban Environments: A Structural Analysis of Urban *Caciquismo* in Mexico." Paper presented at the American Political Science Association Meeting, Chicago, September 1971.

————. "The Political Sociology of Cityward Migration in Latin America: Toward Empirical Theory." Mimeographed. Prepared for *Latin American Urban Annual*, edited by Francine F. Rabinovitz and Felicity M. Trueblood. Vol. 1. Beverly Hills, Calif.: Sage Publications, forthcoming.

Costa, Manuel Augusto. "Migrações Internas no Brasil." Monograph no. 5. Instituto de Planejamento Econômico e Social (IPEA) and Instituto de Pesquisas (INPES). Rio de Janeiro, 1971.

Costa, Manuel Augusto, Douglas H. Graham, Joao Lira Madeira, José Pastore, Nelson L. Araujo Moraes, and Pedro Pinchas Geiger. "Migrações Internas no Brasil." Rio de Janeiro: IPEA-INPES, 1971. Mimeographed.

Costa, Rubens Vaz da. "Apontamentos para a Avaliação da Política de Desenvolvimento Regional do Brasil." Rio de Janeiro: National Housing Bank, 1973.

————. *Crescimento Urbano Acelerado: Desafio da Década de 1970.* 3rd edition. Rio de Janeiro: National Housing Bank, 1972.

————. "Crescimento Urbano do Brasil: Desafio e Oportunidades." Rio de Janeiro: National Housing Bank, 1972.

————. "Economic Development and Urban Growth in Brazil." Rio de Janeiro: National Housing Bank, 1972.

————. *Fast Urban Growth: The Challenge of the '70s.* 4th edition. Rio de Janeiro: National Housing Bank, 1972.

————. "Novas Atitudes e Nova Mentalidade para Enfrentar Os Desafios do Crescimento Urbano." Rio de Janeiro: National Housing Bank, 1972.

————. "Urban Development Strategy and Programs: The Brazilian Case." Text presented before the 24th Congress of the International Chamber of Commerce. Rio de Janeiro: National Housing Bank, May 1973.

————. "Urban Growth: The Foundation of Economic Development." Rio de Janeiro: National Housing Bank, 1973.

Costa-Pinto, L. A., and Waldemiro Bazzanella. "Economic Development, Social Change, and Population Problems in Brazil." *Annals of the American Academy of Political and Social Science* 316 (1958).

Cotler, Julio. "The Mechanics of Internal Domination and Social Change in Peru." In *Masses in Latin America*, edited by Irving Louis Horowitz. New York: Oxford University Press, 1970.

Cuber, John F. "Marginal Church Participants." *Sociology and Social Research* 9 (1940).

Cunha, Paulo Vieira da, and Janice Perlman. "An Empirical Verification of Occupational Mobility of Low Income Workers in Rio de Janeiro." Draft of paper. University of California, Berkeley, 1974.

Dahrendorf, Ralf. *Class and Class Conflict in Industrial Society*. Stanford: Stanford University Press, 1959.

Davis, Kingsley. "The Origin and Growth of Urbanization in the World." *American Journal of Sociology* 60 (March 1955).

————. "The Urbanization of the Human Population." *Scientific American*, September 1965.

Davis, Kingsley, and Ana Casis. "Urbanization in Latin America." *Milbank Memorial Fund Quarterly* 24 (April-June 1946).

Davis, Kingsley, and H. H. Golden. "Urbanization and the Development of Pre-Industrial Areas." *Economic Development and Cultural Change* 3 no. 1 (1954).

Davis, O. A., and A. B. Whinston. "The Economics of Urban Renewal." In *Urban Renewal: The Record and the Controversy*, edited by James Q. Wilson. Cambridge, Mass.: MIT Press, 1966.

Daland, Robert T. "Urbanization and Political Development in Latin America." Paper presented at the Seminar on Social Science and Urban Development, Jahuel, Chile, April 1968.

de Jesus, Carolina Maria. *Child of the Dark*. New York: Signet Books, 1962.

Deutsch, Karl. "The Growth of Nations: Some Recurrent Patterns of Political and Social Integration." *World Politics*, January 1953.

————. "Social Mobilization and Poliitical Development." *American Political Science Review* 55, no. 3 (1961).

Dickie-Clark, H. F. "The Theory of the Marginal Man and its Critics." In *The Marginal Situation*, edited by H. F. Dickie-Clark. London: Routledge and Kegan Paul, 1966.

Dobyns, Henry F. "The Strategic Importance of Enlightenment and Skill for Power." *American Behavioral Scientist* 8, no. 7 (1965).

Doob, Leonard. *Becoming More Civilized*. New Haven: Yale University Press, 1960.

Doughty, Paul L. "The Interrelationship of Power, Respect, Affection, and Rectitude in Vicos." *American Behavioral Scientist* 8, no. 7 (1965).

Doutchy, Paul L. "Behind the Back of the City: 'Provincial' Life in Lima, Peru." In *Peasants in Cities*, edited by William P. Mangin, pp. 30-46. Boston: Houghton Mifflin Co., 1970.

Downs, A. "Uncompensated Nonconstruction Cost which Urban Highways and Urban Renewal Impose Upon Residential Households." In *The Analysis of Public Output*, edited by Julius Margolis, pp. 69-113. New York: Columbia University Press, 1970.

Doxiades Associates. *Guanabara: A Plan for Urban Development.* Document Dox-BRA-A6. Athens, 1965.

Dunn, Edgar S. *Economic and Social Development: A Process of Social Learning.* Baltimore: Johns Hopkins Press, 1971.

Durand, J. D., and C. A. Peláez, "Patterns of Urbanization in Latin America." *Milbank Memorial Fund Quarterly* 43, no. 4, part 2 (1965).

Durkheim, Emile. *The Division of Labor in Society.* Glencoe, Ill.: The Free Press, 1947.

Eckstein, Susan. "Theory and Methods in the Study of Poverty and the Politics of Protest: The Substitution of a Social-Economic Structural Approach for an Individualistic Cultural Approach." Paper prepared for the 1971 Annual Meeting of the American Political Science Association, Chicago, September 1971.

Economic Commission for Latin America. *El Desarrollo Social de America Latina en la Postguerra.* Buenos Aires: Solar Barra Hachette, 1963.

————. "The Growth and Decline of Import Substitution in Brazil." *Economic Bulletin for Latin America* 9, no. 1 (New York and Santiago: March 1964).

————. *Social Change and Social Development Policy in Latin America.* New York: United Nations, 1970.

————. "Structural Changes in Employment within the Context of Latin America's Economic Development." *Economic Bulletin for Latin America* 10, no. 2 (1965): 163-187.

Eisenberg, Paul. "Favela Roquete Pinto and Favela Rute Ferreira: Study and Observations." Mimeographed, 1965.

Eisenstadt, S. N. *The Absorption of Immigrants.* London: Routledge and Kegan Paul, 1954.

Elizaga, Juan C. "Internal Migrations in Latin America." *Milbank Memorial Fund Quarterly* 43, no. 4, part 2 (1965).

Ellis, Herbert C., and Stanley M. Newman. "'Gowster,' 'Ivy-Leaguer,' 'Hustler,' 'Conservative,' 'Mackman,' and 'Continental': A Functional Analysis of Six Ghetto Roles." In *The Culture of Poverty*, edited by Eleanor Burke Leacock. New York: Simon and Schuster, 1971.

Epstein, A. L. "Urbanization and Social Change in Africa." *Current Anthropology*, October 1967, pp. 275-298.

Estado da Guanabara. *Area Prioritária 1: Projeto Habitacional.* Rio de Janeiro: Secretaria de Planejamento e Coordenação Geral, April 1973.

————. *Documento de Prioridades: Programa Desenvolvido Pela CHISAM.* Rio de Janeiro: Secretaria de Planejamento e Coordenação Geral, 1972.

————. *Estudos Cariocas.* Rio de Janeiro, 1965.

————. "Faveladas Removidas e Respectivos Conjuntos." Rio de Janeiro: Secretaria de Planejamento e Coordenação Geral, 1973.

————. "Plano de Malhoria dos Conjuntos Habitacionais." Rio de Janeiro: Secretaria de Planejamento e Coordenação Geral, 1973.

————. "Subsídios para a Política Habitacional de Interesse Social e para Erradicação de Favelas na Guanabara." Rio de Janeiro: Secretaria de Planejamento e Coordenação Geral, 1972.

Estado da São Paulo. "Aspectos Humanos da Favela Carioca." 1960.

Fanon, Franz. *The Wretched of the Earth.* London: MacGibbon and Kee, 1965.

Fava, Sylvia Fleis, ed. *Urbanism in World Perspective: A Reader.* New York: Thomas Y. Crowell Company, 1968.

Federação das Associações de Favelas do Estado da Guanabara (FAFEG). *Relatório do III Congresso Estadual das Associações de Moradores em Favelas.* Rio de Janeiro: FAFEG, 1972.

Fernandes, F. *Sociedade de Classe e Subdesenvolvimento.* Rio de Janeiro: Zahar, 1968.

Field, A. J., ed. *City and Country in the Third World.* Cambridge, Mass.: Schenkman Publishers, 1970.

Filho, Ariovaldo Franco. "Política e Estrategia Social para O Desenvolvimento Urbano." Paper presented at the 13th International Conference of Social Work, Washington, D. C., 1966.

Fonseca, Geraldo Targino, and José Gouveia Viera. "Radiografia da Favela." *Síntese Social,* no. 21 (January-March 1964).

Fortuna, Affonso de Aragão Peixoto, *et al.* "Habitação Popular: O Caso da Cidade Alta." Rio de Janeiro, March 1973.

Frank, André Gunder, ed. *Capitalism and Underdevelopment in Latin America.* New York: Monthly Review Press, 1969.

————. *Latin America, Underdevelopment or Revolution.* New York: Monthly Review Press, 1969.

————. *Lumpen-Bourgeosie: Lumpendevelopment.* Translated by Marion Davis Berdecio. New York and London: Monthly Review Press, 1972.

————. "Urban Poverty in Latin America." *Studies in Comparative International Development* 2, no. 5 (1966).

Frankenhoff, Charles. "Elements of an Economic Model for Slums in a Developing Country." *Economic Development and Cultural Change* 16 (1967): 27-37.

Fried, Marc. "Grieving for a Lost Home." In *The Urban Condition,* edited by Leonard J. Duhl. New York: Basic Books, 1963.

————. "Deprivation and Migration: Dilemmas of Causal Interpretation." In *On Understanding Poverty: Perspectives from the Social Sciences,* edited by Daniel P. Moynihan. New York: Basic Books, 1969.

————. *World of the Urban Working Class.* Cambridge, Mass.: Harvard University Press, 1973.

Fried, Marc, L. Ferguson, P. Gleicher, and J. Havens. "Patterns of Migration and Adjustment: The Boston Negro Population." Institute of Human Sciences, Boston College, November 1969. Mimeographed.

Fried, Marc, and Peggy Gleicher. "Some Sources of Residential Satisfaction in an Urban Slum." *Journal of the American Institute of Planners* 27, no. 9 (November 1961).

Friedland, William H. "A Sociological Approach to Modernization." Mimeographed. Cornell University, 1965.

Friedman, Herbert. "Squatter Assimilation in Buenos Aires." Ph.D. dissertation, Massachusetts Institute of Technology, 1967.

Friedmann, John. "Notes on Urbanization in Latin America." The Ford Foundation, Urban and Regional Advisory Program in Chile, 1964. Mimeographed.

————. "The Phenomenon of Urbanization in Latin America." Mimeographed, n. d. [1965]

314   BIBLIOGRAPHY

————. *Retracking America: A Theory of Transactive Planning.* Garden City, N. Y.: Doubleday, 1973
————. *Urbanization, Planning, and National Development.* Beverly Hills and London: Sage Publications, 1973.
————. "The Role of Cities in National Development." The Ford Foundation, Urban and Regional Advisory Program in Chile, February 1968. Mimeographed.
————. "The Strategy of Deliberate Urbanization." The Ford Foundation, Urban and Regional Advisory Program in Chile, December 1967. Mimeographed.
————. "Two Concepts of Urbanization: A Comment." *Urban Affairs Quarterly* 1, no. 4 (1966).
Friedmann, John, and Thomas Lackington. "Hyperurbanization and National Development in Chile: Some Hypotheses." *Urban Affairs Quarterly* 2, no. 4 (1967).
Friedrich, Paul. "The Legitimacy of the 'Cacique'." In *Local-Level Politics: Social and Cultural Perspectives*, edited by Marc Swartz, pp. 243-269. Chicago: Aldine, 1968.
Fundação Leão XIII. "Favelas of Guanabara." Rio de Janeiro, 1968. Mimeographed.
————. *1967 Report on Favelas of Guanabara.* Divisão de Serviços Sociais e Estatística. Rio de Janeiro.
Furtado, Celso. *Análise do 'Modelo' Brasileiro.* Rio de Janeiro: Civilização Brasileira, 1973.
————. *Development and Underdevelopment.* Berkeley: University of California Press, 1964.
————. *Diagnosis of Brazilian Crisis.* Berkeley: University of California Press, 1965.
————. *Dialética do Desenvolvimento.* São Paulo: Fundo de Cultura, 1964.
————. *A Formação Econômica do Brasil.* Rio de Janeiro: Fundo de Cultura, 1959. Translated into English as *The Economic Growth of Brazil.* Berkeley: University of California Press, 1963.
————. "Political Obstacles to the Economic Development of Brazil." In *Obstacles to Change in Latin America*, edited by Claudio Valez. New York: Oxford University Press, 1965.
Gans, Herbert J. "The Effect of a Community Upon Its Residents: Some Considerations for Sociological Theory and Planning Practice." Paper for the Urban Sociology Colloquium, Rutgers University, May 1961.
————. *Popular Culture and High Culture.* New York: Basic Books, 1974.
————. *More Equality.* New York: Pantheon Books, 1968.
————. *The Urban Villagers: Group and Class in the Life of Italian-Americans.* Glencoe, Ill.: The Free Press, 1962.
Gardner, James. "Urbanization in Brazil." International Urbanization Study, Ford Foundation, 1973.
Germani, Gino. "Aspectos Teóricos de la Marginalidad." *Revista Paraguaya de Sociologia* 9, no. 30 (1972).
————. "Sobre Algunos Aspectos Teóricos de la Marginalidad." Unpublished paper, Harvard University, Center for Population Studies, November 1970.
————. "Assimilación de Immigrantes en el Medio Urbano; Notas Metodológicas." *Revista Latinoamericana de Sociologia* 1, no. 2 (Buenos Aires: 1965).
————. "The City as an Integrating Mechanism: The Concept of Social Integration." In *The Urban Explosion in Latin America*, edited by Glenn H. Beyer. Ithaca, N. Y.: Cornell University Press, 1967.

————. "Emigración del Campo a la Ciudad y sus Causas." In *Sociedad, Economia y Reforma Agraria*, edited by Horatio Gilberti, *et al.* Buenos Aires, 1965.

————. "Inquiry into the Social Effects of Urbanization in a Working Class Sector of Greater Buenos Aires." In *Urbanization in Latin America*, edited by Philip M. Hauser. New York: Columbia University Press, 1961.

————, ed. *Modernization, Urbanization, and the Urban Crisis*. Boston: Little, Brown and Company, 1973.

————. "Social and Political Consequences of Mobility." In *Social Structure and Mobility in Economic Development*, edited by Neil J. Smelser and Seymour Martin Lipset. Chicago: University of Chicago Press, 1966.

Giusti, J. "El Programa de Promoción Popular en Chile. Un Entento de Organización Política de los Sectores Populares." *Revista Latinomericana de Ciencias Sociales* (April 1972).

Goldberg, Milton M. "A Qualification of the Marginal Man Theory." *American Sociological Review* 6, no. 1 (1941), pp. 52-58.

Goldrich, Daniel. "Partnership and Political Integration in Four Lower Class Urban Settlements in Santiago and Lima." August 1967. Mimeographed.

————. "Past Demand-Makers and Their Prospects for Future Demand-Making." February 1967. Mimeographed.

————. "Politics and the Poblador." Mimeographed, n. d.

————. "Toward the Comparative Study of Politicization in Latin America." In *Contemporary Cultures and Societies in Latin America*, edited by D. B. Heath and R. N. Adams. New York: Random House, 1965.

Goldrich, Daniel, Raymond Pratt, and C. R. Schuller. "The Political Integration of Lower Class Urban Settlements in Chile and Peru." *Studies in Comparative International Development* 3, no. 1 (1967-1968). St. Louis: Social Science Institute, Washington University.

Golovensky, David I. "The Marginal Man Concept: An Analysis and Critique." *Social Forces* 30, no. 2 (1952), pp. 333-339.

Gordon, Milton Myron. *Assimilation in American Life: The Role of Race, Religion, and National Origins*. New York: Oxford University Press, 1964.

Grabois, Giselia Potengy. "Considerações sobre o Processo de Inserção do Migrante e Sociedade Urbano-Industrial: Um Estudo de Caso Na Periferia da Região Metropolitana do Rio de Janeiro." Paper presented at O Encontro Brasileiro de Estudo Populacionais, Rio de Janeiro, 1974.

————. "Em Busca da Integração: A Política de Remoção de Favelas no Rio de Janeiro." Paper presented at the Department of Social Anthropology, Universidade Federal do Rio de Janeiro, February 1973.

Graham, Douglas. "Divergent and Convergent Regional Economic Growth and Internal Migration in Brazil: 1940-1960." *Economic Development and Cultural Change* 18, no. 3 (1970).

————. "Migration, Regional and Urban Growth and Development in Brazil: A Selective Analysis of the Historical Record, 1872–1970." Instituto de Pesquisas Economicas, Universidade de São Paulo, 1971.

Graham, Douglas H., and Sergio Buarque de Hollanda Filho. "Interregional and Urban Migration and Economic Growth in Brazil." Mimeographed, n. d.

Green, A. W. "A Re-examination of the Marginal Man Concept." In *The Marginal Situation*, edited by H. F. Dickie-Clark. London: Routledge and Kegan Paul, 1966.

Guglar, Josef. "Migrating into Unemployment in Western Africa." Paper presented at the 11th International African Seminar, Dakar, 1972.

Gutierrez de Pineda, Virgia. *Tradicionalismo y familia. Rasfondo familiar del Menor.* Bogotá: Ascofame, November 1973.

Hagen, Everett E. *On the Theory of Social Change.* Homewood, Ill.: Dorsey Press, 1962.

Halperin, Ernst. "Possibilities for the Export of Revolution in Latin America." Center for International Studies, MIT, 1970. Mimeographed.

Handlin, Oscar. *The Newcomers: Negroes and Puerto Ricans in a Changing Metropolis.* Garden City, N. Y.: Anchor Books, 1959.

———. *The Uprooted.* New York: Grosset and Dunlap, 1951.

Hansen, P. M., ed. *Urbanization in Latin America.* New York: Columbia University Press, 1961.

Harris, Marvin. *Town and Country in Brazil.* New York: Columbia University Press, 1957.

Hauser, Phillip M. "On the Impact of Urbanism on Social Organization, Human Nature, and the Political Order." *Confluence* 7, no. 1 (1958).

———. "The Social, Economic, and Technological Problems of Rapid Urbanization." In *Industrialization and Society*, edited by Bert F. Hoselitz and W. Moore. The Hague: Mouton for UNESCO, 1963.

———. *Urbanization in Latin America.* New York: International Document Service, 1961.

Hauser, Phillip M., and Leo F. Schnore. *The Study of Urbanization.* New York: John Wiley and Sons, Inc., 1966.

Heath, Dwight, and Richard Adams, eds. *Contemporary Cultures and Societies of Latin America.* New York: Random House, 1965.

Herrick, Bruce. "Urbanization and Urban Migration in Latin America: An Economist's View." In *Latin American Urban Research*, edited by F. Rabinovitz and F. Trueblood, pp. 71-82. Beverly Hills, Calif.: Sage Publications, 1971.

Higgins, Benjamin. "The Scope and Objectives of Planning for Underdeveloped Regions." *Documentación del 1 Seminario Sobre Regionalización.* Rio de Janeiro: Instituto Panamericano de Geografia y Historia, Comisión de Geografia, 1969.

Hirschman, Albert O. "Brazil's Northeast." In *Journeys Toward Progress.* Garden City, N. Y.: Doubleday, 1965.

———. *Journeys Toward Progress.* New York: Twentieth Century Fund, 1963.

———. *A Strategy for Economic Development.* New Haven, Conn.: Yale University Press, 1961.

Hobsbawm, E. J. "La Marginalidad Social en la Historia de la Industrializacion Europea." *Revista Latinoamericana de Sociologia* 5, no. 2 (1969).

———. "Peasants and Rural Migrants in Politics." In *The Politics of Conformity in Latin America*, edited by Claudio Veliz. New York: Oxford University Press, 1967.

Hoenack, Judith, and Anthony Leeds. "Marketing Supply and Social Ties in Rio Favelas." Mimeographed, 1966.

Hollingshead, August. "Those on the Bottom." In *Man Alone*, edited by E. and M. Josephson. New York: Dell Publishing Co., 1962.

Hollnsteiner, Mary R. "The People versus Urbano Planner y Administrador." In *Development in the '70s.* 5th Annual Seminar for Student Leaders, The Philippines, March 1973.

————. "Urban Planning: A Curbside View." Paper prepared for the SEADAG Urban Development Panel on "Urban and Regional Planning: Southeast Asian Experience," Bali, Indonesia, April 15-18, 1974.

Holmberg, Allan. "The Changing Values and Institutions of Vicos in the Context of National Development." *American Behavioral Scientist* 8, no. 7 (1965).

Hopkins, Keith. "Housing the Poor." In *Hong Kong: The Industrial Colony*, edited by K. Hopkins. London: Oxford University Press, 1971.

Horowitz, Irving Louis. "Electoral Politics, Urbanization, and Social Development in Latin America." *Urban Affairs Quarterly* 2, no. 3 (1967).

————. *Masses in Latin America*. New York: Oxford University Press, 1970.

————. *Revolution in Brazil*. New York: E. P. Dutton, 1964.

————. "Urban Politics in Latin America." Ithaca, N. Y.: Cornell Center for Housing and Environmental Studies.

Hoselitz, B. F. "The Role of Urbanization in Economic Development." In *India's Urban Future*, edited by R. Turner. Berkeley: University of California Press, 1962.

————. "The City, the Factory, and Economic Growth." *American Economic Review* 45, no. 2 (1955).

Hughes, Everett Cherington, and Helen MacGill Hughes. *Where People Meet: Racial and Ethnic Frontiers*. Glencoe, Ill.: The Free Press, 1952.

Huntington, Samuel. "Political Development and Political Decay." *World Politics* 17, no. 3 (1965).

————. *Political Order in Changing Societies*. New Haven, Conn.: Yale University Press, 1968.

Hurtado, Maria Elena. "Marginalidad Sorpresa." *Revista del Domingo*, Santiago, October 5, 1968.

Hutchinson, Bertram. "The Migrant Population of Urban Brazil." *América Latina* 6 no. 2 (1963).

————. "Urban Social Mobility Rates in Brazil Related to Migration and Changing Occupational Structure." *América Latina* 6, no. 3 (1963).

Ianni, Octavio. *Crisis in Brazil*. New York: Columbia University Press, 1970.

————. *Estado e Capitalismo*. Rio de Janeiro: Editora Civilização Brasileira, 1965.

————. *Industrialização e Desenvolvimento Social no Brasil*. Rio de Janeiro: Editora Civilização, Brasileira S. A., 1963.

Inkeles, Alex. "Making Men Modern: On the Causes and Consequences of Individual Change in Six Developing Countries." *The American Journal of Sociology* 75, no. 2 (1969).

————. "The Modernization of Man." *Modernization: The Dynamics of Growth*, edited by Myron Weiner. New York: Basic Books, 1966.

————. "Participant Citizenship in Six Developing Countries." *The American Political Science Review* 63, no. 4 (1969).

Instituto Brasileiro de Geografia e Estatística. *Censo Demográfico Guanabara*. VIII Recenseamento Geral, Série Regional, Vol. I, Tomo XVII. 1970.

————. *Censo Demográfico: Rio de Janeiro*. VIII Recenseamento Geral, Série Regional, Vol. I, Tomo XVI. 1970.

Instituto de Desenvolvimento da Guanabara (IDEG). *A Interpenetração das Areas Faveladas e Areas Industriais no Estado da Guanabara*. Rio de Janeiro, 1968.

Islam, Nurual. "Concepts and Measurements of Unemployment and Underemployment in Developing Economies." *International Labor Review* 80, no. 3 (1964): 204-256.

Jaffe, A. J. and J. N. Froomkin. "Economic Development and Jobs: A Comparison of Japan and Panama, 1950-1960." *Estadística* 24, no. 92 (1966): 577-592.

Jaguaribe, Hélio. "Dependência e Autonomia na América Latina." Paper presented at the Conference on Latin American Social Sciences, Lima, 1968.

Kahl, Joseph A. *The Measurement of Modernism: A Study of Values in Brazil and Mexico.* Austin: University of Texas Press, 1968.

Kain, J. F. "Journey to Work as a Determinant of Residential Location." *Papers and Proceedings of the Regional Science Association* 9 (1962): 137-143.

Kerckhoff, A. C. "An Investigation of Factors Operative in the Development of the Personality Characteristics of Marginality." Ph.D. dissertation, University of Wisconsin, 1953.

Kerckhoff, Alan C., and Thomas C. McCormick. "Marginal Status and the Marginal Personality." *Social Forces* 34, no. 1 (1955): 48-55.

Klassen, Leo H., and L. S. Burns. "The Position of Housing in National Economic and Social Policy." In *Capital Formation in Latin America.* Washington, D. C.: Pan American Union, 1973.

Kluckhohn, Florence, and Fred L. Strodtbeck. *Variations in Value Orientations.* Evanston, Ill.: Row, Peterson and Co., 1961.

Koenigsberger, Otto. "Apresentação." V Ciclo Sobre Planejamento Urbano, Ministério do Interior, SERFHAU, Rio de Janeiro, 1969.

Koth, Marcia, Julio Silva, and Albert Dietz, *Housing in Latin America.* Cambridge, Mass.: MIT Press, 1964.

Kowarick, Lucio. "Capitalismo, Dependência e Marginalidade Urbana na América Latina: Uma Contribuição Teórica." *Estudos Cebrap*, no. 8 (April-June 1974): 79-96.

————. "Marginalidade Urbana e Desenvolvimento: Aspectos Teóricos do Fenômeno na América Latina." Ph.D. dissertation, Universidad de Sao Paulo, 1972.

Kuznetzoff, Fernando. "Housing Policies or Housing Politics: An Evaluation of the Chilean Experience." Draft of paper. Department of City and Regional Planning, University of California, Berkeley, 1974.

Lamb, Curt. "The New Group Life of the Poor." Yale University, n. d. Mimeographed.

————. *Political Power in Poor Neighborhoods.* Cambridge, Mass.: Schenkman Publishers, 1975.

Lambert, Denis, and Armand Mattelhart. "L'urbanisation Accelerée de l'Amerique Latine et la Formation d'un Secteur Tertiare Refuge." *Civilisation* 15 (1965).

Langoni, C. G. *Distribuição da Renda e Desenvolvimento Econômico do Brasil.* Rio de Janeiro: Editora Expressão e Cultura, 1973.

Langsten, Ray. "Remoção: A Study of the Rehousing of Urban Squatters in Rio de Janeiro." Preliminary draft, June 1973.

Lathrope, D. E. "Some Notes on the Culture of Poverty," Institute on Poverty and Social Problems, September 21, 1964.

Leacock, Eleanor Burke, ed. *The Culture of Poverty.* New York: Simon and Schuster, 1971.

Leal, Victor Nunes. *Coronelismo, Enxada e Voto.* Rio de Janeiro: Livraria Forense, 1949.

Leeds, Anthony. "Brazilian Careers and Social Structures: An Evolutionary Model and Case History." Institute of Latin American Studies Offprint Series, no. 15. Austin: The University of Texas, n. d.

————. "The Concept of the 'Culture of Poverty': Conceptual, Logical, and Empirical Problems, with Perspectives from Brazil and Peru." In *The Culture of Poverty*, edited by Eleanor Burke Leacock. New York: Simon and Schuster, 1971.

————. "Electricity and Power Structure in Rio Favelas." Mimeographed, n. d.

————. "Future Orientation: The Investment Climate in Rio Favelas." Mimeographed, n. d.

————. "Locality Power in Relation to Supra-Local Power Institutions." In *Urban Anthropology*, edited by Aiden Southall and Edward Bruner. Oxford: Oxford University Press, 1973.

————. "Significant Variables Determining the Character of Squatter Settlements." *América Latina* 12, no. 3 (1969).

Leeds, Anthony, and Elizabeth Leeds. "Brazil and the Myth of Urban Rurality: Urban Experience, Work, and Values in 'Squatments' of Rio de Janeiro and Lima." Paper presented at the St. Thomas Conference, November 1967. Mimeographed.

————. "Brazil in the 1960s: Favela and Polity, the Continuity of the Structure of Social Control." In *Brazil in the Sixties*, edited by Riordan Roett. Nashville, Tenn.: Vanderbilt University Press, 1972.

Leeds, Elizabeth Rachel. "Forms of 'Squatment' Political Organization: The Politics of Control in Brazil." M. A. thesis, University of Texas, 1972.

Leeds, Anthony, and David Morocco. "Carnival Groups: Maintainers and Intensifiers of the Favela Phenomenon in Rio de Janeiro." Mimeographed. 1966.

Leighton, Alexander H. "Poverty and Social Change." *Scientific American* 212, no. 5 (1965).

Lerner, Daniel. *The Passing of Traditional Society*. Glencoe, Ill.: The Free Press, 1964.

————. "Toward a Communication Theory of Modernization." In *Communications and Political Development*, edited by Lucian W. Pye. Princeton, N. J.: Princeton University Press, 1963.

Lewis, Oscar. *The Children of Sanchez: Autobiography of a Mexican Family*. New York: Vintage Books, 1963.

————. "Cruz Moves to a Housing Project." In *La Vida*. New York: Vintage Books, 1968.

————. "The Culture of Poverty," *Scientific American* 215, no. 4 (1966): 19-25.

————. *Five Families*. New York: Random House, 1958.

————. *Life in a Mexican Village: Tepoztlan Restudied*. Urbana, Ill.: University of Illinois Press, 1951.

————. "Urbanization Without Breakdown." *Scientific Monthly* 75 (1952).

————. *La Vida: A Puerto Rican Family in the Culture of Poverty—San Juan and New York*. New York: Random House, 1965.

Leys, Colin. "Politics in Kenya: The Development of Peasant Society." Institute for Development Studies, Discussion Paper no. 102. Nairobi, Kenya: University of Nairobi, December 1970. Mimeographed.

Linz, Juan J. "An Authoritarian Regime: Spain." In *Cleavages, Ideologies, and Party Systems*, edited by E. Allardt and Y. Littunen. Helsinki: Transactions of the Westermark Society, 1964.

Little, Kenneth. *West African Urbanization*. Cambridge: Cambridge University Press, 1970.

Lopez, Juarez Brandão. "Aspects of the Adjustment of Rural Migrants to Urban

Industrial Conditions in Sao Paulo, Brazil." In *Urbanization in Latin America*, edited by Philip M. Hauser, pp. 234-248. New York: Columbia University Press, 1961.

————. *Desenvolvimento e Mudança Social Formação da Sociedade Urbano-Industrial no Brasil*. Vols. 1, 2 and 3. Sao Paulo, Brazil.

————. "Some Basic Developments in Brazilian Politics and Society." In *New Perspectives of Brazil*, edited by Eric N. Baklanoff. Nashville: Vanderbilt University Press, 1968.

Lutz, Thomas McKinley. "Self-Help Neighborhood Organizations, Political Socialization, and the Developing Political Orientations of Urban Squatters in Latin America: Contrasting Patterns from Case Studies in Panama City, Guayaquil, and Lima." Ph.D. dissertation, Georgetown University, 1970.

Machado, Luiz Antonio. "Labor Markets and Political Propensities of Marginal Groups: A Tentative Theory of Marginality Theory." Unpublished manuscript, November 1971.

————. "A Política na Favela," *Cadernos Brasileiros* 9, no. 3 (1967).

Mangin, William P. "Latin American Squatter Settlements: A Problem and a Solution." *Latin American Research Review* 2, no. 3 (1967).

————. "Tales from the Barriadas." In *Peasants in Cities*, edited by W. P. Mangin, pp. 55-61. Boston: Houghton Mifflin Co., 1970.

————. "The Role of Regional Associations in the Adaptation of Rural Migrants to Cities in Peru." *Sociologus*, no. 9 (1959).

Mannheim, Karl. *Ideology and Utopia*. Translated by Louis Wirth and Edward Shils. First published in 1936. New York: Harcourt, Brace and World, Inc.

Mann, J. W. "The Problem of the Marginal Personality." Ph.D. dissertation, University of Natal, 1957.

Mannoni, Dominique O. *Prospero and Caliban: The Psychology of Colonization*. New York: Praeger, 1956.

Mar, José Matos. "Migration and Urbanization—The Barriadas of Lima: An Example of Integration into Urban Life." In *Urbanization in Latin America*, edited by Philip M. Hauser, pp. 170-190. New York: Columbia University Press, 1961.

————. "Urbanización y Barriadas en América del Sur." Lima: Instituto de Estudios Peruanos, 1968.

Marca, Edmo Lima de. "Base de Incidência do Percentual do FGTS." Rio de Janeiro: National Housing Bank, 1973.

Margúlis, Mario. *Migracion y Marginalidad en la Sociedad Argentina*. Buenos Aires: Paidos, 1968. SIAP series, vol. 10.

Marshall, Thomas H. *Class, Citizenship, and Social Development*. Garden City, N. Y.: Doubleday Books, 1963.

Martini, George. "Internal Migration and its Consequences: The Case of Guanabara State." Ph.D. dissertation, Brown University, 1969.

Martins, Carlos Estevan, and Fernando Henrique Cardoso. "La Favela: Estratificación Interna y Participación Política." Paper presented at the Conference on La Marginalidad en América Latina, Santiago, November 1970.

Martins, Luciano. "The 'Manu-Military' Self-Sustained Growth in Brazil." Notes for discussion, Workshop on Brazilian Development, Yale University, April 1971.

Marx, Karl. *Capital*, Part 7, Chapter 23.

Mata, Milton da. "Migrações Internas no Brasil: Aspectos Econômicos e Demográficos." *Relatório de Pesquisa*, no. 19. Rio de Janeiro: IPEA, 1973.

Mattelart, Armand, and Manuel A. Garreton. *Integración Nacional y Marginalidad: Ensayo de Reginalización Social de Chile.* Santiago, 1965.

Matza, David. "The Disreputable Poor." In *Social Structure and Mobility in Economic Development*, edited by Neil J. Smelser and Seymour Martin Lipset. Chicago: Aldine, 1966.

McClelland, David Clarence. *The Achievement Motive.* New York: Appleton-Century-Crofts, 1953.

Meares, Mable Sellars. "Rural Investment and its Effect on Rural-Urban Migration in Latin America." M.A. thesis, George Washington University, 1971.

Medina, Carlos Alberto de. "A Favela como uma Estrutura Atomística: Elementos Descritivos e Constitutivos." *América Latina* 12, no. 3 (1969).

———. *A Favela e o Demagogo.* São Paulo: Imprensa Livre, 1964.

Mello, Diogo Lordello, and Cleuler de Barros Loyola. "Alguns Aspectos Institucionais de Marginalidade." Paper presented at the Conference on La Marginalidade en América Latina, Santiago, November 1970.

Merrick, Thomas William. "Labor Absorption and the Traditional Urban Sector." Mimeographed, n. d.

Merrill, Robert N. "Toward a Structural Housing Policy: An Analysis of Chile's Low Income Housing Program." Ph.D. dissertation, Cornell University, 1971.

Merton, Robert, ed. *Social Theory and Social Structure.* New York: The Free Press, 1957.

Michelena, José Silva. "Conflict and Consensus in Venezuela." Ph.D. dissertation, Massachusetts Institute of Technology, 1968.

Miller, Neal, and John Dollard. *Social Learning and Imitation.* New Haven: Yale University Press, 1941.

Miller, S. M. "Poverty, Race, and Politics." In *The New Sociology*, edited by J. Horowitz. New York: Oxford University Press, 1964.

Millikan, Max F., and Donald L. M. Blackmer. *The Emerging Nations.* Boston: Little, Brown and Co., 1961.

Miner, Horace. "The Folk-Urban Continuum." *American Sociological Review* 17 (October 1952).

Mitchell, J. Clyde. *The Kalela Dance.* The Rhode Livington Papers, no. 27. Manchester: Manchester University Press, 1956.

Modesto, Hélio. "Planejamento Governmental e Urbanização." *Revista de Admin. Municipal* 7, no. 38 (Rio de Janeiro: 1966).

Moog, Vianna. *Bandeirantes and Pioneers.* Translated by L. Barett. New York: George Brazilier, 1964.

Morse, Richard. *From Community to Metropolis: A Biography of Sao Paulo.* Gainesville, Fla.: University of Florida Press, 1958.

———. "Internal Migrants and the Urban Ethos in Latin America." Paper presented at the Seventh World Congress of Sociology in Varna, Bulgaria, September 1970. Mimeographed.

———. "The Lima of Joaquin Capelo: A Latin American Archetype." *Journal of Contemporary History* 4, no. 3 (1969).

———. "Recent Research on Latin American Urbanization: A Selective Survey with Commentary." *Latin American Research Review* 1, no. 1 (1965).

———. "Trends and Issues in Latin American Urban Research, 1965-1970." *Latin American Research Review* 6, no. 1 (1971).

———. "Urbanization in Latin America." *Latin American Research Review* 1, no. 1 (1965).

Muira, Yuki. "A Comparative Analysis of Operational Definitions of the Economically Active Population in African and Asian Statistics." *U. N. Population Conference*, vol. 4. Belgrade: 1965.

Muñoz Garcia, Humberto, Orlando de Oliveira, and Claudio Stein. "Categorias de Migrantes y Nativos y Algunas de Suas Características Sócio-Económicas." National University, Mexico City, February 1971. Mimeographed.

———. "Migración y Marginalidad Occupacional en la Ciudad de México. Mimeographed, n. d.

Murmis, M. "Tipos de Marginalidad y Posición en el Proceso Productivo." *Revista Latinoamericana de Sociologia* 5, no. 2 (1969).

Muth, R. "Urban Residential Land and Housing Markets." In *Issues in Urban Economics*, edited by H. S. Perloff and L. Wingo, pp. 286-333. Baltimore: Johns Hopkins Press, 1968.

National Housing Bank. *CHISAM: Metas Alcançadas e Novos Objetivos do Programa*. Rio de Janeiro: Guavira Publicidade, Ltda., n. d.

———. *Economic Development and Urban Growth in Brazil*. Rio de Janeiro, 1972.

———. *National Housing Bank: A Brazilian Solution to Brazilian Problems*. Rio de Janeiro, n. d.

———. *Plano Nacional de Habitação Popular*. Rio de Janeiro, 1973.

Nelson, Carlos. "The Brás de Pina Experience." Massachusetts Institute of Technology, 1971. Mimeographed.

———. "The Possibilities of Developing Policies Supporting Autonomous Housing Action in Underdeveloping Countries: The Brás de Pinha Redevelopment Project." Massachusetts Institute of Technology, 1971. Mimeographed.

Nelson, Joan. *Migrants, Urban Poverty, and Instability in Developing Nations*. Center for International Affairs, Occasional Papers in International Affairs, no. 22. Cambridge, Mass.: Harvard University, 1969.

———. "Urban Growth and Politics in Developing Nations: Prospects for the 1970s." Pearson Conference Document, no. 31, 1970.

"Northeast Brazil." *Realities*, no. 161 (April 1964): 60-67.

Nun, José. "La Marginalidad en América Latina." Mimeographed, n. d.

———. "Superpoblación Relativa, Ejército Industrial de Reserva y Masa Marginal." *Revista Latinoamericana de Sociologia* 69, no. 2.

Nun, José, Miguel Murmis, and Juan Carlos Marin. "La Marginalidad en América Latina: Informe Preliminar." Working paper. Instituto Torcuato di Tella, Buenos Aires, 1968.

Oliveira, F. "A Economia Brasileira: Crítica a Razão Dualista." *Estudos CEBRAP*, no. 2 (October 1972); p. 82. Translated into Spanish as "La Economia Brasileña: Crítica a la Razón Dualista." *El Trimestre Económico* 40, pp. 441-484.

O'Neil, Charles. "Some Problems of Urbanization and Removal of Rio Favelas." Mimeographed, 1966.

Ozyurelli, Oya. "Dynamics of Urban Family and Rural Kin Relations in a Transitional Setting: A Study of Two Turkish Communities." May 1973. Mimeographed.

Parisse, Lucien. *Favelas de L'agglomeration de Rio de Janeiro*. Strasbourg: Université de Strausbourg, Centre de Géographie Appliquée, 1970.

————. *Favelas do Rio de Janeiro: Evolução-Sentido*. Rio de Janeiro: CENPHA, 1969.

————. "Las Favelas en la Expansión Urbana de Rio de Janeiro." *América Latina* 12, no. 3 (1969).

Park, Robert E. "Human Migration and the Marginal Man." *American Journal of Sociology* 33, no. 6 (1928), pp. 881-893.

Parsons, Talcott. *The Social System*. Glencoe, Ill.: The Free Press, 1951.

Parsons, Talcott, and Edward A. Shils. *Toward a General Theory of Action*. Cambridge, Mass.: Harvard University Press, 1954.

Pastore, José. "Satisfaction Among Migrants to Brasília, Brazil: A Sociological Interpretation." Ph.D. dissertation, University of Wisconsin, Madison, 1968.

Patch, Richard. "Life in a Callejon: A Study of Urban Disorganization." American Universities Field Staffs, West Coast South America Series, vol. 8, no. 6, New York, 1961.

Pearse, Andrew. "Some Characteristics of Urbanization in the City of Rio de Janeiro." In *Urbanization in Latin America*, edited by Philip M. Hauser, pp. 191-205. New York: Columbia University Press, 1961.

Peattie, Lisa R. "The Concept of 'Marginality' as Applied to Squatter Settlements." Department of Urban Studies and Planning, Massachusetts Institute of Technology, n. d. Mimeographed.

————. "The Ethnography of Economic Development." Ph.D. dissertation, University of Chicago, 1968.

————. "The Informal Sector: A Few Facts from Bogota, Some Comments, and a List of Issues." Draft of paper. Massachusetts Institute of Technology [1974].

————. "Social Issues in Housing." Joint Center for Urban Studies, Massachusetts Institute of Technology, 1966. Mimeographed.

————. "Some Notes on the Problems of Urbanization." Department of Urban Studies and Planning, Massachusetts Institute of Technology, n. d. [1967]. Mimeographed.

————. "The Structural Parameters of Emerging Life Styles in Venezuela." In *The Culture of Poverty*, edited by Eleanor Burke Leacock. New York: Simon and Schuster, 1971.

————. "'Tercialization,' 'Marginality,' and Urban Poverty in Latin America." Draft of paper. Massachusetts Institute of Technology [1974].

————. *View from the Barrio*. Ann Arbor: University of Michigan Press, 1968.

Perlman, Janice E. "Dimensões de Modernidade Numa Cidade em Franco Desenvolvimento, Estudo do Caso de Belo Horizonte." *Revista Brasileira de Estudos Políticos*, no. 30, 1971.

————. "The Fate of Migrants in Rio's Favelas: The Myth of Marginality." Ph.D. dissertation, Massachusetts Institute of Technology, 1971.

————. "Methodological Notes on Complex Survey Research Involving Life History Data." Institute of Urban and Regional Development, Monograph no. 18. University of California, Berkeley, 1974.

————. "Poverty, Personality, and Political Power." Massachusetts Institute of Technology, January 1966.

————. "Psycho-Cultural Dimensions of Modernization." Honors Thesis, Department of Anthropology, Cornell University, 1965.

————. "Rio's Favelados and the Myths of Marginality." Institute of Urban and Regional Development, Working Paper no. 223. University of Calfornia, Berkeley, 1973.

Perlman, Janice E., and Philip Raup. "Style of Evaluation of the Venezuelan Middle and Upper Classes." Massachusetts Institute of Technology, 1966. Mimeographed.

Perlman, Janice E., Anthony Leeds, and John Turner. "Housing Priorities, Settlement Patterns, and Urban Development in Modernizing Countries." *Journal of the American Institute of Planners* 34, no. 6 (1968).

Petiz, Maria Lucia de Paula. "A Utilização do Método de D.O.C. Num Programa de Melhoramentos Físicos na Favela de Catacumba." Pontífica Universidade Católica, Instituto Social, Rio de Janeiro, November 1963.

Petras, James, and Maurice Zeitlin, eds. *Latin America: Reform or Revolution?* New York: Fawcett World Library, 1968.

Pompermayer, Malori J. "Authoritarianism in Brazil." Paper presented at the Workshop Conference on Brazil Since 1969: Political and Economic Development Theories Re-examined. Latin American Studies Center, Yale University, April 1971.

Pontífica Universidade Católica do Rio de Janeiro. "Três Favelas Cariocas: Mata Machado, Morro União, Brás de Pina-Levantamento Sócio-Econômico." Rio de Janeiro, 1967.

Pontual, Ricardo. "Racionalidad Formal versus Racionalidad Sustantiva en el Proceso de Planificación del Desarrollo Urbano." Paper presented at the Regional Conference on the Politics of Urban Development, México D. F., July 1972.

Portes, Alejandro. "Los Grupos Urbanos Marginados." Santiago, June 1969. Mimeographed.

————. "Leftist Radicalism in Chile: A Test of Three Hypotheses." *Comparative Politics* 2 (January 1970).

————. "The Urban Slum in Chile: Types and Correlates." *Ekistics* 202 (September 1972), pp. 175-180.

————. "Urbanization and Politics in Latin America." *Social Science Quarterly* (December 1971): 697-720.

Poulantzas, Nicos. "As Classes Sociais." *Estudos CEBRAP* 3 (January 1973).

Prado, Caio, Jr. *História Econômica do Brasil.* 7th edition. Sao Paulo: Editora Brasiliense, 1962.

Projecto de Evaluación de los Superbloques. Caracas: Banco Obrero [1962].

Pye, Lucian W. *Aspects of Political Development.* Boston: Little, Brown and Co., 1966.

————. "The Political Implications of Urbanization and the Development Process." In *The City in Newly Developing Countries: Readings on Urbanism and Urbanization*, edited by Gerald Breese. Englewood Cliffs, N. J.: Prentice-Hall, Inc., 1969.

————. *Politics, Personality, and Nation Building: Burma's Search for Identity.* New Haven: Yale University Press, 1962.

Quijano, Anibal. "Dependencia, Cambio Social y Urbanización en Latinoamérica." Social Affairs Division, Economic Commission for Latin America, 1967.

————. "La Formación de un Universo Marginal en las Ciudades de América Latina." In *Imperialismo y Urbanización en América Latina*, edited by M. Castells. Barcelona: Gustavo Gili, 1973.

————. "Notas Sobre el Concepto de Marginalidad Social." Santiago: CEPAL, División de Asuntos Sociales, October 1966.

Rabinovitz, Francine. "Urban Development and Political Development in Latin America." In *Comparative Urban Research: The Administration and Politics of Cities*, edited by Robert T. Daland. Beverly Hills, Calif.: Sage Publications, 1971.

Rabinovitz, Francine, and Felicity M. Trueblood, eds. *Latin American Urban Research*. Beverly Hills, Calif.: Sage Publications, 1971.

Rainwater, Lee. "Fear of the House-as-Haven in the Lower Class." *Journal of the American Institute of Planners* (January 1966).

Rath, João. "Cidade de Deus." *Ultima Hora*. Rio de Janeiro, October 1969.

Ray, Talton F. *The Politics of the Barrios of Venezuela*. Berkeley and Los Angeles: University of California Press, 1969.

Redfield, Robert. *The Folk Culture of Yucatan*. Chicago: University of Chicago Press, 1959.

————. "The Folk Society." *American Journal of Sociology* 52 (1947).

————. *The Little Community and Peasant Society and Culture*. Chicago: The University of Chicago Press, 1963.

————. *The Primitive World and Its Transformations*. Ithaca, N. Y.: Great Seal Books, 1953.

Redwood, John III. "Internal Migration, Urbanization, and Frontier Region Development in Brazil since 1940." Honors thesis, Harvard University, 1968.

Rempel, Henry. "The Determinants of Rural-to-Urban Labor Migration in Kenya." Preliminary draft. Dept. of Economics, University of Manitoba, February 11, 1971.

República Federativa do Brasil. *Projeto do II Plano Nacional de Desenvolvimento (PND): 1975-1979*. Brasília: 1974.

Reynolds, Clark W., and Robert T. Carpenter. "Housing Finance in Brazil Towards a New Distribution of Wealth." Stanford Food Research Institute, 1974. Mimeographed.

Rios, José Artur. "Aspectos Sociais dos Grupamentos Subnormais." CENPHA, Rio de Janeiro, May 1967.

————. "El Pueblo y el Político." *Política*, no. 6 (Caracas, 1960).

————. "Social Transformation and Urbanization: The Case of Rio de Janeiro." Rio de Janeiro, Catholic University, 1970. Mimeographed.

Rios, José Arthur, L. J. Lebret, Carlos Alberto Medina, and Hélio Modesto. "Aspectos Humanos das Favelas Cariocas." *O Estado de S. Paulo*, April 13, 1960.

Roberto, Mauricio. *Plano de Desenvolvimento Local Integrado*. Municipio de Duque de Caxias, Estudo Preliminar.

Roberts, Brian. *Organizing Strangers*. Austin, Texas: University of Texas Press, 1973.

Rockefeller, Margaret Dulany. "Voluntary Associations and Social Evolution: A Case Study of Brazilian Favela Associations." Department of Social Studies, Radcliffe College, March 1969. Mimeographed.

Roett, Riordan, ed. *Brazil in the Sixties*. Nashville, Tenn.: Vanderbilt University Press, 1972.

Rogers, Everett M. *Diffusion in Innovations*. New York: Free Press of Glencoe, 1962.

————. *Modernization Among Peasants: The Impact of Communication*. New York: Holt, Rinehart and Winston, 1969.

————. "Motivations, Values, and Attitudes of Subsistence Farmers." Paper presented at Agricultural Development Council Conference, March 1965.

Rokeach, Milton. *The Open and Closed Mind.* New York: Basic Books, Inc., 1960.

Rosen, Bernard C. "Socialization and Achievement Motivation in Brazil." *American Sociological Review* 27, no. 5 (1962).

————. "The Achievement Syndrome and Economic Growth in Brazil." *Social Forces* 42 (March 1964).

Ross, Marc Howard. "Conflict Resolution Among Urban Squatters." Department of Political Science, Bryn Mawr College, n. d. Mimeographed.

Rostow, W. W. *The Stages of Economic Growth.* Cambridge: Harvard University Press, 1963.

Rush, Barney S. "From Favela to Conjunto: The Experience of Squatters Removed to Low-cost Housing in Rio de Janeiro, Brazil." Honors thesis, Harvard College, March 1974.

Ryan, Edward J. "Personal Identity in a Lower Class Slum." In *The Urban Condition,* edited by Leonard Duhl. New York: Simon and Schuster, 1963.

Ryan, William. *Blaming the Victim.* New York: Pantheon Books, 1971.

Sá, Francisco, Jr. "O Desenvolvimento da Agricultura Nordestina e a Função das Atividades de Subsistência." *Estudos Cebrap* 3 (January 1973).

Safa, Helen Icken. "From Shanty Town to Public Housing: A Comparison of Family Structure in Two Urban Neighborhoods in Puerto Rico." *Caribbean Studies* 4, no. 1 (1964).

————. "Puerto Rican Adaptation to the Urban Milieu." In *Race, Change, and Urban Society,* edited by P. Orleans and W. R. Ellis, Jr. Beverly Hills, Calif.: Sage Publications, 1971.

Sahato, Gian S. "An Economic Analysis of Migration in Brazil." *Journal of Political Economy* 76, no. 2 (1968).

Salmen, Lawrence F. "Housing Alternatives for the Carioca Working Class: A Comparison Between Favelas and Casas de Comodos." *América Latina* [1970].

————. "Urbanization and Development." In *Contemporary Brazil: Issues in Economic and Political Development,* edited by H. Rosenbaum and W. Tyler. New York: Praeger, 1972.

Santos, Theotonio dos. "Brazil, the Origins of a Crisis." In *Latin America: The Struggle with Dependency and Beyond,* edited by Ronald Chilcote and Joel Edelstein. New York: Schenkman Publishing Co., 1974.

————. "The Structure of Dependence." In *Readings in U. S. Imperialism,* edited by K. T. Fann and D. C. Hodges. Boston: Porter Sarges Publications, 1971.

Schlichtmann, Laura, and Janice E. Perlman. "Labor Force Participation Among Lower-Class Women in Brazil." Draft of paper. University of California, Berkeley, 1974.

Schmitter, Philippe C. *Interest Conflict and Political Change in Brazil.* Stanford University Press, 1971.

————. "New Strategies for the Comparative Analysis of Latin American Politics." Paper for the Latin American Studies Association, New York, November 1968.

————. "The Portugalization of Brazil." Paper prepared for Workshop on Brazilian Development. Yale University, April 1971.

Schnore, Leo F. "The Statistical Measurement of Urbanization and Economic Development." *Land Economics* 37, no. 3 (1961).

Schnore, Leo F., and Henry Fagin. *Urban Research and Policy Planning.* Vol. 1. Beverly Hills, Calif.: Sage Publications, Inc., 1967.

Schuh, G. Edward, and Morris Whitaker. "Migration, Mobility, and Some Problems of the Labor Market in Brazil." Latin American Seminar on Development in Agriculture, Bogota, November 1968. Mimeographed.

Schwarz, Roberto. "As Idéias Fora do Lugar." *Estudos Cebrap* 3 (January 1973).

Seeley, John R. "The Slum." In *Urban Renewal: People, Politics, and Planning*, edited by Jewell Bellush and Murray Hausknecht. Garden City, N. Y.: Doubleday Anchor Books, 1967.

———. "The Slum: Its Nature, Use, and Users." *Journal of the American Institute of Planners* 25, no. 1 (1959).

Selznick, Phillip. *TVA and the Grass Roots: A Case Study in the Sociology of Formal Organizations*. Berkeley: University of California Press, 1949.

Sewell, Granville Hardwick. "Squatter Settlements in Turkey: Analysis of a Social, Political, and Economic Problem." Ph.D. dissertation, Massachusetts Institute of Technology, 1964.

Silberstein, Paul. "Favela Living: Personal Solution to Larger Problems." *América Latina* 12, no. 3 (1969).

Silva, Luiz Antonio Machado da. *As Linhas de Análise das Favelas*. Rio de Janeiro: CODESCO, 1967.

———. "O Significado do Botequim." *América Latina* 12, no. 3 (1969).

Silva-Michelena, José A. "Conflict and Consensus in Venezuela." Ph.D. dissertation, Massachusetts Institute of Technology, 1968.

Silveira, Carlos E. "A 'Análise do Modêlo Brasileiro' de Celso Furtado." *Estudos Cebrap* 3 (January 1973).

Simmel, George. "The Stranger." In *The Sociology of George Simmel*, edited by Kurt Wolff. New York: The Free Press, 1950.

Singer, Paulo I. "Força de Trabalho e Emprêgo no Brasil: 1920–1969." Cadernos CEBRAP, no. 3. São Paulo: CEBRAP, 1971.

———. "Migrações Internas: Considerações Teóricas Sobre O Seu Estudo." Mimeographed, n. d.

———. "O Milagre Brasileiro: Causas e Consequências." Caderno no. 6. São Paulo: CEBRAP, 1972.

———. "Urbanización, Dependencia y Marginalidad en América Latina." In *Imperialismo y Urbanización en América Latina*, edited by M. Castells. Barcelona: Gustavo Gili, 1973.

Sjoberg, Gideon. "Cities in Developing and Industrial Societies: A Cross-Cultural Analysis." In *The Study of Urbanization*, edited by Hauser and Schnore. New York: John Wiley and Sons, 1966.

———. "The Origin and Evolution of Cities." *Scientific American* 213, no. 3 (1965).

———. "The Rural-Urban Dimension in Preindustrial, Transitional, and Industrial Societies." In *Handbook of Modern Sociology*, edited by Robert Faris. Chicago: Rand McNally and Co., 1964.

———. "Rural-Urban Balance and Models of Economic Development." In *Social Structure and Mobility in Economic Development*, edited by Neil J. Smelser and Seymour Martin Lipset. Chicago: University of Chicago Press, 1966.

Skidmore, Thomas E. *Politics in Brazil, 1930-1964: An Experiment in Democracy*. New York: Oxford University Press, 1967.

Slotkin, J. S. "The Status of the Marginal Man." *Sociology and Social Research* 28, no. 1 (1943): 47-54.

Smith, David Horton, and Alex Inkeles. "The OM Scale: A Comparative Socio-Psychological Measure of Individual Modernization." *Sociometry* 29, no. 4 (1966).

Smith, T. Lynn. "Urbanization in Latin America." In *Urbanism and Urbanization*, edited by Nels Anderson. Netherlands: E. J. Brill, 1964.

Soares, Glaucio. "The New Industrialism and the Brazilian Political System." In *Latin America: Reform or Revolution*, edited by James Petras and Maurice Zeitlin. New York: Fawcett Publications, 1968.

————. "The Politics of Uneven Development: The Case of Brazil." In *Party Systems and Voter Alignments: Cross-National Perspectives*, edited by Seymour M. Lipset and Stein Rokkan. New York: The Free Press of Glencoe, 1967.

Soares, Glaucio, and R. L. Hamblin. "Socio-economic Variables and Voting for Radical Left: Chile 1952." *American Political Science Review* 61 (December 1967).

Solow, A., and L. Vera. *Panorama del Problema de la Vivienda en América Latina.* Washington, D. C.: Pan American Union, 1952.

Sovani, N. V. "The Analysis of 'Over-Urbanization.'" *Economic Development and Cultural Change* 12, no. 2 (1964).

Stavenhagen, Rudolfo. "Marginality, Participation, and Agrarian Structure in Latin America." *Bulletin* 7 (June 1970).

————. "Seven Fallacies About Latin America." In *Latin America: Reform or Revolution?*, edited by James Petras and Maurice Zeitlin. Greenwich, Conn.: Fawcett Publications, 1968.

Stepan, A., ed. *Authoritarian Brazil: Origins, Policies, and Future.* New Haven: Yale University Press, 1973.

Stokes, Charles. "A Theory of Slums." *Land Economics* 38, no. 23 (1962).

Stonequist, Everett V. "The Problem of the Marginal Man." *American Journal of Sociology* 41, no. 1 (1935), pp. 1-12.

Storh, W., and Paul Pederson. "Urbanization, Regional Development, and South American Integration." The Ford Foundation, Urban and Regional Development Advisory Program in Chile, April 1968. Mimeographed.

Strassman, Paul W. "Innovation and Employment in Building: The Experience of Peru." *Oxford Economic Papers* 22 (July 1970).

Sunkel, Osvaldo. "Subdesarrollo, Dependencia y Marginalización: Proposiciones Para un Enfoque Integrador." Santiago, November 1970. Mimeographed.

Tavares, M. C. *Da Substituição de Importações ao Capitalismo Financeiro.* Rio de Janeiro: Zahar, 1973.

Tavares, M. C., and J. Serra. "Una Discusión Sobre el Estilo del Desarrollo Recente de Brasil." *El Trimestre Económico*, no. 152 (November-December 1971).

Tilly, Charles. "Race and Migration to the American City." In *The Metropolitan Enigma*, edited by James Q. Wilson. Cambridge, Mass.: Harvard University Press, 1968.

————. "A Travers le Chaos des Vivantes Cites." Revised version of paper presented to the Sixth World Congress of Sociology, Evian-les-Bains, September 1966.

Tolosa, Hamilton. "Macro-economia da Urbanização Brasileira." *Pesquisa e Planejamento Econômico* 3, no. 3 (1973): 585-644.

————. "Política Nacional de Desenvolvimento Urbano: Uma Visão Econômica." *Pesquisa e Planejamento Econômico* 2, no. 1 (1972): 143-156.

Tomasek, Robert D., ed. *Latin American Politics: Studies of the Contemporary Scene.* 2nd edition. Garden City, N. Y.: Anchor Books, 1970.

Toness, Odin A., Jr. "Power Relations of a Central American Slum." M. A. thesis, University of Texas, 1967.

"Too Large a Victory." *The Nation* 211, December 14, 1970.

Toro, Alvaro Lopez. "Notas sobre los fenômenos migratórios del Valle del Cauca." In *Las migraciones internas*, edited by Cardona G. Ramiro, pp. 103-116. Editorial Andes, 1970.

Trindade, Mário. *Habitação e Desenvolvimento*. Rio de Janeiro: Vozes Ltds., 1971.

Turner, John C. "Barriers and Channels for Housing Development in Modernizing Countries." *Journal of the American Institute of Planners* 33, no. 3 (1967).

————. "Four Autonomous Settlements in Lima, Peru." Paper presented at the Latin American Colloquium, Department of Sociology, Brandeis University, May 1967.

————. *Uncontrolled Urban Settlement: Problems and Policies*. Pittsburgh: University of Pittsburgh Press, 1966.

Turner, John C., and Robert Fichter, eds. *Freedom to Build*. New York: The Macmillan Company, 1972.

Turner, John, and Rolf Goetz, "Environmental Security and Housing Input." *Carnegie Review* (October 1966).

United Nations. *Improvement of Slums and Uncontrolled Settlements*. New York: United Nations, 1971.

United Nations Committee on Housing, Building, and Planning. *World Housing Survey*. January 31, 1974.

Universidad Católica de Chile. Comite Interdisciplinario de Desarrollo Urbano. "La Docencia y la Investigación en el Campo de la Urbanización: La Experiencia del CIDU." Paper presented at the Seminar on Social Sciences and Urban Development in Latin America, in Jahuel, Chile, April 1968.

————. Comite Interdisciplinario de Desarrollo Urbano. "Notas Bibliográficas sobre el Processo de Urbanización en America Latina a partir de 1965." Compiled by Carmen Barros, n. d.

Valentine, Charles A. *Culture and Poverty: Critique and Counter-Proposals*. Chicago and London: University of Chicago Press, 1968.

————. "The 'Culture of Poverty': Its Scientific Significance and its Implications for Action." In *The Culture of Poverty*, edited by Eleanor Burke Leacock. New York: Simon and Schuster, 1971.

Vargas, Fundação Getúlio. "Mao-de-obra e Construção de Edifícios no Estado da Guanabara." Centro de Estudos e Treinamento em Recursos Humanos, Rio de Janeiro, 1972.

Vekemans, Roger. "Una Estrategia Para La Miseria," DESAL, Santiago, 1967.

————. "Marginalidad, Incorporación, y Integración." DESAL, Santiago, Boletin no. 37, May 1967.

Vekemans, Roger, and I. Silva F. *Marginalidad en América Latina: Un Ensayo Diagnostico*. Barcelona: Herder, 1969.

————. *Marginalidad Promoción e Integración Latinoamericana*. Buenos Aires: Ediciones Troquel, 1970.

Veliz, Claudio, ed. *The Politics of Conformity in Latin America*. New York: Oxford University Press, 1967.

Vernez, Georges. "Bogota's Pirate Settlements: An Opportunity for Metropolitan Development." Ph.D. dissertation, University of California, Berkeley, 1973.

————. "El Proceso de Urbanización en Colombia." *Revista de la Sociedad Interamericana de Planificación* 5 (September 1971).

Vianna, Oliveira. *Populações Meridionais do Brasil*. Fifth edition in two volumes. Rio de Janeiro: José Olympio, 1952.

Wachtel, Howard M. "Looking at Poverty from a Radical Perspective." *Review of Radical Political Economics* 3, no. 3 (1971).

Wagner, Bernard, David McVoy, and Gordon Edwards. "Guanabara Housing and Urban Development Program." Report and Recommendations by AID Housing and Urban Development Team, July 1966. Mimeographed.

Ward, Barbara. "The City May Be as Lethal as the Bomb." *New York Times Magazine*, April 19, 1964.

———. *The Rich Nations and the Poor Nations*. New York: W. W. Norton and Co., 1962.

———. "The Uses of Prosperity." *Saturday Review*, August 29, 1964.

Weber, Max. *The City*. Glencoe, Ill.: The Free Press, 1958.

———. *The Protestant Ethic and the Spirit of Capitalism*. 1958 edition. New York: Charles Scribner's Sons, 1904–1905.

Weffort, Francisco C. "State and Mass in Brazil." In *Masses in Latin America*, edited by Irving Louis Horowitz, pp. 385-406.

Weiner, Myron. "Urbanization and Political Extremism: An Hypothesis Tested." Massachusetts Institute of Technology, n. d. Mimeographed.

———. "Urbanization and Political Protest." *Civilizations* 27, no. 2 (1964).

———. "Violence in Politics in Calcutta." *Journal of Asian Studies* 20, no. 3 (1961).

Wells, John. "Distribution of Earnings, Growth, and Structure of Demand in Brazil, 1959-1971." Working paper. Centre of Latin American Studies, University of Cambridge, n. d.

White, Morton, and Lucia White. *The Intellectual Versus the City*. Cambridge, Mass.: Mentor Books, 1964.

Whyte, William Foote. *Street Corner Society: The Social Structure of an Italian Slum*. Chicago: University of Chicago Press, 1965.

Wilkening, Eugene, and João Bosco Pinto. "Migration and Adaptation in New Settlement Areas." Land Tenure Center, no. 25. University of Wisconsin, 1966. Mimeographed.

Wilkening, E. A. "Comparison of Migrants in Two Rural and an Urban Area of Central Brazil." Land Tenure Center Research Paper, no. 35. University of Wisconsin, Madison, 1968.

———. "The Role of the Extended Family in Migration and Adaptation in Brazil." Paper presented at the Annual Meeting of the Rural Sociological Society, San Francisco, August 1967.

Wingo, Lowdon, Jr. "Recent Patterns of Urbanization Among Latin American Countries." *Urban Affairs Quarterly* 2, no. 3 (1967).

Winnick, L. "Economic Questions in Urban Redevelopment." *American Economic Review* 51 (May 1961).

Wirth, Louis. "Urbanism as a Way of Life." *American Journal of Sociology* 44 (July 1938).

Wolfe, Eric R., and Edward Hansen. "Caudillo Politics: A Structural Analysis." *Comparative Studies in Society and History* 9 (1967).

Wolfe, Marshall. "Recent Changes in Urban and Rural Settlement Patterns in Latin America: Implications for Social Organization and Development." Pittsburgh Conference, November 1966. Mimeographed.

————. "Some Implications of Recent Changes in Urban and Rural Settlement Patterns in Latin America: Summary." Mimeographed, n. d.

Worth, Robert M. "Urbanization and Squatter Resettlement as Related to Child Health in Hong Kong." *American Journal of Hygiene* 78, (1963), pp. 338-348.

Wright, Rolland H. "The Stranger Mentality and the Culture of Poverty." In *The Culture of Poverty*, edited by Eleanor Burke Leacock. New York: Simon and Schuster, 1971.

Yap, Lorene. "Rural-Urban Migration and Economic Development in Brazil." Mimeographed, 1970.

Yeh, Stephen H. K. *Homes for the People.* Singapore: Statistics and Research Department, Housing and Development Board, 1972.

Zachariah, K. C. "Bombay Migration Study: A Pilot Analysis of Migration to an Asian Metropolis." *Demography* 3, no. 2 (1966), pp. 378-393.

Zeitlin, Maurice. "Political Generations in the Cuban Working Class." In *Latin America: Reform or Revolution?*, edited by James Petras and Maurice Zeitlin. New York: Fawcett Publications, 1968.

Index

CATACUMBA, a *favela* near the chic neighborhoods of Copacabana and Ipanema in Rio de Janeiro, was razed by the Brazilian government in 1970. This community was home to nine thousand people, and is one of the several *favelas* intensively studied by Janice Perlman in preparation for the writing of this book. The panorama reproduced here on the case and endpapers was assembled from a series of nine photographs of Catacumba taken by Dr. Perlman.